Chronology of Classic Horror Films

The 1930s

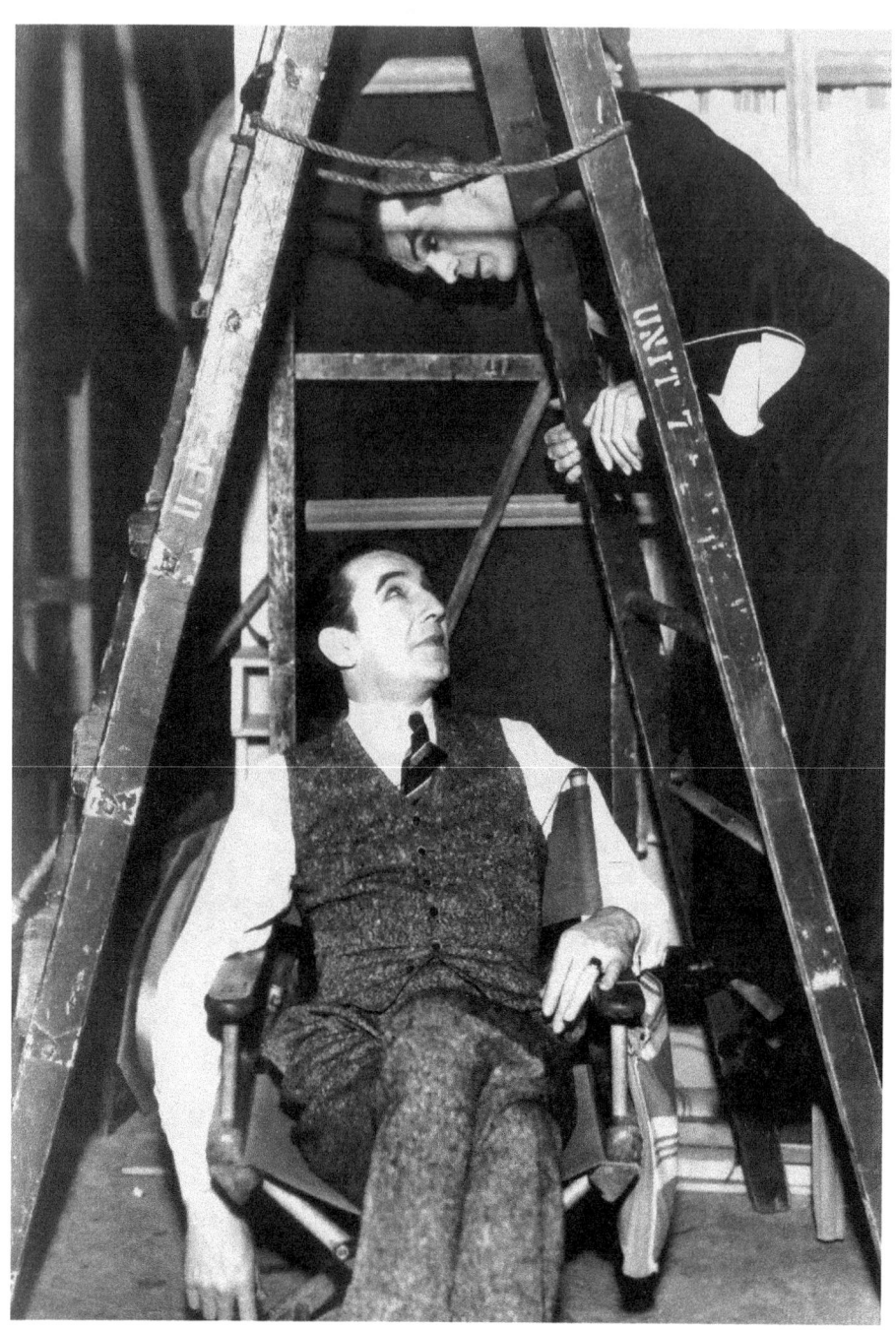
Bela Lugosi and Boris Karloff on the set of *The Black Cat*

Chronology of Classic Horror Films

The 1930s

by Donald C. Willis

Midnight Marquee Press, Inc.
Baltimore, MD, USA

Copyright © 2019 Donald C. Willis

Cover Design: A. Susan Svehla
Interior layout: Gary J. Svehla
Copy Editor: Janet Atkinson

Midnight Marquee Press, Inc., Gary J. Svehla and A. Susan Svehla do not assume any responsibility for the accuracy, completeness, topicality or quality of the information in this book. All views expressed or material contained within are the sole responsibility of the author.

Without limiting the rights under copyright reserved above, no part of this publication may be reproduced, stored in or introduced into a retrieval system, or transmitted, in any form, or by any means (electronic, mechanical, photocopying, recording or otherwise), without the prior written permission of the copyright owner or the publishers of the book.

ISBN 978-1-64430-082-4
Library of Congress Catalog Card Number 2019951475
Manufactured in the United States of America

First Printing: October 2019

Dedication

For David—a world of films

Table of Contents

8	Introduction: To Classic Horror
22	Itinerary: *Oh, the places you'll go!*
29	Highlights of 1929-1930
35	1929-1930
61	Highlights of 1931
62	1931
96	Highlights of 1932
99	1932
158	Highlights of 1933
160	1933
197	Highlights of 1934

199	**1934**
222	**Highlights of 1935**
225	**1935**
263	**Highlights of 1936**
265	**1936**
297	**Highlights of 1937-1938**
299	**1937-1938**
309	**Highlights of 1939**
311	**1939**
342	**Afterword**
344	**Acknowledgments**
345	**About the Author**

INTRODUCTION:
To Classic Horror

"Someone told me upon hearing of this title [*Golden Horrors*], what—oh, no, not another book detailing the Golden Age of Horror Cinema"—Gary J. Svehla review of Bryan Senn's *Golden Horrors*, Midnight Marquee 52:54 (1997). Two decades on ...

The details! Why do the horror movies from the 1930s and 1940s seem virtually inexhaustible—to me, personally, and to us, collectively—whether as art, entertainment, film history, personal history or sociology? No single reason. Many reasons. One of the most significant being, simply, the details, the images, and those still-reverberating moments: [scattered spoilers] the light from the tower window reflected in the Monster's eyes, in *Frankenstein*. Legendre's curious non-reaction to the "dreadful emptiness" in Madeline's eyes (he knew what he would see there), in *White Zombie*. Joseph August's shot of Juanita's haunting eyes, subtly highlighted in the dark, in *Black Moon*. Jacqueline defiantly drumming her finger on the armchair, in *The Seventh Victim*, as the Palladists—the ultimate passive-aggressives—confront her. The fireplace glow illuminating the trailing gowns of the vampire women, as they glide towards Renfield's inert body, in *Dracula*. The strange shafts of light from the roadside bonfire, in the Spanish-language *Dracula*. Svengali's luminous eyes and the unstoppable camera—doors and windows can't slow it down—suggesting his uncanny power over Trilby, in *Svengali*. The light affecting the tuft of wolf's hair on the slide, in *The Undying Monster*, science segueing into the supernatural. Simone Simon's Irena dejectedly slumping down against the door, which separates bride from groom, in *Cat People*. The poor Monster's hopeful patting of his "bride's" hand, in *Bride of Frankenstein*. Kong periodically, gently, placing Ann on various rocks and ledges, in *King Kong*.

More: The sobbing emanating from the courtyard, in *I Walked with a Zombie*. Sibyl singing the killing "Little Yellow Bird," in *The Picture of Dorian Gray*. The seemingly supernatural hum/howl of the wind, which accompanies Mora and Luna everywhere, in *Mark of the Vampire*. The malevolent Ygor playing his flute/horn and getting under everyone's skin, in *Son of Frankenstein* and *The Ghost of Frankenstein*. Vollin's climactic, complete, crazy-armed mental disintegration, in *The Raven*. Siamese twin Daisy channeling sister Violet's fiancé's kiss, in *Freaks*. The unscrupulous Dr. Mirakle and the prostitute lost in the dark and fog of Paris, in *Murders in the Rue Morgue*. The mind cyclone—all corpses, helmets, horrible noise, and rampaging ectoplasm—in *The Devil Commands*. Skipper, the adorable mutt, following around the ape with his master's brain, on the ape's mangling rounds, in *The Monster and the Girl*. (Compare Corky and Dynamo Dan in the more mundane *Man Made Monster*.) The matching

A behind-the-scenes look at the towering laboratory set for *Bride of Frankenstein*

draped-in-cobwebs "ghost" bits in *The Last Warning* and *Who Killed Aunt Maggie?* The shadow of the Bat on the wall altering and shrinking, then separating from the Bat himself, in *The Bat Whispers*. Gorman responding to wife Evelyn's undisguised disgust for him, with the perversely romantic: "What is it that makes me love you so?," in *Murders in the Zoo*. Good dog Wilbur nuzzling Dracula's robe, in *Abbott and Costello Meet Frankenstein*. John Alton's shots of the eerily lovely moonlit sea, in *The Amazing Mr. X*. The tracking shot with the grave robbers,

Director Edgar Ulmer discusses the script with actor Bela Lugosi on the set of *The Black Cat* (1934).

through the gorgeously Gothic graveyard, in *Frankenstein Meets the Wolf Man*. Charles Laughton lolling obscenely in self-satisfaction as Moreau, in *Island of Lost Souls*. The sudden roar of the train on the trestle, in *The Leopard Man*—or, when is a train a "bus"? The shots of the now really broken battlements of Castle Dracula, in *Dracula's Daughter*. The exhilarating trip through time and space—in the friendly confines of the planetarium—in *The Invisible Ray*. The cry of the monstrous hound alarming the populace, in *The Hound of the Baskervilles* (1939). The expanding, advancing, illuminated face of Woodford's "ghost," in *The House of Fear* (1939).

Yet more: The organist at midnight, in *Ghost Valley*. The piano in the dead of night, in *The Beast with Five Fingers*. The shadow of a man thrown huge upon the facade of a house, in *Miss Pinkerton* (the same shot used in the remake *The Nurse's Secret*). The stiff, outstretched arms of the murder victims seated around the dinner table, in *The Thirteenth Guest*. The deliciously ghastly, step-by-step application of the monster flesh, in *Doctor X*. The perverse murder-scene image of Myrna Loy's Ursula (she's the murderer) leaning languidly against the outside of the train-cabin-of-death wall, in *Thirteen Women*. The inspired introductory: "He went for a little walk" understatement, in *The Mummy*. Kharis' dark holes of eyes, in *The Mummy's Hand*. Amina/Ananka's gown, ethereally radiant in the moonlight, in *The Mummy's Ghost*. The sunlight reviving the afraid-of-the-dark Ananka in *The Mummy's Curse*. Max Steiner's scoring of the exciting climactic hunt, in *The Most Dangerous Game*. James Wong Howe's bravura track through the winding, unending corridors of the Egyptian rock temple, in *Chandu the Magician*. Karloff's voice and Beethoven's Seventh breathlessly ushering us up the spiral metal staircase, in *The Black Cat* (1934).

And more: The row of waiting coffins below the veranda, in *The Ninth Guest*. The off-screen howling ruining the dinner party, all tuxes and gowns, in *WereWolf of London*. The eyes of the statue of Sekhmet glowing and the music shrieking—in an early "bus"—in *Charlie Chan in Egypt*. Scattered night sounds disturbing the otherwise silent, 7-minute climactic sequence, set in and around the tunnel tomb, in *Isle of the Dead*. The climactic Concerto for Unhinged Mind conflagration, in *Hangover Square*. The housekeeper periodically bringing in the envelopes with the dreaded orange pips, in *The House of Fear* (1945). Sir Lancelot singing the story of Saint Sebastian/San Sebastian, in *I Walked with a Zombie* and *Zombies on Broadway*—his calypso ballad, by turns, gossipy, threatening, and lyrical. The madman "seeing" Helen sans mouth, in *The Spiral Staircase*. Professor Forbes fleeing the feathered serpent while counter-productively clutching the feather lure, in *The Flying Serpent*. Lon Chaney, Jr. as the monster doing Lugosi/Ygor's smirk (it's Ygor's brain, now, in the monster's skull), in *The Ghost of Frankenstein*. The unseen nighttime horrors in the wide, empty streets of Chicago, in *Fingers at the Window*.

And: Larry Talbot, tied to the chair, asking his father, hopefully, "But you're going to stay with me, aren't you?," in *The Wolf Man*. The Phantom's cape stylishly billowing behind him, as he dashes about, in *Horror Island*. The deceased Gail walking off into the clouds, in *Topper Returns*. Karen Morley's Jenny's response when the subject of love is brought up: "Yes, I've read about that," in *The Phantom of Crestwood*. The foreboding line: "Saul is why we have to keep Morgan," in *The Old Dark House*. The ghoulish "grin" on the face of the skull of Genghis Khan, in *The Mask of Fu Manchu*. The goofy maniac threatening to tear the viewer "limb from limb," at the end of *Night of Terror*. The hell-choir's unnerving shrieking over the opening credits, in *Supernatural*. The somehow melancholic bit in which the invisible man borrows the scarecrow's clothes, in *The Invisible Man Returns*. The kaleidoscopic green lights and shadows, in the first and best shot of *Dr. Cyclops*. Karloff's Kravaal's ominous line (regarding his fellow human beings on the island), "I have laboratory animals here," in *The Man with Nine Lives*. The shrouded corpse in the mortuary rising to confront Enid, in *Midnight Warning*. The moments before Mrs. White threatens to open the door to the Unknown, in *The Monkey's Paw*.

A close-up of the "horror eyes" of Ellman for *The Walking Dead* (1936)

Plus: The ocarina, in *Dead Men Tell*: a little midnight music. The cat making itself comfortable in Abigail's coffin, in *The Black Cat* (1941). Mantan Moreland buoyantly leading a pack of zombies, in *King of the Zombies*. John Alton's lighting of the "ghost" in the netting, in *The Ghost Goes Wild*—he makes it look like writhing ectoplasm. The all-out Hammer-like horror scene in the woods, in *The Red House*. The zombie-like last moments of the apparent suicide victims, in *The Garden Murder Case*. The close-ups of Ellman's horror eyes as he plays oddly intimidating sweet music for his targeted victims, in *The Walking Dead*. The gorilla rising from behind the headboard, in *Seven Footprints to Satan*. The scads of vampiric little duckbills of the deep, in *The Mysterious Island*. The ghostly-white Umbrella Man as, striding towards the camera, he looms larger and larger and larger, in *London by Night*. Lighting effects turning the little old lady (Elspeth Dudgeon) into the gnarled, witch-like Octopus, in *Sh! The Octopus*. Jekyll *enlarging* into Hyde, in *Dr. Jekyll and Mr. Hyde* (1931). Hyde's taunting: "You have that cooped-up feeling" to Ivy, in *Dr. Jekyll and Mr. Hyde* (1941). The nerve-jangling blares of the horror horn, in *Murder by the Clock*. James Wong Howe's light-and-shadow play culminating in the face of the murdered man becoming huge, in *The Spider*. The crazily cavorting, seemingly unoccupied shirt, in *The Invisible Man*. The glowing death mask floating down the dark hall, in *Before Dawn*. The sea monster suddenly rearing up, in *The Son of Kong*. Peter Lorre's Gogol's love-struck-little-boy looks at Frances Drake's Yvonne, in *Mad Love*. Lorre's stranger slipping scarily easily into a lost, blank look, in *Stranger on the Third Floor*. Lorre's Einstein's so wanting to please everyone, in *Arsenic and Old Lace*. Karloff's Gregor addressing the pear, preparatory to murder, in *The Black Room*.

Some more: A disciplined Lugosi (as Ygor) not succumbing to the temptation to over-emphasize "they said" in "I stole bodies—they said," in *Son of Frankenstein*. The terrified mind reader suddenly detecting the thoughts of a killer, somewhere in the theater audience ("Someone here is thinking murder!"), in *Charlie Chan at Treasure Island*. Quasimodo's lament: "Why was I not made of stone like these?," in *The Hunchback of Notre Dame*. The near-subliminal, quietly unnerving "vocal ambiance" sound effects, in *The Cat and the Canary*. A man "scared to death" by a "ghost," in *The Witness Vanishes*. The white-marble look of the face of stage star Angela Merrova, in *The Return of Doctor X*—she looks "like something dead." Noble Johnson's forbiddingly blank-eyed zombie lying in bed, simply turning his head to look towards our already-terrified heroes, in *The Ghost Breakers*. Lugosi's mad doctor's indulgent smile at his splendid new killer bat, in *The Devil Bat*. Bernard Herrmann's willies-inducing musical introduction for Simone Simon's Belle, in *All That Money Can Buy*. Thunder clapping and shadows crisscrossing Milton Parsons' cadaverous face, in *Hold That Ghost*. The mock-macabre Parsons staring out from beneath the coffin lid, in *The Hidden Hand*. The materialization of the kneeling skeleton, in *Night Monster*. The twisted, tormented look on the ape-man Noel's face, as he tries to throttle the dog, in *Dr. Renault's Secret*.

Finally: The vampire-cloaking fog billowing into the children's bedroom, in *The Return of the Vampire*. Isabel's rejection of Ted unintentionally sending him into his ghoul state, in *The Mad Ghoul*. The zombie Lila's echo voice, in *Revenge of the Zombies*. The lightning bursting through the window, in *Sherlock Holmes Faces Death*. The image of her phantom-friend Irena lingering, even after young Amy goes into the house, in *Curse of the Cat People*. The running, jumping, never-standing-still, phosphorescent marsh "monster," in *The Scarlet Claw*. The oddly elegant ectoplasm effects—and the cold room—in *The Uninvited*. The truly imaginative shot of the shadows of Morel's puppets—fabricated in the image of his victims—haunting him, in *Bluebeard*. The nightmare lady who "seems to be a part of the fog that drifts through the window," in *Shadows in the Night*. The seemingly animated shadow which appears about to choke the card cheat, in *The Vampire's Ghost*. The loveliness of the street singer's voice acting as counterpoint to the prevailing unloveliness, in *The Body Snatcher*. Elspeth Dudgeon doing the boogie! boogie! boogie! as the "old woman in black," in *The Woman Who Came Back*. The strangler appearing as something burning and smoking, in *Strangler of the Swamp*. The visitation of the ghost-in-retrospect, in *The Fatal Witness*. The shadow of the fleeing Edelmann looming larger and larger, until it's positively gigantic on the wall, in *House of Dracula*. The secret of the crying baby revealed as ..., in *The Unknown*. The climactic, Lewton-happy leopard scene, in *The Devil's Mask*. The smartly-executed "bus" when Fosco abruptly enters the house, throwing open the curtains, in *The Woman in White*. The huge shadow of an apparently ambulatory cat's claw traveling down the hallway, in *The Creeper*.

Plus at least a thousand and one more such moments, in the treasure-trove of 1930s and 1940s horror. I tried to limit myself to one moment, or scene, per film. And of course the better movies are more than moments—see the individual chapters. Generally, I didn't pick the most famous bits from their respective movies—but you can't ignore the skeleton in the drawing room in *Night Monster*.

Inexhaustibility—another reason we return to the 1930s and 1940s. Notice how these classics, these fine films one and all—well, maybe every other one and all—seem to change from one viewing to the next, from one viewer to the next. Well, of course, they don't. We do. "New" eyes, different eyes. Beast with a million eyes, as it were ...

Retakes. Or, Chameleon Movies. Our "first take" of, say, *White Zombie* (1932) is just that, a first impression. There's always—with a second viewing—a second take, a third take, and so on. (Of course, some movies—say, *Strange Adventure* [1932]—are hardly worth one take.) As Svehla notes, "The movies seem to evolve and stay vital ... The final word [on them] has *not* been printed and, in my opinion, never will be."

Admission. I have now written four separate times on one pretty undistinguished sf/horror movie, *The Man with Nine Lives* (1940). (Do I, maybe, in some warped way, love its very tackiness? Beside the point ...) It's not as if it's like new to me each time that I see it—it's just a (slightly) different experience. Different ideas, or impressions, bob to the surface as I watch each time—and I may not be done with it yet. (I'm not saying that I've changed my opinion of

Bela Lugosi as Dracula and Dwight Frye as Renfield, from *Dracula* (1931)

The Man with Nine Lives, just as I haven't changed my [more positive] opinion of, say, *Island of Lost Souls* [1932], also over several viewings. The two films won't be trading places any time soon.)

"My Pip is probably not the same as your Pip"—Hugh Laurie's Mr. Watts regarding Dickens' *Great Expectations*, in *Mr. Pip* (2012).

There are, in fact, or in effect, as many Pips as there are people who have read *Great Expectations*. And there are, similarly, as many Frankensteins as the number of people who have seen *Frankenstein* over the years, since 1931. For small, representative examples of this daunting array of experiences, or viewpoints, see the quoted material at the end of many of the entries in the book. (Check, for instance, the quotes regarding *Dracula's Daughter* and *Curse of the Cat People*.) Or see the myriad posts under any popular topic on the Classic Horror Film Board, online. See, there, for example, the unending debate regarding the merits, or not, of *Dracula* (1931). Larry Winters did not know what he was starting, so many years ago, in *Garden Ghouls Gazette*, with his "*Dracula*—Tin God of Classics." (A tip of the hat to Cinecurrent)

Chameleons or Elusive Elephants? One reason, I think, for our varying estimations of the movies we love—in other words, those movies to which we return again and again—is that there are so many aspects to them, so many formal and informal elements, which go into even the simplest of them. Can we be aware, that is, at all times, during every movie, in every scene, of the actor's face, his or her way of reaching for a peach pie, the lighting of the pie, the setting, the background music, the sound, camera movement, camera placement, editing? Pretty much no. We see one thing in one scene; someone else sees something else, hears something else. Yet, we're both right. Blind man, elephant. Trunk, tail. Human eyes and ears can't take in everything and process it all at once.

Of course, in the era of Rewind, we're getting closer to the possibility of Cinematic Omniscience, though this requires stopping the film, not just watching it straight through. The magic of Rewind and Pause, helped me, for instance, detect sometimes almost subliminal sight/sound effects in scenes in, notably, *Isle of the Dead*, *The Black Cat* (1934), *The Raven* (1935), *The Cat and the Canary* (1939), *Bluebeard*, *House of Dracula*, *The Woman Who Came Back*, and even, God help me, *Black Dragons*, though in the latter case, it's clearly expedience, not esthetics, at work, in the scene in question.

Our "Golden Age of Horror Cinema" coincided with the advent of sound, which phenomenon had several consequences: most notoriously, dead scenes in pictures without musical scores, such as *Mystery of the Wax Museum* and *Dracula* ... exciting experimentation with that very silence, in some scenes, in films such as (again) *Dracula*, *The Mummy*, and *Mark of the Vampire* (see just below) ... fun with sound effects in films like *Doctor X*, *White Zombie*, *The Old Dark House*, and *Midnight Mystery* ... and stardom for Bela Lugosi, Lionel Atwill and company, actors who thrived on dialogue. In the second half of the Golden Age (which began in 1939), producer Val Lewton revitalized the genre, combining experimentation with silence with the silence-punctuating Lewton "bus," and evocative musical scores by Roy Webb and Leigh Harline.

The Mundane Magic of Re-viewing and Rewinding—Revisited. Or, Another Part of the Elephant. It was only with my third or fourth re-viewing of Universal's *Dracula* (1931), for this book, that I began to realize that the power of some of the early scenes in Castle Dracula was derived, in part, from the absence of music and dialogue. It's in the context of that very soundlessness—in a sound film—that the supernatural, in *Dracula*, seems to flourish. (This revelation may occur, for the more alert, on first or second viewing.)

If director Tod Browning happened on this esthetic tactic by accident—the accident of film history that early talkies often lacked musical scores—he capitalized on this accident in his follow-up vampire picture at MGM: *Mark of the Vampire* (1935), which features mesmerizing sequences with neither music nor dialogue, just the sound of unearthly wind, or whirring. This wind becomes, in effect, the sound of the undead, or (as it turns out)—SPOILER DEAD AHEAD—the mock undead. The sound of another world. (In *Doctor X* and *The Monkey's Paw* [both 1932], the sound of wind more or less takes the place of background music, but it's a more ordinary wind.)

A frame-grab of Boris Karloff disintegrating at the conclusion of *The Mummy* (1932)

Back at Universal, Karl Freund utilized a similar hushed quality for virtually silent scenes in *The Mummy*, although the film does have a (very spare) musical score. In one sequence, the camera snakes around the display case and comes upon the revived mummy Imhotep (Boris Karloff) poring over the sacred Scroll of Thoth—a forbidden ritual—in a secluded corner of the Cairo Museum. The uncanny "eavesdropping" nature of the shot seems to make the viewer complicit in the act. It's a unique experience. By contrast, the corresponding flashback sequence with Imhotep and the scroll, set in ancient Egypt, is floridly scored, exciting, yes, but unremarkable.

This secret of silence, or virtual silence, in sound films was well learned by Lewton. In his 1940s films, silence—or at least the absence of music—sometimes complements, sets up, the renowned Lewton "bus." See, for instance, sequences in *Cat People*, *I Walked with a Zombie*, *Isle of the Dead*, and *The Leopard Man*. The "boo!" of the "bus" may be what's best remembered, but the preliminaries are spellbinding: the wind in the cane in *Zombie*, the occasional

Bela Lugosi plays Count Mora in *Mark of the Vampire* (1935).

night sounds in *Isle*, the clacking of high heels on a sidewalk at night, in *Cat People*. Choreographed sounds. Background "music." (The night wanderings of Jacqueline, in Lewton's *The Seventh Victim*, more conventionally, feature background music.)

By contrast, the silence—or absence of a musical score—in other early Golden Age horror pictures—*Strange Cargo*, *Island of Lost Souls*, *Mystery of the Wax Museum*, *The Dragon Murder Case*—is just there, not used. And music is sorely missed, as it also is in the dialogue sequences in *Dracula* and *Mark of the Vampire*. Lewton—the best of both worlds: night (unsettling sounds) or day (Roy Webb or Leigh Harline music) …

On another technical front: If sound was a fresh and exciting phenomenon in early-1930s horror pictures, black-and-white cinematography had already been refined and perfected in silent films, and could make those talking pictures—even the Bs—look scary great, if acting and dialogue in those same pictures were sometimes erratic. Karl Freund (*Dracula, Murders in the Rue Morgue*), Robert Planck and Ray June (*The Bat Whispers*), Charles Stumar (*The Mummy*), John Stumar and L.W. O'Connell (*Return of the Vampire*), Arthur Edeson (*The Old Dark House*), Jack Mackenzie (*Isle of the Dead*), Nicholas Musuraca (*Cat People* and *The Seventh Victim*), J. Roy Hunt (*I Walked with a Zombie*), James S. Brown, Jr. (*Shadows in the Night* and *Strangler of the Swamp*), John Alton (*The Amazing Mr. X*), etc., created unique night worlds which could harbor anything dead, living, or ambiguous. A review of almost any given horror film from the era could end with: "But the photography was good."

In terms of narrative, it was an era of unfeeling, oblivious scientists and entrepreneurs—and beyond that, cold Fate—and, at the other end of the emotional spectrum, all-too-sensitive monsters and minions. On the one hand, the various doctor Frankensteins, Dr. Pretorius (*Bride of Frankenstein*), Dr. Moreau (*Island of Lost Souls*), Dr. Mirakle (*Murders in the Rue Morgue*), the invisible, omnipotent Jack Griffin, Carl Denham (*King Kong*), Atwill's Eric Gorman (*Murders in the Zoo*), and, more impersonally, the blandly bleak background panoramas of James Whale's two *Frankenstein* films; on the other hand, the Frankenstein Monster, Renfield (*Dracula*), the invisible, *tormented* Jack Griffin (two sides, same coin), Kong, Irena Dubrovna (*Cat People*), Larry Talbot (*The Wolf Man*), Moreau's creations.

That "unfeeling," above, though, isn't quite fair, if the "oblivious" is more than fair. Henry Frankenstein (Colin Clive) is so wildly enthusiastic about his new creation that he suffers a nervous breakdown; he then abandons his newborn. Ernest Thesiger's Pretorius all but passes out cigars as he eagerly presents his tiny living beings to Henry; but they're little more than toys to him. The manic-depressive Moreau (Charles Laughton) frets over his creations, as a gardener might fret over the health of his prize azaleas. Denham exults in his new exhibit, but pragmatically uses Kong's love for Ann Darrow (Fay Wray) to capture him.

The particular genius of Whale and his writers and crew was to get the audience caught up in the monster's story and, at the same time, get us caught up in the process of his creation, and his "bride's" creation, get us involved in the scientist's story, too, splinter our identification, our rooting interest. The monster and the doctor: twin, competing protagonists, like Kong and Denham. No villains, just a suggestion of the mixed blessing of existence. And of course, in *The Invisible Man*, the film versions of *Dr. Jekyll and Mr. Hyde*, *The Wolf Man*, *Cat*

***Svengali* (1932) stars John Barrymore in the title role.**

People, and *The Picture of Dorian Gray* (1945), hero and "monster" are one and the same.

In simpler filmic universes—in 1930s and 1940s horror—out-and-out villainy could be transfixing, too: think Moreau, Mirakle (Bela Lugosi), Murder Legendre (Lugosi, *White Zombie*), Fu Manchu (Boris Karloff, *The Mask of Fu Manchu*), Poelzig (Karloff, *The Black Cat*). The general, unfortunate flip side: nonentities of heroes, as played by, say, Richard Arlen, Leon Ames, Lewis Stone.

Special case: the romantic monster. Think *Dracula*, *The Mummy*, *Svengali*. In essence, the monster is, again, the hero. It's a matter of ends vs. means.

The "monster" half of the equation derives from the necessity of getting the beloved through that one narrative door, to romantic bliss—to wit, death, or a death-like trance.

Then there's *The Monster and the Girl* (1941), which is a very special case ...

I attempted to read or re-read all the source novels and stories for the films herein—to discover how the filmmakers got from here to there. (Admission: The second time around, I had to give up on *The Moonstone*.) One finding: Over-industrious scriptwriters almost invariably reworked their source material drastically, if occasionally to good effect—e.g., *The Ninth Guest*, *Bride of Frankenstein*, *The Devil Commands*, *The Picture of Dorian Gray*. Brazenly, some movies even *rewrote* the movies upon which they were based—*Curse of the Cat People*, *Jungle Woman*, *Jungle Captive*, *The Mummy's Curse*, *Devil Bat's Daughter*. If you want to get really crazy: *Jungle Captive* rewrote *Jungle Woman*, which, in turn, rewrote *Captive Wild Woman*. Why? Why not?

See the yearly Highlights comments for a continuation, in effect, of this introduction. See, especially, the comments for 1931, 1932, and 1942.

But first, our Itinerary ...

Notes. A scene has fairly recently been restored to *Frankenstein* (1931); a score has been added to *Dracula* (1931).

Flux. On a related subject—or, Upgrades and Downgrades. This is not to say that I haven't changed my estimation of certain films, specifically some 1940s horrors. Up, way up, for me: *The Picture of Dorian Gray* and *I Walked with a Zombie*. Down a bit: *The Uninvited* and *The Body Snatcher*. No big changes for me, in recent times, on 1930s favorites: *Bride of Frankenstein*, *King Kong*, *White Zombie*, *Island of Lost Souls*, and *The Invisible Man*, though I have waffled a little on *The Mummy* and *Mark of the Vampire*, and have belatedly welcomed *The Black Cat* into the fold. Okay, the latter is the one big change.

For the record, there were "busses" in pictures before *Cat People* (1942)—in, for instance, *Charlie Chan in Egypt* (1935), *The Thirteenth Chair* (1937), and *The Black Doll* (1938).

More recent examples of movies with little, if any, background music include *My Night at Maud's* (1969), *Le Fils* (2002), *American Sniper* (2014), and *Time out of Mind* (2014). Both the latter pictures eschew music in order to achieve a semi-documentary feel. Eric Rohmer's film gets its quietly maddening ambiguity, in part, by not providing the viewer with background-music cues. You're on your own. In Jean-Pierre and Luc Dardennes' *Le Fils* (*The Son*), the lack of music for the lengthy unedited shots emphasizes the day-to-day of the carpenter's life, the better to set off the scattered, powerful dramatic moments. (Admittedly, the "day-to-day" requires some viewer patience.)

You hold the first volume of our *Chronology* in your hands: *The 1930s*. The second volume, *The 1940s*, will follow within the next year. And if interest warrants, we may carry on even further.

ITINERARY:
"Oh, the places you'll go!"

A chronological list of place names ... the old dark mansions, museums, towns, cities, countries, islands, etc., in which the following films are set, respectively. There will, for instance, be many visits to New York City, London, and Paris, one to Tibet, one to the Welsh mountains, one to Angkor, etc. Specific locations are preferred—say, the London Wax Museum rather than just New York City, Cliff Manor rather than just New York City, etc. The most popular concocted names of the time seem to have been variations on "Cliff": Cliff Manor, Briarcliff, Stonecliff, Bluecliff, Ravencliff, and Drearcliff.

Woodford's Theatre, Broadway, New York City (*The Last Warning*)
China and Redmoat Grange, Limehouse (*The Mysterious Dr. Fu Manchu*)
The Montague estate, outside London (*Unholy Night*)
The Kingdom of Hetvia (*The Mysterious Island*)
Calcutta (*The Thirteenth Chair*, 1929)
The old Wilson dye works and the moor (*Return of Dr. Fu Manchu*)
Long Island (*Darkened Rooms*)
Hawk Island, "off the coast of Cuba" (*Midnight Mystery*)
Castle Dracula, Transylvania, and Carfax Abbey, London (*Dracula*)
Paris (*Svengali*)
Tivoli Theatre (*The Spider*)
The house of Endicott (*Murder by the Clock*)
The sanitarium on Country Drive (*The Phantom*)
Outside Goldstadt (*Frankenstein*)
London (*Dr. Jekyll and Mr. Hyde*, 1931)
The Crag (*Murder at Dawn*)
Paris (*Murders in the Rue Morgue*)
Boom City (*Ghost Valley*)
The old Mitchell mansion (*Miss Pinkerton*)
122 Mill Road (*The Thirteenth Guest, Mystery of the Thirteenth Guest*)
Cliff Manor, Long Island, and the Academy of Surgical Research (*Doctor X*)
Fog Hollow, on a "cursed island" (*The Most Dangerous Game*)
A temple on the Nile (*Chandu the Magician*)
Melody Manor (*The Crooked Circle*)
West of Zanzibar (*Kongo*)
La Casa de Los Andes (*The Phantom of Crestwood*)
The house of Femm, in the Welsh mountains (*The Old Dark House*)
The lost and buried tomb of Genghis Khan (*The Mask of Fu Manchu*)
The Clarendon Hotel (*Midnight Warning*)

Murders in the Rue Morgue takes us to Paris.

India and London (*The Monkey's Paw*)
The Wayne mansion (*Strange Adventure*)
Paris (*Secrets of the French Police*)
Thebes of old and the Cairo Museum (*The Mummy*)
Tombstone Canyon (*Tombstone Canyon*)
The South Seas (*Island of Lost Souls*)
The London Wax Museum, in New York City (*Mystery of the Wax Museum*)
New York City and Denham's island, or Skull Island (*King Kong, Son of Kong*)
The yacht Dulcina (*Terror Aboard*)
Helldorf Castle (*Secret of the Blue Room*)
Forest Lake, New York (*Before Midnight*)
Marmaros, in ex-Hungary (*The Black Cat*)
The island of San Christopher, the West Indies (*Black Moon*)
Verinder Manor, "in the wilds of Yorkshire" (*The Moonstone*)
The old Stamm estate, New York (*The Dragon Murder Case*)
Outside Cragdale (*The Ghost Walks*)
Castle Mora, Czechoslovakia (*Mark of the Vampire*)
Mountain View Inn (*Air Hawks*)
Tibet and London (*WereWolf of London*)

The majority of *The Invisible Ray* occurs in Africa.

The tomb of Ahmeti (*Charlie Chan in Egypt*)
Silver City (*Vanishing Riders*)
The House of de Berghman (*The Black Room*)
Dominey Hall, Norfolk, England (*The Great Impersonation*)
The Carpathian Mountains and Africa (*The Invisible Ray*)
Colby House, San Francisco (*Charlie Chan's Secret*)
London and Castle Dracula, Transylvania (*Dracula's Daughter*)
Red Rock Tavern (*The Rogues Tavern*)
Angkor (*Revolt of the Zombies*)
Paradise Island, the West Indies (*Love Wanga*)
Paris (*The Devil-Doll*)
Pharatime's Tomb, Egypt (*Mummy's Boys*)
Hawkes Neste, a country estate outside London (*House of Secrets*)
Outside Tower Rock (*Phantom of the Range*)
Rockland State Sanitarium, and Chicago (*Charlie Chan at the Opera*)
The lost city of Lukachuke (*Riders of the Whistling Skull*)
London (*London by Night*)
Octopus Island (*Sh! the Octopus*)

Baldrich Manor (*The Missing Guest*)
The town of Frankenstein (*Son of Frankenstein*)
The moors of Dartmoor (*Hound of the Baskervilles*)
Westchester (*The Gorilla*)
Woodford's Theatre, New York City (*House of Fear*, 1939)
New York City (*Miracles for Sale*)
The old London Evening Sun building (*The Witness Vanishes*)
Treasure Island, California (*Charlie Chan at Treasure Island*)
The Louisiana bayous (*The Cat and the Canary*)
New York City (*The Return of Dr. X*)
Jamaica and New York City (*The Devil's Daughter*)
Paris (*The Hunchback of Notre Dame*)
The Amazon jungle (*Dr. Cyclops*)
Crater Island, near the Canadian border (*The Man with Nine Lives*)
Castillo Maldito, near Cuba (*The Ghost Breakers*)
Briarcliff Manor (*Boys of the City*)
Brownsville (*Haunted House*)
The Batterson Place (*Blondie Has Servant Trouble*)
The Cream Crime Museum (*Charlie Chan at the Wax Museum*)
The tomb of Princess Ananka, Egypt (*The Mummy's Hand*)
Red Creek (*The Ape*)
Wistaria Hall, a "strange old house" in the South (*Who Killed Aunt Maggie?*)
Heathville (*The Devil Bat*)
Bottle Neck (*The Trail of the Silver Spurs*)
The Arizona desert (*The Face behind the Mask*)
Barsham Harbor, on the New England coast (*The Devil Commands*)
The Carrington Estate (*Topper Returns*)
The Suva Star, sailing ship (*Dead Men Tell*)
Somewhere between Cuba and Puerto Rico (*King of the Zombies*)
London (*Dr. Jekyll and Mr. Hyde*, 1941)
The Dunemere estate, East Haven (*The Smiling Ghost*)
Cross Corners, New Hampshire (*All That Money Can Buy*)
Talbot Castle, England (*The Wolf Man*)
Radenhouse (*Among the Living*)
Vasaria (*Ghost of Frankenstein*)
Chicago (*Fingers at the Window*)
Hurricane Point (*Whispering Ghosts*)
Ingston Towers (*Night Monster*)
Billings Tavern, an "old Colonial inn" (*The Boogie Man Will Get You*)
Mapleton, in New England (*The Mummy's Tomb*)
Friendly Mission (*Bowery at Midnight*)
Stonecliff (*The Hidden Hand*)

Horror comes to the quaint village of Vasaria, in *Frankenstein Meets the Wolf Man*.

Hammond Hall, Dannow, Sussex, England (in the book) (*The Undying Monster*)
New York City (*Cat People*)
Reno Red's Ranch (*Haunted Ranch*)
A Cornwall tin mine (*The Mysterious Doctor*)
Llanwelly and Vasaria (*Frankenstein Meets the Wolf Man*)
Wapakoneta Falls, New York (*The Ghost and the Guest*)
Fort Holland, the island of Saint Sebastian, the West Indies (*I Walked with a Zombie*)
The Black Raven tavern (*The Black Raven*)
Whipple's Circus (*Captive Wild Woman*)
The "haunted" house on Elm Street (*Ghosts on the Loose*)
La Sagesse beauty parlor, Manhattan (*The Seventh Victim*)
The Paris Opera House (*Phantom of the Opera*)
The Malayan jungle (*Tiger Fangs*)
Outside New Orleans (*Revenge of the Zombies*)

Musgrave Manor (*Sherlock Holmes Faces Death*)
Dark Oaks (*Son of Dracula*)
Bluecliff Seminary (*The Falcon and the Co-eds*)
Priory Cemetery, London (*Return of the Vampire*)
Fairview Cemetery (*The Mad Ghoul*)
London (*The Lodger*)
Monroe College (*Weird Woman*)
The Castle, in the Arizona desert (*The Lady and the Monster*)
La Morte Rouge, near Quebec (*The Scarlet Claw*)
Thrustlewood (*The Invisible Man's Revenge*)
New York City (*Ghost Catchers*)
Mapleton, in New England (*The Mummy's Ghost*)
The north lands (*Return of the Ape Man*)
Ravencliff (*Shadows in the Night*)
Richmond House (*The Girl Who Dared*)
New Orleans (*Cry of the Werewolf*)
Windward house, outside Biddlecombe, on the Cornish coast of England (*The Uninvited*)
Brooklyn (*Arsenic and Old Lace*)
Tarrytown, New York (*Curse of the Cat People*)
The Royal Theatre (*The Climax*)
Wild Horse Mine (*Wild Horse Phantom*)
Paris (*Bluebeard*)
The village of Reigelberg, Professor Lampini's (traveling) Chamber of Horrors, and Visaria (*House of Frankenstein*)
The Gardner estate (*Ghost Crazy*)
The Louisiana bayou (*The Mummy's Curse*)
San Francisco (*I Love a Mystery*)
The Harper House on Cove Road (*The Jade Mask*)
12 Hangover Square, London (*Hangover Square*)
Fog Island (*Fog Island*)
London (*The Picture of Dorian Gray*)
Drearcliff House, "on the west coast of Scotland," near Inverness (*The House of Fear*, 1945)
Broadway, New York City, and the island of San Sebastian, the West Indies (*Zombies on Broadway*)
London and Brighton, East Sussex, England (*The Brighton Strangler*)
Bakunda, Africa (*The Vampire's Ghost*)
Edinburgh (*The Body Snatcher*)
The Monet Wax Museum (New York City?) (*The Frozen Ghost*)
New York City (*Bewitched*)
London (*The Fatal Witness*)

Visaria (*House of Dracula*)
Eben Rock, Massachusetts (*The Woman Who Came Back*)
The old Kincaid Mansion (*Pillow of Death*)
The Warren home (*The Spiral Staircase*)
San Juan, New Mexico (*The Flying Serpent*)
Domingo, Nevada (*The Spider Woman Strikes Back*)
Wardsley (*Devil Bat's Daughter*)
Paris (*Catman of Paris*)
London (*Bedlam*)
London (*She-Wolf of London*)
The old Murks estate (*Valley of the Zombies*)
The house of Martin, Kentucky (*The Unknown*)
Danbury Acres, New York (*The Time of Their Lives*)
The old Menlo estate (*Spook Busters*)
The village of San Stefano, Italy (*The Beast with Five Fingers*)
The Central City Morgue (*Scared To Death*)
Oxhead Woods, New Jersey (*The Red House*)
The Box O Ranch (*Unexpected Guest*)
McDougal's House of Horrors, Florida (*Abbott and Costello Meet Frankenstein*)
Mahoney Manor, Long Island (*Smugglers' Cove*)
The China Coast Cafe (*Alias Nick Beal*)
The Lost Caverns Hotel (*Abbott and Costello Meet the Killer*)
The Forsythe estate (*Master Minds*)

Highlights of 1929-1930

About half of 1929 and most of 1930 are lost—horror movies, like many other late silents and early talkies, were lost to destruction, intentional or accidental. There was little or no secondary market, thus little incentive for studios to protect and preserve their films after first release.

But three standout films from 1929 and 1930 survive—*Seven Footprints to Satan*, *The Bat Whispers*, and *The Last Warning*. The silent version of *Seven Footprints* is a jack-in-the-box of a movie, a fun house haunted by a drolly-omnipresent gorilla—and its shadow—and some 20 other weird characters that keep jumping out of secret rooms, trap doors, and bookcases. The 70mm version of *The Bat Whispers* features phenomenal shadow play by Robert Planck, Edward Colman, and Harry Zech; Ray June's camerawork for the 35mm version is occasionally stunning, too. In both *Seven Footprints* and *The Bat Whispers*, the characters are more or less incidental. The content of the silent/sound hybrid *The Last Warning* is itself a half-satisfying hybrid, a compromise between Universal's earlier hit *The Phantom of the Opera* and the film's source book, Wadsworth Camp's *House of Fear*. Paul Leni's film is alternately prosaic and spookily poetic.

Dracula and *Frankenstein* were a year or two away, but their respective stars, Bela Lugosi and Boris Karloff, first dabbled in the beyond in sound films in

A group shot of the characters appearing in *Seven Footprints to Satan*

An ad from Universal's *The Cat Creeps* (1930)

1929. Unfortunately, both were miscast, Lugosi in *The Thirteenth Chair*, Karloff in *The Unholy Night*. The performance of the year was Warner Oland's, in *The Mysterious Dr. Fu Manchu*. Oland would go on to major in mystery movies (as Charlie Chan) and minor in horror movies such as *Drums of Jeopardy*, *Before Dawn*, and *WereWolf of London*.

Not surprisingly, stilted dialogue scenes were the rule in 1929, in *Darkened Rooms*, *The Mysterious Dr. Fu Manchu*, *The Unholy Night*, *The Mysterious Island*, and *The Thirteenth Chair*. Yet, some actors—Oland, Roland Young, Neil Hamilton—seemed quite at ease with the spoken word in these same films.

Midnight Mystery, June 1930, had perhaps the earliest imaginative use of sound in a (surviving) terror picture.

You could have been forgiven if, in 1929, you thought that MGM, not Universal, would become the premiere producer of talking horror films—*The Unholy Night*, *The Mysterious Island* (with its several undersea monsters), *The Thirteenth Chair*, all MGM ...

Notable performances: Warner Oland (*The Mysterious Dr. Fu Manchu*), Roland Young (*Unholy Night*), Neil Hamilton (*Darkened Rooms*), Una Merkel (*The Bat Whispers*)

Notable direction: Ben Christensen (*Seven Footprints to Satan*), Paul Leni (*The Last Warning*)

Notable photography: Sol Polito (*Seven Footprints to Satan*), Harry Fischbeck (*The Mysterious Dr. Fu Manchu*), Ira Morgan (*Unholy Night*), Archie Stout (*Darkened Rooms*), Joseph Walker (*Midnight Mystery*), Robert Planck and Ray June (*The Bat Whispers*, the 70mm and 35mm versions, resp.), Hal Mohr (*The Last Warning*)

Notable makeup: Perc Westmore (*Seven Footprints to Satan*)

Notable art direction: uncredited (*Seven Footprints to Satan*), uncredited (*The Mysterious Dr. Fu Manchu*), Cedric Gibbons (*The Mysterious Island*)

Notable effects: J.E. Williamson, James Basevi et al. (*The Mysterious Island*), Edward Colman, Harry Zech (*The Bat Whispers*)

Notable sound: Clem Portman (*Midnight Mystery*)

Notable editing: Robert Carlisle (*The Last Warning*)

Other films of interest:

The Bishop Murder Case (1930)—"It's the beginning of a series of murders, ghastly and inhuman." It's February 1930 and the MGM lion still hasn't started roaring. And there's no musical score. There is a thunderstorm—the prop man was working the aluminum sheeting overtime—a black cat, a line regarding "diabolic hatred," and a "never used" attic. But this is still just a stilted mystery, with Basil Rathbone as Philo Vance. The puzzle of the use of the word "bishop" cannot be guessed, though. Tracking shots help break up the dialogue monotony, and a dead-victims'-hands-in-the air motif provides a touch of the macabre. Ref: *Variety* 2/5/30: "eerie eccentric"; hunchback

The Black Pearl (1929)—*Variety* 3/20/29: "one terrific storm"

Black Waters (1929)—*Forgotten Horrors*: "demonic madman," voodoo drums

Bulldog Drummond (1929)—"You inhuman devils!" Threats of torture. It's Ronald Colman's film, what there is of it.

The Cat Creeps (1930)—*Castle of Frankenstein* 16:28: lost

The Cat and the Canary adaptation regarding a killer with claw-like hands. *Variety* 11/12/30: "Prize part ... the West Indian housekeeper with her spooky manner and voodoo suggestion." *Filmfax* 92:43

The Charlatan (1929)—"Mrs. Deering says you have supernatural powers." A thunderstorm mystery, yes, but with no spookiness, apart from George Robinson's lightning effects ...

Check and Double Check (1930)—"The old Williams house ... supposed to be haunted." The haunted house sequence is just some bumps in the night. Highly resistible Amos 'n' Andy comedy. *PV* 31:10

The Faker (1929)— IMDb: Columbia silent with Warner Oland as Hadrian, the faker

The Furies (1930)—*Variety* 4/23/30: Jekyll-and-Hyde-like lawyer, with his butler as his keeper. *AFI catalog*: horror? CHFB (Phantom XCI): domestic drama ... apparently lost

A lobby card from *Seven Keys to Baldpate* (1929), featuring Richard Dix (center) grabbing the man behind the counter.

El Gato (1930)—Apparently lost Spanish-language version of *The Cat Creeps* (1930). *Filmfax* 92:43

The Gorilla (1930)—Lost remake of lost 1927 silent *The Gorilla*, itself remade in 1939 as *The Gorilla* and apparently reworked as *Sh! the Octopus* (1937). *Variety* 2/25/31: "Hoke situations of the most ancient sort." *Filmfax* 92:41

The Great Gabbo (1929)—"He's fine when he thinks he's Otto." No, not the story of a sixth Marx brother, but of an insane ventriloquist (Erich von Stroheim) who can express his feelings only through his dummy, Otto, who seems to be another person. A fine idea, drastically diluted, principally by criminally overlong musical numbers. Gabbo's best line (to Otto), after a performance: "You were rotten, too!"

The Hole in the Wall (1929)—"This place gives me the creeps." Wild man, "spiritualistic medium," crooks with hearts as big as grain silos. Far-fetched suspense drama ...

House of Horror (1929)—Apparently lost. *Famous Monsters* 23:24. Directed by Ben Christensen. *Variety* 6/19/29: secret panels; "old gags"; "one percent dialogue." Walt Lee: supposedly haunted house. *Filmfax* 92:42: "the weakest reviewed of Christensen's American films"

House of Secrets (1929) —Apparently lost. See *House of Secrets* (1936)

In this lobby card from *Paramount on Parade* (1930), we pit **Fu Manchu (Warner Oland)** against **Sherlock Holmes (Clive Brook)** and **Philo Vance (William Powell)**.

In the Next Room (1930)—*Variety* 4/9/30: "queer and baffling" murders in the "old Gerhart mansion." Plus catalepsy, clutching hands. *Film Daily* 4/16/30: "mysterious mansion ... death dealing cabinet." *Billboard* 4/30: "spooky flashlights ferreting out hidden corners ... heroine who fears her spooky surroundings ... weird noises ... terrific rainstorm." Apparently lost

Ingagi (1930)—IMDb: gorilla abducts virgin

Paramount on Parade (1930)—In one skit, Fu Manchu (Warner Oland) shoots both Philo Vance (William Powell) and Sherlock Holmes (Clive Brook), then (yes) flies off. Silly, but it's a kick seeing Vance, Holmes, and Fu together.

Remote Control (1930)—Ref: *AFI catalog*. *Variety* 12/8/30: "ghost gang." "Fantastic content ... pretty light ... phony spiritualist"—Dave Sindelar, CHFB (Movie of the Day 4/11/2015). As Dave suggests, this is not remotely horrific. The "occultist" angle is used mainly in setting up a series of robberies. There's simply a little talk regarding the "mystic realm beyond." And bad comedies like this don't get better with age. Star William Haines is less amusing than simply annoying. It's December, and the MGM lion is still not roaring …

A Royal Romance (1930)—*Variety* 4/23/30: "haunted castle." *FD* 4/27/30: "creeps and shivers galore."… "spooky scenes." Directed by Erle C. Kenton. *AFI catalog*: haunted castle … countess hiding in secret chamber. "I second Rick's assessment that the film barely qualifies even as a sorta-kinda horror film"—Phantom XCI (CHFB 5/29/15)

The Sea Bat (1930)—Ref: *AFI catalog*: "monstrous sea bat." *Variety* 8/13/30: "immense sea bat." IMDb: manta ray. CHFB (Golden Age Horror 5/10/2013). Semi-horrific scenes with yacht-sized "monster," the "strangest of all strange sea creatures." Boris Karloff hardly gets to say, "Aw, shuddup!" before the ray gets him.

Seven Faces (1929)—*Variety* 11/20/29: waxworks figures seem to come to life …

Seven Keys to Baldpate (1929)—"A woman in white! They thought it was the ghost!" Two brief "ghost" scenes, some atmosphere, constant roaring wind. Richard Dix plays it too cute for comedy, and he's not up to drama.

Le Spectre Vert (1930)—*Catalogue des Films Francais, 1929-1939*: the first French talkie made in Hollywood. *Variety* 5/21/30: "the plot is more and more ghastly." Director: Jacques Feyder. Screenplay: Yves Mirande, from *The Unholy Night* (1929). 105 minutes. Photography: William Daniels. with Jetta Goudal, Andre Luguet, Georges Renavent

Stark Mad (1929)—*Variety* 7/3/29: chained ape, "eerie atmosphere." *AFI catalog*: "strange monster with great hairy talons." Apparently lost

Temple Tower (1930)—*Variety* 5/14/30: "masked menace." Remade as *Bulldog Drummond's Secret Police* (1939). Doctor Kiss (CHFB "Movie of the Day" 3/28/2015): restored in 2015; "plays like a horror film … gruesomely good chills … terrific old dark house atmosphere"

Under Texas Skies (1930)—Sinister Cinema Catalog, 2013/2014. "Mute brute"

The Unholy Three (1930)—"She could make Coolidge talk!" Semi-horrific sequence with a rampaging gorilla; otherwise, not even borderline horror. Lon

Chaney, in his only talking picture, is uncertain with his character Echo's dialogue, but revels in "Mrs. O'Grady's."

Unmasked (1929)—Ref: *AFI catalog*: East Indian mystic hypnotizes woman to kill. Apparently lost

The Witching Eyes (1929)—lost. *AFI catalog*: "curse ... witching hand." Phantom XCI (CHFB): German?

1929-1930

The LAST WARNING

The House of Fear (novel—Wadsworth Camp): "The cat is closer." Long neglected Woodford's Theatre presents a "somber fissure" in the "wall of brightness and animation," which is Broadway. ("It remembers too much.") A "legend of supernatural evil" attends the revival of the play, *Coward's Fare*, last presented 40 years ago by "disagreeable devil" Bertrand Woodford, the actor-director who died mysteriously, during a third-act scene. "Woodford had worked himself to death rather than let any man play his part, and a lot of people felt he never would let any man play it now that he was dead." ("He's afraid of Woodford's spook.") Now, "dragging footsteps" and the "curious, stealthy padding" of a cat herald the death of another actor, Carlton, in the same part, same scene. Dolly, an actress old enough to remember Woodford, swears that a "cat rushed past [her] just as Woodford's cat did the night he died."

Other "spook stuff" here includes the "unearthly ringing" of telephones (the "ghost of a bell") ... a "ghastly light ... gathering shape"... the "indistinct, scarcely outlined" form of Woodford, in a photo taken recently (the "shadow of Woodford") ... Raleigh Joyce, a "psychist," or "spook doctor," with the Society for Psychical Research ... and the wailing of a "hideous or unnatural thing" in a closed apartment room.

Tantalizing details alternate with occasional heavy-handed writing. The re-stagings of the deadly scene make a good mainspring for the plot, but the characters—and the cat—only get you about two-thirds of the way through. Tantalizing: "He saw that all of them ... glanced about the vast stage and the auditorium with its army of shadows, as if expectant of something as yet too remote for definition." The ultimate unraveling of the mystery is interesting, if not compelling. This "clear case of a haunted house" in New York City anticipates both *Double Door* and *Rosemary's Baby*. Doubleday published the book in 1916, and already there's a dialogue reference to Charlie Chaplin.

The Last Warning released Jan. 6, 1929: "We just saw Woodford's ghost!" Broadway star and producer John Woodford dies mysteriously, onstage. Titles: "And Woodford's Theatre Dark—A House of Mystery! Year after Year!" Now, another producer, McHugh (Montagu Love), wants to mount a new produc-

A creepy sequence from *The Last Warning*

tion of Woodford's old play "The Snare," in the "nasty old haunted theater." But the deceased Woodford has other ideas. He, or his ghost, seems to send a telegram to financier Josiah Bunce (Burr McIntosh): "Do not attempt to open my theater." Lead actress Barbara Morgan has a different name: Doris Terry; Quaile has a different occupation (director rather than writer) and a slightly different spelling of his name (it's now "Quayle"), but the Terry-Quayle-McHugh (Laura La Plante/John Boles/Love) relationship is basically the same in book and film.

Some bravura camerawork (Hal Mohr), lively direction (Paul Leni), and ultra-nifty montages (Robert Carlisle, editor) jazz up a flimsy story (Alfred A. Cohn et al.). Universal was apparently torn between the pretty good original here (*The House of Fear*) and their own horror hit, *Phantom of the Opera*. [Insert Spoiler] But this Phantom of the Theater has no grand, dramatic core—i.e., no opera phantom—just a hired hand in a bad Halloween mask. And it retains the two culprits from the book, but little of the latter's insinuating supernatural infrastructure. Although the supernatural is ultimately explained away, the book plays like a ghost story. Quayle and Terry are the hollow core of the movie—their coda is just a formality, which draws attention to that fact.

Some of the action here is prosaic, running around and shouting (this is a talkie-wannabe), but the long shot of the phantom—a figure with a ghost-

Carrie Daumery gets tangled in cobwebs in an eerie scene from *The Last Warning*.

white head—is *The Innocents*-like creepy, while the big dead eye of the thing at the peephole is real grotesquerie. And the woman-draped-in-cobwebs is a spooky coup. Mohr's money sequence: The camera swinging back and forth, on a rope or a cable, representing the phantom swinging on a rope toward, then away from, waiting cops. The huge grasping hands superimposed over the characters, at one point, prove not to be the phantom's, but it's a phantom-like effect. Here, titles flash like neon lights, enlarge to simulate shouting, shrink to simulate whispering, go in/out of focus, and waver as if underwater.

Notes: Barbara Morgan's name becomes, in the movie, the name of the older actress (played here by Carrie Daumery), who was called Dolly Timken, the "barometer" (of evil) and nose-witness to the "wraith of the perfume," in the book.

1931. John Boles—horror-movie star. Or so it might have seemed, at the time, what with this film and *Frankenstein* under his belt.

Odd title for an odd bit: "Stop that dancing!" They're the words of one annoyed Bunce brother, Josiah, to another, Robert (Mack Swain), who's doing some inexplicable, impromptu, amusing moves. A little later, and a little less odd: "Stop that whistling!"

Remade as *The House of Fear* (1939), which we will see.

Universal. D: Paul Leni. SP: Alfred A. Cohn, Tom Reed. Story: Cohn. Adap: J.G. Hawks, Robert F. Hill. Titles: Reed, from Wadsworth Camp's novel *The House of Fear* and a play by Thomas Fallon. Ph: Hal Mohr. AD: Charles D. Hall. Ed: Robert Carlisle. With Laura La Plante, Montagu Love, Roy D'Arcy, Margaret Livingston, John Boles, Burr McIntosh, Mack Swain, Bert Roach, Slim Summerville, Torben Meyer, D'Arcy Corrigan, Charles K. French, Fred Kelsey; 90 minutes

Ref: Hirschhorn/*The Universal Story*.

"The camera swings, swoops and zooms ... Even the title cards use FX"—*PV* 28:15.

"Sound effects are multiple, continuous and in detail, to the extent of reproducing a kiss. Absurd"—*Variety* 1/9/29.

SEVEN FOOTPRINTS TO SATAN

Seven Footprints to Satan (novel—A. Merritt): A vaguely Chinese-looking individual who calls himself Satan—although he is supposedly not *the* devil—"leases" the souls of humans and drugs "slaves" with a super-opiate which "dissolves" the soul. In the present, he is an aesthete who lives for amusement and finds it in the beauty of art and in gambling, but, in the past, he seems to have acted more like *the* devil. In his mansion—which is a "labyrinth of secret passages"—he subjects new victims to a challenge involving Buddha's first seven baby steps. A young woman, Eve Demerest, seems ticketed to become "Mme. Satan," but will she herself first dare to take the challenge? Occasionally inventive fantasy is more than a little absurd, and self-serious but rather lightweight. It's no wonder that the writer-director of the film adaptation scrapped most of the book, keeping just enough to make good the title.

Seven Footprints to Satan released Jan. 27, 1929 (silent version) and Feb. 17, 1929 (sound version). "You're despicable, all of you! Demons! Monsters!" James Kirkham (Creighton Hale) fancies himself a "great explorer," but he hasn't gotten any further than his own backyard. (In the book, Kirkham is an accomplished adventurer.) Then, "in the dark of night," he finds himself a prisoner in a most unusual house. A dwarf (Angelo Rossitto) pops out of a wall. Human and inhuman shadows abound. Open a door, and it's the "mistress of Satan" (Laska Winter), a pinch-faced old lady. Turn around, and there's a gorilla (Charles Gemora) rising from behind the headboard of a bed. ("The Beast of Satan has escaped!") Look up, and there's a hand fingering the framework of an elevated trap door. Enter what at first seems to be one of Dr. Moreau's manimals, who proves to be simply the hirsute Professor Moriarty (William V. Mong), who suffers from an infestation of sideburns. Most bizarrely, the Spider (Sheldon Lewis), all bad teeth, bad hair, and crutches, comes down the stairs. ("Beware the man who walks with crutches!") In one wonder-

fully lively sequence, Moriarty emerges from a trap door in a fireplace, the gorilla jumps out of a trunk, the Spider appears from a secret door, the dwarf tumbles out of a bookcase, and the heroine, Eve Martin (Thelma Todd), is removed (live) from a coffin.

From one angle, the silent version is a more literal *Hellzapoppin'*. From another, it's the wildest old dark house movie until *The Rocky Horror Picture Show* (1975). From yet another angle, Benjamin Christensen out-Bunuels Luis Bunuel—the latter's somewhat similar *The Exterminating Angel* (1962) seems almost a deferential homage. Hero and heroine are just straight men to a puzzling series of half-horrific, half-comic sights, sounds, and violent vignettes. His stern response to mystery: "I prefer to have dinner at home."

The prefatory sequences (some 15 minutes) and the 10-minute, seven-steps finale (from the book) are of little interest. A brief coda attempts to explain the inexplicable, but—like the coda of *Mark of the Vampire*—it's harmless and dismissable. It doesn't diminish what comes before it.

Parlor game: Have fun with the titles of 1929 thrillers: *Seven-Foot Prince to Satan* ... *Seven Footprints to Baldpate* ... *Seven Keys to Satan*. Or not.

Notes: A few years later, Thelma Todd encountered the few zanies that she did not run into here—the Marx Brothers, in *Monkey Business* (1931) and *Horse Feathers* (1932). She also made two other Christensen spookers—*The Haunted House* (1928) and *House of Horror* (1929).

Sheldon Lewis, of course, played Jekyll and Hyde, in 1920. He was also The Thing in *The Phantom* (1931) and The Phantom in *Tombstone Canyon* (1932). He also played one Boris Kosloff in *Lightning Hutch* (1926).

Most droll: the near-omnipresent gorilla, always skulking, creeping, and generally unseen by the other characters.

William V. Mong, Creighton Hale and Thelma Todd are pictured in this lobby card from *Seven Footprints to Satan*.

Kevin McLeod's score for the 2014 English-intertitled Serial Squadron version (silent with sound effects) adds to the comic mysteriousness. The glaring, bleached white faces of the actors in this aged print make them all resemble Lon Chaney, Jr. from *Man Made Monster*.

Sojin, as Satan's announcer, says that there are four steps to salvation and four "false" steps. Square that with "seven footprints."

First National. D, SP, Story: Benjamin Christensen. Titles: Cornell Woolrich, from A. Merritt's novel. Ph: Sol Polito. Mkp: Perc Westmore. Ed: Frank Ware. P: Wid Gunning. With Thelma Todd, Creighton Hale, Sheldon Lewis, William V. Mong, Sojin, Winter Blossom, Ivan Christy, DeWitt Jennings, Nora Cecil (old witch), Harry Tenbrook, Angelo Rossitto, Charles Gemora (gorilla), Doris Dawson (Satan's chosen one), Loretta Young; 60 minutes

Ref: Jim Shapiro.

Variety (4/17/29) missed the fun boat, and their (anonymous) reviewer pretended to be shocked: "An utterly moronic sound film appealing to all the passions ... wholly baffling from start to finish." Baffling is the idea!

Christensen "was a true master of combining thrills with comedy in a sumptuously visual and rhythmically edited way"—Ken Strong, "Lost Horrors!" *Filmfax* 92:41.

"It's much more than just another haunted house comedy"—*PV* 27:10.

"I found *Footprints* riotously funny"—Forrest J Ackerman, *Filmfax* 7:31.

STRANGE CARGO

Strange Cargo released March 31, 1929: "Your aunt's seeing spooks again." A "horrible night" on a yacht a "thousand miles at sea": Inexplicably, lights flicker. ("They ain't nearly as bright as they should be.") The "compass is acting funny," and the telegraph too. A sinister face "with an unearthly glow" appears at a porthole. "Something cold" passes a woman's face. A spirit seems to be rapping during a quasi-séance in the crow's nest. Is it all an "atmospheric disturbance" or "something supernatural"—say, a "seagoing ghost"?

A newspaper ad from *Strange Cargo* (1929)

No, but a Hindu yogi (Otto Matiesen?) is found lying in a cupboard deep in a trance: "I am like dead—from afar the order comes!"

As *Photoplay* noted, in its April 1929 review, "Spooks have come to the talkies." And, as noted above, there are hints of the spookernatural—"hypnotism and magic." But the only decent semi-scare is that face at the porthole. The "disturbance" is left unexplained—50 years later, it might have been explained as the workings of the Bermuda Triangle. ("But it's all very strange, sir—you might say, mysterious.") In what would become a common narrative practice of the talkie era—especially in ghost Westerns—the "ghosts," fake or not, are more talked about than seen.

Flat mystery is pretty much all mike-bound dialogue scenes—stand and talk, stand and talk. And surprisingly little advantage is taken of the new technology, outside the superabundance of talk—you hear the "spirit" rapping, a forlorn foghorn, and sailors singing, accompanied by an accordion. Would-be tingly lines are underlined. ("Holy mother! Which of us will be next?") And it is perhaps an historic first for the classic, "Do you know that when you get angry, you're prettier than ever?" The only voice that stands out belongs

A 1-sheet poster that builds up the mystery aspect of *The Mysterious Dr. Fu Manchu*.

to Walter Matthau sound-alike Ned Sparks. ("I wasn't cut out to be a medium!") But it's nice to see Frank Reicher (as the doctor) not long before *King Kong*.

The elevated "séance" is a novelty, but it's a bust, too, except for the prevailing darkness of the scene. "Spirits from the world beyond," indeed …

Note: There's background music only for the opening sequence.

Pathe. D, SP, Story, P: Benjamin Glazer. Story: also Melchior Lengyel. D: also Arthur Gregor. Titles: John Krafft. Writer: Horace Jackson. Ph: Arthur Miller. AD: Edward C. Jewell. With Lee Patrick, June Nash, George Barraud, Cosmo Kyrle Bellew, Russell Gleason, Frank Reicher, Claude King, Ned Sparks, Otto Matieson; 75 minutes

Ref: Dave Sindelar. IMDb. "Compares favorably with any of the spook dramas produced since the flickers decided to talk"—*Variety* 2/20/29.

The MYSTERIOUS DR. FU MANCHU

The Mysterious Dr. Fu Manchu released Aug. 10, 1929: "Fu Manchu is here, in this house!" The estimable Dr. Fu Manchu (Warner Oland)—once known principally as an "expert on Oriental diseases"—transforms into a "diabolical genius of a madman" when British forces unintentionally kill his wife and son during the Boxer Rebellion of 1900. ("These whites are barbarians, devils, fiends!") But "Uncle Fu" seems the "best and kindest man that ever lived," to his ward, the lovely Lia Eltham (Jean Arthur), who is unaware that she is a "creature of Fu Manchu," hypnotized to kill Fu's enemies, the Petries. Principal settings: China and Limehouse, England.

Seemingly calculated to stir up antagonism between Easterners and Westerners, *The Mysterious Dr. Fu Manchu* is the first and best of the Oland series.

(See also *The Return of Dr. Fu Manchu* [1930] and *Daughter of the Dragon* [1931].) It's certainly not the most enlightened movie, and the casting of the title role is at once its least enlightened and most inspired move: Westerner Oland brings a gravity and grandness to the role, and his performance makes the film still worth seeing. Under Rowland V. Lee's direction, a stilted, declamatory mode prevails among the actors, but Oland methodically slows down his speeches and quietly accents each word in ominous phrases like "the guest tea." True, it's also somewhat of a treat to watch O.P. Heggie—the blind hermit of *Bride of Frankenstein*—as criminologist Nayland Smith. But Jean Arthur is not at all up to her bigger dramatic scenes, which become camp interludes. Production scorecard: gorgeously-lit night scenes, a cool cliff-top, seaside Redmoat Grange—a model, in exteriors—mild wind effects, a "ghastly" mask, a handy mummy case, and two lights-out, scream scenes, courtesy of Lia.

Bonus Fu Manchu line: "Better for them they have a cobra in their midst than that girl."

(aka *Dr. Fu Manchu. The Insidious Dr. Fu-Manchu*) Paramount. D, P: Rowland V. Lee. SP, Dialogue: Lloyd Corrigan, Florence Ryerson. Titles: Joseph L. Mankiewicz. Based on characters created by Sax Rohmer. Ph: Harry Fischbeck. Mus: Oscar Potoker. Cost: Travis Banton. With Warner Oland, Neil Hamilton, Jean Arthur, O.P. Heggie, William Austin, Claude King, Charles A. Stevenson, Noble Johnson, Tully Marshall; 80 minutes

Ref: *PV* 37:16.

The UNHOLY NIGHT

The Green Ghost (screenplay for *The Unholy Night*, by Edwin Justus Mayer): "His face is like a ghost's ... a *green* ghost's ... as though he had arisen from Dracula's coffin!" March 26, 1919, and the "greatest fog London has ever known." The "Thing" has taken advantage of the fog and strangled four men ... The scene then switches to the Montague estate, in the countryside near London. The tale is told there of Sir Roger Montague, who died from a disease that "turned him quite green." Now people believe that they hear the "Green Ghost wailing." But "what invisible, unseen *Thing*" haunts the "grim and ghostly" library? In the climax, a "mood of weird spiritualism" pervades a séance attended by a "Phantom Regiment." Plus there's catalepsy ("Mallory, the Ghost") and an incidental floating head at an earlier séance. Scripts like this generally make for dry reading—one keeps wanting to see and hear the scenes that they describe. But there's an occasional touch of offhand near-poetry here ("Yawning hour of midnight") and the unusual use of an actress' name—in such camera instructions as "Big Closeup of Polly Moran" (page 33)—as the character's name. In the film itself, she's just Polly, the maid.

The Unholy Night released Sept. 14, 1929: "Then, if the living fail us, we must call on the dead to help us!" The movie pretty much follows the script—

A lobby card featuring Boris Karloff from *The Unholy Night* (1929)

fake ghosts and floating heads, but real hypnotism and catalepsy. This is such an early talkie that the MGM lion's roars are not heard. The actors playing the officers here all seem to have the same declamatory voice. Only Roland Young adds a little personality, though near the end, he too goes "dramatic" and gets a case of the bug eyes. Like most of his fellow actors, Boris Karloff is hampered by the need to enunciate for the mike, and he further suffers from the strain of affecting a Middle Eastern accent. Based on this film, one would not have predicted world fame for him in two years. The film is a showcase for broad, bad acting. Even the climactic appearance, at the séance, of the Phantom Regiment is a bit of a letdown, almost prosaic, though the ghostly singing of "Auld Lang Syne," which precedes their appearance, is tantalizing. The floating head (from the script), and the wraith (not from the script) of the credits sequence, however, are certainly eerie enough. The long track (photography by Ira Morgan) revealing body after body of the officers in their respective rooms is quite ambitious, condensing time as it does—it ellipses such intervening moments as the opening of bedroom doors, the cries of discovery, etc. Also impressive: the track up to the fire in the fireplace, at midnight, in the otherwise darkened room. In the script, the Phantom Regiment appears beside, or behind, Monty (Young), rather than in front of the séance audience.

See also "Le Spectre Vert" (Other films of interest, 1930.)

MGM. D: Lionel Barrymore. SP: Edwin Justus Mayer. Story: Ben Hecht. Adap: Dorothy Farnum. Titles: Joseph Farnham. Ph: Ira Morgan. Mus: William Axt. AD: Cedric Gibbons. Cost: Adrian. With Ernest Torrence, Roland Young, Dorothy Sebastian, Natalie Moorhead, Sydney Jarvis, Polly Moran, George Cooper, Sojin, John Miljan, John Loder, Lionel Belmore, Boris Karloff; 95 minutes

Ref: IMDb. *Film Comment* 7/89:38: regarding Sojin.
PV 32:16: director Lionel Barrymore's 100th credit.
"It's an all-talker and 100% lemon"—*Variety* 10/16/29.

The MYSTERIOUS ISLAND

"*The Mysterious Island*" or "*L'Isle Mysterieuse*" (novel—Jules Verne) [SPOILERS below]: "I have seen nothing, and yet there *is* something there!" Civilization is rekindled, or rebuilt, brick by brick, in miniature, by five "colonists," on a lost island (dubbed Lincoln Island) in the Pacific. An admirable feat—by the colonists, and Verne—but the tenuous story and characterization strand the myriad taming-the-frontier details. The colonists are bland ciphers of heroes. Every breakfast is noted, every discipline described, from shipbuilding to metallurgy to glass blowing to carpentry to astronomy to ... brick-making.

A lobby card depicting the "creatures of the deep," from *The Mysterious Island* (1929)

At worst, there are exclamation points and vapid comments: "It is true that the enterprise might succeed, but it might also fail." The climactic volcanic eruption is the descriptive high point ("a Niagara of molten fluid"). Finally, Verne weaves a bit of Captain Nemo magic, and explains the hints of the supernatural and a "marine monster" as mere science fiction—"electric balls" and a reprise for the Nautilus. In fact, there are no monsters here—a surprise, as the movies based on this book generally feature all-out, no-doubt-about-it monsters.

The Mysterious Island released Oct. 5, 1929: Off the coast of the Kingdom of Hetvia "lies Count Andre Dakkar's island stronghold," Mysterious Island, actually a "submerged volcano." Dakkar has invented diving-ships which take their passengers "into a new world, amid green shining caverns," at the bottom of the sea, where the "people of the abyss"—distant cousins of humans ("almost like men")—proliferate. For unexplained reasons, the giant, horned, finned sea-bottom lizard is their enemy, and the gigantic killer-octopus ("a sluggish monster of terrific strength") is their ally. Diving-ship No. 1 zaps the lizard with an electric ray. Bonus: a very incidental, large, creepy, crab-like sea creature. Only at the end does the movie's story come close to intersecting the story of the book: The dying Dakkar is buried "deep in the graveyard of the sea"—in his diving-ship—as Nemo (aka Dakkar), in the book, goes down with his submarine.

Fortunately, the future of sound films was not riding on the success or failure of *The Mysterious Island*. Silent sequences with intertitles alternate, haphazardly, with static dialogue scenes. Poor Lionel Barrymore scratches and gestures like crazy, apparently trying to distract from the fact that he's reading from off-screen cards, in those dialogue scenes. Then, like magic, in the silent sequences, he sheds most of his mannerisms. Technology is the name of the game here, whether within the film, in the plot and its premises, or behind the scenes, in the making of this very early talkie. At one point, the two technologies—within and without—are one, when Nikolai, under the sea, talks on the

The adorable, intelligent, duck-billed, bug-eyed over-amped little creatures of *The Mysterious Island*

ship's phone, and Dakkar, above, hears him—and we hear him: no subtitles or intertitles. ("Diving-ship No. 1 reporting.") The sound effects were probably pretty exciting in 1929: rifle fire, the sound of galloping horses, the sound of a battering ram ramming the submerged diving-ship, and—forerunner of scads of mad-scientist-lab sound effects—the crackling of the shiny, porcupiney "telephones," as they rev up.

The film divides, fairly handily, into forgettable political intrigue, on dry land, and fun, somewhat surreal, undersea action. The very forgettable Baron Falon (Montagu Love)-Countess Sonia (Jane Daly)-Nikolai (Lloyd Hughes) romantic triangle effectively kills its part of the movie. The intelligent, duck-billed, bug-eyed, over-amped little "creatures of the deep" look adorable (Angelo Rossitto plays one of them), and seem to switch sides, from enemies of the surface people, to their friends—or maybe they're just neutral—and back to enemies, or predators, after the "bloodless creatures" become maddened by the blood spilled by the humans. (A hint of briny vampirism here.) They might be a horde of Huey, Dewey, and Louies. ("They're all around us—thousands of them!" Well, hundreds.) In very long shot, they look like an avant-garde troupe of tiny, silhouetted ballet dancers. The diving-ships would be more at home in a bathtub.

Notes: Score one for the spectacle of the incidental, but intriguing, sunken "war galley of ancient Rome," "manned" by the skeletons of chained slaves.

Lucien Hubbard rates writing and directing credits here, but Maurice Tourneur and Ben Christensen also put in time at the helm.

The movie retains little of Verne—just the diving-ships, Dakkar (aka Nemo, in the book, where he was not at all, however, the main character), and the island, without bricks. It's not just a mysterious island. It's Mysterious Island, like Mystery Mountain, in *The Brain from Planet Arous* (1957). So that should be the title. No *The* ... This isn't Jules Verne.

MGM. D, SP: Lucien Hubbard, from the novel by Jules Verne. Ph: Percy Hilburn. Mus: Martin Broones, Arthur Lange. AD: Cedric Gibbons. SpFX: J. Ernest Williamson. TechFX: James Basevi, Irving Ries, Louis H. Tolhurst; With Lionel Barrymore, Jacqueline Gadsdon, Lloyd Hughes, Montagu Love, Harry Gribbon, Snitz Edwards, Gibson Gowland, Dolores Brinkman, Karl Dane, Robert Dudley, Bob Kortman, Angelo Rossitto, Harry Tenbrook; 95 minutes.

Ref: IMDb.

Bill Warren, *Keep Watching the Skies!*

Inspector Delzante (Bela Lugosi) hovers over a roomful of guilty-looking suspects, in *The Thirteenth Chair* (1929).

A lobby card from *The Thirteenth Chair* shows Margaret Wycherly (top left) and Leila Hyams

The THIRTEENTH CHAIR

The Thirteenth Chair released Oct. 19, 1929: "Why, what she's asking is too horrible!" In Calcutta "Spirit medium" Mme. LaGrange (Margaret Wycherly) "has done things that cannot be explained," and Edward Wales (John Davidson) hopes that her "power of some sort" can solve the murder of a friend. "Things happen in the dark," promptly, of a séance or two: Madame speaks in voices, she sets one lady to screaming, and Wales is stabbed to death. ("This is horrible! Horrible!") In the climactic séance, the "dead body of Edward Wales" seems to speak: "I've come a long way." (Again: "Oh! This is horrible! Horrible!") Apparently written as a vehicle for his actress wife, Wycherly, Bayard Veiller's play *The Thirteenth Chair* becomes a film vehicle for her and for Bela Lugosi (as Inspector Delzante), as well. And if the movie creaks, it's also a wonderful document, a portrait of Lugosi when he was still playing Count Dracula on stage, but before he played the role in film. His forceful, even bullying Delzante is a mixture of circus ringmaster, standard movie detective, and, pretty inevitably, the Count, down to the hand and arm gestures.

Inauspiciously, Lugosi's first words onscreen, apparently, were "Hmm! Highly connected in official circles?" In fact, this line is just Delzante quoting the Commissioner (Clarence Geldert). An historic, then, but otherwise unmemorable moment. Lugosi, of course, gloried in words, spoken words, and he has a bounty of them here. But it's the extraordinary fighting the ordinary, Lugosi vs. Veiller's fairly carefully crafted but mundane writing. ("We merely wanted her admission she was ... there!") Lugosi's occasional, extravagant gestures simply underline the emptiness of the thing. His absurdly rich accent unfortunately puts Veiller's dialogue in neon lights. His scenes with Mme. LaGrange verge on camp duets, though they still have a "power of some sort." Retrospectively, of course, we can see signs of a unique talent in Lugosi's performance, but one would, at the time, have hardly forecast a grand future for this mostly miscast 47-year-old actor.

Wycherly's Madame LaGrange is folksy, disarming, canny, with something of the showman in her ("Things happen in the dark"), plus more than a little Stella Dallas, as she agonizes over and sacrifices herself for her daughter (Leila Hyams). Merritt B. Gerstad's track up to LaGrange—from long to medium shot—as she prays disconsolately for the power to clear Helen, proves just as effective a means of underlining an important speech as Lugosi's occasional near-growl of a delivery. ("Take her to the matron!")

Surprisingly, the film has one shock scene, which does not date—the use of Wales' dead body, propped up in a chair (a "beastly outrage"), presumably the 13th, for the concluding séance. ("We're not going to sit in the dark with that, are we?") It's the very outrage of it all, which is so satisfying.

Complete with a crazy confession of guilt, which would do a *Perry Mason* episode proud. ("I went mad. The rotten, rotten beast!")

Notes: The 7th and 8th-listed players in the opening credits—Lugosi and Davidson, respectively—would be reunited, in 1941, in *The Devil Bat*, with Lugosi's name now listed above the title.

Holmes Herbert repeats his role of Sir Roscoe Crosby in the 1937 remake.

Balmiest staging ploy: the dagger stuck in the ceiling. In the first shot of said dagger, the latter seems to be moving upwards, but closer inspection reveals that it's the camera that's moving, downwards.

Still stuck in the silent era, the MGM lion's roars here (as also in *The Unholy Night*) are inaudible.

Odd question, out of context: "Do you know who killed you?"

MGM. D, P: Tod Browning. SP: Elliott J. Clawson, from Bayard Veiller's play. Ph: Merritt B. Gerstad. Title Mus: William Axt. AD: Cedric Gibbons. Ed: Harry Reynolds. Cost: Adrian. With Margaret Wycherly, Leila Hyams, Conrad Nagel, Helene Millard, Holmes Herbert, Mary Forbes, Bela Lugosi, John Davidson, Moon Carroll, Lal Chand Mehra; 72 minutes

Ref: *Variety* 1/22/30.

PV 20:13: "Lugosi has a cool major role."

"Lugosi becomes dominant, calculating, and far more serious than the detective of Veiller's play"—Gary Don Rhodes, in *Bela Lugosi*, p95.

DARKENED ROOMS

Darkened Rooms (novel—Philip Gibbs): "A nice evening for the spooks!" Brixton, a London suburb. "Spook merchant" Emery Jago ("I'm a hypnotist") has "uncanny gifts"—specifically, telepathy and hypnosis. And his assistant, and lover, Belle, can see the future in her crystal ball. But Jago starts "mixing up fraud with [these] gifts of super-sensibility." He claims he is possessed by a dead man, and, at a séance, conjures up a "spirit" concocted with "soft wax" and an "enlarged photograph," and the deception is exposed, or nearly so. ("The dead came back!") Gibbs' book has more ghostly and quasi-ghostly phenomena than does the movie adaptation: Belle, for instance—in the book—gets "the creeps" in a country house apparently haunted by an "old lady." And it's not badly written ("this brief little life of ours [is] just an hour in a wayside inn on the way—home"), but it resolves, unsatisfyingly, into a flat love-beyond-death tale, though with a tantalizing coda.

Darkened Rooms released Nov. 23, 1929. "I can make 'em see pink elephants if they'll pay me enough money." Some SPOILERS here. With the aid of books like *The Key to Hypnotism* and *Secrets of Spiritualism*, ambitious young Emory Jago (Neil Hamilton), of Jago's Photographic Studio, plans to convince rich kid Joyce Clayton (Doris Hill) that her dead brother Dick is speaking to her from beyond the "gates of the spirit world." At a séance—complete with rising table—at the Claytons' Long Island estate, Jago's mediumistic assistant Ellen (Evelyn Brent)—the "grandest little spirit"—indeed seems to pass on a message

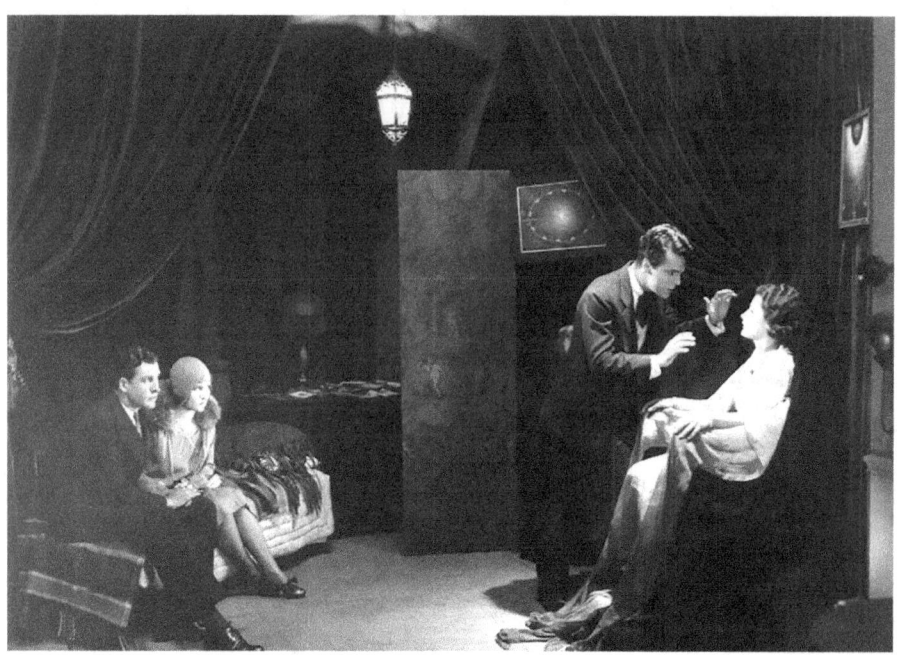

Neil Hamilton hovers over the transfixed Evelyn Brent, in *Darkened Rooms* (1929).

from Dick to Joyce. Jago thinks that it's "hypnotic suggestion" which allows him to do anything he wants with Ellen, but it's actually love which motivates her.

Ultimately, she uses his budding belief in his own powers ("Sometimes, I'm almost afraid of what's behind that thin veil") to scare him away from spiritualism: She hires indigent actor Bert Nelson (Wallace MacDonald) to "play ghost" and expose the fraud to Joyce. In an effective Archie Stout long shot, the "ghost" of Dick appears at the top of the stairs. ("I've come to warn you and to save you.") Breathlessly, Emory tells Ellen of his illumination: "Suddenly, I tell you, we saw it! There it was in the room, just a few feet away. And it spoke! I'm through monkeying with that stuff forever!"

Sincere very early talkie is dramatically pat. And the spectacle of the "ghost" would more likely encourage than discourage a rookie spiritualist. Hamilton is the only actor who seems comfortable with dialogue, while Hill and David Newell, as Joyce's sweetie Billy, are the least comfortable. Film jettisons most of the source book and doesn't come up with much to replace what was lost. The Patrick J. Kearney-Melville Baker script doesn't even make it clear if the dead Dick was, in fact, Joyce's brother. MacDonald became one of the key producers of 1940s shockers, such as *The Devil Commands*, *The Face behind the Mask*, and *The Unknown*. Brent starred in the Josef von Sternberg silents *Underworld*, *The Last Command*, and *The Dragnet*, and she makes the most here of one of her few good lines: "Tough racket bein' a girl and broke." Gale Henry has a choice early bit, as Madame Silvara. The latter discourages a customer from taking money in the semi-sacred crystal-gazing parlor, but, upon stepping into the next room, immediately asks him for two dollars.

Paramount. D: Louis Gasnier. SP: P. Kearney, M. Baker, from Philip Gibbs' novel. Ph: A. Stout. Mus: Karl Hajos. Cost: Travis Banton. With Evelyn Brent, Neil Hamilton, Doris Hill, David Newell, Gale Henry, Wallace MacDonald, George Beranger, E.H. Calvert; 66 minutes

Ref: *AFI catalog*.

"Largely a misfired curiosity"—Dave Sindelar (*Movie of the Day* 11/21/2003).

"Will offend no one, except perhaps Conan Doyle"—*Variety* 12/18/29.

The RETURN OF DR. FU MANCHU

The Return of Dr. Fu Manchu released May 2, 1930: "Fu Manchu alive!" This sequel begins with one wedding and a funeral—neither quite carried

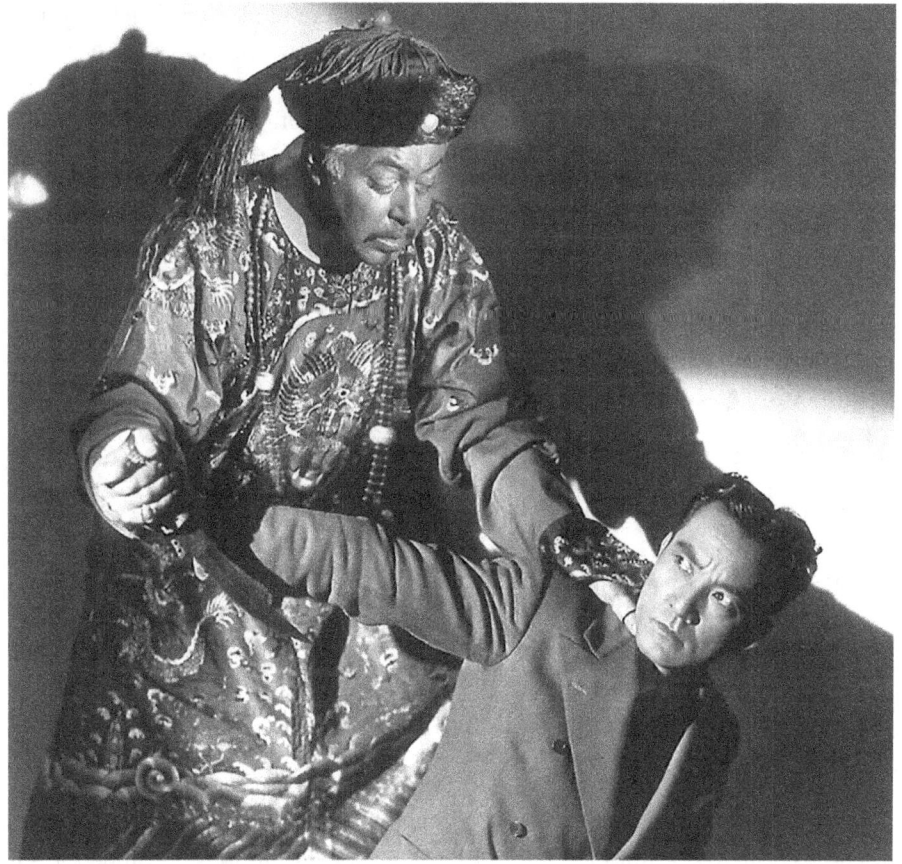

"Fu Manchu (Warner Oland) alive!" in *The Return of Dr. Fu Manchu*

to completion—and a monologue recap of the original, *The Mysterious Dr. Fu Manchu*. And, yes, Fu (Warner Oland) is alive—the potion he took at the end of the latter movie was less a poison, apparently, than a death-semblance serum. ("Your Shakespeare used it in *Romeo and Juliet*.") He employs the same potion on his enemies, then buries them. ("Then they really die!") With a second potion, he both punishes an assistant who fails in his task ("The potion paralyzes the brain immediately—you soon will be completely demented") and controls Lia Eltham (Jean Arthur): "I have taken her mind ... "

Fu sets up his laboratory in the "old Wilson dye works." His "powerful opponent," Nayland Smith (O.P. Heggie), praises him: "Before Fu Manchu went insane, he was a magnificent scientist, working for mankind": but Smith still, in another part of the movie, carelessly uses the word "Chinaman." Unlike *The Mysterious Dr. Fu Manchu*, *The Return of Dr. Fu Manchu* has a rushed feel to it, and possesses little or no historical or artistic value.

In one long sequence, Fu Manchu and Nayland Smith face off across the former's table, but this centerpiece is not quite the grand duel it was supposed to be, partly because Oland approaches his role here almost perfunctorily. His use of his hands for emphasis and punctuation is less effective than in the original, and his delivery is less measured. His best line: "I do considerable dissecting myself!" Jean Arthur picks up where she left off, that is, awkwardly. ("You fiend!") As our hero, Neil Hamilton is better than she at corny dramatics, and is thus less campy, less amusing.

Bonus line regarding Fu Manchu: "Harding has got Fu!"

(aka *The New Adventures of Dr. Fu Manchu*) Paramount. D, P: Rowland V. Lee. SP: Lloyd Corrigan, Florence Ryerson. Characters created by Sax Rohmer. Sequel to *The Mysterious Dr. Fu Manchu*. Sequel: *Daughter of the Dragon*. Ph: Archie Stout. Sd: Gene Merritt. With Warner Oland, O.P. Heggie, Jean Arthur, Neil Hamilton, Evelyn Hall, William Austin, Nora Cecil, Olaf Hytten, Tetsu Komai; 73 minutes

Ref: *PV* 37:16.

Eames/*The Paramount Story*.

MIDNIGHT MYSTERY

Midnight Mystery released June 1, 1930: "Don't scream so loud, my darling—you might split your silly throat." A "bloodthirsty maniac" ruins a house party set in a mansion where the "wind wails through the corridors," on Hawk Island, a "little, rock-bound island, off the coast of Cuba." ("Isn't that wind just too thrilling?") Technically venturesome early talkie creates a cacophony of chatting party guests, piano music, screams, the sound of gunshots, roaring wind, thunder, clanging buoys, and the wailing of a "ghost." ("Never hear anything over that thunder.") Clem Portman did the sound recording, and he obviously had a ball.

Fiendish-perfect-crime tale is ingenious, in its gnarled little way, but the story doesn't yield much in the way of workable material for the actors, except for some campy exclamations. The idea of people who are "thrilled with murders" and hoping for something "nice and gruesome" would be done better in, say, the prologue to *Bride of Frankenstein* and in Hitchcock's *Shadow of a Doubt*. Minor dramatic coup: the bringing into the kitchen (from outside) of the corpse. It really sours the mood of the breakfast crowd.

Hugh Trevor, as Gregory, is terrible; the other actors are simply insubstantial. Betty Compson (Sally) starred in Sternberg's silent *The Docks of New York*, and was Mrs. Kessler/the "ghost" to Bela Lugosi's Kessler in *Invisible Ghost*. Lowell Sherman (Tom) was also a director—he did, among others, *She Done Him Wrong*, *Morning Glory*, and *Night Life of the Gods*. Associate producer Bertram Millhauser is noted more for his scripts for *The Garden Murder Case*, *Sherlock Holmes Faces Death*, *The Spider Woman*, etc. Joseph Walker—Frank Capra's director of photography on most of his 1930s films—creates two impressive effects: the flash-lighted face of the "ghost" in the otherwise completely dark room, and the huge, monstrous shadow of the killer as the latter drags the dead body across the room.

Radio Pictures. D: George B. Seitz. SP: Beulah Marie Dix, from Howard Irving Young's play *Hawk Island*. Ph: Joseph Walker. AD: Max Ree. Ed: Otto Ludwig. Sd: Clem Portman. Cost: Walter Plunkett. SpFX: Lloyd Knechtel. P:

A montage of stills from *Midnight Mystery*

William LeBaron. With Betty Compson, Lowell Sherman, Raymond Hatton, Hugh Trevor, June Clyde, Ivan Lebedeff, Rita La Roy, Marcelle Corday, Sidney D'Albrook; 69 minutes

Ref: "People are all like puppets working to the ends of the director ..."—*Variety* 6/4/30.

The BAT WHISPERS

The Circular Staircase (novel): "That night the Sunnyside ghost began to walk again." Mary Roberts Rinehart's early (1907) version of *The Bat* features just about everything in the later work, except The Bat. And the latter is missed. The mystery business here is complicated enough, but both puzzle and solution are only mildly interesting. There are occasional taking human and comic touches, but the story is still pretty small beans. Here, Cornelia Van Gorder is called Miss Rachel Innes, who narrates. Lizzie is Liddy. Here, the Flemings are the Armstrongs. As in *The Bat*, bank loot in a secret room is the crux. But instead of a garage fire—a stable fire. Instead of a "gleaming eye," a "burning eye." Some of the "goin's-on ... as ain't natchal" in the "spook factory" of Sunnyside (cf. Cedarcrest) have not been repeated in any of the extant "Bat" re-workings. These thrills include a man "scared to death" by a "ghost."... a graveyard exhumation ... and a "woman in white" gliding down a hall. The very popular book was filmed in 1915, and its next incarnation was as a stage play, in 1917, which added The Bat.

The Bat (novel, 1920 or 1926): "The Bat's supernatural, Anderson." "The haunts and the banshees" seem to prowl Cedarcrest, the estate which feisty spinster Cornelia Van Gorder has rented for the summer. ("Spooky sort of place in the dark, isn't it?") But Miss Cornelia knows that it's the arch-criminal The Bat who reigns there—it's "the Bat's home country." Mary Roberts Rinehart's venerable mystery is a bit musty now, but it's sufficiently twisty and not badly written. One prime frisson: the "phone call from nowhere." The in-house phone rings, but the gathered principals who hear it ring realize ... "But we're all *here*." The climactic plot-and-character reversal is well engineered, but will not be a surprise to anyone who has seen the movie versions. Stereotypes include a skittish Irish maid and a Japanese butler with "beady little black eyes." Lizzie's nervousness is overused, but it's she who gets the line: "I saw a *gleaming eye!*" At the end, there's a satisfying explanation for this phenomenon.

The Bat (1926 film): "The house is haunted—we've sent four detectives." This silent adaptation of the 1917 play by Mary Roberts Rinehart and Avery Hopwood features supremely atmospheric architecture. Cedarcrest's staircases, dining room, attic, roof, towers, etc. star—they are, respectively, tall or long or large or otherwise imposing. The sets dwarf the characters, though these near-nonentities are easily dwarfed. The house—as designed by William Cameron Menzies and photographed by Arthur Edeson—is alive; the people ar-

Four intense men and three pointed guns, from *The Bat Whispers* (1930)

en't. And as directed by Roland West, the movie is one long scare sequence—it may still hold the record for number of lights-out scenes. Unfortunately, the big-eared, bat-head mask is pretty hokey—The Bat is more in danger of becoming a pinata than it is of scaring anyone. Coolest creepy line/title: Louise Fazenda's Lizzie's "Candles won't stay lit here—something blows 'em out." Coolest deployment of a line/title: The Bat's "Give me that blueprint!"—his shouted words vividly inhabit the beam of flashlight light, which he's angling down the staircase toward Richard Fleming (Arthur Housman). The movie makes it too clear, from the beginning, what the "gleaming eye" is—there's no mystery.

The Bat Whispers (70mm version): released Nov. 13, 1930. "He rolls things down the stairs, and there's no one there to make 'em roll." The mysterious Bat does indeed whisper, whether he's secreted behind a huge wall portrait or prowling around in an attic, and one onlooker describes him as a "ghost," all in white and without a face. At any rate, The Bat has at least lost those ridiculous bat ears from the silent version.

This first sound version of *The Bat* is half-creaky, half-canny "spookism." The play with shadow and silhouette is, at times, very sophisticated; dialogue sequences are stilted. The change of visual tactics from the silent version is

Who is the Bat? From *The Bat Whispers*

striking: instead of the intimidating height of the tall rooms and windows ... we have the formidable width of the 70mm frame. If the fast tracking through models and sets is fun, it generally seems mere gussying-up of tired material. But the movie is also rife with imaginative shadow play.

Or, I should say, the movies are rife—*The Bat Whispers* is really two movies, at first glance almost identical, scene for scene, line for line, gesture for gesture. The intention seems to have been to create a carbon copy rather than to re-imagine the film for a different format. But, on closer inspection, differences in the staging between the two versions—some minute, some significant—become apparent. In the Robert Planck-photographed 70mm version, for instance, Una Merkel's Dale bangs on a wall, at one point, with her right fist closed; in the comparable moment in the Ray June-photographed 35mm version, she hits it with an open right palm. Apparently, just a detail which the script girl happened to miss.

But other differences are of more note, particularly in the two showcase shadow sequences. In one—in the 70mm version—the shadow of the Bat on a wall alters and shrinks—as if supernaturally imploding—then separates from the Bat himself, as the latter walks toward the camera ... and Dale. In the 35mm version, the shrinking shadow is not as impressive an effect, partly because it's half-hidden, screen right, by other, more mundane shadows, which all-but-obliterate the startling "separating" effect. Here, the shadow seems just a shadow.

In the other standout sequence, the 35mm version holds its own. Again, Planck makes the Bat's shadow on walls and doors seem supernaturally distinct from the Bat himself. The shadow fingers and wrists are crooked, bent in macabre ways, and the huge figure seems to ooze across the walls, enlarge, then disappear into a corner, only to reemerge and shrink, as shadow hand and human hand meet at a light switch. Oddly, it seems surprising when these hands connect up—the animated shadows here, as noted above, have a life of their own and seem not to need human assistance. In June's photography, in this scene, the shadow hands seem a little more ordinary—human-hand-generated—but when the shadow Bat reaches that corner it seems to be suddenly spliced in two, in a fun-house-mirror-like effect. The 70mm scene is superlative, but the 35mm version is quite good, too.

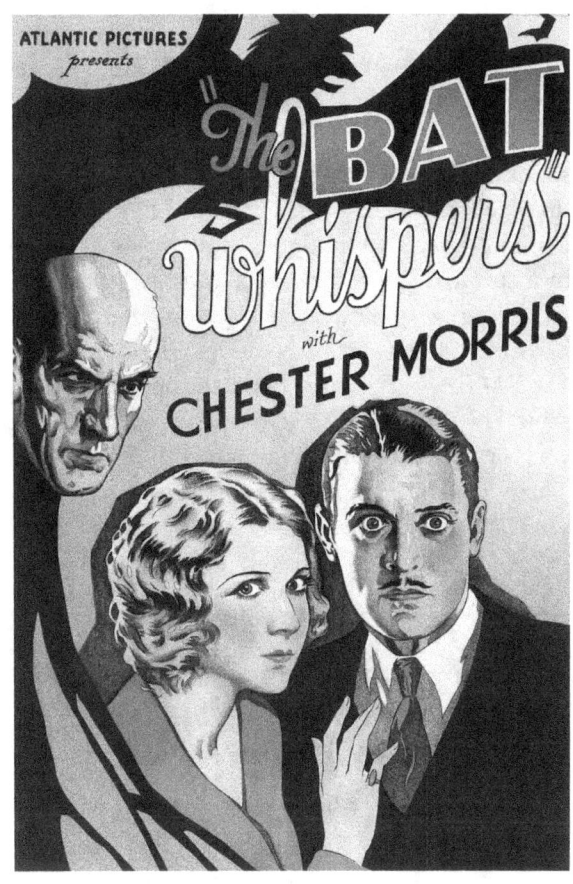

The Bat Whispers (35mm version): "Nobody can stop ghosts." Admittedly, the actors—in generally closer shots—make more of an impression in this version. Chester Morris' Anderson seems even stranger. The fluttery-voiced Una Merkel—a milder form of ZaSu Pitts—seems sweeter. Gustav von Seyffertitz seems craggier. Hard to believe, but Maude Eburne is even more grating. And the sheriff's comical clicks of his tongue are more emphatic. But their material, for the most part, is just as dated.

A tip of the non-Hatlo hat to Dave Sindelar.

UA. D, SP: Roland West, from the play by Mary Roberts Rinehart and Avery Hopwood. Ph: Robert H. Planck (70mm); Ray June (30mm); (asst) Stanley Cortez. Settings: Paul Crawley. Ed: Hal C. Kern, James Smith. SpPh: Edward Colman. Mkp: S.E. Jennings. P: Joseph M. Schenck. With Chester Morris, Grayce Hampton, Una Merkel, Maude Eburne, Gustav von Seyffertitz, William Bakewell, Spencer Charters, Sidney D'Albrook, S.E. Jennings, Ben Bard (The Unknown); 83 minutes

Ref: "Still an impressive movie"—Gary Johnson, imagesjournal.com

The Bat (1959): "So many unexplainable things have happened here." A "man without a face"—The Bat—prowls a "spooky old house," "The Oaks," and kills with steel "claws." Abysmal. The look of the thing is flat and unspooky, and Agnes Moorehead wears her role of Cornelia van Gorder like a dress, which does not fit her at all. She seems uncomfortable. Vincent Price is smooth in a role that goes more or less nowhere. [SPOILER]: His doctor—in a strictly legal sense—gets away with murder, but some extra-legal karma catches up with him. And, in one scene, it's revealed that the doctor seems to be working on a sort of Neo-Devil-Bat.

The Bat ... "Spooky place in the dark, isn't it?" 1960 TV adaptation presented by the *Dow Hour of Great Mysteries* is more bearable than the 1959 movie version, but also can't do much with the rather thin Rinehart material. Early cheat scene has The Bat and the actor supposedly in the campy costume in the same shot. Even the thunderstorm is pretty mild. "The eye!"

Highlights of 1931

You're a fan of classic horror. Imagine, if you can, a time before *Dracula* and *Frankenstein*, 1931 ... Neither can I. It's our life. So nice to have something to which we can wholeheartedly lay claim. The Golden Age began, in earnest, in 1931, with *Dracula* and *Frankenstein*, and unofficially ended with Dracula and the Frankenstein Monster, in 1948 (*Abbott and Costello Meet Frankenstein*). Of course, there were enduring classics—silent and sound—before *Dracula*. And the boom wartime years ended two or three years before A&C met Frankenstein's monster, Dracula, and Larry Talbot. *Dracula* and *Frankenstein* also initiated the *second* half of the Golden Age, in 1938, when they were re-released, and their renewed success helped end a dismaying two-year drought. An argument could be made that *Dracula* and *Frankenstein* have been the most influential of all horror movies. *Abbott and Costello Meet Frankenstein* did not launch another Golden Age, but it did start a trend—at least at Universal and Monogram—of monster-comedies.

The most important names in the first half of the Golden Age were James Whale, Tod Browning, Boris Karloff, and Bela Lugosi. Other possible nominees: Karl Freund (*Dracula, The Mummy, Murders in the Rue Morgue, Mad Love*) and Lionel Atwill (*Doctor X, Mystery of the Wax Museum, Murders in the Zoo, Secret of the Blue Room, Mark of the Vampire*). Of course, Carl Laemmle, Jr. at Universal, was producer for all of them, at one time or another. He, if anyone, could be called the King of the Golden Age.

About half of the horror films of 1931, it seems, were taken from the classics—*Dracula, Drácula* (Spanish-language), *Frankenstein, Svengali* (from *Trilby*), and *Dr. Jekyll and Mr. Hyde*. The year also saw, in effect, two Fu Manchu movies—*Daughter of the Dragon* and *The Drums of Jeopardy*—neither one, however, actually based on the Sax Rohmer novels. Warner Oland plays Fu Manchu in *Daughter of the Dragon* and Dr. Karlov in *Drums of Jeopardy*, but Karlov is a clone of Fu Manchu.

Fox released the first of what would become its annual magic and mystery movie—*The Spider*. Next up: *Chandu the Magician*, in 1932, then *Trick for Trick*, 1933.

Notable performances: Boris Karloff, Colin Clive, Dwight Frye (*Frankenstein*), Bela Lugosi, Frye (*Dracula*), Pablo Alvarez Rubio (Spanish-language *Dracula*), Warner Oland (*Drums of Jeopardy, Daughter of the Dragon*), John Barrymore (*Svengali*), Fredric March, Miriam Hopkins (*Dr. Jekyll and Mr. Hyde*)

Notable direction: James Whale (*Frankenstein*), Tod Browning (*Dracula*), Rouben Mamoulian (*Dr. Jekyll and Mr. Hyde*)

Notable writing: Garrett Fort et al. (*Frankenstein*)

Notable photography: Arthur Edeson (*Frankenstein*), Karl Freund (*Dracula*), George Robinson (Spanish-language *Dracula*), Arthur Reed (*Drums of Jeopardy*),

Barney McGill (*Svengali*), Karl Struss (*Dr. Jekyll and Mr. Hyde, Murder by the Clock*), Victor Milner (*Daughter of the Dragon*), James Wong Howe (*The Spider*)

Notable art direction: Charles D. Hall (*Frankenstein* and *Dracula*), Fay Babcock (*Drums of Jeopardy*), Anton Grot (*Svengali*)

Notable costumes: Earl Luick (*Svengali*), Vera West (*Dracula*), uncredited (*Daughter of the Dragon*), Travis Banton (*Dr. Jekyll and Mr. Hyde*)

Notable makeup: Johnny Wallis [uncredited] (*Svengali*), Jack Pierce (*Frankenstein, Dracula*), Wally Westmore (*Dr. Jekyll and Mr. Hyde*)

Notable special effects: Kenneth Strickfaden, John P. Fulton (*Frankenstein*)

Notable camp: finale, *Murder by the Clock*

Other films of interest:

A Dangerous Affair—HSF4: virtually a lost film, though some of it exists at the Library of Congress. Flimsy script, atmospheric Teddy Tetzlaff photography, a Ghost Gang, an "army of phantoms," a "moving light," and Charles Middleton as a mock-menacing, clubfooted lawyer

The Mad Genius—Someone coming into this cold might think that John Barrymore was just an old bore. Well, here, he is. Barrymore and Boris Karloff ("Fedor! Fedor!") have a scene or two together. Yes, it's Svengali Meets Frankenstein. And there's the line "Have you ever heard of ... Frankenstein, the monster created by man?" But this is not even borderline horror.

The Monster Kills—HSF1: no monster

The Mystery of Life—Glut/CMM: footage from *Ghost of Slumber Mountain*

Secret Witness—ape, murder, no horror. Ref: *FD* 12/30/31. *AFI catalog. Motion Picture Herald* 10/17/31

1931

DRACULA

Dracula ... Bram Stoker's venerable novel is still pretty readable. On the subjects of evil and the horrific, he's often inspired. The "dreadful bag" with the "living thing within it": the latter, a treat for the Count's vampire women, is as suggestively, deeply disquieting as the "little graves in the garden" speech in Hawthorne's short story "Young Goodman Brown." On the subjects of the good, the sweet, and the brave, however, Stoker huffs and puffs. The selflessness of the several protagonists—Mina and Jonathan Harker, Dr. Van Helsing, Dr. Seward et al.—is of course intended as counterpoint to the absolute selfishness of the vampires. But that selflessness reduces a little too frequently to the maudlin of "poor, poor dear Madam Mina" and the camp of "How can women help loving men when they are so earnest, and so true, and so brave!"

Perhaps Stoker's most surprising stroke of all, though, belongs to poor dear Mina, who is, after all, in fact, so wholly good, so truly Christian, or

Count Dracula (Bela Lugosi) stands alongside three of his earth boxes outside Carfax Abbey.

spiritual, that she has compassion for the Count: "Just think what will be his joy when he, too, is destroyed in his worser part that his better part may have spiritual immortality." She's a sweetheart, but her imaginative leap here is way beyond the blandly sweet. Certainly, no one else in the novel—and probably no one reading the novel—would even think of entertaining the idea that the ultra-unscrupulous Dracula had a "better part"! The only other suggestion of such a phenomenon is Van Helsing's observation that "this evil thing is rooted deep in all good." [BOOK SPOILER]:   Not surprisingly, Mina's own "worser part"—she bears the mark of the vampirized on her forehead—disappears when Dracula dies. But her belief in the survival of good in even the worst is borne out by Van Helsing's witnessing of the "gladness" evident in the vampire wives just before the "final dissolution," and in her own witnessing of the "look of peace" on the face of Dracula "in that moment of final dissolution." Dear, dear!

Stoker, in fact, introduced at least three memorable characters in his book—Dracula, his pathetic disciple Renfield—who haplessly fights against his master's baleful influence—and Mina. *Nosferatu* (1922), the Murnau version of

Count Dracula's three brides in the unholy basement of Carfax Abbey

Dracula, produced perhaps the finest screen Dracula; the 1931 *Dracula*, perhaps the finest Renfield.

Dracula released February 14, 1931: It's more or less a given that *Dracula* divides, roughly, into two movies—the opening 18 minutes, set principally in Castle Dracula, Transylvania, and the "Oh, John!" scenes, set in the Seward Sanitarium, near London. But there's at least one wild card here—Dwight Frye's pathetic, compelling Renfield: His best (mad) moments come well into the film.

It's a great 18 minutes, courtesy of director Tod Browning, cinematographer Karl Freund, and art director Charles D. Hall. You keep asking yourself, did I see what I thought I saw? Scattered odd flares—or are they illuminated mists?—in the dirt in the basement. A bee thing crawling out of a miniature casket. An unexplained skeleton hand in a coffin. Meandering critters—possums, armadillos—which seem to have wandered out of similar scenes in the silent *Nosferatu*. Bare branches of trees growing through broken windows *into* the castle. And the god-damnedest great spider web, which separates the living from the undead, on the imposing stone staircase: Dracula (Bela Lugosi) can walk through it without disturbing it, but Renfield has to fight his way through it with his cane.

In one rapt scene, gliding, long-gowned vampire women (Dorothy Tree, Cornelia Thaw, Geraldine Dvorak), swirling moonlit fog, a self-opening door, and the tracking camera (up to Renfield, unconscious on an area rug, and Dracula, standing above him) create a sense of otherworldly movement. And note how the light from the fireplace comes to illuminate the backs of the trailing gowns of two of the three vampire women approaching Renfield's body. Glorious.

No sounds of footsteps in the castle of the armadillos. In the sequences set in and around the poorly maintained castle (a "ruined abbey") and the scenic Borgo Pass, there's no music (except that of the "children of the night") and little dialogue until the virtually silent spell is broken by Lugosi's famous, "I am Dracula." Some early-1930s films like *Dracula* and *Frankenstein*, the same year, though not silents, had no musical scores. There were advantages and disadvantages, aesthetic side effects to these commercial decisions.

On the advantage side: The silent Castle Dracula scenes are spellbinding. (Somewhat less so: the comparable sequences in the Spanish-language version, where music accompanies a hand reaching out of a casket in the castle cellar; rinse and repeat for the abbey cellar, later—twice.) The Philip Glass revised version's scoring of these scenes is actually quite good ... tactful, unsettling. But something unique is lost, a sense of the supernatural created by that very silence, and by the movement of the camera, the gliding brides, the nasty little incidental animals. Glass' music is somehow a bit distracting, even domesticating. The ideal *Dracula* soundtrack might retain much of the Glass score, but leave the silent scenes alone.

The spell of silence returns, now and then—in the unscored original—in later scenes with Dracula in Carfax Abbey, on the great lawn, and on the sanitarium patio. The film is not quite that easily divided into the poetic and the prosaic, the castle and the sanitarium. [FILM SPOILER]: The conclusion, set in the cellars of Carfax Abbey, has brief passages with Dracula leading Mina there which recall the early scenes in Castle Dracula. But the windup is more notable for Renfield's last stand, on the long, winding staircase: "I can't die with all those lives on my conscience!" But he does ... Unfortunately, the stilted Van Helsing-Harker exchanges really kill the atmosphere.

Browning created a similar, intermittent, supernatural ambiance in his 1935 *Mark of the Vampire*. There, he seemed to fudge a bit, and had the vampire scenes "scored" with weird wind sounds—night music, as it were. Clearly, however, it was not a commercial decision—in fact, it's a brilliant compromise between pure silence and music. And it's unlikely that theater organists, in

Dracula (Bela Lugosi) huddles near one of his earth boxes.

1927, left the vampire scenes alone, musically, in the silent version of *Mark of the Vampire, London after Midnight*. Music, in fact, accompanies the stills that illustrate these lost images in the recently reconstructed edition of the movie.

Not until Val Lewton—and sequences in films like *I Walked with a Zombie* and *Isle of the Dead*—are dialogue and music again so evocatively jettisoned, in favor of silence and camera movement. Browning and Lewton seemed attuned to a special filmic, pictorial value created by the conjunction of silence and movement—whether tracking (camera) or walking (character). Not absolute silence: Animal squeaks and howls haunt the castle-cellar scenes in *Dracula*, the unique sound of the wind-whipped cane field backgrounds the walk with the zombie, and the long, silent sequence in *Isle of the Dead* is punctuated by bird cries and the sound of dripping water. By contrast, the complete absence of sound effects in the cellar sequence of the Spanish-language *Dracula* makes it seem as if someone just forgot to turn on the mikes. Sight and sound effects make the comparable Browning and Lewton scenes seem inhabited, rooted.

Dracula first appears as the castle coachman, but it's Lugosi's "I am Dracula" which really marks his grand entrance. And, sporadically, Lugosi makes a grand Dracula. He injects something magisterial into lines like: "My blood now flows through her veins." He has fine sardonic fun, taunting, respectively, Renfield, David Manners' stodgy Harker, and Edward van Sloan's pedantic Professor Van Helsing—he delightedly emphasizes, for instance, the words "rather grim" in the line, "In my humble efforts to amuse your fiancée, Mr. Harker, I was telling her some rather grim tales of my far-off country."

But Lugosi's Dracula threatens to reduce to bits and pieces, including Freund's overused "forbidding" close-ups of his face, and stagy dialogue scenes in which Manners, Van Sloan, and company threaten to bring Lugosi down to their level—although Freund does his best to counteract the staginess with a moving camera and commanding long shots. Finally, however, it must be admitted that only Lugosi could make an experience out of a line like: "We will be leaving tomorrow evening," in which each syllable is drawn out, savored, relished, as if so much depended on each word. And if, as seems possible, it could be argued that the silent scenes with Bela and his "brides" are more entrancing (in the sense of "hypnotic") than his dialogue scenes, still, who would be without the latter?

If Lucy (Frances Dade) seems to succumb rather easily to the charm and romance (and fangs) of Count Dracula of Transylvania, and to the idea of the "broken battlements" of his castle there, and apparently has no compunction about vampirizing little girls (this subplot reduced to one chilling shot), Renfield—at the other end of the self-torment spectrum—is a most reluctant vampire. In fact, he insists that he only wants the blood of little things, like flies, spiders, and rats, though there are suggestions that when he leaves his room "for hours" at a time, he attacks humans, and he is, at one point, seen crawling towards the throat of a maid who has fainted and fallen to the floor. He is torn between loyalty to his master, the Count, ("He promised me things!") and horror at becoming part of the latter's plan to make Mina (Helen Chandler), the heroine, his new vampire bride. ("Not her!") He fears death, or rather judgment after death: "I can't die with all those lives on my conscience! All that blood on my hands!" His abject terror at being overheard advising Van Helsing and company—overheard, that is, by Dracula, in bat form—is most heart-rending. ("I told them nothing!")

Frye's inspired performance ultimately makes Renfield, rather than Mina, the dramatic center of the movie. Chandler has a lovely plaintive voice, but hasn't the presence of Frye. She can't dominate scenes (except, by default, those with Manners), while, in his later "madman" mode, Frye holds his own, even with the master, Lugosi. It's a marvel. It's Renfield who most vividly channels the tale's moral demons. Demon Conscience makes Mina want to send Harker away, and makes Renfield urge those in charge to send *him* away. ("Send me far away!") If Dracula and Lucy and his other "brides" incarnate the lure of the vampire, of eternal life and love, Renfield and, to a lesser extent,

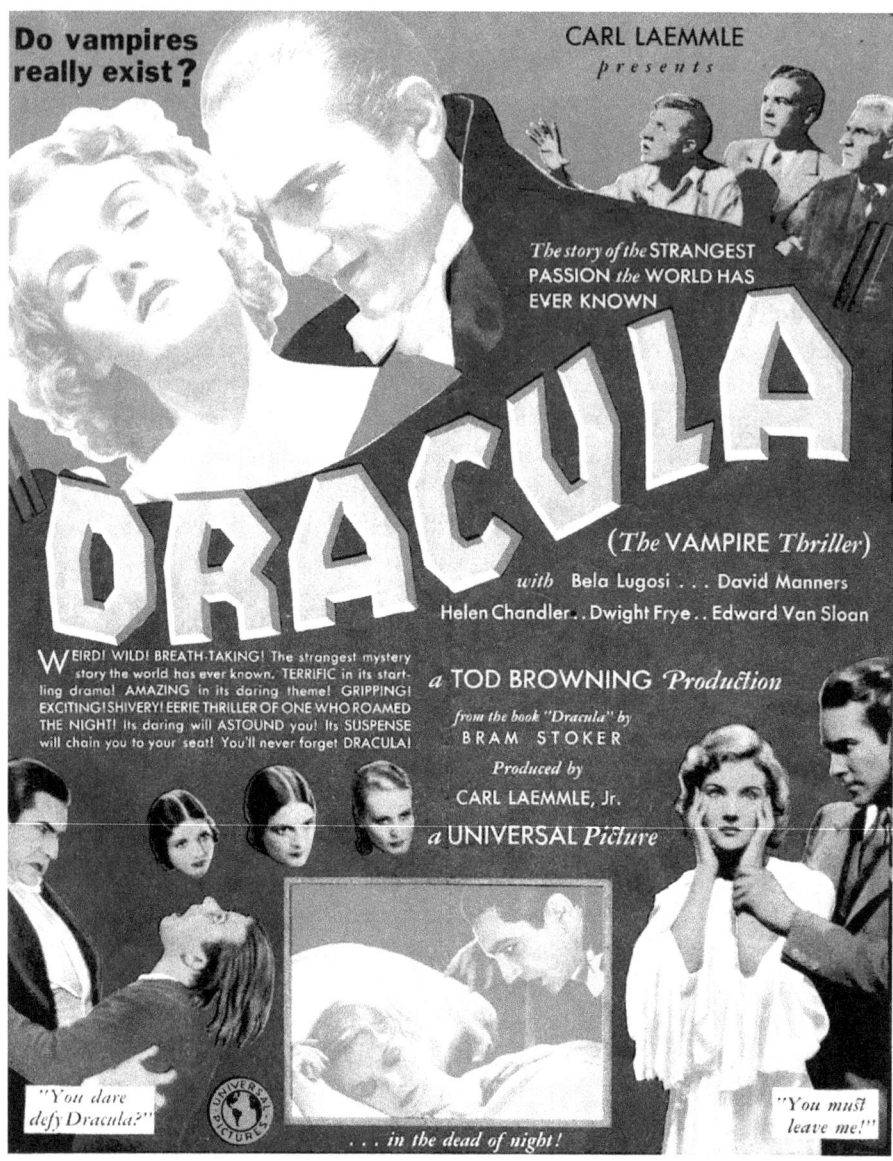

Mina suggest the cost of this supernatural endeavor, the lives, the blood, the children necessary to perpetuate it.

"Yes—Nosferatu, the undead, vampires!" Ironically, it's Harker who, at one point, makes the best case—unwittingly—for vampirism, when he remarks how radiant Mina looks: "Mina, you're so like a changed girl! Oh! you look wonderful!" Mina: "I feel wonderful! I've never felt better in my life!" She looks and feels wonderful, of course, because she has just drunk blood (off-screen) from Dracula—a truly perverse Stoker idea: "He opened a vein in his arm and he made me drink." In effect, she vampirizes the vampire. Does wonders for her complexion—her skin is as lustrous as her Vera West satin gown. Rarely have makeup and costuming been so insidiously seductive. Unlike the single-mindedly romantic Lucy, however, she feels un-wonderful about her thirst for the blood of others, i.e., Harker's. She knows—if he does not—why she's looking really good to him. One bite, and you've got a real eternal triangle ...

A tormented, Renfield-like character appears in Universal's next edition of the Dracula saga, *Dracula's Daughter* (1936): Dracula's daughter herself, Marya Zaleska (Gloria Holden). The spirit of poor Renfield also infuses the reluctant werewolves of Universal's first, failed, full-length foray into the subject of lycanthropy, *WereWolf of London* (1935). True, four years before *WereWolf of London* and 10 years before *The Wolf Man*, Dracula transformed, at will, into a bat and a wolf, respectively. That's the big difference: Glendon's, Yogami's, and Talbot's respective transformations are not at all willed. And Renfield is Larry Talbot is Irena Dubrovna, respectively, in perhaps the two most influential American horror movies of the 1940s—*The Wolf Man* (1941) and *Cat People* (1942). All that blood on their hands.

Dracula explicitly expresses fondness for his castle's "broken battlements." Music also backs the ghostly doings in Carl Dreyer's *Vampyr* (1932).

Van Sloan's careful, precise pronunciation apes Lugosi's, which slows their scenes together down to a crawl, and Van Sloan hasn't the charisma to command our patience.

Other notes: Very briefly, Lucy becomes an early-talkie "woman in white," in her undead state; at the end, Mina, too, does the walk in white.

By the time of *The Black Cat* (1934), David Manners was a looser, more engaging actor—his Peter Alison is actually one of the highlights of that film. Here, he's a stiff.

Fashion notes by Mo.

Universal. D, P: Tod Browning. SP: Garrett Fort, from the novel by Bram Stoker and the play by Hamilton Deane and John L. Balderston. Ph: Karl Freund. AD: Charles D. Hall. Ed: Milton Carruth. Cost: Vera West. Mkp: Jack Pierce. Sd: C. Roy Hunter. Mattes: John P. Fulton. With Bela Lugosi, Helen Chandler, Dwight Frye, David Manners, Edward van Sloan, Herbert Bunston, Frances Dade, Joan Standing, Charles K. Gerrard, Moon Carroll, John George, Michael Visaroff, Cornelia Thew, Dorothy Tree, Geraldine Dvorak; 85 minutes

Ref: "*Dracula*'s first 16 minutes ... are as potent as any in 1930s horror ..."—Frank J. Dello Stritto, "The *Dracula* That Never Ends," *Cult Movies* 27:41.

"The stage role of Seward has far more depth (and lines) than the screen characterization, particularly developing the doctor's feelings as he witnesses the transformation of his daughter Mina"—Jim Coughlin, "The Supporting Players of Universal's *Dracula*, *Midnight Marquee* 49:63.

Scarlet Street 26:38: "Him and Me," David J. Skal's first encounter with the 1931 *Dracula* ("there wasn't any music"), and more.

Scarlet Street 26:48: "To the Manners Born," Rick McKay interview with David Manners ("[Tod Browning] was never on the set").

Cult Movies 13:35-37: *Dracula* (1931): "Addenda to the Children of the Night," by Garydon Rhodes.

"[Charles D. Hall's] attention to detail helps create a sense of creeping decay tempered with echoes of bygone grandeur"—Steve Kronenberg, "Staged Fright—The Art Directors of Horror's Golden Age," *Monsters from the Vault*, Spring '97: 6-28.

"a remarkably effective background of creepy atmosphere ... Its kick is the real emotional horror kick"—*Variety* 2/18/31.

S.F. Chronicle 11/1/99: (headline) "The Undead, Live at the Paramount"—article regarding Philip Glass conducting his score for *Dracula*.

"Purists argue that Browning's original decision was the best one—to enhance the horror by eerie sound effects instead of underlining it with music"—Roger Ebert, *Great Movie Reviews*.

"It was only when I watched it with the Philip Glass soundtrack that I was able to last through the whole thing"—Dave Sindelar.

The DRUMS OF JEOPARDY

The Drums of Jeopardy (book): "There was a God, yes, but his name was Irony." Harold MacGrath's uneven but engaging 1920 novel ranges, in tone, from the genuinely stirring to the gruffly sentimental. Its hearty mixture of intrigue, romance, and politics seems very much of its time, which is to say that the book is both a little dated and very valuable as a socio-political document. Alternately, it overreaches ("The ability to laugh, that's America") and gets it just right: the kinda Proustian "We wear masks, we inherit generations of masks." In the middle of arrant nonsense, a gem: "We reach zenith sometimes, but we never stay there." Foolishness and wisdom, intertwined. At times dismissable, ultimately embraceable, *The Drums of Jeopardy* is chiefly remembered as the apparent source of a certain Mr. Pratt's screen name—Boris Karloff. MacGrath's Boris Karlov is a "species of madman" compared, at one point, to Torquemada, at another, to Quasimodo, and at yet another, to a werewolf. He likes to torture, but his exploits are more suggested than described. This is not a horror story, though another bit player here is called Mr. Rathbone. In its race-consciousness, the book also seems very much of its pop-culture time. The American character, the Irish character, the Russian character, and the British character are in the narrative forefront, and, in the background, lurk loaded words like "Chinamen," "Jap," and "whitest."

The Drums of Jeopardy released March 2, 1931: "I'll kill you all!" The Tiffany film *The Drums of Jeopardy* retains only the title of the book, a few char-

Warner Oland hovers in *The Drums of Jeopardy* (1931).

acter names (including "Boris Karlov")—and in one scene, or the beginning of one scene—it even changes the drums from emeralds to rubies. Obviously, the producer, Phil Goldstone, was not interested in an adaptation of the Mac-Grath book. What he wanted was a Fu Manchu movie, and he pretty much got it. Paramount's Fu Manchu, Warner Oland, plays the casually intimidating Dr. Karlov. And Florence Ryerson, the co-author of *The Mysterious Dr. Fu Manchu* and *The Return of Dr. Fu Manchu*, wrote the script for *The Drums of Jeopardy* which—creaky as it is—actually proves to be a somewhat better Oland vehicle than was *The Return of Dr. Fu Manchu*. Substitute "Petroffs" for "Petries" and you have the plot, as well as Karlov's enemies list. Then, add some *The Bat/The Cat and the Canary* atmospherics, including a fair scare with a dressmaker's dummy. Credit Arthur Reed and Fay Babcock, respectively, for the spooky photography and art direction elements such as a "bad storm," meandering mists, and the three-shot (far, medium, medium-close) intro to Dr. Karlov—obscured by chemical vapors—and his lab. Subsequent historical ironies: Boris Karloff himself would play Fu Manchu the following year, in *The Mask of Fu Manchu*. And Oland and Karloff would co-star in *Charlie Chan at the Opera* (1936). Wallace MacDonald, who plays the cad Gregor Petroff, would go on to produce some nifty 1940s thrillers such as *The Devil Commands*.

(*Mark of Terror*—reissue title): Tiffany. D: George B. Seitz. SP: Florence Ryerson, from Harold MacGrath's novel. Ph: Arthur Reed. Mus: Val Burton.

AD: Fay Babcock. Ed: Otto Ludwig. Cost: Elizabeth Coleman. P: Phil Goldstone. With Warner Oland, June Collyer, Lloyd Hughes, Clara Blandick, Hale Hamilton, Wallace MacDonald, Mischa Auer, Julia Swayne Gordon, Ruth Hall, Robert Homans, Murdock MacQuarrie, Harry Semels; 75 minutes

Ref: *PV* 2:9.

"Story closely follows the pattern and construction of *Dr. Fu Manchu* ... strictly small timey"—*Variety* 4/15/31.

DRACULA (Spanish-language)

Dracula released April 24, 1931: Universal's Spanish-language version of the Browning film utilizes an occasional shot from the mother film, but features different actors, a different director (George Melford), and a different cameraman (George Robinson). Either Robinson was not as talented, at this point in his career, as Karl Freund, or he did not have as big an allowance. He manages two impressive tracking shots in the opening scenes—and one, the introductory track up to Dracula (Carlos Villarias), on the stone staircase, is worthy of the master. But the coach ride to the castle is too well-lit, and thus less disorienting, and you can see the string dangling the bat above the horses. It's just a coach ride, not a netherworld experience. The roadside bonfire, which casts up strange shafts of light, though, is an atmospheric touch.

Dracula is introduced rising from his coffin in a hokey puff of smoke, like a stage magician, and the spectral flares—which helped make the cellar scene in the Browning so memorable—are missing, though you get an extra shot of the vampire women, and alternate shots of the possum and the bee. The scenes in the great, decaying staircase room are, again, too well lit and lack the intricate gradations of light and darkness of the Browning film. The swimming shadowy patches at the top and sides of the frame make the master shot, in the latter, more mysterious, less like simply a nice shot of a great set, and the contrasts between the moonlit pillars and windows, and the deep, deeper, deepest shadows—in the English-language version—create myriad points of visual interest. It's the difference between a set and a world evoked. And the "brides" here simply scramble over to Renfield's prone body—no real lighting or gliding effects. Here, it's they, not Dracula, who bite Renfield.

[SPOILER]: The concluding Carfax Abbey cellar scenes offer a couple of atmospheric bonuses: Dracula carrying Eva down not one but two flights of stone steps (the first, apparently, the Castle Dracula steps, modified). And three long shots of woman-in-white Eva walking away from the Count's sleeping body.

Four popping eyes don't help the Dracula-Renfield (Pablo Alvarez Rubio) staircase scene, and two more popping eyes provide unintentional laughs aboard the Vesta. The rather ordinary-looking Villarias might be a headwaiter rather than a count, or The Count, and he's just a camp casualty when he

In the Spanish-language version of *Dracula* (1931), Count Dracula (Carlos Villarias) is tricked into looking into a mirror by Professor Van Helsing (Eduardo Arozamena), in this Universal lobby card.

tries to imitate the Lugosi Stare of Horror. If anything, he reminds you that, yes, there was definitely something special about Bela Lugosi. When Dracula, offscreen, is first announced at the sanitarium, Villarias walks in, and it seems, for a second, that this can't be the Count, just someone ushering him in. But, no—get used to it—he's Dracula. The momentary confusion may arise from the fact that we have the same scene in the Lugosi *Dracula*, and we're used to Lugosi entering when Dracula is announced.

Meanwhile, Eduardo Arozamena haplessly takes Edward Van Sloan as *his* inspiration, for Professor Van Helsing. He acts, or overacts, with his eyebrows. Lupita Tovar is sweet but a bit monotonous, as Eva (the Mina role), and she overdoes her "coming out" scene (after drinking from Dracula's arm). As Harker, Barry Norton is at least not as deadly as David Manners. And, again, Harker unwittingly makes the case for vampirism: "You look like a different woman," he tells Eva, after she drinks Dracula's blood.

Again, the best performance is by the actor who plays Renfield—partly because he does it his way rather than imitating Dwight Frye. As noted above, Alvarez Rubio gets off to a wobbly start as the sane Renfield, an Oxford graduate. He's too quickly unbalanced by the undead state of affairs. But though he's not quite on the level of Frye, he's a convincing madman ("un loco"), and he perhaps puts over the "thousands, millions of rats" monologue better than Frye. He even rates an additional, moving scene with Van Helsing, in which he begs the latter, "Save me! Save my soul!" Finally, however, this version's extra half hour tells. Each scene goes on a little too long, and even Alvarez Rubio wears out his welcome.

Notes: No sequence with the flower seller in this version. Barry Norton made a career out of playing a "party guest" or "nightclub patron" in movies—IMDb lists him in at least 60 such roles!

Universal. D: George Melford. SP: Baltasar Fernandez Cue, from Bram Stoker's novel *Dracula* and the Hamilton Deane-John L. Balderston play. Ph: George Robinson. AD: Charles D. Hall. With Carlos Villarias, Lupita Tovar, Barry Norton, Pablo Alvarez Rubio, Eduardo Arozamena, Jose Soriano Viosca, Carmen Guerrero; Bela Lugosi et al. (*Dracula* footage); 104 minutes

Ref: " ... outshines its famous and classic cousin"—Bryan Senn, *Filmfax* 57: 38-9.

"The classic *Dracula* is more compact, sparser in dialogue and more subdued in acting styles [than the Spanish-language version]"—Frank J. Dello Stritto, "The *Dracula* That Never Ends," *Cult Movies* 27:42.

"This *Dracula* is so familiar, but also very different and sometimes better"—*PV* 10:48.

"If Tod Browning's direction of the Lugosi version looks dull enough without comparison, it withers completely when viewed against Melford's work"—Bill Littman, "*Dracula* Espanol," *Midnight Marquee* 37:75, 143-148.

"American director Melford actually improved upon Browning's version—it is better paced and more imaginatively photographed"—Stephen Jones, *Essential Monster Movie Guide*, p114.

SVENGALI

Trilby (novel—George Du Maurier): "When you heard her sing ... you heard Svengali singing with her voice ... " Paris, the 1850s. Principals: Young British painter Little Billee—"so weak of body, so strong of purpose"—"whose pinnacle ... is now the highest of all—the highest probably that can be for a mere painter of pictures!"... the mysterious Svengali, the "greatest [singing] master that ever lived!" and a "sticky, haunting, long, lean, uncanny, black spider-cat"—a "demon, a magician," ... and the beautiful Trilby—adored by all, especially the above principals—once tone-deaf, but, under the spell and training of Svengali, "there was no end to her notes, each more beautiful than the other—velvet and gold, beautiful flowers, pearls, diamonds, rubies—drops of dew and honey; peaches, oranges, and lemons! ... the unconscious Trilby of marble, who could produce wonderful sounds ... and love [Svengali] at his bidding with a strange, unreal, factitious love ... just his own love for himself

Trilby (Marian Marsh) is brought under the hypnotic control of Svengali (John Barrymore), from the 1931 film adaptation, *Svengali*.

turned inside out ... and reflected back on him, as from a mirror." After his death, she again becomes "tuneless." But his power over her continues from beyond the grave: The presence of a large, framed photograph of Svengali—"his big black eyes ... full of stern command" prompts her to the "most astounding feat of musical utterance ever heard out of a human throat."

Is it art or pop? Whatever *Trilby* is, it's full of exclamation points and absolutes ... a reflection of the youthful high spirits—and low spirits—of its protagonists, Trilby, Little Billie, and his artist friends, Taffy and the Laird. It wears its heart on its sleeve, its hat, its coat. Alternately bitter and sweet, the book occasionally forces the tone. But it gets the flavor of a particular time and place, even as it seems to be digressing. The flurries of alternate words and phrases: repetition and variation can be very engaging, as can the protagonists' "good, honest, innocent, artless prattle—not of the wisest, perhaps, nor redolent of the very highest culture ... nor leading to any very practical results; but quite pathetically sweet from the sincerity and fervor of its convictions ..." In the book, Svengali is an important but supporting actor—his story is told, at the end, in a nutshell, by his assistant Gecko, who also, of course, loved Trilby.

Trilby (1915 silent film): "Trilby's soul belonged to him." Here, Svengali (Wilton Lackaye) comes "out of the mysterious East"; in the book, he was

apparently European. His early announcement regarding his intentions is also pretty much the film's bare-bones plot: "Trilby is tone deaf. She can no more sing than that fiddle can play itself, but under my power, she will be the greatest contralto the world has ever known." But Svengali, "weakened by the constant strain of keeping Trilby under the spell, becomes subject to heart attacks, during which Trilby's former self comes to the surface." ("Svengali has hypnotized her with his devil's tricks.") Flavorless adaptation of the book ends on a bland happy note—no bitter, no sweet. The title cards, at least, could have used a little Du Maurier. The film's one visual coup: "That bird of evil omen" Svengali, and two more "Svengalis," in a folding mirror, surrounding and "dominating" Trilby. Odd precursor: the vulture's head, which becomes Svengali's head, in the title card illustrating the words "Svengali, the vulture." Compare both the beast in *The Vulture* (1966) and the Kramer-headed turkey in an episode of *Seinfeld*.

Svengali released May 22, 1931: "Don't look at me like that, Svengali!" J. Grubb Alexander's screenplay pretty much jettisons the characters of Little Billie (Bramwell Fletcher), Taffy (Lumsden Hare), and The Laird (Donald Crisp)—which means that most of the book is gone. Only Trilby (Marian Marsh) has a major role in both book and (1931) film. And Svengali (John Barrymore)—"Polish or something"—is now a co-starring role, but Barrymore can't get much traction with Alexander's generally flimsy dialogue. At first, he seems to be a villain, a monster. Using only those haunting hypno-eyes with the flick-on lights, he forces a woman (Carmel Myers) to drown herself. When he convinces the spellbound Trilby that she is not good enough for Little Billie, he fakes her death and hypnotically transforms her into a European singing sensation. But the repeated use of his power is draining the life out of him ("Your headache is here in my heart"), and he's defeated by her "manufactured love" for him. [SPOILER]: During her last concert, he collapses, and prays, "Oh, God, grant me in death what you denied me in life—the woman I love." God seems to answer his after-death wish: She dies with his name on her lips, and he perks up, momentarily, before he, too, dies.

A happy ending—for the villain of the piece. Or is he a villain? His love for Trilby, his mental and physical suffering—and his apparent triumph in death—seem, magically, to transform Svengali into the film's hero. Finally, yes, despite all odds, Barrymore's hokey, impish Polish accent—and Svengali's touching disintegration—yield an unexpected but satisfying fade-out. It's nothing like Du Maurier, but it's just as good, in its own perversely happy way. Destroying and Rebuilding the Classics 101 ...

If it's true, as Pauline Kael wrote, that director Archie Mayo couldn't quite "get a performance out of [Marian Marsh]," it's also true that her face is very good at blank expression, necessary when Trilby is, for instance, repeating "Svengali, Svengali, Svengali." She looks absurdly like a big, live doll, in (initially) her gendarme outfit. Her slightly plump face can be ridiculously sweet, as framed by bangs and Little-Girl curls. In her early scenes, Trilby has a most disarming, childlike forthrightness. It's a fine introduction to the character. Later, with her hair more conventionally brushed back and tied up, she's still pretty, yes, but almost ordinary—the Trilby Doll effect is gone. It's all Svengali by then ...

In the finest and most famous sequence, Svengali hypnotizes Trilby, from afar, to come to him. As the wind whistles, Barney McGill's camera tracks back from a close-up of Svengali's power eyes, across his room and (somehow) through the window pane and out, across the housetops. Then it tracks forward and enters wind-opened glass doors, and prowls across her room, to Trilby, asleep in bed. It is—in effect, at least—one long shot, and it's wonderfully suggestive of hypnotic forces at work. When she snaps out of it, in Svengali's room, and sees him, he has his regular eyes back.

Note: In an hilarious footnote to *Svengali*, Carole Lombard's Lily Garland fumes: "I'm no Trilby!" as Barrymore's Oscar Jaffe enters, with a Svengali flourish, in a scene in *Twentieth Century* (1934).

WB. D: Archie Mayo. SP: J. Grubb Alexander, from George L. Du Maurier's novel *Trilby*. Ph: Barney McGill. Mus: David Mendoza. AD: Anton Grot. Mkp: Johnny Wallis. TechFX: Fred Jackman, H.F. Koenekamp. Ed: William Holmes. Cost: Earl Luick. With John Barrymore, Marian Marsh, Donald Crisp, Bramwell Fletcher, Carmel Myers, Luis Alberni, Lumsden Hare, Paul Porcasi, Henry Otto; 81 minutes

Ref: IMDb.

"I always find myself wondering what Bela Lugosi might have done with this role"—Dave Sindelar (2/14/2002).

MURDER BY THE CLOCK

Murder by the Clock (book by Rufus King): "Glory, be, sir—what with this bringing back of the dead … " French-Canadian Police Lt. Valcour—an "oldish fellow"—attempts to solve the case of an apparently dead man revived by adrenaline. ("Suspended animation and catalepsy were all right as figures of speech, but the human illustration was rather ghastly.") Okay murder mystery has its grace notes and occasional insights into the human mystery, but the horror element is pretty much limited to the above. ("Endicott lives … ") The climactic unraveling of the mystery is properly involving, and the "Five Years Later" coda is a quiet stunner. One of those grace notes: "Her words were fragments of stone chipped from some elemental quarry of granite like conviction and harsh purpose." All this and an "extraordinary scream" and a passing reference to Lon Chaney.

Murder by the Clock, released July 21, 1931: "I don't want to see dead people!" [SPOILER ADVISORY]: Good camp finally starts taking over from

In this lobby card, Regis Toomey stands over the fallen Lilyan Tashman, as the suspense builds in *Murder by the Clock* (1931).

bad camp here in the last 20 minutes or so, when death by strangulation comes to seem a very temporary state, and the action gets frantic and amusing. First, adrenaline revives Herbert Endicott (Walter McGrail), of the house of Endicott. ("His pulse is going again! He's alive!") Then, the ghostly figure of Mrs. Endicott (Blanche Friderici), the family matriarch, appears at a window, as the horn signaling her apparent, recent revival in the crypt blares. Mixed responses: "Mrs. Endicott—she's risen from her grave!" "Maybe she was buried alive." "We're not dealing with ghosts!" Uproariously—from a certain angle—the sight of one apparent returnee from the dead seems to return another to death.

Somewhere between the book and the movie—there was a Charles Beahan play in between—everything worthwhile was lost. It's about 50 minutes in before incidents from the book even begin making their way into the movie. At the heart of the fiasco: the Laura (Lilyan Tashman)-Herbert-Tom (Lester Vail) love triangle, a treasure-trove of wonderful bad acting. Laura is a femme fatale in the worst, most fatale way, dramatically-speaking. She's a manipulator, like the book's Mrs. Endicott, but too obviously and repetitively. Irving Pichel's performance, as the "halfwit" Phillip Endicott ("Knives!"), is hardly on a level with Dwight Frye's Renfield, but it's a step above the camp trio.

The movie's one notable invention: the horror horn. The "horrible" thing sounds something like an all-clear siren, and successfully jangles the nerves of characters and viewers alike. (No credit for sound or sound effects.) One highlight of Karl Struss' atmospheric photography: the out-sized shadow of a man, hands outstretched, as he's about to strangle old Mrs. Endicott. The second most alarming visual effect: Laura's form-fitting gown.

A tip of the non-Hatlo hat to Dave Sindelar.

Notes: At one point, a scrap of a major-league baseball game, in progress, is heard on a radio: "Lefty Grove pitching ... " In 1931, Grove had one of the greatest years ever for a pitcher, winning 31 games and losing only four.

At another point, Lt. Valcour (William "Stage" Boyd) professes that he's looking for a "murderer whose mind works like a clock." Officer Cassidy (Regis Toomey): "Murder by the clock!" The basis for the book's title is more prosaic. Each chapter is pegged to a time of day, or night, from 8:37 p.m. to 7:11 a.m., with an epilogue at "8:37 p.m.—Five Years Later."

Paramount. D: Edward Sloman. Adap: Henry Myers, from Rufus King's novel and Charles Beahan's play. Ph: Karl Struss. With William "Stage" Boyd, Lilyan Tashman, Irving Pichel, Regis Toomey, Sally O'Neil, Blanche Friderici, Walter McGrail, Lester Vail, Martha Mattox, Charles D. Brown, Lenita Lane, Willard Robertson; 76 minutes

Ref: "Impressive looking, complicated Paramount feature"—*PV* 27::10. "The eerie stuff laid on in layers"—*Variety* 7/21/31.

"This forgotten horror may actually be an early form of film noir"—Dave Sindelar (*Movie of the Day* Archive 9/4/2003).

DAUGHTER OF THE DRAGON

Daughter of the Dragon released Sept. 5, 1931: "I am the daughter of Fu Manchu!" Dr. Fu Manchu (Warner Oland) seems to have penciled in a generation or two more to his original vow of vengeance on the Petries; and, out of left field, a daughter of the doc himself, Princess Ling Moy (Anna May Wong), turns up. ("Fu Manchu, coming here from the grave?") In order to redeem the honor of the House of Fu, she must "become" a man, when her father dies (in what was surely the longest death scene on film in 1931): "The vengeance shall be mine—I will be your son." However, the voice of Fu returns to her in pep talks: "We shall never rest until you kill him who remains." Warner Oland, too, seems resurrected, from his static performance in *The Return of Dr. Fu Manchu*. He makes his words count here. ("I, your father, am Fu Manchu!") And he rates one dandy set piece: Upstairs, in his foes' mansion, he claps his hands, and the drugged Sir John Petrie (Holmes Herbert) tumbles down a flight of stairs, dead, to the collective dismay of the first-floor assembled.

"The golden dragon stirs in his sleep." The "man-daughter" half of the movie begins well, too, when the Princess, in a glittering gown, bows to the banner of the bloody family dragon, as the camera pans deliberately up from her back to the banner (Victor Milner, photography), and an ominous gong sounds. Visually, at least, the film is a fine showcase for Anna May Wong, who is striking to behold, but uncertain as an actress here. (The next year, she would find her dramatic niche, under Josef von Sternberg's direction, in *Shanghai Express*.) Unwisely, dialogue writer Sid Buchman gives her long, Oland-like lines.

Bramwell Fletcher (center) appears unhinged by Anna May Wong and her henchman, from *Daughter of the Dragon* (1931).

("Death will first awaken Petrie from sleep, and then end his lingering horror with a short life," roughly.) Ultimately, the eternal-triangle, or rectangle, plot makes a strange hash of the performances of Wong, Sessue Hayakawa (the Japanese actor as Chinese detective Ah Kee), Bramwell Fletcher (as Ronald Petrie), and Frances Dade. Fletcher's first personal camp line (when the Princess demonstrates a face-eating acid): "You wouldn't dare do that!" His next (twice!): "Anything but that!"

Sax Rohmer's novel, *Daughter of Fu Manchu*, reads less like the basis of the movie than like, simply, a variation on the Fu's-daughter idea. Book and film have very little in common, apart from a few character names. Even the daughter's name is different—it's Fah Lo Suee (which means "Sweet Perfume") in the book. For the most part, the Rohmer is pretty dreadful, a riot of exclamation points intended to manufacture excitement. ("Nayland Smith was doomed!") The most surprising and intriguing part: the very end, in which Dr. Fu Manchu is revealed to be, almost, a Good Guy, who reins in his daughter's excesses. Here, he is, at once, "the world's greatest criminal, the world's supreme genius—and a man of his word." In his own words: "I worked for my country. I saw China misruled, falling into decay … " Fah Lo Suee's mystery weapon-drug—which "produces strange delusions"—proves to be "Cannabis indica"—marijuana, which was apparently pretty powerful back in 1930. ("I was a giant in a microscopic room!")

Paramount. D, Adap: Lloyd Corrigan. Adap: also Monte M. Katterjohn. Dial: Sidney Buchman, from Sax Rohmer's novel *Daughter of Fu Manchu*. Ph: Victor Milner. Sd: Earl S. Hayman. Assoc P: Robert Harris. With Anna May Wong, Warner Oland, Sessue Hayakawa, Bramwell Fletcher, Frances Dade, Holmes Herbert, Lawrence Grant, Harold Minjir, E. Alyn Warren, Olaf Hytten, Tetsu Komai, Nella Walker; 70 minutes

Ref: *PV* 2:9. UCLA Film Archive.

"The dialog is mostly amateurish and inept"—*Variety* 8/25/31.

"There are some exciting sequences in this one"—Dave Sindelar.

The SPIDER

The Spider released Sept. 27, 1931: Stage magician Chatrand the Great (Edmund Lowe) and his amnesiac partner Alexander (Howard Phillips) are into "magic, conjuring, and mind reading." [SPOILER]: In the two-part pay-off sequence, ghostly figures appear above the trance-bound Alexander, like an ethereal dance troupe. Photographer James Wong Howe has fun here with light and shadow, but this striking imagery at first seems rather irrelevant, until the huge face of the murdered John Carrington (Earle Foxe) appears. ("You shall stand face to face with the dead!") Psychology and showmanship, aimed at making the killer—in the theater audience—confess. Perry Mason, medium. Then, in a "new kind of third degree," Chatrand forces Alexander's mind

to detect the murderer's mind, in the theater audience, in this forerunner of *Charlie Chan at Treasure Island*. ("His thoughts are dominating this theater.") The magic acts and amnesia plot are just a pretext for this hokey but fun sequence. The earlier scene in which Alexander cries "I remember!" and the theater goes dark, a gun is fired, helping to whip up a little excitement.

Lowe's is just one of several stolid performances. Though Chatrand's stage illusions are okay, Lowe hasn't the requisite flair. He might be auditioning for the role of Chandu the Magician, which he would play the following year, but Wong Howe's highlighting of his face and hands only reminds one that Lowe is not Bela Lugosi, who might have made this movie more of a collector's item. Carrington is the uncle of Lois Moran's Miss Sweetie, or rather Beverly Lane.

Notes: The 1945 remake is not at all horrific.

The only spider in the movie is a spider ring, which the killer is wearing. (Chatrand: "I see a hand. On the hand is a spider ring!")

"Chatrand" is so spelled on the Tivoli Theatre marquee, on the stage curtains, and on a poster or two outside the theater. However, it's spelled "Chartrand" in a newspaper sub-head. But everyone seems to be calling him "Chatrand."

The scene in which Sonya seems to become a literal talking head anticipates a scene in Werner Herzog's *Aguirre: The Wrath of God* (1972).

The film's title is written, letter-by-letter, in a sort of neon longhand, like spirit writing writ large.

Fox. D: Kenneth MacKenna, William Cameron Menzies. SP: Barry Conners, Philip Klein, from the play by Lowell Brentano and Fulton Oursler. Ph: James Wong Howe. Mus: Carli Elinor;(uncredited) Hugo Friedhofer et al. Ed: Alfred DeGaetano. Sd: Alfred Bruzlin. With Edmund Lowe, Lois Moran, El Brendel, John Arledge, George E. Stone, Earle Foxe, Howard Phillips, Purnell Pratt, Ruth Donnelly, Ward Bond, Joyce Compton, Warren Hymer; 59 minutes.

Ref: *PV* 33:12.

"Should be a pretty good grossing spookie"—*Variety* 9/8/31.

The PHANTOM

The Phantom released Nov. 1, 1931: "There's nothing to be frightened of in our own home." Supreme Pictures capitalizes on the 1930 reissue of *The Phantom of the Opera*, as MGM did also, more cleverly, with *The Phantom of Paris* (also 1931), a pragmatically retitled adaptation of *Cheri-Bibi*, by Gaston (*Phantom of the Opera*) Leroux. Our movie here—not so supreme. In the editing chaos herein—courtesy of Ethel Davey—"old quack" Dr. Weldon (William Gould) wants to "be the first" to do some kind of brain transplant, or reshuffle, and finds in heroine Ruth (Allene Ray) a "marvelous subject." Transplant central: a sanitarium on Country Drive. Meanwhile, the actually "harmless" Phantom, or

Thing (Sheldon Lewis), comes out of the closet, literally, wriggling his fingers and cackling as he approaches Ruth. ("This terrible thing crept out ... ")

[SPOILER] The wriggling business is not scary, closer to funny or campy. And perhaps that was the idea, if the last shot of the Phantom is any indication: The revealed look on Lewis' face is charmingly goofy. And the three enthusiastic purveyors of comic relief—Lucy the hyper maid (Violet Knights), Oscar the loony desk clerk (William Jackie), and Shorty the jumpy chauffeur (Bobby Dunn)—are given such long leashes that comedy overwhelms drama and suspense. In the case of Knights, Alan James, the director, had an excuse: She was his sister. ("I'm so scared!") Oscar's introductory scene is more funny strange than ha ha: Hidden behind the desk, he stands up, a little at a time, as if he were being inflated, until he reaches full height. *The Phantom* is pathetic, but unique, an offbeat form of bad.

Supreme Pictures. D, SP: Alan James, aka Alvin J. Neitz. Ph: Lauron Draper. P: Louis Weiss. With Guinn "Big Boy" Williams, Allene Ray, Niles Welch, Tom O'Brien, Sheldon Lewis, Wilfred Lucas, Violet Knights, William Gould, Bobby Dunn, William Jackie; 62 minutes.

Ref: IMDb. "Tough slog. The comedy was killing me"—rvoyttbots, CHFB (Golden Age Horror 6/14/15).

FRANKENSTEIN

Frankenstein (1910 movie): "The evil in Frankenstein's mind creates a monster ... " Victor's (Augustus Phillips) aim is to create the "most perfect human being." But his stew pot yields first, smoke, then a skeletal thing that becomes a Monster (Charles Ogle) that looks like a Dickens ruffian. And this primitive Edison short looks like a photographed stage play. The Monster's movements aren't at all stylized or suggestive of something extra-human. At the end, it

Rare Universal 6-sheet poster from *Frankenstein* (1931)

seems to disappear into a mirror. Kinda cool: the creature sticking his arm out of the closed cabinet. Kenneth Strickfaden, where are you?

Frankenstein released Nov. 21, 1931: "Where should we be if nobody tried to find out what lies beyond?" In a laboratory, in an "abandoned old watchtower close to the town of Goldstadt." For Dr. Henry Frankenstein (Colin Clive), "beyond" is the "great ray that first brought life into the world." With said ray—and a little "chemical galvanism"—he brings life to a piecemeal body that "never lived" (Boris Karloff). He has "all the electrical secrets of heaven" at his fingertips, and yet … he's a brilliant scientist, but he has problems with follow-up, with the non-electrical.

In this out-of-the-way Gothic universe, Frankenstein's hunchbacked assistant Fritz (Dwight Frye) proves to be co-author of the doc's work, on both na-

Dr. Frankenstein (Colin Clive) in the foreground, with Fritz (Dwight Frye) in the background; both dwarfed by the impressive Universal mad lab.

ture and nurture sides: He provides both the abnormal brain (with its "scarcity of convolutions on the frontal lobe") and the bullwhip and torch, with which he torments the creature. Fixated on the idea of creating life, Frankenstein, in his single-mindedness, abdicates responsibility for the quality of that life. At his most pathetic, he distractedly begs Fritz to stop tormenting the Monster. ("Oh, come away, Fritz! Leave it alone! Leave it alone!") He can control the cosmos, but not the hired help, or his own emotions.

"Wait till I bring him into the light." *Frankenstein* puts a unique, surreal spin on a character, which became a type, the visionary, but shortsighted scientist. At the worst moments, Frankenstein's imagination fails him, and others. If the Monster passes the Light test, Henry fails it. Initially left alone in darkness, the Monster instinctively reaches out for the light from a just-opened tower window, gravitating to it like a plant to the sun. Henry is pleased. His test has succeeded: The Monster has responded. But Henry doesn't see that he has actually created a kindred spirit. The test is over, the sunroof is closed—but he doesn't see the sequel unfolding before him, just after the test: the creature's hands supplicating, reaching out to *him*, as if asking where the light went. For the Monster, the daylight is his great ray. Ironically, Henry doesn't realize that he has created something with his own thirst for knowledge, for more. It's more than just alive.

"And you really believe that you can bring life to the dead?" When the Monster first looks up, we see the elusive light reflected in his eyes: the imprint of the soul, as it were. But Henry doesn't follow up, doesn't encourage him, can't see beyond *beyond*. He enthuses not with the Monster, but with his associate: "It understands this time—it's wonderful!" he tells his ex-professor, Dr. Waldman (Edward van Sloan), after he makes the Monster sit down again. He's enthusiastic more for the experiment than for this new, or renewed, being, just a "few days old." He doesn't connect with the latter, and that's the beginning of the end for this curiously extended family. What was needed, at the least, was, say, someone good with puppies, or babies, or gladiolus. Or someone who connected with his own father: "My father never believed in anyone," Frankenstein tells Waldman.

Immediately filling the empathetic void: Fritz assails the Monster with a torch. *He* connects. Fritz takes the initiative that Henry could not. He might almost be acting on the doctor's dismay when the latter learns, belatedly, from Waldman, that the Monster's skull houses a "criminal brain." The chance is lost, if there was a chance with this unholy three: oblivious scientist, mean-minded gofer, newborn with bad brain. (True, Fritz's brain isn't exactly good either, but it is his own.) Waldman is the realist. He tells Henry, "You have created a monster, and it will destroy you!" A lot of good his realism does him, though—it destroys him, Waldman.

"I'm afraid—terribly afraid! Something is coming between us!" Arthur Edeson's camera tracks through the midst of villagers celebrating the wedding of the doctor and Elizabeth (Mae Clarke). This extended shot continues, dissolves into an ominous track with the restless, escaped Monster (that "something") through an orchard. This two-in-one track is a more sophisticated form of foreshadowing than is Elizabeth's premonition, above: In effect, the forward motion of the two tracks fuses, or confuses, two forces—call them (in actor van Sloan's introductory words) the "two great mysteries of creation: life and

The Monster creator (Colin Clive), the Monster (Boris Karloff) and the Monster torturer (Dwight Frye) in the castle dungeon, with its weird angles and impressive shadows

death." And it's Henry—as fiancé and scientist, respectively—who has set both in motion.

The two shots, and the film as a whole—although more in tune with the trappings of death—in fact give the other mystery of creation a little of its due, too: Henry's exultant "It's alive!" and the Monster's reaching for the light are life-affirming, soul-affirming notes, idiosyncratic as they are. Of course, from another angle, Henry's exultation is mere raving, and yields immediately to exhaustion. Later, there is a third fugitive, hopeful note—the Monster's communion with the little girl, Maria (Marilyn Harris). Dashed hopes, however, are what propel the narratives of *Frankenstein* and *Bride of Frankenstein*, not sweet idylls ... Another angle is provided by Charles D. Hall's elaborate sets, which dwarf the characters, and put human—and extra-human—concerns in perspective.

Karloff's Monster is all responses. He reacts automatically to his environment, without thinking, although he does make an imaginative (mistaken) connection between floating flowers and floating Maria's. This devastating whirlwind sequence, of course, presupposes that Maria can't swim, can't float. At ease, afterwards, with nothing to which to respond, the bewildered Monster's arms hang loosely, like empty coat sleeves.

Colin Clive is excellent. He makes Frankenstein's obsessive idealism at once pitiable, admirable, and detestable, makes the doctor's nervous breakdown seem a natural outcome of his single-mindedness. And Frye's grubby eagerness and general scuttling about get under your skin. Director James Whale, however, seems less interested in the other participants—Elizabeth, John Boles' Victor Moritz, Frederick Kerr's Baron Frankenstein—and leaves them rather adrift, as also, at times, the film. The movie's lack of background music is felt during their scenes, not so much in the scenes accompanied by the sounds of thunder and machinery and screaming.

"[The Monster's] demeanor is one of sorrow (it has lost its only friend), guilt, and anger (at itself and perhaps even at little Maria for leaving it)"—John E. Parnum, in *We Belong Dead*, p. 44.

Notes: What are the first words spoken in *Frankenstein*? A sort of trick question. Before the credits begin, Edward van Sloan, as himself, addresses the audience: "How do you do?" He advises that the film might "horrify you." ..

The title refers to the doctor, not to the Monster, or to Baron Frankenstein.

Those are not "ghosts"-in-sheets in the lab, in between procedures. It's just Frankenstein keeping his expensive equipment safely under wraps.

Everyone seems to have been quite proud of the main stone staircase—the characters, including the Monster, go up and down it regularly.

No Una O'Connor in Whale's first horror movie, but he uses incidental skeletons to lighten the mood—at one point, Fritz bumps into one. And the first shot is a long slow pan of the gathered at a funeral, one by one, including, wryly, a shrouded skeleton, prominent in the background. Death attending a funeral.

Universal. D: James Whale. SP: Garrett Fort, Francis Edward Faragoh, from the novel by Mary Shelley, the play by Peggy Webling, and the composition by John L. Balderston. Ph: Arthur Edeson. Mus: B. Kaun. AD: Charles D. Hall. Mkp: Jack Pierce. SpFX: Kenneth Strickfaden, John P. Fulton. Sound: C. Roy Hunter. Cost: Mae Bruce. Ed: Clarence Kolster. With Colin Clive, Boris Karloff, Edward van Sloan, Mae Clarke, John Boles, Dwight Frye, Frederick Kerr, Lionel Belmore, Marilyn Harris, Ted Billings, Jack Curtis, Francis Ford, Mary Gordon, Michael Mark, Paul Panzer, Pauline Moore; 70 minutes.

Ref: *Filmfax* 35:45: friendship of Mae Clarke and Colin Clive.

Filmfax 7:26: laserdisc restoration.

Midnight Marquee 37:123-126 (Gregory Mank).

"Simply stated, the universality of the Frankenstein Monster originates from the simple fact that he is like us at various moments in our lives: disconnected, alienated, frustrated, lonely, rejected, hated, awkward, jealous"—Gary J. Svehla, in *We Belong Dead*, p33.

"Looks like a *Dracula*-plus ... Karloff ... makes a memorable figure of the bizarre [monster] ... a fascinating acting bit of mesmerism"—*Variety* 12/8/31.

DR. JEKYLL AND MR. HYDE

The Strange Case of Dr. Jekyll and Mr. Hyde (story—Robert Louis Stevenson): "Man is not truly one, but truly two." Dr. Henry Jekyll discovers "certain agents" which "have the power to shake and pluck back that fleshly vestment, even as a wind might toss the curtains of a pavilion"—and he becomes, temporarily, and sporadically, one "Mr. Hyde." He finds that he can experience "vicarious depravity" through Hyde's "malign and villainous" exploits, then disappear back into the person of the good doctor, his "city of refuge": "I did not even exist!" Although, as he notes, "the terms of this debate are as old and commonplace as man"—we are all Jekyll and Hyde—he is "radically both" of the "two natures that [contend] in the field of [his] consciousness ... " Ultimately, however, Jekyll runs out of the "impure ... salt" which restores him to himself, or his Jekyll self, and awaits the "doom that is closing on us both ... " And, although Mr. Hyde is generally thought of as pure, indulgent evil, Jekyll, at one point, marvels that Hyde's "love of life is wonderful ... " It's this constant redefining of the Jekyll/Hyde relationship which keeps the original story surprising and fresh, no matter how well we might think we know it.

Dr. Jekyll and Mr. Hyde (1912): Very early, silent, drastically abridged (just 11 or 12 minutes long) version of the tale regarding a Dr. Jekyll (James Cruze) who takes "certain drugs" which turn him into his buck-toothed, bushy-browed, stooped "evil self"—Mr. Hyde (Cruze). "Repeated use of the drugs causes him to change to his evil self against his will." The transformation from Jekyll to

A pressbook herald of *Dr. Jekyll and Mr. Hyde* (1931)

Hyde is just a cut from Cruze in Jekyll makeup to Cruze in Hyde makeup. And already filmmakers are providing Jekyll with a love interest (Florence La Badie). In one sequence—roughly adapted from the Stevenson original—Hyde seems to knock down a girl (Marie Elene), while running through the (apparently English) village.

Dr. Jekyll and Mr. Hyde (1913): "Dr. Jekyll [King Baggot] plans to set free his evil self." His "unheard of experiments" yield Mr. Hyde (Baggot), a "demon souled man" who looks and acts like an irascible, duck-walking spastic. Ideas and incidents taken, sometimes roughly, from the original story, include Hyde's knocking down of the crippled boy, Jekyll's willing all his "worldly possessions" to Hyde, Jekyll irresistibly reverting to Hyde, Hyde's meeting at midnight with Dr. Lanyon (Howard Crampton), and Jekyll's running out of the "antidote." Fairly faithful to Stevenson, but pretty primitive, technically and dramatically. The closest the film comes to wit is Jekyll's note, which reads: "The bearer Mr. Hyde is my best friend. Treat him as myself."

Dr. Jekyll and Mr. Hyde (1920 Pioneer Film): Dr. Jekyll's (Sheldon Lewis) main theory here is that "man has two natures—good and evil." A simple editing cut, and Jekyll is Hyde—an "Apostle of Hell"—who promptly accosts and knocks down a woman and who proves to be an arsonist. Meanwhile, Jekyll's atheism is challenged by his experiences: "Oh, God help me—save me from the penalty of my unbelief ... " Mawkish "Jekyll and Hyde" features mundane chases with Hyde and the cops, and a pleasing use of irises, in and out. Lewis would go on to reprise his wriggling-fingers Hyde as The Thing in *The Phantom* (1931). The oddest story element: One of Jekyll's patients "is the first case of its kind known to medical science. The child is dead and yet alive—it almost proves my theory that there is no soul." But, apparently, there are zombies ...

Dr. Jekyll and Mr. Hyde (1920 Paramount): "Wouldn't it be marvelous if the two natures in man could be separated—housed in different bodies!" Dr. Henry Jekyll (John Barrymore), idealist and philanthropist—chided by Sir George Carew (Brandon Hurst) for being "afraid" of "experience"—concocts a potion which transforms him into the evil, repellent Mr. Hyde (Barrymore). "In the impenetrable mask of another identity, Hyde set forth upon a sea of license— to do what he, as Jekyll, could not do." Until the last 20 minutes or so, this version of the Stevenson story is somewhat of an antique, with Barrymore wildly hammy as both Jekyll and Hyde. There's even a hokey Great Profile pause, at one point. But the concluding sequences are almost startlingly horrific. It must have been quite a ride for unprepared audiences of the time. It's still quite a ride. Hyde's face is never pretty—it's partly those long, long bad teeth— [SPOILER ON THE HORIZON]: but near the end it's lit for horror, and Barrymore's broad bestial grimace, as he rises from the bludgeoned body of Carew, is an inspired glimpse of a human hell. The other wicked highlight: the huge, double-exposure spider, which Jekyll imagines as Hyde, perhaps inspired

In this lobby card, Mr. Hyde (Fredric March) strikes out against Carew (Holmes Herbert), the father of his fiancée, in *Dr. Jekyll and Mr. Hyde*.

by Hyde's spidery fingers. The spider thing rates its own, traveling spotlight. And it scuttles. Carew's advice to Jekyll to experience life proves to be the worst piece of horror-movie advice pre-*Revolt of the Zombies* (1936)—to wit, Cliff's "ride roughshod" nudge to Armand. Yield 1920: Hyde; yield 1936: an army of zombies.

Dr. Pyckle & Mr. Pride (1925 short): Dr. Stanislaus Pyckle's (Stan Laurel) scientific formula turns him into a slightly unkempt "vicious fiend," who stalks the countryside with a peashooter. "I'll call it 'Dr. Pyckle's 58th Variety!'" he cries, anticipating another Heinz reference in the 1962 *The Manchurian Candidate*. A dose of the formula gives his dog a fright wig. Yes, evil here is Bad Hair—for humans and dogs. At his most reprehensible, Mr. Pride takes a boy's ice-cream cone. Stan Laurel's deflating of customarily hyper-dramatic *Jekyll and Hyde* movies is slight but winning. Some good, rubber-legged slapstick signals Pyckle's transformation into Pride. Future director Tay Garnett (*China Seas*) apparently wrote the wry foreword: "We squirm under the tumult of Good and Evil, ever warring within us, yet were Science to separate them, Bad would flourish, Crime run riot—even saxophone players would be tolerated." Ref: Jim Shapiro.

Dr. Jekyll and Mr. Hyde released Dec. 31, 1931: "Now, if these two selves could be separated from each other, how much freer the good in us would be, what heights it might scale. And the so-called evil, once liberated, would fulfill itself and trouble us no more." Dr. Henry Jekyll (Fredric March), however, proves to have been overly optimistic. When "certain chemicals" succeed in turning him into a person of "forbidding appearance," whom he dubs Mr. Hyde (March again), it is the latter that comes to dominate. And Hyde's bedside manner is not the same as Jekyll's.

Sex, drugs, and Bach. At one point, the news that he and his fiancée, Muriel Carew (Rose Hobart), are to be separated for at least another month issues almost directly in Jekyll's taking the Hyde formula—as his servant Poole (Edgar Norton) advises Jekyll to go out on the town. He does, as Hyde, and the latter mercilessly torments music-hall singer/temptress Ivy (Miriam Hopkins). In the context of Muriel's father's (Holmes Herbert) complaints regarding the lovebirds' "impatience," the doctor's "good" comes to seem to mean sexual repression, or suppression. In the context of the narrative as a whole, "so-called evil" comes to mean less sexual liberation than sexual intimidation and violence.

From one angle, then, this is a tale not of Good and Evil but of Evil (repression) and Evil (expression). Jekyll's repressed anger at Carew (he harbors thoughts of strangling him) later becomes Hyde's savage beating of the man. Any so-called good is almost squeezed out. Only (a) Muriel's unyielding, impassioned defense of Henry, a "finer and greater person than any of us"; (b) Henry's relinquishing of her before God, as "penance," and (c) poor Ivy's spirit, together, locate the elusive good. Jekyll's yeoman work in the hospital's "free ward" is meant to do this, but it does so too obviously to have any effect.

As Allen Dart notes (*Fangoria* 300:33), the "scenes of Hyde's psychological and (implied) physical torture of Ivy Pearson are genuinely disturbing ... " And, in fact, we do not see Hyde use his whip on her. We just see him hold her, kiss her, muss her hair. Nastily, he speaks sarcastically of "our great love." He's truly despicable, but what makes these scenes so disturbing is their focus on Hopkins' verge-of-hysteria performance. She is forever holding in that scream. Unlike Ann Darrow in *King Kong*, she can't quite let it out. In Hyde's mock-fond embrace, her grimace of repulsion can't quite even break into a smile for him. And the fact that Ivy has spirit makes it harder to see her broken.

The terrorization of women has been a subject in movies from *Broken Blossoms* to *La Strada* to *The Girl with the Dragon Tattoo* series. Rouben Mamoulian's film is not unique. But the focus on Ivy's bottled-up terror is a brilliant strategy. Call it an early example of the suggestion school of horror and violence. But Mamoulian and writers Samuel Hoffenstein and Percy Heath do not seem to trust us to get the point. They are almost as unrelenting as Hyde. This is a good thing insofar as it can be seen not to let us—or Jekyll—off the hook easily. But this hair-raising moral lesson finally begins to become almost a browbeating.

If Miriam Hopkins were less of an actress, I wouldn't even have to bring this up. But every syllable of Hyde's verbal taunting is reflected in her face—and it's harrowing to watch.

March's fidgety, anxious Hyde is a unique creation. From the get-go, he's pure energy, waiting to be channeled. But not waiting long. His all-lips-and-teeth makeup—which Pauline Kael (not without justification) found "hilarious" (*5001 Nights at the Movies*)—must have inspired Oscar-winner March. At the least, the fact that his mouth is stuffed with teeth helps disguise his voice and makes him sound as well as look gloriously outré.

Hobart is better at Good than is March, partly because his Jekyll is saddled with the "I have gone further than man should go" lines. Even Hyde gets a few cornball lines: e.g. (to Ivy): "I like you when your temper's up!" Jekyll's agonized "I'm one of the living dead" speech is at first pretty moving, but overstays its welcome, though March's delivery throughout seems heartfelt, honest. Holmes Herbert's Lanyon wins the Camp award here, as his eyes bug out while he witnesses Hyde turning into Jekyll.

Notes: There's a little much of symbolic birds, predatory cats, "angels" and "devils" (in the dialogue), and covered pots significantly boiling over.

Hyde's liberation from Jekyll begins on a droll, oddly upbeat note—he stands in the street baring his head and enjoying the pouring rain. For a few seconds, a happy resolution seems to be in the offing.

Other Hollywood stories of sexual repression have been more optimistic, and comedic. Not much Hyde in Katharine Hepburn's Tracy Lord, in *The Philadelphia Story* (1940), nor in Jean Arthur's Phoebe Frost (ah!), in *A Foreign Affair* (1948).

At the end, a cop shoots Hyde, then bends to his right, revealing the skeleton display which Jekyll glanced at, earlier, just before first taking the potion.

That little glance, then, seems to have been a quirky foreshadowing of Jekyll/Hyde's death.

At one point, in the opening subjective sequence (Jekyll's point-of-view), Jekyll's talented eyes somehow effect a dissolve from one shot to the next. The sequence also yields the first of two matching shots of Jekyll and Hyde, respectively, in mirrors—subjective cameos. "Man is not truly one, but truly two!"

For all the fine makeup effects, in all the Stevenson film adaptations, the most impressive transformation may occur here—near the end—in modest medium shot, with Jekyll facing away from the camera, as he "enlarges" into Hyde. He seems at once to get taller, wider, and more formidable.

Paramount. D: Rouben Mamoulian. SP: Samuel Hoffenstein, Percy Heath, from Robert Louis Stevenson's story. Ph: Karl Struss. AD: Hans Dreier. Ed: William Shea. SpMkp: Wally Westmore. Cost: Travis Banton. Sd: M.M. Paggi. With Fredric March, Miriam Hopkins, Rose Hobart, Holmes Herbert, Halliwell Hobbes, Edgar Norton, Tempe Pigott, Tom London, Murdock MacQuarrie, Douglas Walton, Eric Wilton; 98 minutes

Ref: "Runs overtime on footage ... [but] in many passages it is an astonishingly fine bit of interpreting a classic"—*Variety* 1/5/32.

Highlights of 1932

The year 1932 was a Golden Age in itself. The box-office effect of *Dracula* and *Frankenstein* (the "horror series started by Universal's *Dracula*"—*Variety* 7/26/32) had fully kicked in by August of 1932—some 19 horror films were released between August and December. 1932 saw three of the best horror films ever made—*The Mummy*, *White Zombie*, and *Island of Lost Souls*. In fact, the year was pretty much all highlights—even minor thrillers like *The Crooked Circle*, *Secrets of the French Police*, *The Monster Walks*, and *Murder at Dawn* earned their horror creds. Genre luminaries James Whale, Tod Browning, and Karl Freund shared the spotlight with Michael Curtiz, William Cameron Menzies, Victor Halperin, and Erle C. Kenton.

Lugosi and Karloff—the actors who started it all, the year before—followed up with more fine work: Karloff in *The Mummy* and *The Old Dark House*; Lugosi in *White Zombie* and *Murders in the Rue Morgue*. And they also enlivened pulpy fictions like *The Mask of Fu Manchu* (Karloff) and *Chandu the Magician* (Lugosi). It would be another two years before Universal did the dream-team thing and began pairing the two, most successfully in *The Black Cat* (1934).

Musical scores were beginning to become a factor—in, for instance, *White Zombie*, *The Most Dangerous Game*, *Chandu the Magician*, and, to a lesser extent, *The Mummy*. Meanwhile, an onslaught of sights and sounds kept viewers from noticing the lack of music in movies like *Doctor X* and *Island of Lost Souls*.

It was a banner year for ghost Westerns—*Tombstone Canyon*, *Ghost Valley*, *Haunted Gold*. And Long Island was Creep Central in 1932—Cliff Manor and Melody Manor, in *Doctor X* and *The Crooked Circle*, respectively, were both situated there.

Major-studio (MGM) Dud of the Year: *Kongo*.

Notable performances: Charles Laughton, Karloff, Ernest Thesiger, Eva Moore, Brember Wills (*The Old Dark House*), Wallace Ford, Leila Hyams, Angelo Rossitto, Daisy Earles (*Freaks*), Myrna Loy, Kay Johnson (*Thirteen Women*), Zasu Pitts, Christian Rub, Raymond Hatton (*The Crooked Circle*), Lugosi (*Murders in the Rue Morgue*, *White Zombie*, *Chandu the Magician*, *Island of Lost Souls*), Karloff (*The Mummy*, *The Mask of Fu Manchu*), Joan Blondell (*Miss Pinkerton*), Robert Frazer (*White Zombie*), Lionel Atwill, Fay Wray, Lee Tracy, George Rosener (*Doctor X*), Leslie Banks, Fay Wray (*The Most Dangerous Game*), Walter Huston (*Kongo*), Karen Morley (*The Phantom of Crestwood*), Laughton, Kathleen Burke (*Island of Lost Souls*)

Notable photography: Jules Cronjager (*The Monster Walks*), Edward A. Kull (*Murder at Dawn*), Karl Freund (*Murders in the Rue Morgue*), Ted McCord (*Ghost Valley*), Barney McGill (*Miss Pinkerton*), Ray Rennahan (*Doctor X*), Henry Gerrard (*The Most Dangerous Game*, *The Phantom of Crestwood*), James Wong Howe (*Chandu the Magician*), Robert B. Kurrle (*The Crooked Circle*), Arthur Edeson (*The*

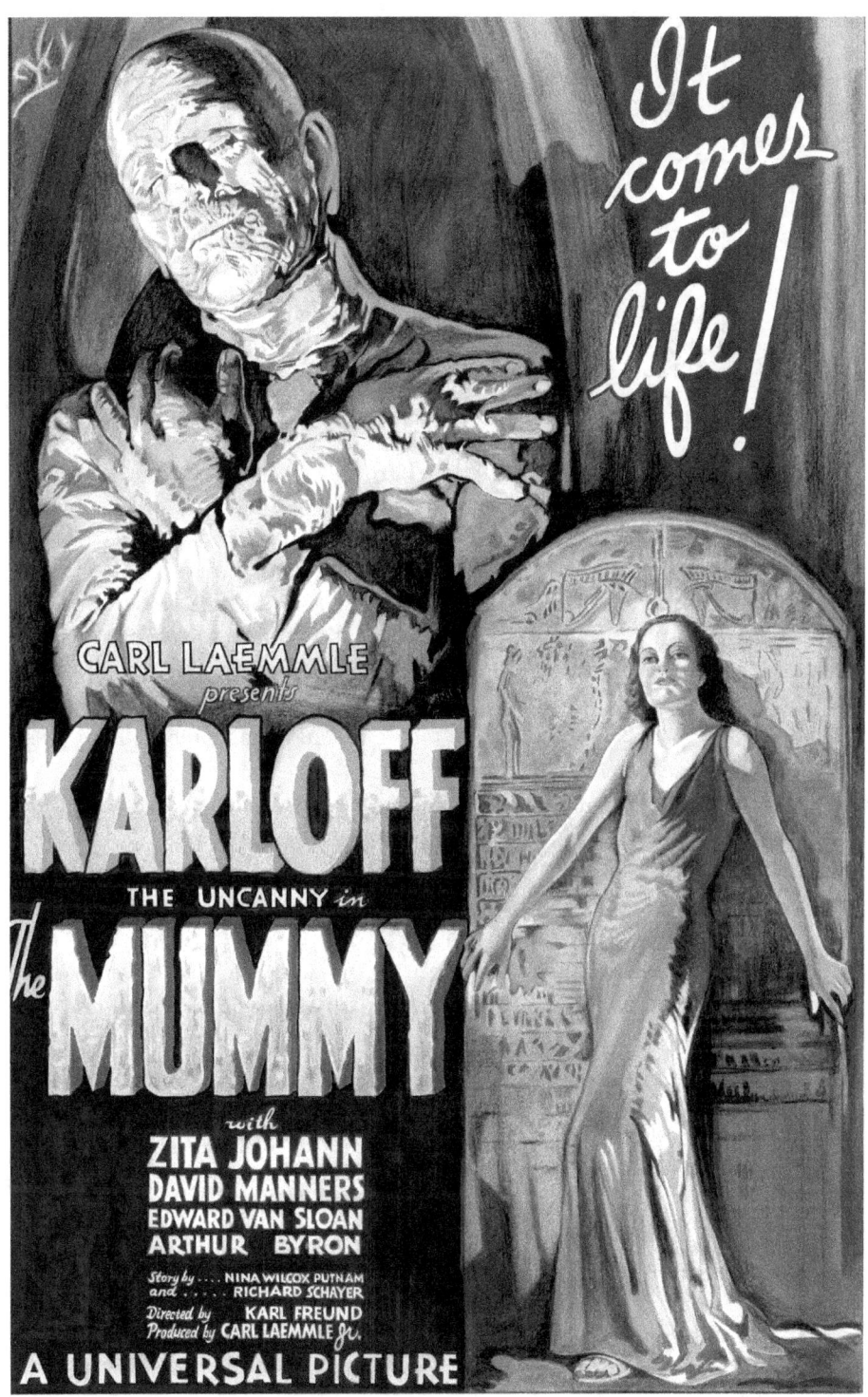

The 1-sheet poster from *The Mummy*

Lugosi from *Murders in the Rue Morgue*

Old Dark House), Alfred Gilks (*Secrets of the French Police*), Nicholas Musuraca (*Haunted Gold*), Charles Stumar (*The Mummy*)

Notable directing: Tod Browning (*Freaks*), Victor Halperin (*White Zombie*), Michael Curtiz (*Doctor X*), William Cameron Menzies, Marcel Varnel (*Chandu the Magician*), James Whale (*The Old Dark House*), Karl Freund (*The Mummy*), Erle C. Kenton (*Island of Lost Souls*)

Notable writing: Garnett Weston (*White Zombie*), James Creelman (*The Most Dangerous Game*), Robert Tasker, Earl Baldwin (*Doctor X*), Benn Levy (*The Old Dark House*), John Balderston (*The Mummy*), Waldemar Young, Philip Wylie (*Island of Lost Souls*)

Notable art direction: Charles D. Hall (*Murders in the Rue Morgue* and *The Old Dark House*), Carroll Clark (*The Most Dangerous Game, Ghost Valley*), Ralph Berger (*White Zombie*), Willy Pogany (*The Mummy*), Max Parker (*Chandu the Magician*)

Notable Makeup: Perc Westmore (?), Max Factor (?) (*Doctor X*), Wally Westmore, Charles Gemora (*Island of Lost Souls*), Jack Pierce (*The Mummy*)

Notable gowns: uncredited (*White Zombie*), uncredited (*Doctor X*), Vera West (*The Mummy*)

Notable music: Max Steiner (*The Most Dangerous Game, Thirteen Women*), James Dietrich (*The Mummy*)

Notable sound: George F. Hutchins (*The Monster Walks*), Douglas Shearer (*Freaks*), uncredited (*The Thirteenth Guest*), Robert B. Lee (*Doctor X*), L.E. Clark (*White Zombie*), Hedgcock and Hunter (*The Old Dark House*), Hans Weeren (*Tombstone Canyon*)

Notable editing: Fred Bain (*Murder at Dawn*), Harold McLernon (*White Zombie*)

Notable special effects: Howard Anderson (*White Zombie*), uncredited (*Chandu the Magician*), Warren Newcombe, Kenneth Strickfaden (*The Mask of Fu Manchu*)

Notable unfurling of a movie's title: *White Zombie, Chandu the Magician, The Most Dangerous Game*

Other films of interest:

Almost Married—Bill Warren. *Variety* 7/26/32: a "belated starter in the horror series started by Universal's *Dracula* ... implausible story ... nice photographical flashes." *AFI catalog*: "horror ... print viewed." Rick (CHFB 5/29/15): "legitimate, if close to the borderline, horror film." D: Menzies, Varnel. Regarding a lunatic pianist. Rare

Behind the Mask—torture scene with mad doc Edward Van Sloan. Enjoyably outlandish!

Central Park— Escaped lunatic (John Wray)—"strong as on ox and crazy as a loon"—throws zookeeper to lion, in a scene that might be an outtake from *Murders in the Zoo*. Pleasing scenes with Joan Blondell and Wallace Ford, but an over-involved scam plot takes over ...

Sinister Hands—"Mother's having her swami over tonight to put on a séance for us." Well, call it a séance, but it's just chalk and a darkened room. Lights-out murder, a magic slate, and a poking hand. Filmed with an eye on cheap. Two eyes. Not even semi-horror.

6 Hours To Live — Professor's "new ray" brings back the dead—for six hours. Second half of film is over-ambitious, but fairly compelling.

Strangers of the Evening —"How can a man be alive without a face?" Stiff comedy with one scare scene, or bit, in which a supposedly dead man awakes and scares a morgue attendant. ("Holy smacks! It was terrible!")

1932

The MONSTER WALKS

The Monster Walks released Feb. 10, 1932: Commonwealth Pictures' cut-rate version of *Murders in the Rue Morgue*. ("It's Yogi, Mr. Earlton's ape.") During one of his periodic visits to Berkeley's Pacific Film Archive, the late William K. Everson defended the Lugosi *The Ape Man* by noting that, however inept the production, it delivered the horror goods to fans. It didn't cheat. By the same token, *The Monster Walks* doesn't skimp on the horrific details. Ape cries as well as peals of thunder enliven the soundtrack. A clutching paw leaves "horrible marks" on the throat of one murder victim. In the climactic scene, a "strange boy" (Mischa Auer) whips Yogi into a frenzy (easy, since Yogi is never far from frenzy), as the bound-and-gagged heroine (Vera Reynolds) awaits her fate.

[SPOILER]: A "hopeless paralytic" (Sheldon Lewis) proves to be the villain—no, it's not synthetic flesh, though, just a handy confederate in the wings. Jules Cronjager's able camerawork and lighting provide some Gothic atmosphere. And the dialogue attempts to reinforce the simian threat. ("Why, with his tre-

mendous strength, anything is possible!") But acting and dialogue are at best mild camp, as actors pause for dramatic—actually, comic—effect. ("Yes—very sudden.") And, unwisely, director Frank Strayer doesn't speed the talk along. Listen to Yogi. He's saying that *The Monster Walks* should have been a silent film ...

Commonwealth Pictures. D: Frank Strayer. SP: Robert Ellis. Ph: Jules Cronjager. AD: Ben Dore. Ed: Byron Robinson. Sd: George F. Hutchins. P: Cliff P. Broughton. With Rex Lease, Vera Reynolds, Sheldon Lewis, Mischa Auer, Martha Mattox, Sidney Bracey, Willie Best; 57 minutes.

Ref: "Suffers both from poor dialog and trite development ... Mischa Auer is the most effective figure"—*Variety* 5/31/32.

MURDER AT DAWN

Murder at Dawn released Feb. 15, 1932: "He was hanging on a hook!" Dr. Farrington (Frank Ball) rents The Crag ("that old place") in order to work on the VXO Accumulator, an invention that he maintains will produce "unlimited power, direct from the sun—and it works equally well with artificial light ... Free power! Do you hear? Free power—setting millions of wage slaves free!" Free, one assumes, from wages—to paraphrase a Groucho punch line. Scene for scene, however, *Murder at Dawn* finds itself more concerned with skulking than with science. Skulkers, in fact, seem to outnumber non-skulkers. They even spy on one another. And continuity is such that, at one point, one skulking gent seems to be in two places at once. Only the number of disappearing, supposedly dead bodies rivals the number of skulkers. Two of the vanishing bodies, however, turn out to be the same body, and not dead, and—in one of the two cases—not even a body, just a dummy. Scorecards at the gate …

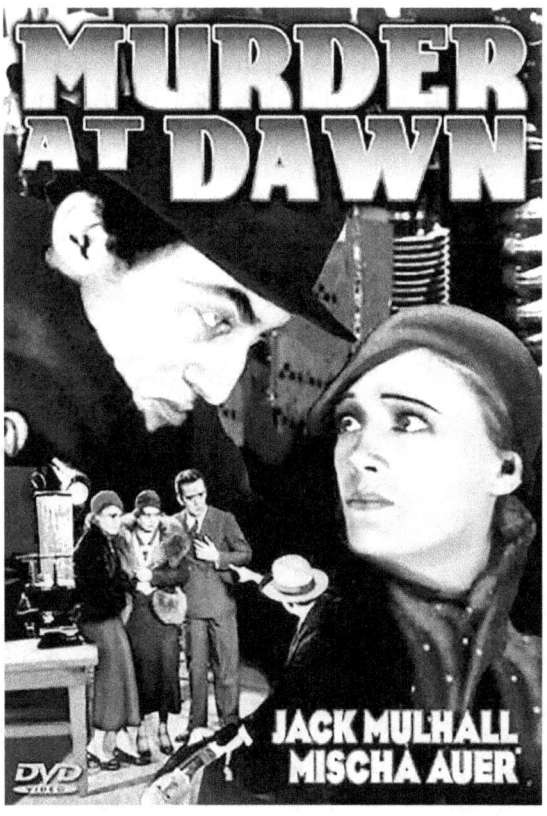

If this movie is scrappy, elementary, and moronic, it's also (as suggested) rather lively. In a phrase, or clause, it's Mischa Auer (Henry, the caretaker), Martha Mattox (the housekeeper), and beaucoup shadows. Who could ask for more from a dime (i.e., the budget)? Mattox has that forbidding-old-lady look. If she runs into trouble with the dialogue, she neatly snaps off her best line: "There ain't no telephone!" In fact, the best thing going is simply Edward A. Kull's camera tracking with Mattox, as she carries a lone flickering candle through The Crag.

Auer's caretaker functions, effectively, as a sort of Phantom, caped and capped, and throwing huge shadows above and behind him. He's "that crazy caretaker" and the "guy with the cape," and of course he "must be insane!" [NEAR-SPOILER]: And he's also the answer to pretty much every narrative question. Meanwhile, hero Jack Mulhall doesn't seem to know what to do when he's not talking. Eddie Boland is the stereotypical comic drunk, and George Reed is the stereotypical comic black man.

The title refers to the less noble use of the accumulator. Should the morning sunlight hit the latter, through the tower-room window, electricity would kill the doc's daughter (Josephine Dunn). And there is a bit of suspense in the well edited (Fred Bain) and alternated shots of the sun itself, the sunlight at the window, the accumulator, and the (bound) doc looking worried, worried.

Note: The Crag features one of the less impressive mad labs, though Kenneth Strickfaden fashioned the electrical gizmos.

Big 4 Films. D: Richard Thorpe. SP: Barry Barringer. Ph: Edward Kull. Ed: Fred Bain. SpFX: Kenneth Strickfaden. Sd: Earl Crain, Sr. With Josephine Dunn, Jack Mulhall, Eddie Boland, Marjorie Beebe, Martha Mattox, Mischa Auer, Phillips Smalley, Crauford Kent; 62 minutes.

Ref: IMDb.

"Even the "B"-audiences will be apt to scoff"—*Variety* 4/5/32.

"Some forgotten horrors have been forgotten for very good reasons"—Dave Sindelar (8/18/2002).

FREAKS

The Show: "You're hired as freaks ... not vampires!" For its first eight minutes, *The Show* (1927) plays like Tod Browning's personal preview of *Freaks*. The most alarming creature: the forbidding Edna Tichenor as Arachnida, the Human Spider, with six pretty-convincing huge spider legs above and behind her head. ("She eats flies on week days ... and butterflies on Sundays!") Tichenor—Luna, the Bat Lady, in *London after Midnight*—was perhaps the screen's first (silent) scream queen. Also featured: Zela the (top) half lady (Zalla Zarana) ... Neptuna, The Queen of the Mermaids (Betty Boyd) ... and The Living Hand of Cleopatra (just a writhing hand sticking out of a wall). At the end, Lionel Barrymore's villain unleashes the "deadliest of all poisonous reptiles," a true leapin' lizard from Madagascar, which looks like an iguana. The story is mainly syrupy, with a blandly happy ending. Barrymore and John Gilbert are not exactly subtle here. And Human Spiders apparently don't rate eight legs.

A pressbook herald from *Freaks*

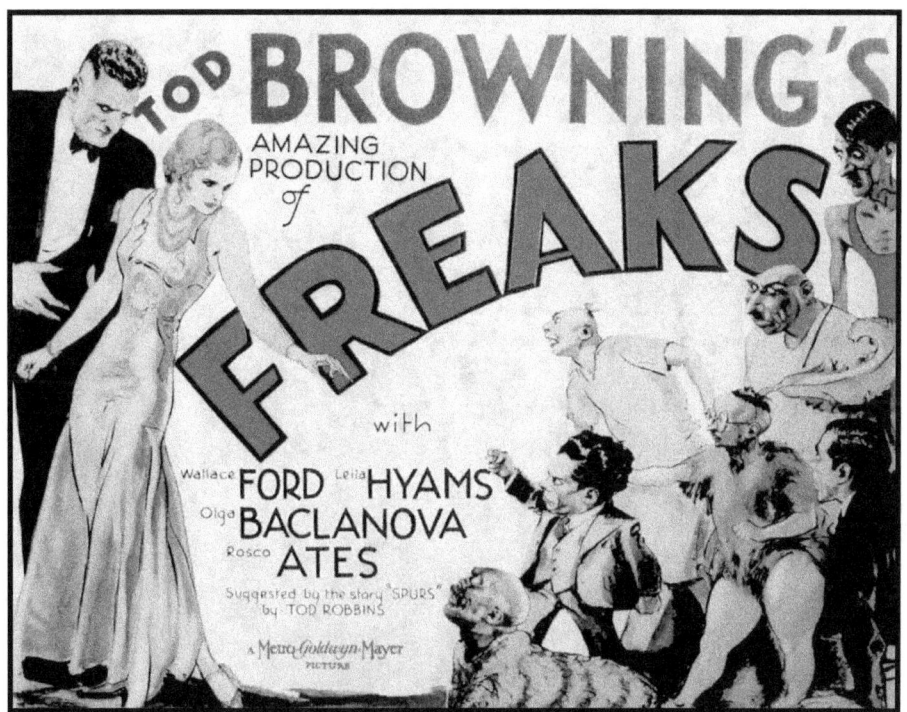

Half sheet poster from *Freaks*

"Spurs" (short story by Tod Robbins): "I always make people pay to laugh at me!" *Freaks* completely rewrites Robbins' story, but it's quite faithful to its tone of mutual loathing. The dwarf Jacques Courbe's revenge on his ex-beloved and her lover is as nastily inventive as the movie's climactic revenge scenes. Suspense highlight: the "steady *pit-pat, pit-pat*" of Courbe's wolf-dog St. Eustache, as the sound comes "nearer, [grows] more distinct" to the ex-lovers. It's the printed-page equivalent of John Williams' shark music.

Freaks released Feb. 20, 1932: [SPOILERS]: "You are about to witness the most amazing, the most astounding living monstrosity of all time." For circus high-wire star Cleopatra (Olga Baclanova), Hans the midget (Harry Earles) is "only something to laugh at"—until she discovers that he has come into a hefty inheritance. She marries him, then starts to subject him to a slow death by poison. At the end, in the woods, the "code of the freaks" leads Hans' circus friends to perform radical surgery on the "peacock of the air." She is reduced to a quacking, or crowing, bird-thing, with a finely feathered torso and tail. ("One of us!")

Indulge this unique film's drama of mutual disgust between the "beautiful big woman" Cleo and the "big homely brute" Hercules (Henry Victor), on one hand, and between the diminutive Hans and Frieda (Daisy Earles), initially his fiancée, on the other. Baclanova and Victor play too broadly and obviously,

The family of oddities, Johnny Eck sitting atop the table, from *Freaks*

and Harry Earles' performance is pretty stilted. Only Daisy Earles' touching scorned woman survives the melodramatics.

It's the day-to-day details—in effect, the sideshow—which make *Freaks* unique. Because the day-to-day of Siamese twins, living torsos, pinheads, and dwarfs is anything but mundane. A few scenes are all that's needed to suggest myriad complications in the love lives of the twins, Daisy and Violet Hilton (using their own names). ("Hook up our dress.") And the scenes are light and comic. Beyond comic: Daisy channeling Violet's fiancé Mr. Rogers' kiss. (The actor seems to be uncredited, even on IMDb.) Director Tod Browning sometimes stops the show altogether in order to allow his subjects to do their thing—e.g., the living torso (Prince Randian) lighting a cigarette. At other times, an unemphasized detail will win the day—e.g., the armless woman (Frances O'Connor)—in medium shot—pulling back a blanket with her foot so that Phroso (Wallace Ford) can get a look at the bearded lady's (Olga Roderick) baby girl. ("And it's gonna have a beard.")

The sounds of thunderstorm and harmonica ominously introduce the second most famous scene in *Freaks*. (The most famous, of course: the revelation of the Cleo-bird.) Browning is in his horror element, as the empathetic Madame Tetrallini's (Rose Dione) "children"—pre-Zippy pinheads, dwarfs, torsos—crawl through the mud, wielding knives and advancing on the wounded Hercules, and others run through the night rain after Cleopatra. It's a most satisfying finish to a payback story. For the house of pain in *Island of Lost Souls*, we substitute a forest of pain. An eye for an eye, a feather for a feather. Wisely, however, Browning ends the film with a Hans and Frieda reunion, a perhaps necessary move after scenes of collectively scary freaks. Hans and Frieda: reassuring.

Angelo Rossitto, who plays Angeleno—the eyes and ears of the freaks—had perhaps the longest career anyone has ever had in horror and science fiction movies, from *Seven Footprints to Satan* (1929) to *The Offspring* (1987)—almost 60 years. Memorably, in the 1940s, he partnered with Bela Lugosi, in *Spooks Run Wild* (1941), *The Corpse Vanishes* (1942), and *Scared to Death* (1947). A true dream team ... Another dwarf actor here, Jerry Austin, had a choice role as Cupidon, in the 1945 *Saratoga Trunk*. In one of the more sympathetic, non-freak roles, Wallace Ford is ingratiating as a "cheap clown," and Leila Hyams is fine as pal to his Phroso and an advocate for freaks.

Note: The "horsey-back ride": Hans on Cleo: originates in Robbins' story.

MGM. D: Tod Browning. SP: Willis Goldbeck, Leon Gordon. Dial: Edgar Allan Woolf, Al Boasberg Ph: Merritt B. Gerstad. Ed: Basil Wrangell. With Wallace Ford, Leila Hyams, Olga Baclanova, Roscoe Ates, Henry Victor, Harry Earles, Daisy Earles, Rose Dione, Daisy and Violet Hilton, Edward Brophy, Matt McHugh, Angelo Rossitto, Prince Randian; 52 minutes

"*Freaks* may be one of the most compassionate movies ever made"—Andrew Sarris.

"As a horror story in the *Dracula* cycle, it is either too horrible or not horrible enough"—*Variety* 7/12/32.

MURDERS IN THE RUE MORGUE

The Murders in the Rue Morgue (story—Edgar Allan Poe). [literary SPOILERS]: A pair of "fearfully mutilated" bodies is found in a house in Paris' Quartier St. Roch, and the keenly analytical C. Auguste Dupin deduces that only the "beast of Cuvier"—an "Ourang-outang," from the Indian Archipelago, as it transpires—could satisfactorily account for both the savageness of the murders and the "absence of motive" regarding same ... A murder mystery without a real murderer—just an imitative ape incited by the sight of blood. And it's an intriguing puzzle, with an even more intriguing solution. But it's a disembodied puzzle, without character or story. Our unnamed "I" here, who narrates, and Dupin prefigure Watson and Holmes, but Conan Doyle fleshed out the characters. *Murders* is a complete success, if an odd, modest one.

Murders in the Rue Morgue released Feb. 21, 1932: "They say he was a scientist or something"—or the "funny old man at the sideshow who owns the ape." At any rate, "he isn't an ordinary man." Paris, 1845. The unscrupulous Dr. Mirakle's (Bela Lugosi) experiments in evolution involve combining the blood of his ape Erik with that of a woman. After discarding (and that's the word)

Dr. Mirakle (Bela Lugosi) towers over all, in this lobby card from *Murders in the Rue Morgue*.

the body of a woman of the night (Arlene Francis), whose blood was "rotten," he comes upon a woman, Camille (Sidney Fox), whose blood is "perfect."

The film is bits and pieces of Poe's story, wrong-headed improvements on same, and Lugosi. He's a "show in himself" (as Camille notes), beginning with the absurd eyebrows, or eyebrow. *Murders in the Rue Morgue*, in fact, is at least halfway to a fine vehicle for Lugosi, no small feat considering that Mirakle was not even in the original. (It's less successful as a vehicle for Fox, ill served by atrocious sweet-talk with Leon Ames' renamed Pierre Dupin.)

One problem (besides the sweet talk) is that the Tom Reed-Dale Van Every script can't quite define the sides of its strange romantic triangle. Obviously, it's love at first sniff for Erik, the "beast with a human soul," who must content himself with doting on Camille's bonnet, initially: There are iron bars between the two. Mirakle seems to make light of his attraction: "You liked her, didn't you, Erik?" But it seems to be dead-serious jealousy that incites Erik, first to try to throttle Pierre, then, near the end, to kill Mirakle, preparatory to carrying Camille away across the roofs of Charles D. Hall's Paris.

[SPOILERS]: Erik, yes, finds her perfect, too, which enables Mirakle to use him to corral her. This beauty-killed-the-beast story (Pierre ultimately shoots down Erik) would be done better, the next year, in *King Kong*. The problem here is that the triangle's third side is occupied—not to say crowded—by both Pierre and Mirakle. Rectangles don't work, at least not when the movie's raison d'être, Lugosi/Mirakle, dies five minutes early, and leaves Monsieur Sweet Talk to take care of Erik and the loose dramatic ends.

The movie's most harrowing sequence—Dr. Mirakle drawing and testing blood from the prostitute—is also its most exhilarating. It's a nightmare of screaming (her) and shouting (him). But it's also a whirlwind showcase for Lugosi and his favorite movie toys—the microphone and the camera. He jumps from one out-sized emotion—anger, snarling impatience, rage, despair—to the next. It's less a dramatic spectacle than a chaotic, surreal one-man show.

When Mirakle sees that his subject is dead, he's crushed. Is it disappointment? Maybe. Compassion? Maybe not. Maybe just surprise, sudden awareness of something beyond his manic-depressive imagination. Something Outside. The sequence ends in quiet anguish for Mirakle, when he mutters, in long shot, "Will my search never end?" Is this a long-odds attempt to elicit audience sympathy for this most callous of characters? Or is it just a logical concluding note in this Symphony, or Cacophony, of a Madman? What a year for sadistic fiends—Mirakle, Moreau, Fu Manchu ...

"I tried to bring Poe's prose style into the dialogue, but the director thought it sounded stilted, so he and his assistant rewrote scenes on the set"—John Huston, *An Open Book*. Who was right—Huston or director Robert Florey? In the end, it may not have mattered much—at least in the case of Lugosi. Mirakle's sweet talk has a decidedly macabre tinge: (to Camille, regarding Erik) "He has an eye for beauty." A hundred actors, for instance, could have spoken the innocuous phrase "a lady in distress?," and it would have remained innocuous. But Lugosi succeeds in making each harmless syllable insinuating, intimidating. It's a cockeyed elocution lesson. Perhaps only Groucho Marx could have given the words as distinctive a spin.

Note Lugosi's early speech regarding heresy: "Heresy? Do they still burn men for heresy? Then burn me, monsieur!" The ripe, sarcastic tone he later perfected for his Ygor, in *Son of Frankenstein*, first appears here. In print, the line: "Do you think your little candle will outshine the flame of truth?" is metaphorical hokum. But Lugosi's sarcastic accent on "little" and his stern, self-righteous underlining of "the flame of truth" make this rhetorical question high adventure. What begins in kitsch, ends—about 10 words later—in art, or in something rather novel, midway between the two.

Even an ordinary line like (to Camille): "There is something you must know" abruptly turns extraordinary, with Lugosi's insistence on the "know," as if he (or Erik) had some great arcane knowledge to impart. But she doesn't bite: "Are you insane, monsieur?" The great genius is lately getting only static, despite his flair for the darkly dramatic. Mirakle's gorilla patter, at the carnival, is charming (did Huston create the ape language?), but he perhaps misses the

Dr. Mirakle experiments on "woman of the streets" Arlene Francis.

apish subtext of lust, or he wouldn't seem so startled when Erik advances on him, near the end.

"It's the hair of an ape." The sequence with Pierre at the microscope trying to find the cause of the several deaths is pointless. (Insert sketch labeled "Red blood cell of the gorilla.") We have already seen the results of the "bad blood." Also pointless: lines like Dupin's "I wonder what Dr. Mirakle is up to." We already know what he's up to. And the tantalizing mystery in the Poe story, regarding the language that the witnesses describe hearing coming from the murder scene, evaporates here since we already know its source.

Cinematographer Karl Freund doesn't fool around when it comes to night shots and coaches. As with the early sequence in *Dracula*, he shoots the Paris night sequence with Mirakle and the prostitute in a sea of darkness and fog. It's visually quite disorienting. The coach, the lamppost, and the players are virtually the only solid objects swimming in this sea. Paris itself has disappeared and given way to Mirakle's nightmare tableau here. All kin, somehow: the dark, the fog, the doctor ... Later, a minor Freund coup: the massive shadow of Erik's hand on Camille's bedstead, behind her.

Notes: The intoxicating shot in which Camille swings on the swing before and with the camera (also, one assumes, on a swing) anticipates a similar scene in Jean Renoir's enchanting *Day in the Country* (1936).

Ten years later, a specialist in incidental ghouls such as Milton Parsons or Skelton Knaggs would have played D'Arcy Corrigan's morgue keeper.

Erik is a gorilla (Charles Gemora) in long shot, but only an insert of a snarling chimpanzee in close shots. This imposture is most damaging, perhaps, in the scene in which Camille, in bed, screams at chimp Erik. A little alarming, maybe, but not at all scary. Not for nothing are there no movies with titles like "Chimpanzee at Large," "Congochimp," "The White Chimpanzee," "Bride of the Chimpanzee."

Arlene Francis is better remembered for her 25 years on the "What's My Line?" TV series.

Universal. D, Adap: Robert Florey. SP: Tom Reed, Dale Van Every, from the short story by Edgar Allan Poe. Add. Dial: John Huston. Ph: Karl Freund. AD: Charles D. Hall. Mkp: Jack Pierce. SpFX: John P. Fulton. Ed: Milton Carruth. Sd: C. Roy Hunter. With Sidney Fox, Bela Lugosi, Leon Ames, Bert Roach, Betty Ross Clarke, Brandon Hurst, D'Arcy Corrigan, Noble Johnson, Arlene Francis, Herman Bing, Iron Eyes Cody, Charles Gemora, Harry Holman, Torben Meyer, Tempe Pigott, Michael Visaroff, Polly Ann Young; 61 minutes

Ref: "[Lugosi] often transforms overacting into an art form"—Bryan Senn, *Cult Movies* 15:67.

"The fact that [the prostitute's] blood is diseased is a shock to [Mirakle]?"—Dr. Maniac review, *Scary Monsters* 26:74-79.

"Features a triumphant Bela Lugosi performance"—Gary J. Svehla, *Midnight Marquee* 50:82.

"As bad as Sidney Fox and Leon Ames are, they play like Vivien Leigh and Laurence Olivier compared to Madge Bellamy and John Harron in *White Zombie*"—Gregory Mank, in *Bela Lugosi*, p50.

"*Dracula* and *Frankenstein* having softened 'em up, this third of U's baby-scaring cycle won't have the benefit of shocking them stiff"—*Variety* 2/16/32.

GHOST VALLEY

Ghost Valley released May 13, 1932: "Seen any ghosts around here yet?" Boom City, Nevada, a "ghost city for the last 30 years." A plot to "scare the girl into selling" the mine—the girl being Jane Worth (Merna Kennedy)—is behind highly exaggerated reports of an "ape man, a brute as big as a telegraph pole." The great line here is: "They've hired me to impersonate myself." It's made to make sense in context, but even there it doesn't pay to think about it too much.

Apart from the reliable excitement of riders on fast horses, this compact Tom Keene Western features a variety of spooky settings, including a cave and a church. ("The place is probably haunted.") Ted McCord's lighting and Carroll Clark's art direction make pews and pulpit, in the latter, look haunted

all right. Highlights: a phantom vs. the comic relief (Harry Bowen) in Bronson Caverns, and the unnerving sounds of an organist at midnight (a killer aural shiver) in the supposedly empty church. Two other small visual coups: the hovering shadow of a pair of clutching hands, and a glowing lantern carried down a street in the dark of night. Plus some big bothersome cobwebs, a black cat, a skull, and constant wind sound effects, in and around Boom City, during the night—unfortunately, there are few wind sight effects to back them up. As *Variety* noted, "The kids will love it."

RKO Pathe. D: Fred Allen. SP: Adele Buffington. Ph: Ted McCord. AD: Carroll Clark. Ed: William Clemens. Sd: Earl Wolcott. With Tom Keene, Merna Kennedy, Kate Campbell, Mitchell Harris, Harry Bowen, Harry Semels, Billy Franey, Ted Adams; 54 minutes

Ref: "Not enough story to get in the hair of fast action. Will score"—*Variety* 8/30/32.

MISS PINKERTON

Miss Pinkerton (novel—Mary Roberts Rinehart): "The house was eerie that night." Mystery set in the "old Mitchell mansion" proves fairly forgettable. It's not really even an old-dark-house story, though there are scattered hints of "ghostly figures," and a cat under a bed is good for a passing scare. The height of horror: "something blacker than darkness," on a landing, which frightens our heroine, Miss Adams, aka Miss Pinkerton. ("It looked like a ghost.")

Miss Pinkerton released July 30, 1932: "He did not walk through that door like a ghost!" Fans of the book were no doubt pleased that the movie adaptation followed Rinehart pretty closely. (The movie does make more obvious the budding romance between Joan Blondell's Miss Adams and George Brent's inspector.) The movie is in fact slightly more tolerable than the book, mainly because shadows seen can be more vivid than shadows described. The black-clad killer/skulker here is not really a full-fledged phantom. It's the over-sized shadows that he throws on walls—and the screams he elicits—which get this picture into, or near, the realm of the horrific.

If much of *Miss Pinkerton* is strictly mystery-business, direct from the book, it's also true that, before a word is spoken, we see an unknown light source casting the huge shadow of a man on the front of the "old Mitchell mansion." And, before a word is spoken, we hear screaming. The most enterprising, even experimental visual: The camera tracks up to Miss Adams, as she spots someone and screams, then it tracks away from her. Fade to black. Then, the camera tracks up to the mysterious Hugo (John Wray), the one she saw. It's at least a nice try at visually approximating the experience of fear and fainting. Barney McGill Deluxe.

McGill's second most unusual contribution: the very brief illumination of the eyes of the killer, who's otherwise all in black. (At least, it's apparently supposed to be his eyes that light up, in medium shot, but the lighting effect seems to be located closer to his mouth.) Earlier, McGill creates some cool, spiky tree-branch shadows around the outside of the kitchen window. And, at one point, there's a strange, not very realistic glow, or gleam, from a fireplace, which glow may have been intended to be unrealistic, or surrealistic.

Joan Blondell makes her Scream Queen bid, most forcefully, and Elizabeth Patterson and Blanche Friderici do some shrieking, too. Blondell is generally quite personable, though she has a couple of Bug Eyes moments. Wray and Friderici (as Mary) do their best to appear *forbidding*. Robert Tasker added a lot of passable snappy dialogue.

Notes: There's also some strange "knocking" or "creeping" in the mansion.

WB-FN. D: Lloyd Bacon. Adap: Niven Busch, Lillie Hayward, from Mary Roberts Rinehart's novel. Addl Dial: Robert Tasker. Ph: Barney McGill. Mus: Bernhard Kaun. AD: Jack Okey. Ed: Ray Curtiss. P: Hal Wallis. With Joan

Blondell, George Brent, Ruth Hall, John Wray, Elizabeth Patterson, C. Henry Gordon, Holmes Herbert, Mary Doran, Blanche Friderici, Nigel De Brulier, Lucien Littlefield, Allan Lane, Stanley Blystone, Walter Brennan, Don Dillaway, Harry Strang, Lyle Talbot, Luana Walters; 66 minutes.

Ref: "The settings are extremely well done for atmosphere"—*Variety* 7/12/32.

"It was so big, so terrible!" The 1942 remake, *The Nurse's Secret*, is just an indifferent mystery, without the intimidating shadows. Apparently, cinematographer James Van Trees was not allowed to get creative with the lighting. A big, howling dog is as spooky as this one gets, though Leonard Mudie as Hugo is grim-looking enough. The two opening shots are from *Miss Pinkerton*. In this version, the inspector and the nurse are already an item.

WHITE ZOMBIE

The Magic Island (book —W.B. Seabrook): "I will show you dead men working in the cane fields." Only two of this book's four parts concern voodoo ("The Voodoo Rites") and zombies ("Black Sorcery"), but they're well written, if a little patchwork. Ingredients include love-ouangas (Haitian charms—"midnight and moonlight were in it"), Damballa (the "ancient African Serpent god"), the Virgin Mary (invoked to intercede with the "old African gods"), pentagrams, Baron Samedi (the "spirit of the graveyard"), a requiem mass for a "dreadful, dead he-goat," baptized voodoo drums, a vampire (here called a Loup Garou), and other elements of "horror-beauty." The interpolated anecdote regarding Ti Joseph and his cane-field crew of "poor unhappy zombies" is a terrific little tale relating to the "ragged edge of things, which are beyond either superstition or reason." ("The eyes were the worst.") "Toussel's Pale Bride" is another little gem of a horror story. ("She seized a candle ... and saw the man was dead.") *Magic Island* actually has slightly closer ties, or more ties, to *I Walked with a Zombie* (which see) than it does to *White Zombie*.

White Zombie released Aug. 4, 1932: "But the soul is gone!" Deep in the heart of Lugosi-land ... The creators of the visually adventurous, intoxicating, if uneven *White Zombie*—Garnett Weston (story and dialogue), Victor Halperin (director), Edward Halperin (producer)—apparently did nothing else quite like it, before or after. There was apparently something in the air in the early 1930s, a unique aesthetic crossroads, when the art of black-and-white cinematography had been perfected (principally in silent films), and sound was still an exciting experiment. However, the air made no guarantees. Just look at the Halperins' next thriller, *Supernatural* (1933).

White Zombie is nothing if not ambitious, visually. Zombies here, for instance, don't just walk—they travel single file, picturesquely (in long shot), in silhouette, across the rims of hills. When we see the drunk, maddened hero, Neil (John Harron)—his bride, Madeline (Madge Bellamy), has apparently just

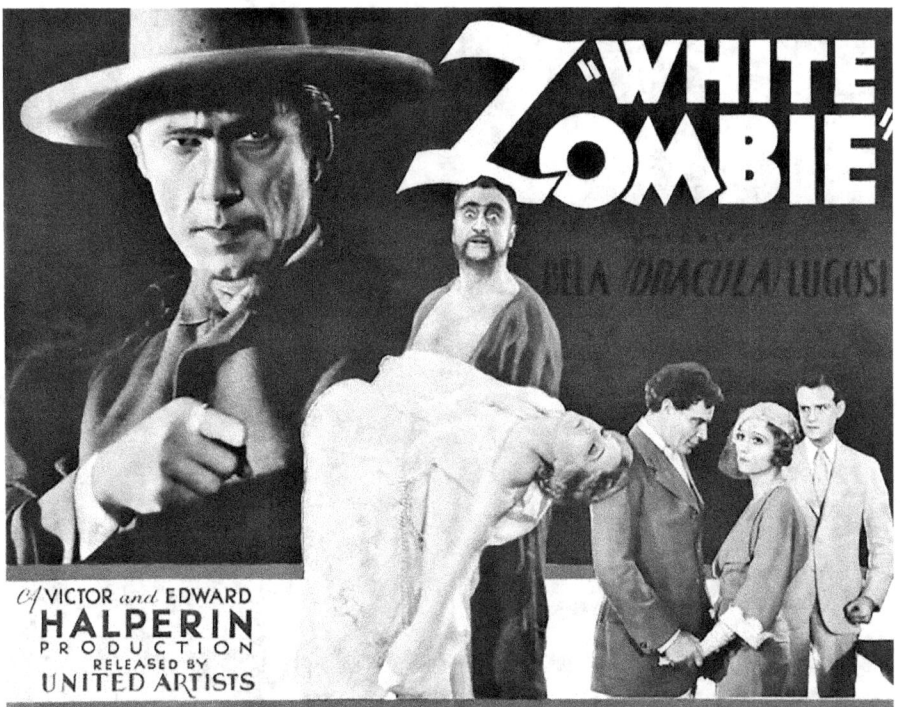

died—the other dancing, drinking bar patrons are only shadows. In the film's poetic shorthand, they are only irrelevant (for him) happy couples. Later, a series of dissolves (Harold McLernon, editor) takes us, first, from outside zombie-wrangler Legendre's (Bela Lugosi) "house of the living dead"; then to a shot of an imposing stone stairway, then inside, where towering columns, walls, and windows dominate (Ralph Berger, art director; Howard Anderson, special effects). Still later, some kitschy but oddly elegant wipes splice together Neil (way down below, on the beach) with Madeline (way up high, at the chateau's balcony railing), and a fancy "curtain up" wipe replaces him, in one shot, with her, in the next.

The first zombie movies were, at times, surprisingly beautiful (it's that "horror-beauty")—I am thinking, mainly, of *White Zombie* and *I Walked with a Zombie* (1943), but also of moments in *Revenge of the Zombies* (1943) and *Voodoo Man* (1944). The principal focus of beauty, as established by *White Zombie*: the walking, white-gowned zombie woman, seen, in various incarnations, in all four of the above films. Vivid background flourish: Madeline—in her flowing, silk-chiffon evening-dress overlay (fashion notes: Mo)—dashing across the house's great room, in long shot. And, just before this: the flowing thing again, as she glides down and across a stone hall and stairway. Killing detail here: the gliding gown drapes itself over—even caresses—the stone steps. This may be the ultimate Woman in White movie …

Murder Legendre (Bela Lugosi) directs a member of his army of zombie workers.

Note, however, that it takes at least two distinct, unacknowledged phenomena to help create the flowing and gliding effects. One: Legendre's hypnotic powers apparently extend to doors, which open (and close) before (and after) his trance-bound subjects pass through doorways. It makes visual, if not voodoo sense: A gliding zombie can't stop to deal with doors, knobs, and handles without wrecking the gliding effect. Two: Vividly illuminating Madeline's gown and—in a gliding-squared effect—casting her elegant shadow high against a stone wall, is a very bright light, source unknown. A third note, regarding the final stage of her enchanted run: To get the winged angel of death effect (she was programmed to dispatch Neil with Legendre's dagger)—during her flight down the outdoor steps—Madeline's arms are outstretched, and the floating overlay becomes her "wings."

If Legendre's thick eyebrows are over the top, campy, Lugosi himself here is more often than not restrained. The scene: In the great room, Legendre is whittling a zombie control doll and addressing Beaumont (Robert Frazer, who gives the film's second-best performance), beside him, miserably mute and helpless, a recent victim of a zombie potion. The line: "You see, you are the first man to know what is happening—none of the others ... did." Slight verbal accents on "happening," "none," and "others." Only the pause before the word accentuates "did." In fact, Lugosi speaks the word in a clipped and quiet manner. Typically, Lugosi will draw out key words, embellish them, relish them, extend them. Here, he shrinks "did" down to its nasty (in context) core, the better to suggest (along with Beaumont's presence, or absence) the ghastly nature of what happens to his victims, aware or not.

The scene: Legendre's sugar-cane mill, manned by zombies. ("They are not worried about long hours.") The players: Legendre and the pre-zombie Beaumont. The subject: Legendre's first encounter, earlier in the evening, with Madeline and Neil, from whom Beaumont wants to pry her, with Legendre's help. The line: "I looked ... into her eyes." The import (found in the line which follows): "She is deep in love ... but not with you." At the end of the movie, Madeline delivers its great line (more on that later), but Lugosi's almost whispered, strangely reverent delivery of "I looked ... into her eyes" makes this simple sentence the effective center of *White Zombie*. That whisper seems to be one of quiet awe—awe (the subsequent line suggests) in the presence of a power to rival voodoo—namely, love. The scene, however, is not sentimental about love or Legendre. When the latter tells Beaumont how he plans to corral Madeline, he has to whisper the details in his ear, and Beaumont responds with a horrified "No! Not that!" (Shades of Dwight Frye's Renfield.) Legendre is enough of a romantic that he believes in love, or acknowledges it, but business is business ...

The scene: Legendre, the trance-bound Madeline, and Beaumont, in the great room, in the complement to the mill sequence. The action: Legendre holds her hand in his, looks down at this sweet suggestion of love (in some alternate universe), then looks up, into her eyes, again, and is not surprised—the expression on Lugosi's face may change slightly, but he already knows that instead of love, he will see nothing. For him, it's a non-reaction shot. Beaumont: "Better to see hatred in them than that dreadful emptiness."

Madeline's tremendous line, at the end, is simply, "I dreamed," spoken when she first awakens from her zombie state, after Legendre dies. In an instant, it filters the entire picture through her. It's like a magic rewind button, a very fast rewind. How did the action unfold, as seen, or felt, from the other side? From inside those apparently empty eyes? All we know is that she seems to have a piece of Legendre's power herself, refracted: When Neil senses her presence, far above him, at the balcony railing, it's certainly not *his* doing. It's as if she's in a dream, from which she can occasionally peek out, but not awaken.

The movie's action is not a dream, but it's sometimes dreamlike. Things happen for no clear reason; Legendre and Beaumont say things that don't

Pressbook herald from *White Zombie*

make obvious sense. Madeline's flight through the chateau, for instance, ends with her at the edge of a cliff—is this the Madeline core of Madeline the zombie compelled to jump, to atone for attempting to stab Neil? Or is this just a natural way to conclude her flight? Or (a third, strong possibility) is this foreshadowing? Soon, some eight characters, in all, will (a) jump, (b) fall or (c) be pushed off said cliff to their deaths. *Hamlet* on a dime.

One of the eight—who is pushed by Beaumont, who, in turn, falls with him—is Legendre, whose vulture follows him down, diving and screeching and ... to quote the Cary Grant character in *Monkey Business* (1952), "What's the vulture doing?" It's less a pet to Legendre than a familiar, though it almost, at times, seems like his alter ego. Legendre dies; the vulture dies, too, it seems. At one point, Beaumont—addressing Legendre, in the room, and the vulture, outside the window—cries, somewhat inexplicably, "The vulture! You! No, not that!" Maybe it's more unsettling not to know what, exactly, or even roughly, is on Beaumont's fevered mind here, or on Legendre's.

Legendre is fond of invoking "the future," but is at best provocatively vague about it. "I have other plans for mademoiselle!" he taunts Beaumont. But do they involve the vulture or Beaumont or Legendre himself, or all of the above? Legendre's expressed disdain for the zombie Madeline would seem to preclude a sexual liaison between the two. Perhaps he was thinking about (among other never-stated things) his upcoming assignment for her: Kill Neil. "I have taken a fancy to *you*, monsieur!" he tantalizes Beaumont. Again he seems uninterested in near-necrophilia—his relationship with his zombie regiment, the unholy six, is strictly business. Perhaps he's having perverse fun with Monsieur Beaumont.

Other actor notes: Madge Bellamy's ditzy smile—and, later, her zombie eyes—look as if they were pasted on her face. With the eyes, it's appropriate. Joseph Cawthorn, as Bruner, is supposed to be a sort of folksy Van Helsing, and he's no more tiresome than most Van Helsings.

Two fun, hokey shock scenes: Groom Neil to bride Madeline: "What do you see in the [wine] glass?" She: "I see happiness." Then, she sees Legendre, eyes glowing full voodoo, in the glass. Later, Arthur Martinelli's camera, discreetly, and strategically, eschews following Neil into Madeline's tomb. But we hear his scream when he sees that her body is no longer there.

General Notes: About the only element—apart from zombies and Haiti and an ouanga or two—common to both *Magic Island* and *White Zombie* is the idea (as expressed in the latter) of burying dead bodies in the middle of the road, to foil grave robbers. In the book, we learn that the "poor unhappy dead" are assured "protection" by having their graves "set close beside a busy road or footpath, where people are always passing."

White Zombie is one of the first horror movies to have a full-service musical score, though it's not dramatic, simply atmospheric.

The vulture seems to scream with a distorted, amplified human voice more unnerving even than the rooster's crow in *The Old Dark House*.

The long dialogue sequence between Neil and Dr. Bruner (Cawthorn) shuts down the movie, temporarily, but from a technical angle it's impressive—it's one, long (five minute) take. Shades of *Russian Ark*.

Way cool musical intro: A drum thump punctuates the appearance of each letter of "ZOMBIE," in the title.

The fear which the coach driver (Clarence Muse) exhibits ("Zombies!") is apparently not accurate, or at least not typical: "Haitian peasants are on curiously intimate terms with their dead and seem almost totally devoid of ... terror of graveyards, ghosts, "haunts," and dead bodies ... " (Seabrook p89)

For fans of the original *Famous Monsters of Filmland*, virtually our first, stirring glimpse of *White Zombie* was the "active tableau" pictured in *FM* 16 (1962), page 30. It's a publicity-still anagram of actual scenes from the finished film, with added running and pointing by several characters. The main scene invoked: the one in which Legendre's zombies are carrying Silver (Brandon Hurst) up the stairs to his death.

Sequence in *Dr. Terror's House of Horrors (1943)*.

United Artists. D: Victor Halperin. SP: Garnett Weston. Ph: Arthur Martinelli. AD: Ralph Berger. SpFX: Howard A. Anderson. Mkp: Jack Pierce, Carl Axcelle. Ed: Harold McLernon. Sd: L.E. Clark. P: Edward Halperin. With Bela Lugosi, Madge Bellamy, Robert Frazer, Joseph Cawthorn, John Harron, Brandon Hurst, George Burr Macannan, Clarence Muse; 69 minutes

Ref: *PV* 31:28. "One of the classics of Hollywood's golden age of horror, an eerie, thoroughly disquieting exercise"—David J. Hogan, *Filmfax* 57:66.

Reference to "Martinelli's shadow-land lighting"—Bryan Senn, *Drums of Terror*, p19.

"Lugosi's line readings are some of his best, and some of the best heard in horror films"—John Stell, in *Bela Lugosi*, p56.

"Wonderfully gruesome"—Stephen Jones, *Essential Monster Movie Guide*, p111.

"Victor Halperin goes to Hayti [sic], hotbed of Obi, for the latest addition to the blood curdling cycle, and with good results ... [Lugosi] gives an exceptionally good performance"—*Variety* 8/2/32.

The THIRTEENTH GUEST

The Thirteenth Guest, or The Morgan Mysteries (novel—Armitage Trail): Thirteen years after wealthy Colonel Morgan "died quite suddenly"—just before his birthday celebration—his "grim and gruesome" mid-west home—a "huge black bulk"—seems haunted by "inexpressibly terrifying ... phantom footsteps," a "supernatural spectacle," or "apparition"; a "mysterious strangler," or "demon"; a "floating" head in a window, "eerie echoes," and a "mysterious tower." Only very mildly intriguing mystery uses much repetition in order to achieve novel length. D.A. Winston and police detective Grump prove to be very jittery grown men. And Winston comes off as pretty dense, the better to set up the concluding revelation re Marie Morgan. Richard Matheson borrowed the idea of the cobwebbed banquet table from this book, apparently—or from the film adaptations—for the 1962 *Tales of Terror* ("Morella")—it's not in the Poe story.

Ginger Rogers investigates the cobwebbed banquet table around which all the murder victims will be posed, in *The Thirteenth Guest*.

The Thirteenth Guest released Aug. 9, 1932: Before there was Fred and Ginger, there was Lyle and Ginger, one of the odder teams in motion-picture history. In 1932, Ginger Rogers and Lyle Talbot starred in this film; in 1933, they were paired again in *A Shriek in the Night*. (For the record, she was also in *42nd Street* [1933], which featured Talbot's voice.) And the same production team made both their starring films—Albert Ray (director), Frances Hyland (writer), M.H. Hoffman (associate producer), Tom Galligan and Harry Neumann (photography), L.R. Brown (editor), Gene Hornbostel (art director), and Sidney Algier (production manager).

"The 13th guest never got there." The house at 122 Mill Road has been unoccupied for 13 years, but visitors there find a working phone. It seems that old man Morgan (Charles Meecham) died at his birthday banquet, his wife (Isabel La Mal) had the house sealed, and a phantom killer ("fiendish as the devil") in the present day requires both electricity and telephone service to electrocute his victims. (He uses just enough electricity "to kill ... but not to burn the body.") This first adaptation of the Trail novel is slightly preferable to the book, if only because more of the action takes place in the old house—in the book, only the beginning and the ending are set there.

Unfortunately, there's not much in the way of old-house atmosphere here—mainly just the usual clutching hands and skulking phantoms. However, there's one unexpected frisson: the killer's stationing of his victims at the cobwebbed banquet table, with their stiff arms outstretched, like zombies. Two "Yows!" What distinguishes the phantom killer's scenes is his weird, puzzling screaming (like "Tarzan and the devil and a couple of hyenas thrown in"). At one point, this cloaked, cowled killer actually says, "You little fool!" [SPOILERS]: At first, the movie seems to be pulling a *Psycho*, or pre-*Psycho*, by killing off its lead actress, Rogers, but her character, Marie Morgan, does a "resurrection act," of sorts. Rogers is kinda sweet, and that's about all that's asked of her. At the end, though, she does a decent Hysterical, too. Talbot cruises uneventfully through the movie.

Note: Hyland's script names the 13th guest, but this person then seems to have been counted twice. Yes, this is really "The Twelfth Guest"!

(*Lady Beware*—British title) Monogram. D: Albert Ray. SP: Frances Hyland; (uncredited) Arthur Hoerl, from Armitage Trail's novel. Ph: Tom Galligan, Harry Neumann. AD: Gene Hornbostel. Ed: Leete R. Brown. P: M.H. Hoffman. With Ginger Rogers, Lyle Talbot, J. Farrell MacDonald, Paul Hurst, Erville Alderson, Ethel Wales, James Eagles, Crauford Kent, Phillips Smalley, Lynton Brent, Al Bridge, Bobby Burns, William B. Davidson, Kit Guard, Henry Hall, John Ince, Tom London, Charles Meecham, Harry Tenbrook; 69 minutes

Remake: *The Mystery of the 13th Guest* (1943)

Ref: IMDb. "*The Thirteenth Guest* is a first-rate 'old dark house' mystery"— Jeff Miller, *Filmfax* 61:58.

DOCTOR X

Doctor X released Aug. 27, 1932: "This is a very strange house." Cliff Manor, Blackstone Shoals, Long Island, where the night wind whistles—a "strange, uncanny place." The "moon killer" has murdered and cannibalized six victims in six months, using a "strange surgical knife" imported from Vienna. The victims also show signs of "strangulation ... by powerful hands." Main suspects: five doctors at the Academy of Surgical Research: Dr. Xavier (Lionel Atwill), Prof. Haines (John Wray), Dr. Wells (Preston Foster), Prof. Duke (Harry Beresford), and Dr. Rowitz (Arthur Edmund Carewe).

Long Island of Lost Souls. The headline here is also a [SPOILER]: One of the doctors has created what he calls "synthetic flesh," or "living manufactured flesh." In a sequence which still enthralls, he applies this "flesh" to his head, in effect making a monster before our eyes, step by step, like Jack Pierce. (Max Factor is credited for Mask Effects.) If *Doctor X* has its bare patches, it also has its gung-ho gruesome payoffs, and this may be the most gleefully outrageous of all. The "flesh" begins, on application to the head, with somewhat the texture of clay, and electricity provides the finishing touches, at least to the synthetic hand. Director Michael Curtiz and lenser Ray Rennahan even dare to get a

little surreal and, once or twice, photograph the creation process through the medium of the distorting manufacturing liquid. Disorientation 101.

The first big payoff is head doc Xavier's "psycho-neurological" test to see if one of his medicos is the murderer: "One of us in this room may be a murderer, a man who kills by the light of a full moon, leaving his victim's body mutilated ... a cannibal!" Just one highlight of this early sequence: Atwill's galvanic description of the rising red liquid in the "thermal tubes," which rise indicates faster heartbeat in the subject. Another highlight here: the preview, in effect, of Warners' follow-up film, *The Mystery of the Wax Museum*—the spectacle of the wax-figure models of the murder victims. A third highlight: the hypnotic whirring of the "high-frequency coil." But the test is interrupted by yet another murder.

The script omits the particulars of Xavier's second, climactic psychological test, but the killer again hijacks it, replacing Xavier's butler Otto (George Rosener), onstage, and threatening Xavier's daughter Joanne (Fay Wray). Extra-mile horrific detail: the chronic gasping of the "terrible monster." Prize here, too, for what must be the most hapless attempt on film to garner sympathy for a homicidal, ultra-ugly monster. As he explains: "I'll make a crippled world whole again!" The disconnect!

The lack of a musical score doesn't hurt *Doctor X* as much as it hurts *Mystery of the Wax Museum*. Sound effects (Robert B. Lee) take up much of the slack—sirens, foghorns, wind-whipped branches, rustling leaves, a chiming clock, an almost comically creaking door, the clangings of a train pulling into a station, the crackling of electrical equipment, etc.

The primarily blue/red/brown two-strip Technicolor has the atmospheric effect of tinting-plus. Shadows seem to have a different, richer character in color. Also unnerving: the scudding blue clouds around the omnipresent full moon, and the gusts of blue-white fog (blue, white, and creepy).

As suggested above, Atwill is at his emphatic best. That gloriously outraged delivery informs the essential Atwill line here: "Meddling fools!" Lee Tracy's reporter Lee Taylor serves two main purposes. He lightens the tone, and in effect conducts us on a comic-horrific tour of this curious night world— the morgue, the academy, the waterfront, Cliff Manor. That said, the byplay between Lee and Joanne does get a bit wearing. Wray's Joanne's repeated concern for her father is just convincing enough to ground the action, which is otherwise swamped by comedy and horror. Speaking of the latter, Rosener is memorable as Warners' Dwight Frye, or as Taylor puts it, "Old man bad luck." He's a bit monstrous himself, in appearance, but cedes that territory handily to the Fake-Flesh Monster when the latter slides in behind him and takes over …

The final Maximum Horror extra mile: The lamp Taylor flings at the moon killer sets him on fire, and he falls out a high window to the beach below, a flaming, screaming human meteor.

Notes: The credits read "Photographed by Technicolor"—as if the company were an individual, a concept ahead of its time. Same goes for the credits of *Mystery of the Wax Museum*.

Even the chiming clock gets in on the chills—that oddly unnerving ascending moon-face at top of same announces 11 o'clock and midnight, respectively. And, yes, it also reinforces the full moon motif.

Fashion note by Mo: Fay Wray's most fetching costume is the short, blue-green satin robe over the nightgown.

WB. D: Michael Curtiz. SP: Robert Tasker, Earl Baldwin, based on the play *Terror* by Howard W. Comstock and Allen C. Miller. Ph: Ray Rennahan. Mus: Bernhard Kaun. AD: Anton Grot. Mkp: (uncredited) Ray Romero, Perc

Westmore. SpPhFX: Fred Jackman, Jr. Ed: George Amy. Sd: Robert B. Lee. With Lionel Atwill, Fay Wray, Lee Tracy, Preston Foster, John Wray, Harry Beresford, Arthur Edmund Carewe, Leila Bennett, Robert Warwick, George Rosener, Willard Robertson, Thomas E. Jackson, Harry Holman, Mae Busch, Tom Dugan, Selmer Jackson; 76 minutes

Ref: IMDb. Bill Warren. *Scary Monsters* 28:22-26: Tom Triman article.

At the Strand on opening night, many people laughed when sinister hands appeared out of the dark, someone was suddenly dropped through a trap door or a monstrous, weird face came into focus"—*Variety* 8/9/32.

THIRTEEN WOMEN

Thirteen Women (novel by Tiffany Thayer): A "glacier of melancholy psychology ... had moved intrepidly through the Delphian ranks since early December, carrying one after another of these young ladies with it, breaking them, tearing them, grinding sanity from their minds and life from their bodies ..." Dark-skinned beauty Ursula Georgi—half-Javanese and half-Caucasian—employs hypnotism, the power of suggestion, "murder from the grave," and "banshee telephone calls" to wreak revenge on former fellow members of the Delphian Society at Mount Albans Seminary, in the Bronx. In fact, some of the Delphians—a "group of susceptible women"—did "sneer at color" and make Ursula's stay at Mount Albans a miserable one. Susceptible they may be, but suggestion and hypnotism seem to work a little too easily and powerfully here. Thayer has undoubted insights into human nature, but his worldly wisdom and sophistication come off as too calculated. His writing is more over-clever than witty. And with a cast of thirteen women and several men, the book plays like several short stories strung together, if occasionally compelling stories.

Thirteen Women released Sept. 16, 1932: "It is death I read for you!" Bartlett Cormack and Samuel Ornitz's screenplay quickly dispenses of three of the 13 women—June, May, and Hazel—then turns Helen's scenes into the strongest in

A lobby card from *Thirteen Women*, featuring Myrna Loy and Ricardo Cortez

the movie, and finally tries to funnel Thayer's other women/short stories into one straightforward narrative, again with Laura Stanhope (Irene Dunne)—a "strong character"—at the center of the "Horoscope Murders."

Only the middle gambit, with Helen (Kay Johnson), succeeds. ("No stars are going to twinkle to me into committing suicide.") Swami Yogadachi (C. Henry Gordon) predicts melancholy and suicide for her. Kay Johnson wisely lets the import of lines like: "I haven't laughed in so long" do the work. The film's main problem: the inability of writers and director (George Archainbaud) to imagine either the Good Woman (Laura) or the Evil Woman (Myrna Loy's Ursula). They can't quite decide whether Ursula is Fire or Ice, hot hate or cold revenge—at any rate, she's a "half-breed type—half-Hindu, half-Javanese, I don't know." And she gives people "the willies." The filmmakers do come up with a memorable image for her when she is caught leaning languidly against Helen's cabin wall as she waits for the telltale gunshot. The sequence inspires composer Max Steiner's best work here, an unusual yoking of the plaintive and the relentless, or roughly Helen and Ursula, respectively.

Myrna Loy is effective in silent mode—her thin voice here, though, undercuts her threatening look. Meanwhile, Laura ("Anyone can think themselves into anything!") dwindles into a standard Concerned Mother mode. (Ursula has targeted her son Bobby [Wally Albright] for violent death.) Despite *Thirteen Women*, Loy and Irene Dunne both went on to have pretty phenomenal careers.

Only Jill Esmond (as Jo), Johnson, and Ricardo Cortez (Sgt. Clive) come through unscathed, and, of the three, only Johnson scores an outright fine scene.

The takeaway here: "Suggestion is a very common occurrence in the life of every normal individual ... Waves of certain types of crime, waves of suicide are to be explained by the power of suggestion upon certain types of mind." (Hollingsworth and Hoffenberger, *Applied Psychology*)

Fun facts: In the movie, the seminary is located "north of San Francisco." In the book, "Swami Yogadachi" was simply a guise assumed by Ursula.

The scenes featuring the 12th and 13th women (Phyllis Fraser and Betty Furness) were deleted.

This was the "hers" of the 1931-1932 his-and-hers horror movies of real-life couple Florence Eldridge and Fredric March—the "his" of course was *Dr. Jekyll and Mr. Hyde*.

RKO. D: George Archainbaud. SP: Bartlett Cormack and Samuel Ornitz, from Tiffany Thayer's novel. Ph: Leo Tover. Mus: Max Steiner. AD: Carroll Clark. Ed: Charles L. Kimball. Sd: Hugh McDowell, Jr. Cost: Josette De Lima. Exec P: David O. Selznick. With Irene Dunne, Ricardo Cortez, Jill Esmond, Myrna Loy, Mary Duncan, Kay Johnson, Florence Eldridge, C. Henry Gordon, Peg Entwistle, Harriet Hagman, Blanche Friderici, Leon Ames, Clarence Geldart, Lloyd Ingraham; 73 minutes

Ref: IMDb. "It's all kind of silly"—Dave Sindelar (6/8/2002).

"Deteriorates into an unreasonably far-fetched wholesale butcher shop drama"—*Variety* 10/18/32.

The MOST DANGEROUS GAME

"The Most Dangerous Game" (short story—Richard Connell): Ship-Trap Island, in the Caribbean. After falling off a passing yacht, big-game hunter Sanger Rainsford, from New York City, finds himself in a "chateau on a high bluff," home of another hunter, the slightly mad General Zaroff, a Cossack. Zaroff informs him that, no, the dreaded Cape buffalo is "not the most dangerous" game—rather, it is the animal that is "able to reason" who is the most dangerous ... man. Zaroff proceeds to hunt Rainsford, who employs the Malay man catcher, the Burmese tiger pit, and a Ugandan native trick to defend himself ... Slight, bland novelty item from the man who co-authored both the story for Frank Capra's classic *Meet John Doe* (1941) and the screenplay for the Abbott and Costello *Rio Rita* (1942).

The Most Dangerous Game released Sept. 16, 1932: "I thought that perhaps tonight you would like to see my trophy room." Author and big-game hunter Bob Rainsford (Joel McCrea) is the only survivor of a yacht-wreck on the

treacherous reefs of a "cursed ... island no bigger than a deer park." He finds that he and his host, Count Zaroff (Leslie Banks)—who lives in an old fortress there—seem to be "kindred spirits." But, in his search for a "new sensation," Zaroff has turned to a new prey, humans. ("So that's your most dangerous game.")

A pre-*King Kong* doodle from Cooper and Schoedsack Productions. This is more strange adventure than horror, but scripter James Ashmore Creelman and art director Carroll Clark wisely Gothic it up—the mad pianist/hunter Zaroff inhabits, in effect, Castle Dracula, a lovely old dark chateau set. Instead of Dracula's, "I bid you welcome," Zaroff offers, "Welcome to my poor fortress," as he descends the stone staircase. Then throw in fog and a slew of hounds of the Baskervilles.

Like Max Steiner's score, the movie comes into its own only in the climactic hunting sequence. Earlier: clumsy dramatic Steiner thumps, the worst one hoking up the track down the steps to a close-up of Zaroff. [SPOILERS]: Later: Steiner finally in his finest *King Kong* element, as Henry Gerrard alternates shots of hunter and hunted (Rainsford and Fay Wray's Eve), varies camera angles, and tracks ahead of Rainsford and Eve, then tracks with them, subjectively, as they push through the dense jungle foliage. ("Those animals I hunted—now I know how they felt.") Anti-climactically, Steiner then tries to jazz

up a routine brawl between Zaroff and Rainsford. In the coda, the (remaining) dogs savage Zaroff, of course, but it's still satisfying, if inevitable.

Banks is good, but not quite in the top tier of early 1930s mad docs and gentlemen like Charles Laughton, Bela Lugosi, Colin Clive, and Lionel Atwill. He relies a bit too much on absently fingering the scar on his forehead (inflicted by a Cape buffalo), and, as noted above, Steiner occasionally sabotages his performance. Either Banks' bugging eyes or the music is redundant. Fay Wray is her usual offhandedly-sensuous, effortlessly convincing self, and she gets in some of her signature screaming. Joel McCrea is very uneven, at the mercy of his dialogue—lots of "Why you—!" and "You murdering rat!" and a little of "The boat—quick!" Robert Armstrong, as Eve's brother, is one note, constantly sloshed.

Notes: Zaroff's front-door knocker summons up the title and then the credits. The door opens to reveal the cast.

In the film, the fortress is said to have been built by the Portuguese "centuries ago"; in the story, Zaroff himself built it. In the film, the swamp is called Fog Hollow; in the story, it's called Death Swamp.

The scene of the crew from the sinking yacht, screaming in water heated by the boilers, is a nasty bit, like Kong chewing on the natives.

The 1945 remake, *A Game of Death*, is inconsequential.

The 1956 reworking, *Run for the Sun*, is clumsy storytelling and routine chase sequences. Frederick Steiner's score is a highlight. Dialogue reference to the "hounds of the Baskervilles."

(*Hounds of Zaroff*—British title) RKO. D: Irving Pichel, Ernest B. Schoedsack. SP: James Ashmore Creelman, from Richard Connell's short story. Ph: Henry Gerrard. Mus: Max Steiner. AD: Carroll Clark. Mkp: Wally Westmore. SpFX: Harry Redmond, Jr. PhFX: Lloyd Knechtel, Vernon L. Walker. Ed: Archie Marshek. SdFX: Murray Spivack. Sd: Clem Portman. OptFX: Linwood G. Dunn. Cost: Walter Plunkett. Exec P: David O. Selznick. Assoc P: Merian C. Cooper. With Joel McCrea, Fay Wray, Leslie Banks, Robert Armstrong, Noble Johnson, Steve Clemente, William B. Davidson, Buster Crabbe, James Flavin, Hale Hamilton; 63 minutes

Ref: *The Making of King Kong* p73. IMDb.

"Transforming Zaroff into an arrested adolescent makes the Count unique among 1930s horror villains"—Frank J. Dello Stritto, *Cult Movies* 19:25.

CHANDU THE MAGICIAN

Chandu the Magician released Sept. 18, 1932: "Thou shalt cause them to see what is not there, even unto a gathering of 12 times 12." In this speeded-up serial of a movie, Captain Frank Chandler (Edmund Lowe) joins the "sacred company of the Yogi" and thus has "at his command the wizardry of the East." He is now called "Chandu." (The main yogi's crystal ball provides a wealth of exposition.) Chandu's task: "Conquer the evil that threatens mankind." The evil: Roxor (Bela Lugosi), "last of an ancient family that lived in Alexandria." The threat: that Chandu's brother-in-law Robert Regent (Henry B. Walthall)—a "crazy scientist who lives in one of the rock temples" along the Nile—will weaken and give Roxor the secret of activating the former's death ray.

In this, the *Raiders of the Lost Ark* of its day, co-director William Cameron Menzies and company conjure up fantastical death-ray-in-progress labs, huge stone doors, and canyons forbiddingly littered with skeletons. But they didn't have Industrial Light & Magic at their command. On the other hand, Steven Spielberg and company didn't have Bela Lugosi, who does more with the letter "r" in the following sentence than most actors do with whole scripts: "What will they think when they feel the power of Roxor!" Is it ham or genius? Whatever it is, it's unique.

His Roxor misses the wit of his Legendre (*White Zombie*) or Mirakle (*Murders in the Rue Morgue*), though this quality makes a guest appearance in the line, "If Nadji opposes me—and you ... serve ... me ... well—there shall be a new slave in your harem." Lugosi is certainly in the cornball spirit of the thing, in a role something like his Dr. Vollin, in *The Raven*, though here he's not really campy because he's not serious. Happily unleashed in his longer, vitriolic speeches, he's brought back to earth by the in between scenes, which could have used some retakes. At the end, he gets a well-deserved rest when Chandu freezes Roxor in place.

The evil Roxor (Bela Lugosi) leers as only he can; Lugosi is certainly in the cornball spirit of the thing.

Poor Edmund Lowe isn't bad at the end, when Chandu directly challenges Roxor. ("I have come out of the coffin, from the depths of the Nile!") But, unlike Lugosi, he's not up to the grand gestures. Chandu needed, perhaps, Ronald Colman, especially in the scenes in which Chandu romances Nadji (Irene Ware), in the worst way. But even a calmed-down Lugosi proves not quite right for the role of Chandu, in the serial follow-up *Return of Chandu* (1934). Lowe may actually be the better Chandu. No contest, however, between Lugosi's Roxor and the semi-sequel's arch-villains, the sorcerer-priests Vindhyan (Lucien Prival) and Vitras (Jack Clark), who are pretty bland.

Most thrillingly, James Wong Howe introduces us to each new temple or house with a track up to it, though the structures in question sometimes seem to be simply models. He tracks down to one temple, then into Chandu's induction ceremony therein. Next, he tracks down to the Regent lab. He tracks up to a window of the Regent household. But Howe's most spectacular tracking shot is of course the one way down and way into the rock corridors of the temple. The camera swings right, then left, then right, and keeps going ... somewhat as the cars do on Mr. Toad's Wild Ride at Disneyland.

This early sound film has a corny but full musical score, and much noise and commotion—the sounds of a sandstorm, an astral bell which rings when danger is nigh, screeching birds, the howling of animals, or men pretending to be animals, various explosions, electrical zipping and zapping, and even the gonging of a gong. All this, and the "CHANDU" in the title sparkles.

Fox. D: William Cameron Menzies and Marcel Varnel. SP: Barry Connors, Philip Klein, from the radio series by Harry A. Earnshaw, Vera M. Oldham, R.R. Morgan. Ph: James Wong Howe. Mus: (uncredited) Louis De Francesco et al. AD: Max Parker. Ed: Harold D. Schuster. Sd: Joseph E. Aiken. Cost: Earl Luick. With Bela Lugosi, Edmund Lowe, Irene Ware, Herbert Mundin, Henry B. Walthall, Weldon Heyburn, June Lang, Nigel De Brulier, John George, Dick Sutherland; 71 Minutes

Ref: "While no more convincing than Edmund Lowe, Lugosi becomes infinitely more *fun* to watch"—Bryan Senn, *Midnight Marquee* 57:5-8.

"*Chandu* carries the fantastic, the inconsistent and the ludicrous to the greatest lengths yet achieved by the screen"—*Variety* 10/4/32.

The CROOKED CIRCLE

The Crooked Circle released Sept. 25, 1932: "Tonight, if that clock should strike 13, beware!" Col. Wolters' (Berton Churchill) Melody Manor—"one of the oldest houses on Long Island"—is "full of ghosts," including a "phantom fiddler." ("There's a ghost in the house, and he plays the violin.") And it's the midnight setting for a battle between two crime clubs: Wolters' Sphinx Club, a "band of amateur criminologists," and the Crooked Circle, a band of thieves. Complicating matters: not one, but two quasi-menacing old codgers ... Old Dan (Christian Rub), a "queer old man" given to rasping his words and shaking his forefinger, and Harmon the Hermit (Raymond Hatton): "I always visit the folks in this house the first night—no telling how long they'll be here. Heh heh heh heh! Queer things about this house." Harmon—an "eccentric old musician"—inspires the movie's goofiest line: "A queer-acting hunchback brought in a basket of tomatoes." [SPOILER]: Near the end, a supposedly dead man returns, after an hour or so in suspended animation.

The Crooked Circle may be short on quality, but it certainly has quantity—two clubs, two codgers, and a host of creep elements: "fiddling ghosts," a skeleton ("that awful thing") in the attic, which seems to be stalking Nora Rafferty (Zasu Pitts), a "walking" table, a clock which strikes 13 as the lights go out, a tombstone bearing the words "Died of Fright," trick chairs and graves which make people appear and disappear, sudden shadows (courtesy of Robert B. Kurrle's deft cinematography), and—in the first, startling shot—a darkened skull which seems magically to light. It's still a cool shot, even when you realize that the effect was achieved just by pulling off the skull's cover. Spookiness is always percolating here. If the movie is not exactly a gem, it sticks to business.

For a "B" movie, *The Crooked Circle* boasts an all-star cast: Zasu Pitts, Ben Lyon, James Gleason, Churchill, Roscoe Karns, C. Henry Gordon. But Rub and Hatton seem to be having more fun than most of the stars. Zasu Pitts' constant whimper is a fair substitute for screaming (though she does that, too), and her physical latching on to Gleason's cop is a wry running gag. Blame Old Dan for inspiring her repetition of his "something always happens to somebody" line. The Secret Service's use of a Hindu psychic (Gordon's Yoganda) anticipates, from a certain angle, Mulder and Scully.

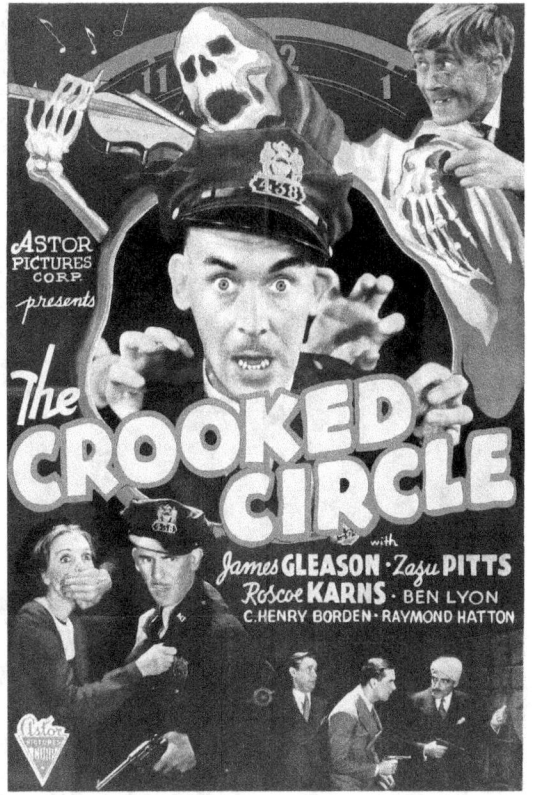

Notes: Scriptwriter Ralph Spence's main claim to fame was his oft-filmed play, *The Gorilla*.

Some years later, Gleason would again play a cop among spooks, in *Arsenic and Old Lace*.

Sono Art—World Wide. D: H. Bruce Humberstone. SP: Ralph Spence. Addl Dial: Tim Whelan. Ph: Robert Kurrle. AD: Paul Crawley. Ed: Doane Harrison. Sd: William R. Fox. P: William Sistrom. With Zasu Pitts, James Gleason, Ben Lyon, Irene Purcell, C. Henry Gordon, Raymond Hatton, Roscoe Karns, Berton Churchill, Spencer Charters, Robert Frazer, Ethel Clayton, Frank Reicher, Christian Rub, Tom Kennedy, Paul Panzer; 70 minutes

Ref: "lumbering and badly-timed haunted house story ... Hint of *Chandu* ... in the shape of a supposed Swami"—*Variety* 10/4/32.

"A supremely silly movie ... but it throws so many creepy suspicious characters at you ... that it keeps you diverted"—Dave Sindelar (7/16/2002).

KONGO

West of Zanzibar (1928): "The Evil Spirit is at it again!" "Dead-Legs" (Lon Chaney) plots terrible revenge on the man (Lionel Barrymore) who attempts to steal his wife (Jane Daly) and who rendered him "this thing that crawls"... on dead legs. The supposed "evil spirit"—a glowing-eyed voodoo "monster" with a touch of Carmen Miranda—is part of his revenge ... The bit of plot is simply a pretext for some pretty impressive Chaney displays of, respectively, Hate, Loathing, Dismay, and various Torments. There's even a time-out for Love,

Walter Huston and Lupe Velez appear in this lobby card from *Kongo*.

but the negative emotions dominate. Barrymore, Mary Nolan, and Warner Baxter get the dramatic scraps.

Kongo released Oct. 1, 1932: "I'm gonna puncture you and let the leeches do the rest!" The crippled, monomaniacal Flint (Walter Huston) plots a complicated revenge on the "man who stole my wife ... the man who kicked my spine in ... the man who sneered" (C. Henry Gordon). "Voodooism will bring me what I want," he intones, as that glowing-eyed "big devil" in the mask returns, in this remake of *West of Zanzibar*. Excruciating tale of love surviving the prevailing "sordidness," "squalor," and "filthy leeches" makes one appreciate the pared-down original. The extra running time (20 minutes or so of it) only brings out the basic unbelievability.

"Abel" in *Variety* (11/22/1932) indicated that the story was dated in 1932: "It's the same story [as the stage play] although accentuated for the screen, and made the more ridic as a result." Hopefully, the DeVonde-Gordon property has been retired forever. This version of it has only occasional camp value, thanks in part to the fact that Conrad Nagel (the dissolute doctor), Lupe Velez (the basically extraneous Tula), and Virginia Bruce (Flint's main victim, Ann) all seem to cherish their respective, impassioned speeches. Ann's parting words to the "thieving cripple" Flint—"I'll try to remember only your courage"—almost gets through the movie's thick film of phoniness; Flint's climactic prayer doesn't come close to getting through. Even Huston's spirited ranting finally gets a little monotonous.

Notes: The unscrupulous Flint has Ann sent to a "house" in Zanzibar, but can't be seen to despoil her himself, thanks to a certain key plot twist.

Bonus: a talking, bodiless head belonging to the supposedly decapitated Tula, in Flint's magic act.

The noisy ceremonies with Flint and the natives are a riot of elaborate masks.

Fun dramatic cheat: Gordon's Gregg seeming at first to sob, but actually laughing, uncontrollably, to kick off the climactic revelations. The real cheat is that we don't get to see his comeuppance.

MGM. D: William Cowen. SP: Leon Gordon, from the play by Chester De Vonde and Kilbourn Gordon. Ph: Harold Rosson. AD: Cedric Gibbons. Sd: Douglas Shearer. Ed: Conrad A. Nervig. With Walter Huston, Lupe Velez, Conrad Nagel, Virginia Bruce, C. Henry Gordon, Mitchell Lewis, Forrester Harvey, Curtis Nero, Everett Brown, Charles Irwin, Sarah Padden; 86 minutes

The PHANTOM OF CRESTWOOD

The Phantom of Crestwood released Oct. 14, 1932: "You don't believe in ghosts, do you?" This creaky old mystery, set in La Casa de Los Andes, features storm, wind and lightning, during breaks in dialogue ... a ghostly face in the night which proves to be a phosphorescent death mask ... a secret tunnel from the house to the nearby sea ... and two deaths by dart.

But it will be for star Karen Morley's performance for which this thriller is remembered. Her Jenny Wren is vulnerability with bite. The script's innocence vs. experience themes live in her and die everywhere else. [SPOILER]: Midway, the film seems ready to pull a *Psycho* and kill her off, but it brings her back in flashbacks. Her best nostalgia-for-innocence line (regarding the subject of love): "Yes, I've read about that."

The horror highlight: a hokey, fun Henry Gerrard track up to the Ghost Face; Second Place goes to another tracking shot down a lightning-lit corridor. NBC and RKO conducted a promo contest for the best ending for the story, but the winning entry was not necessarily the ending actually used.

RKO. D: J. Walter Ruben. SP: Bartlett Cormack. Story: Ruben, Cormack. Ph: Henry Gerrard. AD: Carroll Clark. Ed: Archie Marshek. Sd: Denzil A. Cutler. Cost: Walter Plunkett. Assoc P: Merian C. Cooper. With Karen Morley, Ricardo Cortez, Anita Louise, Pauline Frederick. H.B. Warner, Sam Hardy, Mary Duncan, "Skeets" Gallagher, Robert McWade, Gavin Gordon, Ivan F. Simpson, George E. Stone, Aileen Pringle, Bess Flowers; 76 minutes

Ref: *PV* 38:61. "One episode is overdrawn, the haunting of the girl by the phosphorized death mask of one of her victims"—*Variety* 10/18/32.

"A very entertaining mystery [and] the horror elements are solid and satisfying"—Dave Sindelar (4/15/2003).

The OLD DARK HOUSE

Benighted (novel—J.B. Priestley): "You may have wondered—whether you did well—in coming—even for shelter—out of the storm—into this house—this old dark house." "Somewhere in the wildest Wales." Five travelers are stranded by a ferocious storm in a "very queer house," with "very queer people," including the butler/bodyguard Morgan, a "huge lump of a man ... as gigantic but as brainless as a prehistoric monster" and "as strong as a gorilla," pyromaniac and "ghastly loony" Saul Femm, a "dangerous maniac" who believes in "cleansing by fire," old, bedridden Sir Roderick Femm, who "years and years ago ... did mad things [which] touched all the others" (his "blur" of a face has a "ghostly sheen"), Rebecca Femm, "now with a God ... behind her [who] is vengeful—half-crazed," like her, and poor dear Horace Femm who, though less infected than some of the others by "Femmishness," is "empty and brittle—a shell."

By contrast, Priestley reserves a more positive, romantic optimism for the travelers. Philip Waverton begins as "too married" to Margaret, but the "exciting personal adventure called Philip" eventually kicks in, and the two "begin again." And disillusioned veteran Roger Penderel, thrown together, if very gently, with chorus girl Gladys DuCane, finds in her "somebody you could talk and laugh and cry with, not so very different in most things, indeed strangely like you." If the book keeps losing its way, in, say, the visitors' extended game of Truth—which is rather like an author's game of Exposition—it also keeps righting itself, redeeming itself. Somehow, Priestley makes optimism—even in a house which gets progressively "queerer and darker"—seem the right, logical, only response: "Now it seemed strange that people whose hearts were empty could meet on such a night and talk through this darkness without loving." The book, however, ends with the death of one of the travelers—it's a tempered optimism.

The Old Dark House released Oct. 20, 1932: "Saul is why we have to keep Morgan." If Universal's 1932 Halloween movie is perhaps the least of James Whale's four horror pictures, it's partly because it's in pretty exalted company, and partly because the film's benighted (as in stranded by night) visitors to the

Boris Karloff lurks in the shadows from *The Old Dark House* lobby card.

house of Femm, in the Welsh mountains, are somewhat less interesting than the benighted (as in morally stunted) Femm household itself. The visitors tend to talk out their personal histories; the Femms, more dramatically, suggest their history, by their behavior, by their various vivid neuroses and psychoses.

Horace Femm's (Ernest Thesiger) palpable panic at the visitors' tales of storms and floods—"We may be cut off, shut up in this house!"—instantly conjures up a terrible, if out-of-focus, Femm family history, while his sister Rebecca's (Eva Moore) rabid Puritanism helps bring a little of that history into focus. Her disgust/fascination with guest Margaret Waverton's (Gloria Stuart) fair flesh suggests a kinship with Charles Halton's nosy neighbor ("Look at her legs!") in *Stranger on the Third Floor*. Evil here is more in the mind of the beholder than in the body of the beheld, though the distorting-mirror effects suggest that Rebecca's taunting is getting to Mrs. Waverton, at least for the night: As Rebecca harangues her, various reflections in the scattered bedroom mirrors suggest her, Rebecca's, warped mentality, but the final gargoyle is left for Mrs. W, as she looks at herself in a mirror.

Benn Levy's screenplay presents a family so dysfunctional that the man, Morgan (Boris Karloff), appointed to keep in check the most dangerous family member, Saul (Brember Wills)—a cackling pyro—is only marginally less dangerous than Saul. ("I know things about flames that nobody else in the world knows.") When bedridden patriarch Sir Roderick (Elspeth Dudgeon) first mentions his eldest son's name, Saul, Margaret almost comically shrinks back and cries, "Saul?," as if the very name somehow frightened her. Of course, it's not the name—it's the dismaying revelation that there's another Femm lurking about. When drunk, Morgan is a vicious brute who requires two or three men to hold him down. He, too, takes a turn at terrorizing Mrs. W, who unwillingly plays flame to the insistent household moths. [SPOILER]: The Morgan-Saul relationship ends as it began, in irony—if irony of a different sort—with the brute cradling the dead madman's head and sobbing. Is this unexpectedly moving moment mere perversity, on the parts of Whale and Levy, or a celebration of human mystery?

For the most part, Charles Laughton must talk out his role of Sir William Porterhouse, but he does so empathetically. [SPOILER]: Loud and insecure, Porterhouse proves a not-quite-impossibly generous fellow when he blesses the union of his companion Gladys (Lillian Bond) and Penderel (Melvyn Douglas), an amiable cynic. It's in part the grounding of this not-quite-unbelievable generosity in the fact of Sir William's continuing devotion to his dead wife, which renders his selfless act almost believable. But his magnanimous relinquishing of Gladys proves to be based, also, in unselfish, fatherly feeling for her: The second-most-unexpected emotional breakdown is his raw grief when Penderel seems to have died in a fall. It's only a dramatic aside, but Laughton brings Sir William fully to life in that moment or two. The grief, of course, is for Gladys, not Penderel …

If Laughton and Karloff have the choicest dramatic moments, Moore, Thesiger, and Wills also stand out, and Douglas and Bond do well in more conventional roles—the Penderel and Gladys characters are less conventional and more fully realized in the book. If Levy sees to it that the film doesn't get too bogged down in Truth, or Exposition, he also rather shortchanges the Wavertons, Gladys, and Penderel.

Notes: Horace's "Have a potato" and Roderick's "You see, when you're as old as I am, at any minute you may just die!" are not in the book. Can we credit (uncredited) dialogue writer R.C. Sherriff here? On the other hand, Rebecca's "No beds. They can't have beds" is Priestley's.

William Hedgcock and C. Roy Hunter's whistling-wind effects are many and varied. The old dark but very noisy house; the ultra-shrill intermittent off-screen crowing suggests a rooster from hell.

See also *Strange People* (1933), or *The Old Dark House*, Part II.

Universal. D: James Whale. SP: Benn W. Levy, from J.B. Priestley's novel. Ph: Arthur Edeson. Title Mus: David Broekman. AD: Charles D. Hall. Mkp: Jack Pierce, Otto Lederer. Ed: Clarence Kolster. Sd: C. Roy Hunter, William Hedgcock. SpFX: John P. Fulton P: Carl Laemmle, Jr. With Boris Karloff, Melvyn Douglas, Charles Laughton, Lillian Bond, Ernest Thesiger, Eva

Moore, Raymond Massey, Gloria Stuart, Elspeth Dudgeon, Brember Wills; 72 minutes

Ref: *PV* 31:28-9. IMDb. "At once bleakly horrible and unbearably funny"—David J. Hogan, *Filmfax* 61:52.

"*The Old Dark House* lends itself to almost everything previously pulled with *Dracula, Frankenstein, White Zombie* and the rest of that ilk ... Rialto audience ... was audibly derisive at the love scenes between Douglas and Lilian Bond"—*Variety* 11/1/32.

The Old Dark House (1963): "Something terrible is happening here!" Femm Hall, Dartmoor, England, is "not only alive, but evil ..." ("It's an old house—old and dark.") As Roderick Femm, Robert Morley presides, amusingly, over a family of mild eccentrics. Morgana (Fenella Fielding) is the Femm fatale, and Morgan (Danny Green) is her brute of a father. The idea of a William Castle/Hammer co-production is more pleasing than the actuality. Mystery-comedy is neither funny nor scary. With the obligatory: "You're mad!" For some reason, Castle gets credited twice as director, in the opening credits.

The MASK OF FU MANCHU

The Mask of Fu Manchu (book): "This looks unwholesome, Greville ... " The latter personage is one of two fictional characters within this novel (the other: Dr. Petrie) who are said to have published, respectively, accounts of the exploits of Nayland Smith (former Assistant Commissioner of Scotland Yard) and his nemesis, the "evil and honorable" Dr. Fu Manchu. Sax Rohmer, of course, is the actual author of this middling thriller regarding Fu Manchu's campaign to acquire the mask and sword of 8th-century Islamic prophet El

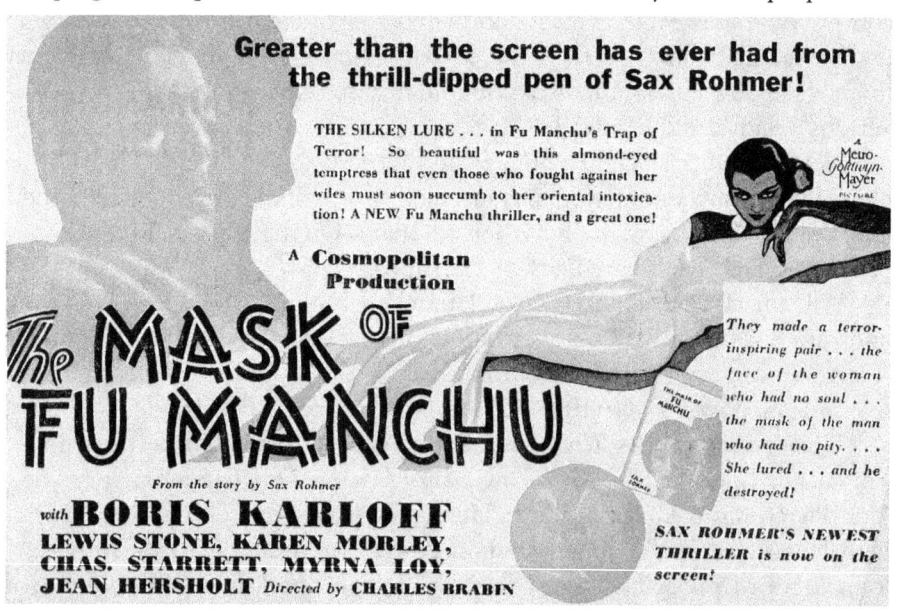

Lewis Stone and Boris Karloff appear in a lobby card from *The Mask of Fu Manchu*

Mokanna, the "Veiled Prophet." The campaign involves an apparition on the Great Pyramid, an elixir of youth, an amnesia drug, and an amazing thread "prepared from the flocculent secretion of *Theridion*—a well known but interesting spider … " Rohmer concludes with a perfectly delightful coda, in which Fu Manchu presents the astonished Shan Greville—and his bride Rima—with gifts, and—in a witty note—acknowledges the finer qualities of his adversaries. Another, earlier highlight: the faint sound of a gong in the absolute quiet of the pyramid.

The Mask of Fu Manchu released Nov. 5, 1932: "He'll declare himself Genghis Khan come to life again!" In 1932, Bela Lugosi played the great mad villain Roxor, in *Chandu the Magician*. That same year, Boris Karloff was Dr. Fu Manchu. The only way to top that would be to co-star them in the same movie. For Lugosi and Karloff, respectively, these were dream roles, or grand nightmare roles. Retrospectively, of course, though, there are problems—e.g., Lugosi was not Egyptian; Karloff was not Chinese. Thespically delightful, racially incorrect. *Chandu the Magician*, however, does not seem overtly racist. There are no rabble-rousing "hideous yellow monster" references in the Fox film. And while the British characters in *The Mask of Fu Manchu* condescendingly profess bafflement with Eastern ways ("Will we ever understand these Eastern races?"), hero Chandu embraces Eastern wizardry.

Fu Manchu (Boris Karloff) with his daughter (Myrna Loy) in *The Mask of Fu Manchu*

The Mask of Fu Manchu is circumscribed fun, and it doesn't help that it generally has the first-take feel of a serial. In fact, MGM's Fu Manchu is more blatantly "hideous" than either Paramount's or Sax Rohmer's. Anyone familiar only with this incarnation of Fu Manchu might find it hard to believe that Warner Oland's doctor was actually a gentleman, and that Rohmer's was "honorable." Forbidding, yes, but honorable and a gentleman.

For the record, there's little actual Rohmer here, except a mask, a sword (or scimitar), the amazing thread, and Fu Manchu's daughter's (Myrna Loy) affection for young Granville (Charles Starrett)—"Greville" in the book. And mask and sword belong to Genghis Khan, not to Mokanna. Oland's Fu Manchu is closer to Rohmer than is Karloff's calculating sadist, but Karloff wields his long fingernails elegantly, and he almost brings off even the accidental rhyming of "What can one so poor as Dr. Fu Manchu do for you?"

Meanwhile, Karen Morley's over-amped earnestness is as campy as Loy's under-amped stolidity, and Lewis Stone is, well, Andy Hardy's father. The horror money scene is the creation and injection of the zombie serum into Granville. ("He will do as I command exactly as though I was doing it!") But more effortlessly weird is a shorter scene set in the "lost and buried tomb of Genghis Khan": The dead one's skeleton bears the sword, while the fabled mask covers only the top front of his skull, which makes him seem to be grinning ghoulishly.

MGM. D: Charles Brabin, Charles Vidor. SP: Irene Kuhn, Edgar Allan Woolf, John Willard, from Sax Rohmer's novel. Ph: Tony Gaudio. Mus: William Axt. AD: Cedric Gibbons. SpFX: Warren Newcombe, Kenneth Strickfaden. Ed: Ben Lewis. Cost: Adrian. Mkp: Cecil Holland. Sd: Douglas Shearer. With Boris Karloff, Karen Morley, Myrna Loy, Lewis Stone, Charles Starrett, Jean Hersholt, Lawrence Grant, David Torrence, Steve Clemente, Willie Fung, Ferdinand Gottschalk, Tetsu Komai, James B. Leong, Chris-Pin Martin, Lal Chand Mehra, Edward Peil, Sr., C. Montague Shaw, E. Alyn Warren; 68 minutes

Ref: "One of [Karloff's] few great horror roles not to include the touch of sadness associated with his other classic genre performances"—"Dr. Cyclops," *Fangoria* 122:33. *Filmfax* 46:40: Kenneth Strickfaden and the high-voltage effects here.

"Audiences are liable to laugh where they oughtn't. The audience at the Capitol did"—*Variety* 12/6/32.

MIDNIGHT WARNING

Midnight Warning released Nov. 15, 1932: "Are you sure, Miss Van Buren, that you have the right hotel?" A classic puzzle in a mostly indifferent Poverty Row thriller. When Enid Van Buren's (Claudia Dell) brother disappears from Suite A of the Clarendon Hotel, the hotel staff denies that he was ever there. As noted in *Forgotten Horrors*, "A well-known story which seems to have originated during the Chicago World's Fair of 1893 is the basis for *Midnight Warning*" and later provided the basis for the 1951 British film, *So Long at the Fair.* Its most recent incarnation: *Flightplan* (2006), in which an airplane subs for the hotel, and a woman's daughter subs for the brother. Other variations include *Bulldog Drummond Strikes Back* (1934), Hitchcock's *The Lady Vanishes* (1938) and its remakes, *Dangerous Crossing* (1953), and *Treacherous Crossing* (1992).

Despite the familiarity of the premise, and the stilted acting of William (Stage) Boyd, Claudia Dell et al., the puzzle still intrigues, and the long climactic sequence set in Klein's Mortuary is quite satisfying horror-mongering. In this "hocus pocus in the basement," a shrouded corpse seems to rise to confront Enid, whom the hotel people want to drive mad. ("You want me to go mad?") It's actually kind of a mean scene, half-spooky and half-campy. A "ghost" voice cries "Enid!" and she screams when she touches a dead foot in the corridor of corpses. Her sanity returns, a little abruptly, in the coda.

Mayfair Pictures: D: Spencer Gordon Bennett. SP: John T. Neville, from Norman Battle's story "Eyes of Mystery." Ph: Jules Cronjager. P: George W. Weeks. With William "Stage" Boyd, Claudia Dell, Huntley Gordon, John Harron, Hooper Atchley, Lloyd Whitlock, Phillips Smalley, Lloyd Ingraham, Henry Hall; 63 minutes.

Ref: IMDb. YouTube.

Forgotten Horrors, pages 69-70: the history of the two William Boyd's.

The MONKEY'S PAW

The Monkey's Paw (short story—W.W. Jacobs): "Wish our boy alive again." Model short horror story is the ultimate in the power of suggestion. [SPOILERS]: If you've been away from Jacobs' story for some time—and/or you're familiar with the 1972 take on the story *Deathdream* (each movie is creepy in a different way)—you might think you remember the appearance of a living rotted corpse at the end. But, no—the "thing outside" is wished away, just in time. It doesn't get more hair-raising than that. Cherishable line: "For God's sake don't let it in."

The Monkey's Paw tradeshown November 1932 (released Jan. 13, 1933): A 48-minute, French-dubbed DVD allowed me to get some idea of the quality of this rare film. A 10-minute prologue set in India features an Indian fakir performing familiar stage-magic tricks with his female assistant, though at one point he "freezes" a British soldier magically. There's background music for this "stage" act, but when the scene switches to London, there's no music at the Whites' home, where most of the action is set.

Sgt. Major Morris (C. Aubrey Smith) brings a monkey's magic, mummified paw from India to Mr. and Mrs. White (Ivan F. Simpson, Louise Carter),

C. Aubrey Smith, Ivan F. Simpson, Bramwell Fletcher and Louise Carter stare intently at the monkey's paw, in this lobby card scene.

in an extended, satisfyingly atmospheric sequence. Candlelight leaves much of the scene in darkness, and the wind whistles outside continuously. There's a sense of unseen forces at work, in and around the house. Mr. White "sees" a monkey's face in the fireplace, and the wind noisily blows open a window when he holds the paw aloft. As the major departs, and snow swirls, he has a vision of a menacing monkey.

As *Variety* notes, the best sequence is the climax, where the curse is wished away before Mrs. White can open the door and confront her son, or his apparent walking, knocking corpse. The knocking is quite enough: Terrific suspense, no shock needed. And this is, rightfully, where this version ends—no "dream tag." (See *Variety* quote, below ...)

Graham John's screenplay pads the plot out to feature length, but preserves the solid core of the tale, and cameraman Leo Tover irises deftly in and out of scenes. The low whistling winds in the night scenes at the old house make the absence of music less noticeable. Fun to see Bramwell Fletcher, as the son, the same year he met Imhotep.

RKO. D: Wesley Ruggles; (uncredited) Ernest B. Schoedsack. SP: Graham John, from the short story by W.W. Jacobs and the play by Louis N. Parker. Ph: Leo Tover, Edward Cronjager, Jack MacKenzie, J.O. Taylor. Mus: (uncredited) Max Steiner. AD: Carroll Clark. Ed: Charles L. Kimball. SpFX: Linwood

G. Dunn, Lloyd Knechtel, Harry Redmond, Sr., Vernon L. Walker. P: Merian C. Cooper, Pandro S. Berman. With Ivan F. Simpson, Louise Carter, C. Aubrey Smith, Bramwell Fletcher, Betty Lawton, Winter Hall, Herbert Bunston, Nina Quartero, James Bell, Sidney Bracey, Nigel De Brulier, John George, Gordon Jones, J.M. Kerrigan, LeRoy Mason, Lal Chand Mehra, Harry Strang; 58 minutes

Ref: *Harrison's* 11/26/32. *Film Daily Yearbook*.

HSF1: 1915, 1923, and 1948 British versions.

Walt Lee. *Filmfax* 92:43.

[Spoiler]: "Sometimes a too effective blood-chiller … One genuinely good moment near the close when the father is forced by his wife to wish his son alive again, and then listens, terror-stricken, to the boy's familiar knock at the door, wishing him back into his grave before the mother can overcome her difficulty with the [door] bolts … banal 'it was a dream' tag"—*Variety* 6/6/32.

STRANGE ADVENTURE

Strange Adventure released Nov. 20, 1932: "You all hate me, but you all want my money." You glean that the phantom prowling the Wayne mansion (a "spooky joint") is supposed to be scary only because the black valet (Snowflake) reacts in terror to his presence. ("What's the matter, Jeff? You look like you've seen a ghost.") The character of Jeff is an unembellished cliché, while the phantom, the cops, and the suspects scoot in and out the hall doorways as if they're part of an extended Marx Brothers routine.

Poor Dwight Frye can't do anything with the nothing here. Lucille LaVerne's appearance, as the housekeeper, is sufficiently forbidding, but another cliché. She was later the witch's voice in Disney's *Snow White and the Seven Dwarfs*. June Clyde's perkiness (or *Jiggle*, 1932) is the closest thing to an interesting actor's gambit. Most of the budget seems to have gone into the phantom's over-sized cape and cowl. Nadine Dore's "scared to death" scene as Gloria Dryden is just part of a distraction from the main murder mystery. The best shot is actually the title-credits shot: Leon Shamroy's camera slowly closes in on the phantom's shadow on a door.

"A Monogram Melodrama"—credits.

(*[The] Wayne Murder Case*—alternate title) Monogram/Chadwick. D: Phil Whitman. Cont: Lee Chadwick. Dial: Hampton Del Ruth. Story: Arthur Hoerl. Ph: Leon Shamroy. Ed: Carl Pierson. Sd: Balsley & Phillips. With June Clyde, Regis Toomey, Lucille LaVerne, Jason Robards, Sr., William V. Mong, Dwight Frye, Nadine Dore, Alan Roscoe, Harry Myers, Eddy Chandler, Fred "Snowflake" Toones, Jack Cheatham, Kit Guard, Harry Tenbrook; 62 minutes

Ref: *Midnight Marquee* 58:26-28.

SECRETS OF THE FRENCH POLICE

Secrets of the French Police released Dec. 2, 1932: "You see how quiet she is now, how much like marble?" Trying to unravel the origins of this patchwork movie proves more interesting than the movie itself. First, the August 12, 1932, estimating script cites Samuel Ornitz's *The Lost Empress* as one of the two sources. It was apparently an unpublished work. The other source cited is "Secrets of the Surete," by H. Ashton-Wolfe. This refers to Ashton-Wolfe's "American Weekly Series," mentioned in the film's credits. And a pre-title shot shows someone opening up a copy of *The American Weekly* and finding an article subtitled "The French Detective Police." "Secrets of the Surete: The French Detective Police," then, is pretty surely the work which the writer of this note on page 81 of the script had in mind: "For mechanics of above device—see Ashton-Wolfe's memoirs." (The device in question yields murder-by-billboard. See below.)

Ashton-Wolfe's two books regarding the Surete—*The Forgotten Clue: Tales and Methods of the Surete* and *The Invisible Web: Strange Tales of the French Surete*—contain nothing about said device. However, *The Forgotten Clue* proves to be a source for several other *Secrets of the French Police* ingredients: the "spoken portrait" ("In a case where no photograph exists, we make one up ..."), an apparent forerunner of the police artist ... the analysis of cigarette ashes found near a dead body ... and the examination of fingerprints.

In addition to the Anastasia story (the "lost empress") and the ways and means of the Surete, the film incorporates elements from *Svengali*, *Murders in the*

Rue Morgue, and *Arsene Lupin*. And in its mysteries of the statuary room, it actually beats *Mystery of the Wax Museum* to the punch. In the film, actual Surete official Ashton-Wolfe becomes Francois St. Cyr (Frank Morgan). (He's still Ashton-Wolfe in the estimating script.) St. Cyr assigns Leon Renault (John Warburton), a pickpocket, to find out what's going on in mad General Han Moloff's (Gregory Ratoff) chateau. (Manchu-Russian mix Moloff has a "magnetic personality," and the "trace of insanity" comes from his father's side.) But the viewer is allowed inside the chateau long before Leon enters it, thus dispelling most of the mystery. What we know before he does: Moloff is employing a parabolic mirror to help hypnotize flower-seller Eugenie Dorain (Gwili Andre) into passing herself off as the lost Anastasia (the *Svengali* angle).

[SPOILERS]: Inexplicably, however, Moloff later abandons this plan and attempts, instead, to turn Eugenie into the "most beautiful statue [he] has ever made." Is this just Another Weird Thing for Moloff to do? Or was *Secrets of the French Police* belatedly trying to sell itself as a horror movie, specifically, Universal's *Murders in the Rue Morgue*? In the estimating script, the Anastasia plan is not abandoned. Moloff is simply apprehended, by the police. In script and film, Moloff, earlier, embalmed and turned his own operative (Kendall Lee) into a statue, though we did not see the embalming process. Pretty tame.

However, in the finished film, we see the beginning of the draining of Eugenie's blood. The film omits two of the script's bizarre inserts, a "wolfhound's head—filling the screen—its monstrous mouth menacingly open—its huge fangs gleaming and dripping," and a "colossally magnified fly—which has been chemically tested so what we see is not gruesome—the chemicals make the fly as brilliant as a jewel" (page 90 of the script). But the inclusion of the beginning of the embalming process more than makes up for these lost inserts, in terms of the horror quotient. *Murders in the Rue Morgue* means, *Mystery of the Wax Museum* ends.

In the script, the above-noted murder device is pretty impressive: "As the car rounds the curve, a terrifying spectre looms up ahead. A tremendous car, driven by a horrible, hunched figure, which has nothing but a blur for a face, is driving head-on into the Duke's car" (page 76 of the script). In the film, no "horrible, hunched figure" is apparent, and the design of the "phantom car" is cartoonish—in fact, the "headlights" jump out like a cartoon character's eyes bugging out. Still, yes, such a spectacle would unnerve the driver of any automobile heading toward it.

Notes: Alfred Gilks' nimble camerawork includes some slick tracking shots.

Moloff, foiled, electrocutes himself on his own electronic gizmo.

"The castle set was previously used for RKO's *The Most Dangerous Game*—" classichorror.free-online.co.uk.

RKO. D: Edward Sutherland. SP: Samuel Ornitz, Robert Tasker. Story: Ornitz, *The Last Empress*, based on the magazine series "Secrets of the Surete: The French Detective Police" by H. Ashton-Wolfe. Ph: Alfred Gilks. AD: Carroll Clark. Ed: Arthur Roberts. Sd: George D. Ellis. SpFX: Harry Redmond, Sr. Cost: Walter Plunkett. Exec P: David O. Selznick. With Gwili Andre, Gregory Ratoff, Frank Morgan, John Warburton, Rochelle Hudson, Christian Rub, Murray Kinnell, Arnold Korff, Kendall Lee, Lucien Prival, Harry Cording, Julia Swayne Gordon; 58 minutes

Ref: *PV* 38:61-62.

HAUNTED GOLD

Haunted Gold released Dec. 17, 1932: "There's something uncanny and weird about everything—this house, and the people in it." Ingredients in this John Wayne "B" ghost Western for Warners include the "mysterious presence" of the Phantom, usually seen as ever-peering eyes at a peephole … a "haunted mine" … the gaunt Benedict (Erville Anderson) and the forbidding housekeeper (Martha Mattox), direct from some Old Dark House … the shadow of a bat … a quasi-clutching hand … a "creepy, spooky dump" … a creepy, spooky graveyard on a hill … and a "million monsters."

Camera ace Nicholas Musuraca makes the most of galloping horses and the shadows of the various "ghosts, spooks, and Phantoms," but young Wayne's performance is uneven—he's not up to exclamations yet. ("What!") Meanwhile, scriptwriter Adele Buffington employs the cliché ever-terrified Black man, Clarence (Blue Washington), as a comic crutch. ("Boss, you like to scared me to death!") And though he's usually just demeaningly jittery, he gets a few scenes in which to play the hero, and Washington suggests here what he could have done with a longer thespic leash. In the opening credits, the names of Wayne and Duke, his horse, come before the title. The horse is talented.

WB. D: Mack V. Wright. SP: Adele Buffington. Ph: Nicholas Musuraca. Mus: Leo F. Forbstein. With John Wayne, Sheila Terry, Harry Woods, Erville Alderson, Otto Hoffman, Martha Mattox, Blue Washington, Bob Burns, Bud Osborne, Slim Whitaker; Ken Maynard (archive footage); 58 minutes

Ref: Dave Sindelar (CHFB Movie of the Day 10/19/14). Recap of "digest version" of *The Phantom City* (1928), the "silent weird Western" on which *Haunted Gold* is based. Includes some 10 minutes of surviving footage plus "footage borrowed by *Haunted Gold*."

The MUMMY

The Mummy released Dec. 22, 1932 (copyright 1933): "Herein are set down the magic words by which Isis raised Osiris from the dead ... In many forms shall we return."—The Scroll of Thoth. "In the desert near Thebes." The message here: You can't go home again, especially if home is 3,700 years

Pressbook herald from *The Mummy* (1932)

ago ... This Universal classic is too somber and serious. It should simply be considered camp by now, yet it still seems, for the most part, to resist such a reduction. Boris Karloff's mummified High Priest Imhotep ("Never saw a mummy like that")—semi-reconstituted as scholar Ardath Bey—and Zita Johann's "partly Egyptian" Helen Grosvenor/Princess of Isis, Anckes-en-Amon, 18th Dynasty, aren't exactly Fun City. One may want *The Mummy* to lighten up a bit, but in the end it has its way. Karloff's gravity and Helen's great torment are just too much, or should have been so. Hard to pinpoint why they're usually not, but ...

"Come out under the stars of Egypt." Start with the camerawork (Charles Stumar, under the direction of Karl Freund). If, dramatically, the film is somewhat erratic, photographically, it's occasionally transcendent. If, glibly, the dialogue conveys the weight of centuries, with its "3,700 years ago" refrain, the camera irresistibly draws you into another world and time, most literally in the crane up from behind Helen and Imhotep, then over them, and down to his Wayback pool, in which he shows her the beginning of their story ("love and crime and death"), in ancient Egypt; most mysteriously, in the way the camera curls around the glass display case containing the princess' coffin, and finds the kneeling Imhotep poring over the scroll he stole. Unearthing the long-hidden, by candlelight ... (There's a parallel sequence in the flashbacks, as the young Imhotep kneels beside the coffin and reads from the same scroll.)

Some of James Dietrich's musical score, too, has a time-travel-to-days-of-old feel to it, as does the plethora of Egyptian artifacts—funerary equipment, caskets, scrolls, talismans, living statues, cauldrons. The intertwining of the (very) old and the new is subtly suggested in the sequence in which the music from the night-club dance floor continues playing over shots of Imhotep, in the Cairo Museum's "room of the princess," chanting; conversely, his chanting is heard over the shots at the club.

Lobby card showing the resurrection sequence where Imhotep (Boris Karloff) is brought back to life, only to drive Bramwell Fletcher insane.

"I loved you once, but now you belong with the dead." Helen, however, ultimately wants 1932, and the continuing odd power of *The Mummy* has something to do with the implication that Imhotep and Helen are both right. The problem is—in the John Balderston script's scheme of things—that Now and Forever is not possible. It's either Now (Helen) or Forever (Imhotep), though her "dreadful modern Cairo" comment hints at some backward-looking wistfulness on her part. As Imhotep advises, Forever does involve a certain "moment of agony." In the manner, somewhat, of Jesus, or Mina, in *Dracula*, she must die and enter the "underworld," temporarily, to get to the "Great Change" place, where their "Thebes of old" love can be reborn. Imhotep puts it quite poetically: "You shall rest ... like the setting sun in the west, but you shall dawn anew in the east, as the first rays of Amon-Ra dispel the shadow." (Amon-Ra is the "king of the gods" here.)

But, as he intones this, he's holding a wicked-looking dagger over her recumbent form, and that vague "moment of agony" begins to seem somewhat less vague, or at least more immediate, than the poetry. ("You shall not plunge my body into ... the bath of Natron," a very hot bath.) Though he's hardly a homicidal psychopath—after all, it worked for him—the pain and wrinkles associated with Forever (she would be a "living mummy like himself") are at least balanced by the pleasure implicit in seizing the day here. In the end, 1932 wins, although David Manners' Frank is hardly the most electrifying representative of the Now. Imhotep and Karloff are Forever; most of the other actors are at best last Tuesday ...

Karloff must make his character felt with minimal movement and vocal inflection, though he alternates between gentle and savage tones. He moves and speaks almost in slow motion—there seems to be an inverse correlation between Imhotep's physical limitations and his mystical powers (those deadly "evil sendings"). By contrast, in the flashbacks to ancient Egypt, circa 1730 B.C., Karloff moves at normal speed, as he narrates his tragic origins, sepulchrally. In her earlier scenes, Zita Johann's distinctive face, delicate voice, and way with a line make both Imhotep's and Frank's attraction to her understandable. ("Do you have to open graves to find girls to fall in love with?") And Manners, midway between *Dracula* and *The Black Cat*, is not as stiff as he was in *Dracula*, but not yet as loose as he was in *The Black Cat*. It doesn't help that the later scenes between Helen and Frank are over-earnest and badly written, or that some of the later dialogue scenes between Imhotep and the princess fall flat, too.

"And once, 10 years ago, he found too much." Tell a boy: "Don't touch that casket!" and it just encourages him. Of course, if Ralph Norton (Bramwell Fletcher)—the "Oxford Chap"—had not touched the casket, it might have been a pretty tepid movie. The declaration that the mummy lives ("It comes to life!" said the ads) is made by the now-mad Norton's balmy-witty "He went for a little walk!"

"The key to [Karloff's] portrayal is its very stillness"—Mark Clark, *Monsters from the Vault* 8:47.

Notes: Now: Helen's elegant silk gown. Not now: Imhotep's original ratty mummy wrappings.

Dietrich's music for the opening shots promises grand adventure, romance, and mystery, and the movie that follows does not disappoint.

Karloff appears "in many forms" here, or at least three: the mummy under wraps ... the stiff, stately walking mummy ... and the young priest, in the flashback, way back. He appears in yet a fourth form, if you count the sculpted face on the cover of Imhotep's sarcophagus, which face looks like Karloff's.

The Mummy is playing on television in the 2009 film *Happy Tears*, and dialogue inspired by it ("death in the name of Amon-Ra") turns up in connection with a mock-curse on an old trunk.

The visions in the pool constitute a sort of supernatural television.

Sweet how the title adorns a pyramid, in the opening credits.

The 1935 East Indian film *Kalkoot* is a reworking of *The Mummy*.

(*Imhotep*—early title) Universal. D: Karl Freund. SP: John L. Balderston. Story: Nina Wilcox Putnam, Richard Schayer. Ph: Charles Stumar. Mus:

James Dietrich. AD: Willy Pogany. Mkp: Jack Pierce. SpFX: John P. Fulton. Cost: Vera West. Ed: Milton Carruth. Sd: Joe Lapis. With Boris Karloff, Zita Johann, David Manners, Arthur Byron, Edward van Sloan, Bramwell Fletcher, Noble Johnson, Kathryn Byron, Leonard Mudie, Leyland Hodgson, C. Montague Shaw; 73 minutes

Ref: Filmfax 87-88:74-77.
Moving Picture Monthly 5/35, 6/35.
Scary Monsters 25:10-16.

"No other film of its era so deftly combines romance, suspense, and mysticism"—Mark Clark, "Ministry of Mayhem: The High Priests of Universal's Mummy Saga," *Monsters from the Vault* 8:47.

"A subtle, intelligent masterpiece"—Bryan Senn, *Filmfax* 57:56-7.

"Why would Isis, goddess of Life, kill?"—Lisa Mitchell, "Mummy Dearest" (*Cult Movies* 17:33-35) regarding the climax of *The Mummy*.

Fangoria 182:24-29: "Unwrapping the Mummy," Bill Warren preview of the updated version.

Midnight Marquee 52:5-13: Paul M. Jensen regarding the "Cagliostro" project: "*The Mummy* retained only a few minor elements" and was more indebted to the book *She*, the play *Berkeley Square*, and *Dracula*, book, play, film.

"Fine Willy Pogany styling and good camera work by Karl Freund"—Robert Bloch, *FM* 10:26.

TOMBSTONE CANYON

Tombstone Canyon released Dec. 25, 1932: "That was the cry of the phantom killer! That's the cry that gave Tombstone Canyon its name! When that cry is heard, somebody always dies!" K.B.S.' Christmas ghost Western. Before werewolves first howled in talking horror pictures, there were, yes, movies like this and *The Thirteenth Guest*, which featured miscellaneous weird cries. In this case, the man who cries is the Phantom (Sheldon Lewis), who is "loco," black-caped, rifle-toting, and disfigured—all of the

above. His cry sometimes sounds like a loud, strangled "Yee haw!" and he also has a sparingly used cackle.

[SPOILERS]: The plot, in the Phantom's handwritten note: "Alf Sykes — You're next —Phantom." Until the end, some mighty pretty countryside is all that keeps that plot going. At the end, the Phantom—or just plain Phantom ("Don't move, Phantom!")—explains all, and there are then dollops of pathos and fulfillment. ("You try not to think too hard of your old dad.")

Notes: Is this a ghost Western ("Let's get out of this place! It's plumb spooky!") or an existential Western? Hero Ken (Ken Maynard): "All I want to find out is who I am."

In the rather complicated opening action sequence, in the canyon, four different factions take potshots at each other—the hero, the heroine (Cecilia Parker), (the) Phantom, and several bad guys.

K.B.S. D: Alan James. Story: Claude Rister. Cont: Earle Snell. Ph: Ted McCord. Sets: Ralph DeLacy. Ed: David Berg. Sd: Hans Weeren. P: Samuel Bischoff, Burt Kelly, Willliam Saal. With Ken Maynard, Cecilia Parker, Sheldon Lewis, Frank Brownlee, Lafe McKee, Edward Peil, Sr., Bob Burns, George Chesebro, Jack Kirk, Leo Willis; 62 minutes

Ref: "Off to a fast pace and never stops running"—*Variety* 4/11/33.

ISLAND OF LOST SOULS

Island of Lost Souls released December 1932: "Say, what is all this mystery about Moreau and his island?" On an "island without a name," in the South Seas, bio-anthropologist Dr. Moreau (Charles Laughton)—a "grave-robbin' ghoul" from Australia—has succeeded in fantastically speeding up the evolution of plants and animals, utilizing plastic surgery, blood transfusions, gland extracts, and "ray baths." ("Strange-looking natives you have here."). Compared to Colin Clive's Dr. Frankenstein, in *Frankenstein*, Laughton's Moreau seems one-dimensional. Or perhaps it's just the fact that we first catch Moreau at a later stage in his respective career, long after the first flush of unblemished enthusiasm. We come upon him only after everything has gone wrong—at least from the point of view of anyone but Moreau. There's little or nothing redeeming about him, at least as a person.

In H.G. Wells' book, *The Island of Dr. Moreau*, the doctor has perfected what he sees as a valuable indifference to pain, at least the pain of others. The movie's Moreau, too, seems oblivious to pain, but—unlike the book's Moreau—he doesn't rationalize it. (Wells' Moreau: "Pain is simply our intrinsic medical adviser to warn us and stimulate us.") He's simply oblivious. The subject of pain as pain seems rarely, if ever, to have occurred to him. He doesn't take pleasure in it, as does Lugosi's Dr. Vollin (*The Raven*). He doesn't like to torture. He just tortures. In one casually cruel scene, he examines a subject's head, as the subject screams. He just doesn't hear the screaming. He's frighteningly focused.

Kathleen Burke (the Panther Woman), Richard Arlen and Charles Laughton strike a pose in this lobby card from *Island of Lost Souls*.

The Waldemar Young-Philip Wylie screenplay slices and dices the Wells. It gets at the same ideas—generally successfully—but generally in different ways. It introduces a major new character, Lota, the Panther Woman (Kathleen Burke), the "only woman on the entire island." Director Erle C. Kenton wrings pathos and outrage out of a scene in which she weeps, as Moreau delights: "You see this? The first of them to shed tears. She is human! I'm not beaten!" (In the comparable Wells passage, Moreau says, "The thing before you is no longer an animal, a fellow-creature, but a problem.") In another sweet-sad scene, Lota examines herself in a mirror, looking for the "flaw" which has repelled the hero, Edward Parker (Richard Arlen). It's her nails, which are reverting to claws. ("She's never seen anything like him.") Her dying, self-sacrificial: "Go back to sea," to Parker, is the film's equivalent of "We belong dead" from *Bride of Frankenstein*.

[SPOILERS]: *Island of Lost Souls* effectively ends with Moreau at the mercy of all his "things," in his House of Pain. In the book, the puma-thing seems to kill him—the movie's ending, in miniature—but the book's best revenge on Moreau is the work of nature: Over time, the Beast People simply revert to their beast selves. And Edward Prendick (the book's name for him) lives out the rest of his life in rural solitude, away from the machinations of man.

Brilliantly, Laughton makes Moreau a creature, principally, of self-indulgence. Disconnect: Moreau throws his arm around Parker as he leads him on show-and-tell of his "less successful experiments." But Parker is anything but his pal: "Moreau, you don't deserve to live!" It's not just what he does—which is heinous enough—it's what he is, or why he does it. He lacks scientific objectivity. When he feels he has failed with Lota ("the stubborn beast flesh creeping back"), he mopes; a few seconds later ("She is human!"), he exults. Manic or depressive, it's all about him, not science, not others. ("My work, my discoveries. Mine alone.") The sequence in which he confides in Parker is not really about sharing—it's an excuse for him

Kathleen Burke plays shy with Richard Arlen, in a publicity shot.

(as drolly played by Laughton) to bask in his own glorious achievements. Parker's reactions be damned. Helplessly, Moreau lapses into a smirk when he imagines how easy it would be to create a woman who talks. He's lost in a sea of himself.

In the film's other standout performance, Bela Lugosi overcomes his Sayer of the Law (i.e., Moreau's Law) makeup fiasco and makes more-than-vivid his scattered lines, especially, of course, "the House of Pain!" It's as if—in one spoken phrase—Lugosi were giving voice to the world's pain—yes, even the despicable Moreau's, as the latter wails, at the end. A tall order, a Wellsian one, in fact: At one point, Prendick writes—of the cries of the "vivisected puma"—"It was as if all the pain in the world had found a voice." In the film, it finds its voice in Lugosi.

At the end, the "crooked creature" (Wells' words) repeats the famous phrase—when Moreau haplessly reminds him of the "house," and the medical instruments are in the hands of his creations—but Lugosi now gives it a triumphant accent. His anguished "J'accuse!" to Moreau, "You made us *things*! Not men! Not beasts! Part man! Part beast! Things!" is an almost breathtaking feat, every phrase emphasized, and yet not overemphasized. Pigeons/roost irony: Moreau was his accuser's Henry Higgins ... Lugosi's commanding bravura

here contrasts with his earlier, matter-of-fact advisory for Moreau: "Law ... no more." The underplaying underlines the finality—bringing down the House of Pain ...

Of the other actors, Kathleen Burke, Paul Hurst, and Arthur Hohl come off best; Arlen and Leila Hyams worst. If the movie is unevenly acted, however, it's still a harrowing achievement.

Notes: The movie has so much to look at that background music is almost not missed. Almost.

No stinting on the variety of makeup for the faces of the beast-men—no two look the same.

England outlawed the showing of the movie for its depiction of vivisection. It wasn't enough, apparently, that the screenplay seems firmly anti-vivisection: The vivisector is depicted as a horrendous person.

In this movie, the asparagus might eat the people.

Fresh-to-the-island Ruth's (Hyams) divinely silly question: "What's there to be afraid of?"

Paramount. D: Erle C. Kenton. SP: Waldemar Young, Philip Wylie, from H.G. Wells' novel *The Island of Dr. Moreau*. Ph: Karl Struss. AD: Hans Dreier. Mkp: Wally Westmore, Charles Gemora. VisFX: Gordon Jennings. With Charles Laughton, Richard Arlen, Leila Hyams, Bela Lugosi, Kathleen Burke,

Arthur Hohl, Stanley Fields, Paul Hurst, Hans Steinke, Tetsu Komai, George Irving, Joe Bonomo, Gemora, Duke York; 70 minutes

Ref: Wikipedia. *Midnight Marquee* 45:20-25. *The Dark Side* 47:45-46.

"Laughton gives us the greatest mad doctor of them all"—Bryan Senn, *Filmfax* 57:50. "Of the entire parade of mad doctors and maniacs that have crept across the screen in horror films, no character can quite match Laughton's Moreau"—Frank Dello Stritto review, *Photon* 25:24-29, 45.

"The overall production still seems slightly stiff and by-the-numbers"—Gary J. Svehla, *Midnight Marquee* 83-84.

"Some horror sequences which are unrivaled"—*Variety* 1/17/33.

"Probably the best horror film ever made"—Mike Weldon.

"Laughton hamming it up in a white jacket and Lugosi having a fine time behind a lot of crepe hair for dear old Paramount"—Robert Bloch, *FM* 10:26.

The Moreau (Marlon Brando) of the 1996 *The Island of Dr. Moreau* is equal parts Moreau, God, Frank Gilbreth, and Dr. Doolittle, with the hyena-swine (Daniel Rigney) as Jesus ("Father—why?"). This strangely humanized Moreau fancies himself a family man, with a "family" which he has created in his laboratory. [SPOILERS]: He deserves a better send-off than the Wells and Laughton Moreau's, but his less-successful experiments/family-members tear him apart and eat him anyway. If, instead, the screenplay had taken its cue from Brando's exquisitely droll "Would you like a biscuit?" scene—in which a midnight snack turns into a tragically futile taming-of-the-beasts melee—the movie might have become a truly unusual, pastoral science-fiction comedy, with (as I see it) neither Moreau nor nature ever quite winning the evolutionary war, but one then the other winning, then quietly losing uproarious little battles. With a little gore. As it is, the film squanders most of its running time on noise and commotion, a new Lota—here called Aissa (Fairuza Balk), an "extraordinary creature" tormented by returning fangs—and a rampant "beasts (and men) will be beasts" theme. The movie ends on an unexpected note, from an unexpected source—Wells' book. Hero Edward Douglas' (David Thewlis) concluding narration began as Edward Prendick's: "Then I look about me at my fellow men. And I go in fear ... I feel as though the animal was surging up through them ..."

Highlights of 1933

The year of *King Kong*. Featuring not one, but three amazing creations—Kong himself, Carl Denham (Robert Armstrong), and Ann Darrow (Fay Wray). For more, see below.

James Whale made it three for three with *The Invisible Man*, arguably the best so far of his Universal horror classics. Again, as in *Frankenstein*, the man with the power is in danger of losing his mind. As Jack Griffin, Claude Rains may be mainly just a voice, but the story is in that voice, and in the most affecting sequence, he somehow uses bandaged hands to express Griffin's particular torment.

Mischa Auer, horror-film star, at least in the early-to-mid '30s, in *The Monster Walks*, *Drums of Jeopardy*, *Murder at Dawn*, *The Flaming Signal*, and *Condemned To Live*. He gives one of his best genre performances in 1933's *Sucker Money*.

Most disappointing horror picture of the year: *Mystery of the Wax Museum*. What *Doctor X* (Michael Curtiz's fun 1932 shocker) did right, Curtiz's *Mystery of the Wax Museum* does wrong.

Charlie Ruggles was the comic bane of horror movies in 1933, in *Murders in the Zoo* and *Terror Aboard*.

One-hit wonders: The Halperins flopped with their follow-up to *White Zombie*—*Supernatural*.

History is made on Poverty Row, as the action of *Strange People* takes place over the span of one hour, and the movie itself runs ... one hour.

Notable performances: Glenda Farrell (*Mystery of the Wax Museum*), Mischa Auer, Mae Busch (*Sucker Money*), Lionel Atwill, Kathleen Burke (*Murders in the Zoo*), Robert Armstrong, Fay Wray, Bruce Cabot, Frank Reicher (*King Kong*), John Halliday (*Terror Aboard*), Paul Lukas (*Secret of the Blue Room*), Dorothy Wilson (*Before Dawn*), Claude Rains (*The Invisible Man*), Frank Reicher (*Son of Kong*)

Notable photography: Ira Morgan (*The Vampire Bat*), James Diamond and William Nobles (*Sucker Money*), Eddie Linden, J.O. Taylor, Vernon L. Walker; (optical) Linwood G. Dunn (*King Kong*), Harry Fischbeck (*Terror Aboard*), Joseph Valentine (*Night of Terror*), Arthur Martinelli (*Supernatural*), M.A. Anderson (*Strange People*), Charles Stumar (*Secret of the Blue Room*), Lucien Andriot (*Before Dawn*), John Stumar (*Before Midnight*)

Notable direction: Edward Sutherland (*Murders in the Zoo*), Ernest B. Schoedsack and Merian C. Cooper, apparently (*King Kong*), James Whale (*The Invisible Man*)

Notable writing: James Creelman, Ruth Rose, Merian C. Cooper (*King Kong*), R.C. Sherriff (*The Invisible Man*), Jack Townley (*Strange People*)

Notable art direction: Carroll Clark, Al Herman (*King Kong*)

Notable visual effects: Willis O'Brien (*King Kong, Son of Kong*), John P. Fulton (*The Invisible Man*)

Notable musical scores: Max Steiner (*King Kong, Son of Kong*)

Notable design: Mario Larrinaga, Byron L. Crabbe (*King Kong*)

Notable sound effects: Murray Spivack (*King Kong, Son of Kong*)

Notable editing: Ted Cheesman (*King Kong*)

Notable costumes: Walter Plunkett (*King Kong*), Travis Banton (*Supernatural*)

Other films of interest:

The Death Kiss—The title and the presence of actors Bela Lugosi, David Manners, and Edward van Sloan are supposed to make you think that this is some sequel to *Dracula*, but it's just a mystery movie. Its only interest as such: The plot involves almost every department in the movie studio therein. Lugosi, billed third, might as well have been an extra. Van Sloan is convincing as a director. Manners' character is an insufferable snot.

The Emperor Jones—ghosts, voodoo drums

The Horror—Rare cheapie. 35-min. fragment at the Library of Congress. John Massey (Leslie King) transforms into an ape-man thing. Plus a gorilla and a mystic. Re-edited apparently as *The Drunkard* (1944). Ref: Phantom XCI, CHFB, "Golden Age Horror" (*The Horror*), 6/17/13. IMDb. HSF1. (FJA poster)

A Shriek in the Night—Here, a janitor does the mad-doctor cackle, and the incinerator sequence is suggestively horrific, but this is not horror.

The Sphinx—"I tell you that guy Breen's a maniac." Routine mystery padded out with semi-horrific bits: a secret room, screaming, a "boogeyman," and a drawing of a sphinx with a man's huge head

Tomorrow at 7—scattered thunderstorm-mystery elements: lights-out scenes on a plane and on a plantation ... forbidding housekeeper ... sinister coroner (Charles Middleton, but this is in his pre-Ming dynasty) ... clutching hand ... annoying comic relief

Trick for Trick—Very rare third and final entry in Fox's magician trilogy, also including *The Spider* ('31) and *Chandu the Magician* ('32). Highlights: magician Azrah's (Ralph Morgan) door-into-nowhere—he seems to be walking on an invisible floor ... Luis Alberni's mad doctor and his lab-created lightning ... and shrieking-wind effects. But the in between scenes get pretty tiresome. Ref: *HSF4*

Wajan, Son of the Witch—tribal chief curses village. Ref: *HSF1*. doctor kiss, CHFB, "Poverty Row," 1/6/10. CHFB, "Movie of the Day" 3/28/15: restored in 2002. *Variety* 4/20/38: "goona goona." *Die Unsel der Damonen*—original German title. *Black Magic: A Story of Bali Island*—1949 British re-release title

Wasei Kingu Kongu—Japanese riff on *King Kong*. Apparently a short. Ref: Wikipedia

White Woman—Ref *Variety* 11/21/33: "gruesome." *PV* 39:12: Decapitation Central

1933

The VAMPIRE BAT

The Vampire Bat released Jan. 21, 1933: "Vampires are at large, I tell you! Vampires!" It's just the beginning of 1933, and already The *Vampire Bat* is a "shiver picture" which seems to be "too late in the cycle to figure in the money." (*Variety* 1/24/33) But shiver pictures proved to have surprising staying power, and *The Vampire Bat* now seems squarely in the middle of a cycle that would occasionally slow, but not wind down, until late 1936.

The movie's disjointed plot comprises scraps of its contemporaries. Lionel Atwill's mad Dr. von Niemann's hypnotic-plus control of henchman Emil (Robert Frazer) comes from *Svengali* and *White Zombie*. Renfield—in the person of Dwight Frye's addled Herman—seems to have wandered in from Dracula, and of course the picture's title and its hints of a "human vampire" want you to think *Dracula*, too. *Murders in the Rue Morgue* might have inspired the rooftop phantom. And the sets are from *Frankenstein* and *The Old Dark House* (*Forgotten Horrors*, p82).

In one respect, however, the movie seems a little ahead of its time: The script also drops hints of werewolves well before Universal's major early forays into lycanthropy. Ira Morgan's tracking shots prove effective scene setters, but

6-sheet poster from *The Vampire Bat*

Edward T. Lowe's dialogue makes dull actors of Melvyn Douglas and even Atwill, though the latter makes the energetic most of his climactic: "Life!—that moves, pulsates, and demands food for its continued growth!" The "life" in question looks like a (pulsating) household sponge and is better described (see above) than seen. By default, Frye and Fay Wray take acting honors.

Camp Lives! Department: (an extra) "Seems strange that a human being should want to play with bats" and (Douglas) "Why should anyone want human blood? Why?"

Note: *The Vampire Bat*—*Special Edition*. Unlike *Dracula* (1931), *The Vampire Bat* did not get a complete musical-soundtrack updating. Sinister Cinema's find, a Spanish-language-dubbed version, though, features about 10 minutes more music than the original English-language edition. The most sustained stretch of music occurs near the end—it's about 7 minutes long, and covers several scenes, sometimes over, or under, dialogue. And it doesn't sound like other film music of the era. Equally unusual: This version's addition, or amplification, of the sound of footsteps. For all the characters. Shoes on floors really resound here. It gets to be distracting, at least once you notice the phenomenon, which might better be reserved for tap dancing.

(*Blood Sucker*—re-release title. *Forced To Sin*—re-release title) Majestic Pictures/Larry Darmour Productions. D: Frank Strayer. SP: Edward T. Lowe. Ph: Ira Morgan. AD: Charles D. Hall. Ed: Otis Garrett. Sd: Dick Tyler. P: Phil Goldstone. With Lionel Atwill, Fay Wray, Melvyn Douglas, Dwight Frye, Maude Eburne, George E. Stone, Robert Frazer, Rita Carlyle, Lionel Belmore, William V. Mong, Fern Emmett, Paul Panzer, Carl Stockdale, Paul Weigel; 65 minutes

Ref: IMDb. "A neglected gem"—Roy Kinnard, *Filmfax* 7:38-41.

"I found this one quite enjoyable, with a great role for Frye"—Dave Sindelar (6/22/2002).

MYSTERY OF THE WAX MUSEUM

Mystery of the Wax Museum released Feb. 18, 1933: "The whole place is a morgue!" 1921, London. When the Wax Museum burns, the face and hands of curator Ivan Igor (Lionel Atwill) are badly burned. 1933, New York City. Igor is now running the London Wax Museum. But who or what is the "horrible thing" in the basement, and why does the Joan of Arc figure look so real?

Mystery of the Wax Museum is the more sedate, respectable version of *Doctor X* (1932), which was also directed by Michael Curtiz and also starred Atwill and Fay Wray. From one angle, *Mystery of the Wax Museum* is an overlong build-up to a pretty okay unmasking scene; from another angle, it's the obvious suspense of a woman (sometimes Fay Wray, usually Glenda Farrell) wandering around a fairly dangerous museum. From either angle, it's exasperatingly thin.

The picture is full of dead scenes, no play on words intended. Blame, first, the absence of a musical score to shape and define the action. Imagine *King Kong* without Max Steiner … By contrast, the 1930 Warners film *Road to Paradise* features an almost-nonstop musical score. Go figure. *Chandu the Magician* could have given *Mystery of the Wax Museum* some of its abundant music and had plenty left over.

Then, blame the absence of an editor to trim overlong dialogue sequences and overlong wandering sequences. (An editor is credited, one George Amy, but that was perhaps a contractual requirement.) Next, blame director Michael Curtiz, though the absence of both a background score and an editor left him rather hamstrung.

It's not really any fault of the actors that the story just lies there. Glenda Farrell isn't bad, but she's monotonously energetic, unchained as she is. It's not the quality of the (very uneven) material that helps elevate her to starring status here—it's mainly the quantity of screen time she's allowed to consume. Fay

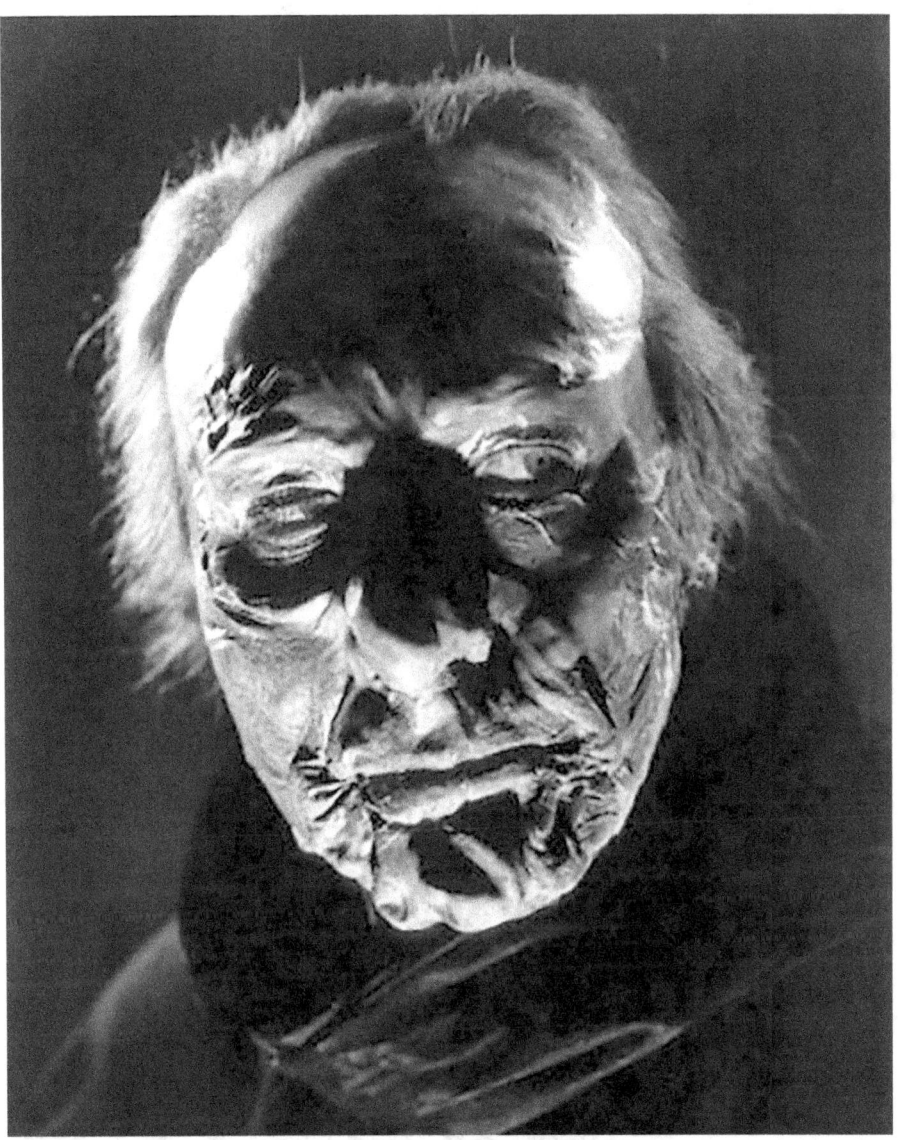

Lionel Atwill as the disfigured, fire-scarred Ivan Igor

Wray, on the other hand, is reduced to the role of incidental screamer. Misery of the Wax Museum.

Atwill's eastern European/Russian accent is less taking than his own familiar voice. Yes, it's hard to believe that he could give a dull performance, but an Atwill without his imperious bluster is almost an ordinary actor. And he's further constrained by the fact that, after the fire, his face/mask must of course be less expressive. Small favors: At least Warner Bros. regular Allen Jenkins isn't in *Mystery of the Wax Museum*; on the other hand, Frank McHugh is.

The 1930s

Newspaper ad from *Mystery of the Wax Museum* (1933)

Most of the thrills are on the mild side—suddenly closing (or opening) doors, human eyes peering through masks, melting wax figures (Joan of Arc a natch for this), corpses sitting up, Mr. Ugly rambling through the basement. The lifelike-display-figures idea would be done better the next year, in *The Black Cat*.

Most helpful sign in the lab: "Wax Temperature."

(*The Wax Works* original title; *Wax Museum*—shooting title) WB. D: Michael Curtiz. SP: Don Mullaly, Carl Erickson, from the play *Waxworks* by Charles S. Belden. Ph: Ray Rennahan. End music: Bernhard Kaun. AD: Anton Grot. Ed: George Amy. Wax Figures: L.E. Oates. Mkp: Perc Westmore, Ray Romero. Cost: Orry-Kelly. Sd: E.A. Brown. SdFX: Rex Wimpy. With Lionel Atwill, Fay Wray, Glenda Farrell, Frank McHugh, Allen Vincent, Gavin Gordon, Edwin Maxwell, Holmes Herbert, Claude King, Arthur Edmund Carewe, Thomas E. Jackson, DeWitt Jennings, Matthew Betz, Wade Boteler, Frank Darien, William B. Davidson, Otto Hoffman, Robert Homans, Milton Kibbee, Robert Emmett O'Connor, Guy Usher, Lee Shumway; 77 minutes

Ref: IMDb. "Witty, exciting, frightening"—Bryan Senn, "The Horror Films of Michael Curtiz," *Midnight Marquee* 58:32.

"A loose and unconvincing story ... [but] a fairly decent job along the *Frankenstein* and *Dracula* lines"—*Variety* 2/21/33.

The film is listed, charmingly, in Andrew Sarris' *The American Cinema*, as *History of the Wax Museum*.

SUCKER MONEY

Sucker Money released March 1, 1933: He: "This place, I expect to see ghosts." She: "I have." Like a newspaper sub-headline, the words, "An expose of the Psychic Racket/A True Life Photoplay" appear below the title in the credits. But, ironically, this "expose" of the swami racket employs its own borderline-supernatural plot elements. The thoroughly unscrupulous and "positively uncanny" Hindu Swami Yomurda (Mischa Auer) is a Svengali who keeps his séance link to the spirit world, Princess Karami (Mona Lisa), in a permanent hypnotic trance. ("Lately, she's been acting awful strange. Kinda gives me the creeps.") Ultimately, he poisons her, but he recruits a new spirit guide by using a strange light in a crystal ball to help him hypnotize "perfect subject" Clare Walton (Phyllis Barrington). ("You will do my bidding.")

In the nuttiest sequence, an obviously projected image on a screen is intended to represent—for a select audience of the ultra-gullible—the uncanny materialization of an event in the recent past of three of the principals. ("Great Scott, that is uncanny!") Yomurda, as the filmstrip concludes: "Ah! the thought wave is broken!" (i.e., the projector is turned off). The most visually impressive "materialization": the young woman's "grandma" appearing in a sea of black. Cinematographers James Diamond and William Nobles also

score with an intimidating close shot of Yomurda—all threatening eyebrows—as he glowers above the poisoned Princess.

"Quite mad at the finish," the dying swami declares, "No one has ever caught Yomurda with the goods," and Auer does his best to put over the requisite mad bravado, but that line is no help. Mae Busch, as the world-weary Mame, is the only other actor that makes a favorable impression. Unfavorable: Earl McCarthy, as the reporter hero Jimmy, is quite helpless with his later, dramatic scenes.

Note: Mischa Auer also appears as Swami Yomurda in the non-horrific *Sinister Hands* (1932), though this is not necessarily the same Swami Yomurda.

(*Victims of the Beyond*—British title) Progressive/Willis Kent. D: Dorothy Reid, Melville Shyer. SP: Willis Kent. Ph: James Diamond, William Nobles. Sets from Republic Studios. Ed: S. Roy Luby. With Mischa Auer, Phyllis Barrington, Earl McCarthy, Ralph Lewis, Mae Busch, Mona Lisa, Al Bridge, J. Frank Glendon, Kit Guard, Harry Todd; 59 minutes

Ref: IMDb. *Harrison's* 5/13/33.

"Painfully creaky"—Dave Sindelar (9/29/2006).

MURDERS IN THE ZOO

Murders in the Zoo released March 31, 1933: "Anti-toxin!" Or, Murder by Mamba, or at least by green-mamba venom, the "swiftest acting venom there is." There's "something peculiar" about "millionaire sportsman" Eric Gorman (Lionel Atwill)—for starters, he seems over-keen on wild animals: "They love. They hate. They kill." And the film visually identifies him, twice, with a tiger.

Eager to please early-1930s horror-movie fans, *Murders in the Zoo* begins with Gorman sewing a man's mouth shut—and the man, Taylor (Edward Pawley), running into gruesome close-up. Later, in answer to a question regarding Taylor, Gorman responds, "He didn't say anything." Atwill gives the line just the lightest, right emphasis. This is in fact a pretty good vehicle for

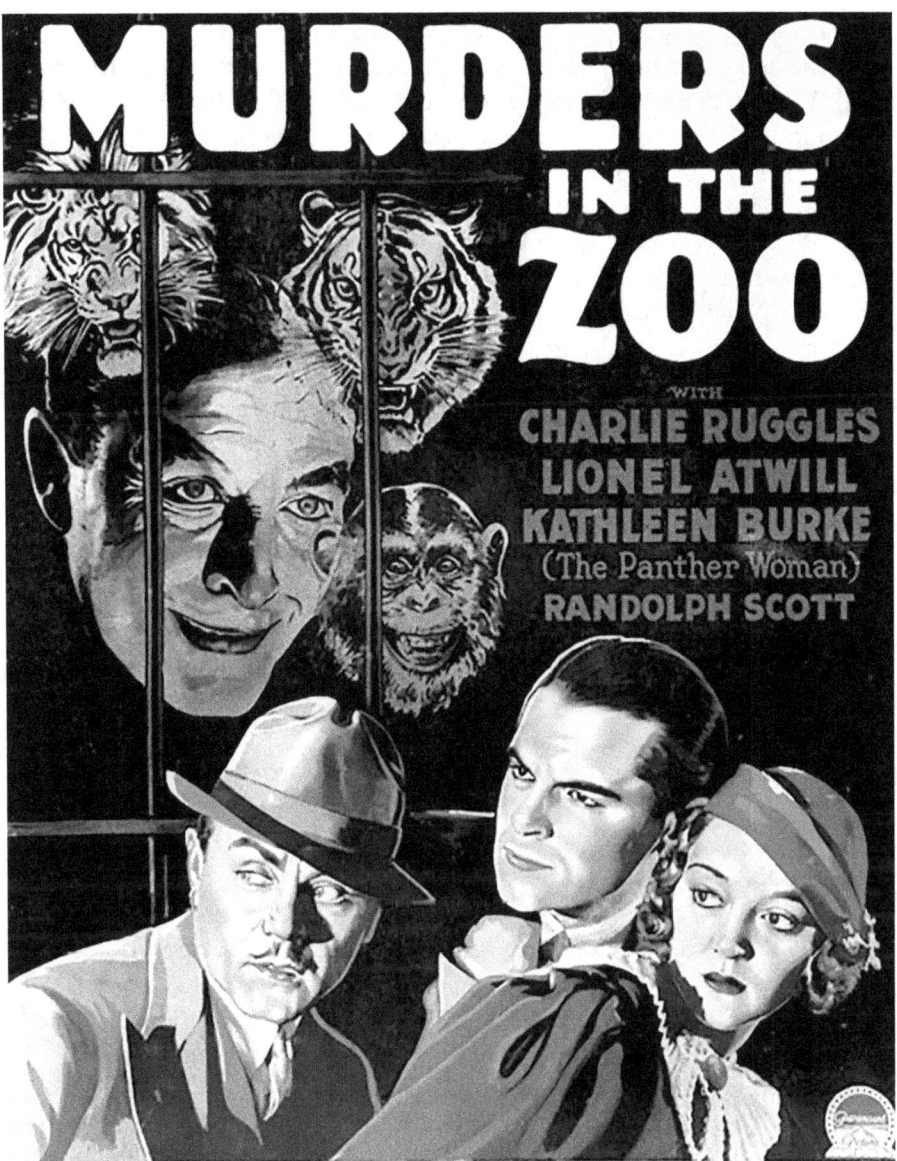

6-sheet poster from *Murders in the Zoo*

Atwill. His scenes with his wife, Evelyn (Kathleen Burke), are among the highlights of the year in horror. She: "I hate you!" He: "What is it that makes me love you so?" She screams in terror. He smiles, curiously. She: disgust. He: mad lust. Perversely sincerely, he coos, "Anything I've done I've done because I love you."

Too much Ruggles. Unfortunately, *Murders in the Zoo* is also a vehicle for comic actor Charlie Ruggles, who gets top billing and the lion's share of footage. He did quite well in Ernst Lubitsch comedies of the time, but here he has weak material, and his impishness quickly wears thin. Oater star Randolph Scott (Woodford) also did *Supernatural* the same year. Gail Patrick (Jerry) went on to play in some notable comedies, such as *My Man Godfrey* (1936) and *My Favorite Wife* (1940), and also did the bizarre *The Madonna's Secret* (1946) and executive produced the original *Perry Mason* TV series. In 1934, John Lodge (Roger Hewitt) played opposite Dietrich in Sternberg's exhilarating *The Scarlet Empress*. Director Edward Sutherland did Abbott and Costello's first (*One Night in the Tropics*) and one of John Barrymore's worst (*The Invisible Woman*).

Notes: A sheen of nostalgia may seem to overlay *Murders in the Zoo*, in part because Kathleen Burke was The Panther Woman in Paramount's 1932 horror extravaganza *Island of Lost Souls*.

The thrilling music over the title—as well as the track back from the zoo door under said title—make *Murders in the Zoo* one exciting title.

(*Murder at the Zoo*—working title) Paramount. D: A. Edward Sutherland. SP: Philip Wylie, Seton I. Miller. Ph: Ernest Haller. Mus: R.G. Kopp, John Leipold. With Lionel Atwill, Gail Patrick, Charles Ruggles, Randolph Scott, John Lodge, Kathleen Burke, Harry Beresford, Jane Darwell, Samuel S. Hinds, Ethan Laidlaw, Edward McWade, Syd Saylor, Phillips Smalley, Edwin Stanley, Duke York; 62 minutes

Ref: IMDb.

"A total of three murders, plus an attempted fourth, meaning Gorman is batting .750 in his league"—*Variety* 4/4/33.

KING KONG

The Lost World (1925, 92-minute version): "I'd give my entire personal fortune to get that beast to London—alive!" Despite the similarities in story and the fact that Willis O'Brien did the animation for both movies, no one could have predicted the achievement of *King Kong* based on the occasional charm of *The Lost World*. The brontosaurus "running wild" in the streets of London—in the climactic scenes here—best suggests what was to come some eight years later: It's still a pretty alarming sequence. Otherwise, this tale of an Amazon "mystery world" is fatally split between dinosaur spectacle and human drama, or attempts at same: mutual dilution. Prime O'Brien details include the snakelike movement of the bronto's long neck, and his sneer ... the sudden appearance of the pterodactyl ... the slobber in the allosaur's mouth ... and the glowing eyes of *something* in the dark of night. The recurrent cuts to Bessie Love reaction shots are welcome camp.

King Kong released April 7, 1933: "I've got enough trouble without a love affair to complicate things." "Tough egg" Carl Denham (Robert Armstrong) sets forth with a large crew aboard The Venture to "make an outdoor picture," somewhere "way west of Sumatra," in the East Indies. In fact, he's in search

6-sheet poster from *King Kong* (1933)

of Kong, the "biggest thing in the world"—a "kind of a gorilla" roughly as big as a house. The human inhabitants of what comes to be called "Denham's island" keep Kong at bay behind a "colossal" wall and gate. But they appease him by offering up Denham's picture's prospective star, Ann Darrow (Fay Wray), as a sacrifice. Denham's comment regarding first mate Jack Driscoll (Bruce Cabot) might apply to Kong as well: "Some big, hard-boiled egg gets a look at a pretty face and, bang, he cracks up and goes sappy!"

On the surface, *King Kong* is a lot of good scary fun, but it's also surprisingly fatalistic. It's prefaced by an "old Arabian proverb": "And lo, the beast looked upon the face of beauty. And it stayed its hand from killing. And from that day, it was as one dead." We can actually see the instant that beauty stops this beast, in their first scene together: He seems about to beat his chest, but becomes puzzled by something in the chained Ann's screams. He can only make helpless (stop) motions with paws and arms …

Kong will take any means to protect Ann (Fay Wray)

And here one sees, in retrospect, why poor Bruce Cabot was saddled with that embarrassing (for the actor), tongue-tied interlude with Fay Wray, on the ship—an unusual false move for this movie. Kong, above, is reenacting, most charmingly, the very same scene with Ann. But what Kong does, visually, Jack has to do with unfortunate dialogue. Jack, in fact, is Kong, writ small. Both are in thrall of the "face of beauty." Like Kong, he does almost everything that he does, after meeting her, for her. His all-at-sea love scene is necessary, but it could have been done better. The first Kong/Ann scene could not have been done better.

Big Love. Kong's subsequent feats of strength and skill—he saves Ann, in turn, from a tryannosaurus, a snake-like thing (an elasmosaurus), and a pterodactyl—are a measure of his feeling for her. He's passion writ gigantic—he busts through a giant gate (on the island) and tears free of very-heavy-duty, chrome-steel chains (in New York City) to get to her, to protect her. Change of scene; no change of heart, or fixation. But if he only has eyes for her, she only has screams for him, first, last, and always. He terrifies her. That's it. Their relationship does not develop. It intensifies, through reiteration. In one scene, he tries to tickle her, but she's still just straining to wriggle out of his grasp. Even at the very end, when Kong is picking her up, lovingly, one last time, she is kicking her legs furiously, in abject terror. The girl can't help it; neither can he.

And of course it wasn't really the planes or beauty that killed the beast—it was Denham, and his endless entrepreneurial enthusiasm, his drive for "money and adventure and fame." But he's not quite the villain. He's not quite God. (According to Denham, the public is God: "The public must have a pretty face to look at!") He's not quite a matchmaker. He's a little of each, and more than a little of the showman. He's forward motion of a different kind than Kong or Ann Darrow. Reflective, he's not. While the Skipper (Frank Reicher) is lamenting regarding "all those men lost" in the prehistoric jungle of Kong, Denham is enthusing regarding the "biggest thing in the world." *King Kong* is precariously pitched between celebration and condemnation of Denham. He's a great guy, but …

The various dinosaurs behind the wall are as single-minded as Kong, Ann, and Denham—they're all cranky, aggressive. This may not be veristic dino detail, but it makes for a harrowing midsection of the movie, some 25 minutes of nonstop nightmare action. Kong places Ann gently atop a tree trunk. Along comes a tyrannosaurus. Kong places her gently on a ledge in his home-base cave. Along comes the snake-thing. Kong places her gently on his rock balcony. Along comes the pterodactyl. This clockwork predictability, or inevitability, just seems the natural, Darwinian-squared order of things here. Ironically, Kong's paw might be the safest place for Ann. The other denizens of Denham's jungle would not be so gentle. They're not taken with her, not cowed by her screams. This survival-of-the-fiercest story might not be bearable if it weren't also a great, surreal love story. Kong dies, tragically, but he lives a great love story, or simian passion play.

Grand Central Station: In one sequence, Kong is up above, fishing with his paw for Jack, who is hiding in an outcropping near the top of an apparent spider pit. Jack does not see the lizard beastie climbing towards him, at the same time, from below. Meanwhile, not far away, Ann does see the tyrannosaurus that has seen her. And all this is happening in pretty much the same packed moment. The bit-part lizard thing gets its own distinctive hiss/snarl. The tyrannosaurus has a kind of prissy yap. Kong himself of course has an assortment of roars, yelps, and throaty challenges. (Sound effects: Murray Spivack.)

One quietly active diorama, or dinorama, illustrates the range of animation wizard Willis O'Brien and company: Jack walking, foreground right; the defeated tyrannosaurus lying in mid-range; and Kong fussing about something, way in the background. The frosting: incidental (apparently animated) birds darting this way and that. All in the same intricately-orchestrated shot. Just an in between, getting-us-from-here-to-there shot. Goodness. In another linking shot, the shadow of Kong on tree branches heralds his actual appearance in said shot, as he carries Ann to his cave lair. They didn't have to do the shadows. But they did—for the stegosaurus, the bronto, the snake-lizard, and the pterodactyl, too. Goodness.

Two other prime animated details: the "death throes" of the spike at the end of the stegosaurus's tail, and the snaking back and forth of the tail of the snapping-turtle T Rex. Then there are a few shots, which the effects team might like to have back. The Kong head in close-up, for instance, tends to look like a big kid mugging for the camera. And when the crew passes the felled stegosaurus, it looks like just what it is—actors looking at an image on a screen.

Two informal, oval tree-and-bushes "frames" prove wildly successful at setting off, first, the stegosaurus, and, later, Kong and the tyrannosaurus. The frame-within-the-frame effect is curiously Currier and Ives charming, and reinforces the movie's fairy-tale-horror feel. Other design notes: Kong's lair features volcanic puffs of smoke, odd rock formations, all degrees of light and dark, but no apparent kitchen. And there's a fascinating, almost subliminal detail: the tiny, foreground flames, apparently flaring up from some unseen pool of lava, as Kong takes on Mr. Snake-Thing. (The lost lava-pool sequence!) (Settings: Carroll Clark, Al Herman. Art technicians: Mario Larrinaga, Byron L. Crabbe, largely responsible for the film's "inimitable visual style" [*The Making of King Kong*, p136].)

The breakneck pace of much of the latter half of the movie might make it seem as if Max Steiner's musical score is simply one crescendo after another. But there are crescendos and there are crescendos, and Steiner scores each Kong/dinosaur battle differently, gives each its own, appropriate flourishes. Steiner's main Kong theme—suggesting vulnerability, out-sized (so to speak) emotion, and the grim inevitability of an old proverb—gives *King Kong* some of its magnificence. The four-minute Overture—a mini-*King Kong* symphony—is a fine work in and of itself. Musical moments to cherish in the movie proper include a three-second "lament" for the fallen stegosaurus, skillfully sandwiched between the prevailing passages of "trek" music ... and the sweet, low-key music over the introductory shot of the harbor, which says it's pretty much a day like any other New York City day: Oh! There's the Empire State Building ...

Robert Armstrong is pretty nearly perfect here. He can seem excited and calm, at the same time—his Denham never lets his over-sized ambitions overwhelm him, though they may lay waste to the countryside. Armstrong lets you see how Denham makes everyone go along with him, if sometimes grudgingly. And Fay Wray's sweet sensuousness makes you see how everyone falls for her—"everyone" meaning mainly Kong and Jack. And her first, "test" scream, on the ship, isn't unnerving just for Jack—she sounds as if she's just seen four or five of the horsemen of the apocalypse. It's her screaming almost as much as O'Brien's animation which gives one the willies. Kong is a picnic compared to the half-formed hellish visions her voice initially raises here.

Notes: Peter Jackson's envisioning of the lost spider-pit sequence is true to the original *King Kong* in at least two ways: It's unrelenting horror, and the pit creatures are all shrill things. Chief nasties: a lanky crab monster, a roaring speed demon of a spider, and a big-mawed tentacled ugly. Lots of very unpleasant wriggling, writhing, and scampering. Especially revolting: The crab picks up one bloke off a small hill, and, at the same time, a lizard beauty grabs a second victim. Bonus: a styracosaurus up above the pit. Fun detail: We see the lizard thing from *King Kong* just beginning its climb up to Jack, from the pit bottom.

That same year the Halperins' *Supernatural* began with quotes from Confucius, Mohammed, and the New Testament.

File under Nastily Inventive Uses of a brontosaurus's long neck: Having it snake around a tree trunk in order to pluck off the Venture crew member dangling on the other side of the trunk.

File under Deceptively Lulling: The lovely first shot of the Venture setting out to sea, seemingly going nowhere, with harmless-looking clouds in the background.

At several points during the ceremony before the gate, the native dancers beat their chests with the ape arms they're sporting—someone is familiar with Kong's m.o.

Camp: The Man Who Grimaces look on Jack's face as he sees Kong for the first time, through the window in the gate.

For the good of the plot: Despite the natives' lively, expressed interest in the "golden woman," Denham fails to place a watch on Ann on board the Venture that night.

Kong and the bronto don't seem to be meat-eaters. They pick up victims with their teeth apparently just to silence them.

The big wall keeps Kong and ambulatory dinosaurs away from the village. But there had to have been periodic Pterodactyl Alerts.

More notes: Although the credits do not list a director, producers Merian C. Cooper and Ernest B. Schoedsack apparently co-directed (*The Making of King Kong*, p107). "Cooper ... produced and directed with Schoedsack"—*Variety* 3/7/33.

Thank, principally, Cooper for that "breakneck pace"—he ruthlessly cut the film from 14 reels to 11 (*The Making of King Kong*, pp181-182).

RKO. D, P: Merian C. Cooper, Ernest B. Schoedsack. SP: James Ashmore Creelman, Ruth Rose. Story: Cooper, Edgar Wallace. Ph: Eddie Linden, Vernon L. Walker. Mus: Max Steiner. PD: Carroll Clark. VisFX: (sup) Willis O'Brien; Marcel Delgado, Linwood G. Dunn, Orville Goldner et al. SdFX: Murray Spivack. SpFX: Harry Redmond, Jr., Harry Redmond, Sr. Ed: Ted Cheesman. Cost: Walter Plunkett. With Fay Wray, Robert Armstrong, Bruce Cabot, Frank Reicher, Sam Hardy, Victor Wong, Noble Johnson, Steve Clemente, James Flavin, Roscoe Ates, Reginald Barlow, Dick Curtis, Ruby Dandridge, Earl Dwire, Betty Gale, Ethan Laidlaw, Vera Lewis, Carlotta Monti, Paul Porcasi, Syd Saylor, Harry Strang, Madame Sul-Te-Wan, Harry Tenbrook, Blue Washington, Bill Williams; 100 minutes

Ref: "Highly imaginative and super-goofy ... A most tolerant audience at the Music Hall broke down now and then ... [laughing] in the wrong way ... but on the whole was exceedingly kind"—*Variety* 3/7/33.

She (1935): "Here burns the Flame of Life." In the "far, far north," the semi-immortal Queen of Kor, She (Helen Gahagan), believes explorer Leo (rhymes with "mayo") Vincey (Randolph Scott) is her love of 500 years ago, John Vincey, returned to her. And She has been lonely, shouldering as she has the "burden of immortality." ... Merian C. Cooper production is comparable in scope and ambition to his *King Kong*, but has little of the latter's excitement. Gahagan, like Scott, is at the mercy of overripe dialogue—lots of "endless

time" and "little mortal life." And Helen Mack, as Tanya, is no more convincing championing the Life and Love of the Average Man and Woman. The last half, at least, is decent camp, thanks to the hilarious Busby Berserkeley choreography, aided and abetted by one of Max Steiner's less compelling scores. An incidental highlight of the dancing: the madly grinning drummer. Benjamin Zemach rated on Oscar nomination as Best Dance Director, natch.

King Kong Appears in Edo (Japanese, 1938): Ref: IMDb. YouTube: extant few minutes of "suitmation."

One Million B.C. (1940): The first post-*Kong*-duo dinosaur feature in the U.S., apparently. Like *Son of Kong*, it's not a horror movie, but it does have monsters, including a tyrannosaurus, a "mighty mastodon," a small (rubber) triceratops, actual lizards made to look big, an armadillo with a horn or two, and a dimetrodon/lizard. "Strange figures and forms" on a cave wall tell the story of an "ancient people," specifically the Rock People and the Shell People. A guy (Victor Mature) from the former, a tribe of meanies, meets a gal (Carole Landis) from the latter, a tribe of nice-ies. The guy discovers singing, laughter, collective hunting-gathering, and finally sex. Co-themes: the power of kindness and the badness of meanness. Exasperating morality play owes more to Tarzan and Jane than to *King Kong*, though the various dinosaur roarings and rantings seem taken from *King Kong*. The script's humaneness does not seem to extend to lizards. The basically antiquated, ultra-dramatic score by Werner R.

Heymann occasionally lets up and becomes less overbearing and sweeter. The effects illustrate the dictum that there's nothing like obvious back projection to take you right out of a movie.

Tarzan's Desert Mystery (1943): The "mysterious things" in the "fever-medicine jungle" (an hour into the movie) include tussling "dinosaur" lizards from *One Million B.C.*, strange tentacled plants, and a giant cave-spider. Perhaps because Tarzan (Johnny Weissmuller) had already taken on Nazis (*Tarzan Triumphs* [1943]), it was decided to have him take on a giant spider, too, here. (Otto Kruger's "Hendrix" is really "Heinrich.") Cheetah has a big (generally comic) role in this one. Thank goodness—the human actors have precious little with which to work. Passably creepy: the cave littered with bones, and the spider in the shadows. When it emerges from the shadows it looks like a shiny low-slung motor vehicle with a lot of legs.

The White Gorilla (1945): "When the white gorilla and the black gorilla met, the jungle vibrated with their wild battle cries." "Odd coloring" makes the fearsome white gorilla an outcast among the other gorillas. The two main gorillas are called "monsters," but their lackluster duels hardly qualify them as such. And the "Cyclops" in the Cave of the Cyclops proves to be only an idol or two. Executive producer Louis Weiss' Silents Preservation Society (not an actual society) here uses much footage from the 1927 silent serial *Perils of the Jungle*, narrated in the Jerry Warren manner.

Unknown Island (1948): The "home of monsters" here is a 10-mile-square "taboo island rising out of the sea," in the South Pacific. The "horrible animals as big as houses" on same include a couple of rather stolid brontos, an aggressive "hairy monster" (a giant sloth), a "fin-backed lizard," or dimetrodon—a Funny Face with a toothy mouth and bulging eyes—and a "whole slew" of comically wobbly, horned tyrannosaurus-types. The climactic sloth-vs.-"tyrannosaurus" fight echoes, faintly, the bout between Kong and the tyrannosaurus, and features a little dino-gore. Even Cinecolor and much growling and snarling can't help these pathetic dinosaurs (and sloth). Richard Denning's John Fairbanks' abject reminiscent fear, at the beginning—just after the war, he was stranded on the island—promises much, but Howard Anderson and Ellis Burman's effects deliver zilch. Barton MacLane's lively gruff act, as Captain Tarnowski, provides the atmosphere. It's an entertaining cliché. ("I ain't leavin' here till I get one of those big babies alive!") Place name: the Port of All Nations Cafe. Steamer name: The Pelican, a "floatin' pigpen."

Jungle Jim (1948): "Devil doctors!" Yes, it's Tarzan (Johnny Weissmuller) vs. Superman (George Reeves), or rather Jungle Jim vs. the craven Bruce Edwards. This slapdash jungle thriller features a few minutes with a long river-monster with a dinosaur-like head and a tail like a tentacle. Jim easily removes the tail from the beautiful doctor's (Virginia Grey) leg, and that's that. The cute, lively little dog Skipper, which goes on the safari, gets more screen time than does the

monster. The "witch doctor cult," which practices human sacrifice, also gets short shrift.

Mighty Joe Young (1949): "I shoulda left you in Africa where you belonged." Entrepreneur Max O'Hara (Robert Armstrong) brings a "dangerous gorilla" from Africa to his Golden Safari night club, where Joe Young begins a smash act onstage with his young protector Jill (Terry Moore). Laughs-and-tears tale is pretty elementary, but Willis O'Brien's animation of Joe is fascinating. It's all determinedly innocuous, but in some ways O'Brien's new gorilla is a better "actor" than was his original, Kong, or his son. The face and body seem more effortlessly expressive. Joe's at once like nothing you've ever seen before and yet is perfectly plausible, at home, as Jill's "pet." Of the human actors, Ben Johnson comes off as most appealing. There was a remake.

Africa Screams (1949): In an apparent nod to *King Kong*, *Africa Screams* features one sequence with a "big ape," orangutang gargantua, as tall as a palm tree and with a "face almost human." It momentarily bleaches natives' faces white with fear, and makes Lou Costello's eyebrows dance. Abbott and Costello are onscreen a lot here, but better laughs are to be found in their other movies. Funnier than Abbott, Costello, Shemp Howard, or Joe Besser: a gorilla (Charles Gemora) with a fondness for Lou. Bud highlight: one of his most extended lamentations over the (not really) lost Lou. A bit with Lou imitating the gorilla's outstretched arms faintly recalls similar imitations in *Abbott and Costello Meet Frankenstein*, from the year before.

King Kong (1976): "Lights! Camera! Kong!" In the South Pacific, a "bank of fog that doesn't change a whit in 35 years" harbors a "gigantic, turned-on ape" and, incidentally, a giant snake. Kong here is personality-minus, except for the starry eyes. He doesn't so much walk as stroll. The climactic sequence—in which Dwan (Jessica Lange) tries to save Kong ("Don't put me down!")—would be more effective if he were generating a little more star power. This remake is the '33 *King Kong* filtered through the '46 *Beauty and the Beast*: Here, beauty comes to love the beast. And this "warmer" *King Kong* could have succeeded in its own way, but miscalculations abound. Instead of Carl Denham: the one-dimensional, villainous Wilson (Charles Grodin), whom Kong dispatches with one huge, well-planted foot. Cardboard karma. And Jeff Bridges' Jack Prescott ends up as just an audience-manipulation device—"Assholes!" he yells, helpfully, at the helicopter assassins of Kong. Sweet and lovely: Kong letting Dwan take a shower by holding her in his hand under the waterfall. Pauline Kael: "This film can stand in one's affections right next to the original version." Well, maybe right next to *The Son of Kong* ...

TERROR ABOARD

Terror Aboard released April 14, 1933: "This is some kind of a devil ship." Indeed: The Dulcina, a yacht, sets sail on Friday the 13th ... the ship's cat is black ... seagulls are seen flying upside down above the ship, and, more importantly, mad Maximilian Kreig (John Halliday)—under indictment by a grand jury for forgery and grand larceny—is systematically killing everyone on board, crew and guests alike. ("This woman was frozen to death.") When a party from the ship City of Hope boards the yacht, the latter at first seems abandoned, "running wild." ("The boat is haunted!")

The contrast between Kreig's cold-blooded murders and his dapper self is an extra turn of the horror screw. But Kreig doesn't really come off as the master manipulator he's supposed to be. We are meant to think, Fiendish! But we're more likely to be thinking, Mechanical, as the manipulated are usually pretty easily led to the slaughter. And, despite lines like: "There's something loose aboard this ship, something that ain't human nor natural!"... there's scant spookiness or mystery since we know who's doing it.

As the steward, Charlie Ruggles proves no funnier than he did in *Murders in the Zoo*, the same year. His closest-to-funny line: "I'm going in the next batch." Bobby Dunn has a couple of amusing bits as a cross-eyed sailor.

Notes: The abandoned, fully set dinner table the boarding crew finds on the Dulcina recalls a similar scene in 1932's *The Thirteenth Guest*.

Smooth camerawork by Harry Fischbeck provides some atmosphere.

Fiendish detail: Kreig keeps a scorecard of his victims.

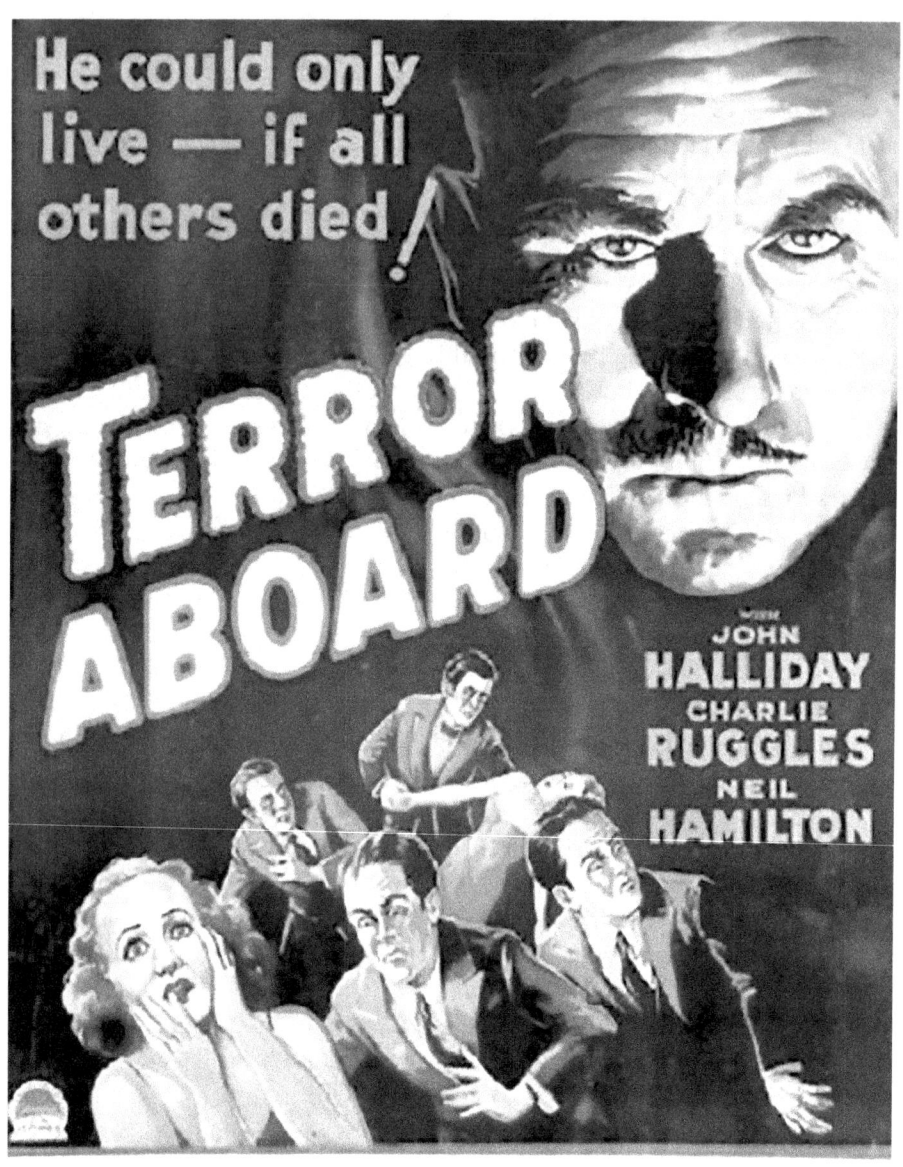

(*Dead Reckoning*—working title) Paramount. D: Paul Sloane. SP: Manuel Seff, Harvey Thew. Story: Robert Presnell, Sr. Ph: Harry Fischbeck. Mus: Herman Hand, John Leipold. AD: Wiard Ihnen. Ed: Eda Warren. Cost: Travis Banton. Sd: M.M. Paggi. P: William LeBaron. With John Halliday, Charles Ruggles, Shirley Grey, Neil Hamilton, Jack LaRue, Verree Teasdale, Stanley Fields, Leila Bennett, Morgan Wallace, Thomas E. Jackson, William Janney, Paul Hurst, Frank Hagney, Clarence Wilson, Paul Porcasi, Bobby Dunn, Eddie "Rochester" Anderson; 69 minutes

Ref: *Fangoria* 100:8.
Weldon 2.
IMDb.
Walt Lee.
Jim Shapiro.

NIGHT OF TERROR

Night of Terror released April 24, 1933: "The maniac has murdered again!" A slouch-hatted maniac (Edwin Maxwell) with the "distorted face of a madman" has killed 12 people, all of them "after sundown." Other ingredients: a fluid for the supposed "suspension of animation"—the "death sleep ..." Sika (Mary Frey), a medium given to trances ... and Degar (Bela Lugosi), her husband, who's given to discouraging her from going into trances.

The good news is sparse: the opening credits unfolding as if inside a crystal ball ... the happy camp introduction of Degar, glaring through an opening in a paneled door ... the foolish but somehow memorable coda, with the believed-dead maniac: "I am the maniac! If you dare tell anyone how this picture ends ... I'll climb into your bedroom window tonight and tear you limb from limb!"

The movie has a slapped-together feel, as if it were written up, shot, and edited very quickly. If there were any fun to be had here, the tired, insistent racist treatment of black chauffeur Martin (Oscar Smith) would have killed

it. Fondly noted, however: Lugosi's relish of words like "murder," and Joseph Valentine's occasional slick work with shadows.

(*He Lived To Kill*—working title; *Terror in the Night*—working title). Columbia. D: Ben Stoloff. SP: William Jacobs, Beatrice Van, from Willard Mack's story "The Public Be Damned." Ph: Joseph Valentine. Ed: Arthur Hilton. P: Bryan Foy. With Wallace Ford, Sally Blane, Bela Lugosi, Bryant Washburn, Tully Marshall, Gertrude Michael, George Meeker, Mary Frey, Matt McHugh, Edwin Maxwell, Otto Hoffman; 65 minutes

Ref: "Even the usually reliable Lugosi doesn't make this film worth seeing"—John Stell, "Hail Columbia?," *Monsters from the Vault*, Spring 1997:40.

"Comes too late in the cycle to be an outstander ... Entire cast works hard, but it's not much good"—*Variety* 6/27/33.

SUPERNATURAL

Supernatural released May 12, 1933: Art Deco horror in the penthouse. Three supernatural forces are at work in *Supernatural*. The spirit of Ruth Rogen (Vivienne Osborne)—the executed "notorious strangler," as the headlines put it—takes possession of the body of socialite Roma Courtney (Carole Lombard), in order to exact revenge on Paul Bavian (Alan Dinehart), the spiritualist who betrayed her. Meanwhile, the spirit of Roma's recently deceased twin brother John (Lyman Williams) tries to protect her from Bavian and Rogen. It's left unstated, but perhaps implied that John stays near Roma after his death, at least in part because they're twins, and close.

Finally, Bavian himself stages séances—complete with "spirits" and "independent writing"—which prove to be fake, although he seems to be onto something when his (fake) spirit of John accuses estate manager Hammond (William Farnum) of (real) murder. If there is supposed to be a point to this mixing of real and fake spiritualism—including real and fake spirits of John Courtney—Garnett Weston's script (with Harvey Thew and Brian Marlow) fails to locate it. This good spirit/bad spirit idea anticipates *The Uninvited*.

Here and there, there are good beginnings of excitement, such as Arthur Martinelli's track up to Dr. Houston's (H.B. Warner) penthouse lab, as lightning flashes and rain cascades. But the shrill, clumsy score does not help, although the shrieking choir over the opening credits promises something pretty feverish. It sounds like a supernatural catfight, or a chorus of the damned.

The actors are all one-note, except Lombard, who's two—Roma and the Ruth-possessed Roma. As the latter, Lombard flattens her voice and arches her eyebrows. Her best scene is as the pre-Ruth Roma, in John's room, which is haunted, literally, if tenderly, by John. The family dog King brings John his slippers—apparently, he too sees (as does the viewer) that the spirits here wear clothes ... This sequence also sports an eerie-sweet, plaintive musical theme. Lombard's gowns do great things for her bare back, and vice versa, and the

Carole Lombard looks sinister in *Supernatural* (1933)

imposing close-ups of her "Ruth Rogen" eyes do scary things which naturally recall the close-ups of Bela Lugosi's eyes in the Halperins' previous, superior movie, *White Zombie*.

Notes: I like the irrelevant descriptive real estate note in the newspaper story: "Ruth Rogen yesterday confessed she killed each of her three lovers after a riotous orgy in her sensuous Greenwich Village apartment."

Note that Ruth Rogen continues her campy evil cackling even after she leaves Roma's body.

Although she, too, is one-note, Beryl Mercer's (the landlady) death throes are pretty harrowing.

Paramount. D: Victor Halperin. Story, Adap: Garnett Weston. SP: also Harvey F. Thew, Brian Marlow. Ph: Arthur Martinelli. Mus: Karl Hajos et al. Cost: Travis Banton. P: Edward and Victor Halperin. (Art Direction uncredited). With Carole Lombard, Alan Dinehart, Vivienne Osborne, Randolph Scott, H.B. Warner, Beryl Mercer, William Farnum, Willard Robertson, George Burr Macannan, Eddy Chandler, Frank O'Connor; 65 minutes

Ref: "The Jekyll-Hyde transposition in the femme gender is ... forced to depend on ... fainting spells, smirks, she-devil facial expressions and double exposure"—*Variety* 4/25/33.

"Astonishingly unlikely storyline"—David J. Hogan, *Filmfax* 57:61.

"Great scale models were used for the Manhattan sky line, elevated trains and a yacht"—*PV* 41:17.

"Spiritual activity positively gallops throughout"—John Soister, in *Cinematic Hauntings*, p291.

STRANGE PEOPLE

Strange People released June 17, 1933: Or, Constant Thunder. "Do you realize that death may lurk around the nearest corner, ready to breathe its chilly breath into your heart?" Jurors who, "about a year ago," found a man guilty of murder find themselves, on a stormy evening, at the old dark house of the murdered man. "It couldn't be a coincidence that we all meet here tonight!"

Ghastly ingredients include a skulking, bug-eyed creep, a lights-out murder, almost comically constant, if rather half-hearted thunder, a "staring" corpse, a mysterious form rising (in long shot) from a loft in a barn, a coffin in said barn, a hushed scene in a darkened house—as the occupants wait for an intruder to enter—and a lot of screaming. Oddly, though, the most bloodcurdling scream proves to be coming from one of those big, old-fashioned radios. Near the end, it seems that almost everyone's running around the secret passageways and stairs.

Deceptive-appearances are fun in Jack Townley's script. (He also did the dismal *Mummy's Boys*, 1936, and *The Disembodied*, 1957.) The early stages of the story turn out to be simply a demonstration of the unreliability of circumstantial evidence. ("How do I know that you're a real policeman? I don't trust anybody in this place.") This is not as fun a find as an actual lost Universal horror picture would be, but—as the credits note—*Strange People* was "produced at Universal City," and M.A. Anderson seems to have had a grand time photographing the *Old Dark House* set from every possible angle and with every possible kind of shadow. (The stairs get a real workout.)

Surprisingly, it seems a kind of history was made at Chesterfield with *Strange People*, which is about the earliest known film to be shot in "real time." The action takes place between 8 p.m. and 9 p.m., and the running time is 61 minutes, including about a minute total for the beginning credits and "The End." At the beginning, a tower clock chimes 8 o'clock; 30 minutes in, it marks 8:30, and in the last shot, it chimes 9 o'clock. And rain seems to be pouring down every minute of that hour ... No jump-cutting here.

A very young Walter Brennan plays a radio repairman who stutters, an early-talkie cliché. Jack Pennick ("Just the plumber") appeared in over 30 John Ford films.

Note: Later "real time" films include *Rope* (1948), *High Noon* (1952), *Cleo from 5 to 7* (1962), and *Nick of Time* (1995).

A tip of the hat to Dave Sindelar.

Chesterfield. D: Richard Thorpe. SP: Jack Townley Ph: M.A. Anderson. AD: Edward C. Jewell. Ed: Vera Wood. P: George R. Batcheller. With John Darrow, Gloria Shea, Hale Hamilton, Wilfred Lucas, J. Frank Glendon, Michael Visaroff, Jack Pennick, Lew Kelly, Mary Foy, Frank LaRue, Stanley Blystone, Walter Brennan; 61 minutes

Ref: *AFI catalog*.

SECRET OF THE BLUE ROOM

Secret of the Blue Room released July 20, 1933: "This ghost seems to have human features." In Helldorf Castle, three people have died in a "room that's been locked for 20 years," and 1 a.m. seems to be the witching or ghosting hour ... One victim, a detective, died with a "look of agonized horror" on his face; "heart failure, caused by great fright."

This tantalizing "scared to death" mystery is never solved, but, in the present, one man (William Janney) disappears from the boo room, and one (Onslow Stevens) is killed there. ("Have we a ghost in our midst?") "Haunted house" thriller has a fine cast—Lionel Atwill, Paul Lukas, Edward Arnold, Gloria Stuart—and a smooth but unexciting script, by William (*Bride of Frankenstein*) Hurlbut. Chief problem: Everything happens at 1 a.m., in the "ghost room," but nothing much happens before or after, or anywhere else, although Charles Stumar's restless camera helps disguise that fact. Photographic highlight: the

huge shadow on the wall behind Stuart's terrified Irene von Helldorf. Another highlight: the "Someone is ringing from the [vacant] blue room" frisson.

An underplaying Atwill delivers the 20-years-ago exposition capably, and Lukas comes off best of all as the urbane Capt. Walter Brink. [SPOILER]: The killer proves to be both the "victim" whose body is not found, and the movie's worst actor. In a pleasing concluding shot, Paul, the butler (Robert Barrat), closes the castle doors on "us," the visitors.

Remakes: *The Missing Guest* and *Murder in the Blue Room*. *Secret of the Blue Room* itself is in fact a remake of the 1932 German film *Geheimnis des Blauen Zimmers*, starring Theodor Loos, Wolfgang Staudte, and Else Elster (as Irene von Hellberg). Directed by Erich Engels, written by Erich Philippi, and "made in Germany for Universal" (*Variety* 9/19/33). There was also a 1933 Czech version, *Zahada Modreho Pokoje*, in which "Helldorf" became "Hellford." Anyone for anagrams?

Universal. D: Kurt Neumann. SP: William Hurlbut. Ph: Charles Stumar. Mus: Heinz Letton. AD: Stanley Fleischer. Cost: Vera West. With Lionel Atwill, Gloria Stuart, Paul Lukas, Edward Arnold, Onslow Stevens, William Janney, Robert Barrat, Muriel Kirkland, Russell Hopton, Elizabeth Patterson; 66 minutes

Ref: www.deutscher_tonfilm.de.

IMDb.

doctor kiss, CHFB 8/9/2009 (Universal Horrors)

The FLAMING SIGNAL

The Flaming Signal released July 25, 1933: "It's awful—just think of raising a dead man!" Scrappy, isn't it? Impoverished production is more Rin Tin Tin than *The Mad Ghoul*—the first-listed cast member is Flash, a dog. The movie does, however, feature a full-fledged horror sequence, the revival of the dead high priest (Mischa Auer). Henry B. Walthall, as the father: "Did you hear the man say that the priest would come back to life?" Marceline Day, as the daughter: "I heard it—gave me the shivers!" The scene in which he sits up is actually a fairly decent shock moment.

The other relative highlight: the close-up of the ghastly-masked native who leads the bearers of the high priest's dead body. The back-from-the-dead native ritual looks like simple calisthenics, but the monotony of the drumming builds a little suspense. Noah Beery is just a raspy growl of a voice, but that's enough to cop acting honors here. Camp moments help—John Horsley's hero to Day: "But Sally, we're starting a new day, you and I and Flash!" Woof?

Imperial. D: George Jeske, Charles E. Roberts. SP: Roberts. Story: William G. Steuer. Ph: Irving Akers. Mus: Lee Zahler. Ed: Laurence Creutz. P: William Berke. With Flash [yes] the Dog, John David Horsley, Marceline Day, Noah Beery, Henry B. Walthall, Carmelita Geraghty, Mischa Auer; 64 minutes

Ref: *Forgotten Horrors*.

IMDb.

BEFORE DAWN

The Death Watch: "Well, miss, you can't get people to stay in a house that's supernatural." Edgar Wallace's short novel was the source for *Before Dawn*. Spooky ingredients include the death watch, a small beetle whose clicking supposedly portends death ... a "horrible-looking man" who seems to walk through a wall and who makes "hideous noises." ... a "woman in white" who seems to kill a dog just by lifting her hand ... and various "howlings and shriekings."

Scorecard: good creepy clues ... arbitrarily inserted romance ... serviceable mystery plot. The most interesting element is the death watch, a curious but real-life insect: "From somewhere near at hand the death watch was tapping rhythmically, noisily, ominously." In real life, however, its clicking—as it bores into wood—probably does not spell death, any more than a woodpecker's pecking would. At one point, one of the bad guys misleadingly suggests that the clicking is really the tapping of a murderer at his victim's door.

Before Dawn released Aug. 4, 1933: "He touched me with his hand ... his dead hand." The same year, some of the *King Kong* team at RKO also made this horror drama—Merian C. Cooper (executive producer here), Edgar Wallace (his short novel was the source), Max Steiner (musical director), Carroll Clark and Van Nest Polglase (art department), and actor Frank Reicher (as Joe Valerie). And *Before Dawn* has promising ingredients, as well as personnel: the floating death-mask of thug Joe Valerie ("It's him—back from the dead!"), the psychic Mlle. Mystera ("I'm really clairvoyant"), or Patricia (Dorothy Wilson); and Warner Oland's avaricious Dr. Cornelius.

But the development of the plot is lackadaisical, and there's much (dull) ado about a missing million in gold. Oland seems uncertain whether he's playing a villain or just a colorful character. And Dorothy Wilson is more effective with face than voice at capturing her genuine psychic's defensiveness, defiance, and discouragement, although her *Curse of the Demon*-like trance-talking seems to inspire her, and you feel her enthrallment. ("I can't open my eyes!") She assists the police with her powers, an idea anticipating *Fear* (1990).

Director Irving Pichel and lenser Lucien Andriot's one genuine coup: the glowing death mask [SPOILER] which floats down the otherwise-completely-dark hall, toward Jane Darwell's helpless Mrs. Marble, who falls downstairs, breaks her neck, and dies. ("Something in the dark, at the top of those stairs ... a horrible face.") It is not explained how the mask is lit, nor how the hall is rendered completely dark, by the perpetrator, but it's the end, not the means which counts here. In a worthy sequel to this scene, the mask returns to scare the housekeeper, Mattie (Gertrude Hoffman), as the camera moves into a close-up of what seems to be a still, or freeze frame, of her open, screaming mouth.

Note: The movie uses very, very little from the book: the heroine's first name, Patricia ... the name Chesterford, in the book a house in England, in the movie a town in the U.S ... the hidden-loot plot element ... and the general idea of fake supernatural phenomena. But book and movie sport different phenomena. In 1933, author Wallace was aced out in both this picture and *King Kong* ...

RKO. D: Irving Pichel. SP: Garrett Fort; (uncredited) Ralph Block, Marion Dix, from Edgar Wallace's novel *Death Watch*. Ph: Lucien Andriot. AD: Carroll Clark, Van Nest Polglase. Ed: William Hamilton. Sd: Philip Faulkner, Jr. With Warner Oland, Stuart Erwin, Dorothy Wilson, Dudley Digges, Gertrude Hoffman, Oscar Apfel, Frank Reicher, Jane Darwell, Stanley Blystone, Ed Brady, Pat O'Malley; 60 minutes

Ref: *Variety* 10/24/33. IMDb.

"Pretty predictable ... minor, fun, but merely okay"—Dave Sindelar (11/4/2003).

The INVISIBLE MAN

The Invisible Man released Nov. 13, 1933: "The whole world's my hiding place!" For those familiar with the stirring James Whale/R.C. Sherriff movie, H.G. Wells' novel *The Invisible Man* reads, surprisingly, like *The Invisible Man*

Pressbook herald from *The Invisible Man* (1933)

Claude Rains is more than merely a frenzied voice in *The Invisible Man* (1933)

on a Leash. Carefree he's not. Invisibility seems almost wasted on him. The book is nothing if not responsible, cautious: The sober Wells is concerned less with the too-exciting possibilities of invisibility than with the science of it, and the drawbacks of it, for his morally stunted, invisible protagonist. ("He is pure selfishness.") Somewhat daringly, by contrast, the filmmakers allow you to feel that mad Jack Griffin(Claude Rains) just might—with invisibility and ingenuity—become Emperor of England, of Europe. Verging on reckless, they let you live the fantasy, for a while …

Film or book, it's basically the same story. Yet, where the movie's Griffin seems so powerful, in the book, he seems oddly helpless, more prone to delusions of persecution than to delusions of grandeur. ("I had not reckoned that, transparent or not, I was still amenable to the weather and all its consequences.") The movie's Griffin seems omnipresent, and in effect, he is. Kemp (William Harrigan), Mr. Nervous: "He may be here now, beside us, or in the garden, looking through the window, or in a corner of my bedroom, waiting for me, waiting to kill me!"

In the film, Griffin is so maddened by a side effect of chemical invisibility that even his moving speech regarding his motivations—which begins with unexpected tenderness ("For you, Flora")—ends in drug-induced delusions of grandeur. ("The nation that wins my secret can sweep the world with invisible armies!") Rains' inexorably rising excitement—reflected in his voice and in the gloved hand with which he alternately cradles his bursting head and distractedly pushes at his knee—makes the speech Griffin's life in miniature. The power of invisibility is too great for him to control; it controls him. Frank J. Dello Stritto rightly calls this "one of the truly great scenes of the horror genre" (*Cult Movies* 17:29).

But if the movie is somewhat more ambitious than the book, it's also more flawed. The "Flora, dear" scenes apparently did not much engage Whale, nor anyone else, and unhappily recall the Henry/Elizabeth/Victor triangle from *Frankenstein*. Dr. Cranley (Henry Travers) and his daughter Flora (Gloria Stuart)—two characters not in the book—contribute mostly-disposable human-interest "improvements" on the Wells novel. Drama here must be made with Rains' expressive voice and hands, whether gloved or bandaged, since it's certainly not to be found in Stuart's conventional hand-wringing.

The movie's special off-angle appeal lies partly in the fact that hero and villain are one, though the "poor struggling chemist" hero is basically past tense. Griffin is both doctor and "monster," which simplifies things, or over-simplifies them. Although no less involving than *Frankenstein* or *Bride of Frankenstein*, *The Invisible Man* lacks a certain philosophical dimension, or reduces same to an afterthought. Griffin's distraught lament: "God knows, there's a way back!" is heartfelt (thanks to Rains) but lost in macabre fun. If Griffin's murder of a "stupid little policeman" is unambiguously contemptible, the viewer is encouraged to root for his methodical revenge on the "dirty little coward" Kemp, who, by comparison, makes Griffin look, if not exactly good, at least not craven.

John P. Fulton's effects satisfy and sometimes even startle—and prove a match for H.G. Wells' nimble, elegant descriptive phrases. Prime example of

Who would think that gauze and goggles would be so unsettling? Jack (Claude Rains) slowly goes insane.

Universal's magician at work: the holes where the eyes should be, as Griffin unwraps the bandages from his face. ("Look! He's all eaten away!") And the maniacally-dancing shirt is an inspired invention, only just suggested by the "convulsed ... garment" in the book.

   Notes: Look closely for fine actor Dwight Frye. He's an incidental reporter here, necessarily his least memorable role in a Whale horror picture.

   Listen closely for the grudging admiration of the bobby whose plan (wet paint on the top of the wall) for catching the invisible man is rejected in favor of his sergeant's (dirt): "Oh, I see. Pretty good." Lovely throwaway.

   Identify closely with the invisible Griffin when he enters a bank, then leaves with a drawer-full of "Money! Money! Money! Money!"

   The novel has its wry moments, too, like Colonel Adye's response to Kemp's suggestion to scatter "powdered glass ... on the roads": "It's unsportsmanlike." Would that Sherriff had found a way to incorporate Wells' epilogue regarding the inn's landlord into the movie, the landlord who has hidden Griffin's written-in-code working notebooks: "Once I get the haul of them—Lord! I wouldn't do what *he* did; I'd just—well!"

Universal. D: James Whale. SP: R.C. Sherriff, from H.G. Wells' novel. Ph: Arthur Edeson. Mus: Heinz Roemheld. AD: Charles D. Hall. Ed: Ted Kent. Mkp: Jack Pierce. SpFX: John P. Fulton. MinPh: John J. Mescall. SdSup: Gilbert Kurland. P: Carl Laemmle, Jr. With Claude Rains, William Harrigan, Una O'Connor, Gloria Stuart, Henry Travers, Forrester Harvey, Holmes Herbert, E.E. Clive, Dudley Digges, Harry Stubbs, Donald Stuart, Merle Tottenham, Ted Billings, Walter Brennan, John Carradine, D'Arcy Corrigan, Dwight Frye, Mary Gordon, Violet Kemble Cooper, Crauford Kent, John Merivale, Monte Montague, Jameson Thomas; 71 minutes

Ref: "Universal, which has shown a liking for screamers, and had the nerve to put the first one over, is delivering something here which will more than satisfy audiences"—*Variety* 11/21/33.

Filmfax 37:24,26: Wesley G. Holt review of the laserdisc version.

"Solid story ... an improvement on Wells' original ... sheer joy, mixing mirth and menace"—Tom Weaver, *100 Years of Science Fiction*, p5.

BEFORE MIDNIGHT

Before Midnight released Nov. 18, 1933: "Fresh blood!" Forest Lake, a "little town about 50 miles from New York [City]." Inspector Trent (Ralph Bellamy)—"one of the best detectives in the country"—solves the Arnold case, which is told in flashback ... Wealthy Edward Arnold lives in the shadow of a family curse ("the fear haunted me") involving the mysterious appearance of blood below a portrait, and an old grandfather clock (the "death clock"), which legend has it stops one minute before the murder of the head of the household. When wind from a terrific thunderstorm blows open a window, the clock indeed stops, and Arnold falls down, dead.

The attending physician (played by Arthur Pierson) declares, "Death was caused by fright—it's the superstition.

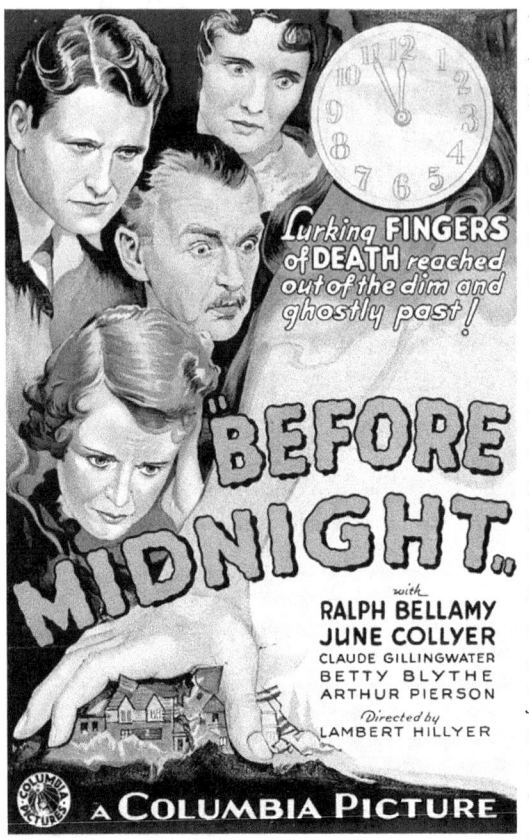

When the clock stopped, he was seized with fear, and, having a weak heart, it killed him." [SPOILER]: Trent, however, discovers that the means of death was a dose of cyanide. ("I don't believe in ghosts.") It transpires that one man used the "curse" to kill another …

John Stumar's (*The Return of the Vampire*) photography carries the atmospheric scenes—most of which occur in the first 15 minutes—and makes good the line: "Why, at night, this house seems to become alive!" In the most ambitious pictorial touch, the poisoned man's head obscures the face of the clock, just before he collapses. Momentarily, his face "becomes" the clock's face. Three points. The second-most-ambitious visual effect: the half-darkened, half-glistening Buddha incense burner, which also seems to "become alive." The exterior flora seems to have been chosen for its photogeneity. John's brother Charles shot the 1932 *The Mummy*, *Secret of the Blue Room*, *WereWolf of London*, and *The Raven* (1935).

Unfortunately, Lambert Hillyer's (*The Invisible Ray*, *Dracula's Daughter*) direction is stilted. The actors have so little with which to work that they're self-conscious, almost comically so at times, and that leaves a lot of dead air. Bellamy survived this movie to take on a similar role in *The Wolf Man* and a memorable comic-butt role in Howard Hawks' *His Girl Friday*. Betty Blythe had the title role in the 1925 *She*, but here she's just another lost acting soul. In less than six seconds, the uncredited Fred Toones (aka "Snowflake") is reduced to the usual quivering stereotype—a record, perhaps.

I omit the name of the actor who plays Arnold, above, because "Arnold" is not who he seems, at first, to be. Robert Quigley's flat script even includes an "I'll tell! I'll tell!" scene, in which a knife in the back silences the prospective teller. The most amusing cliché: the peals of thunder that punctuate dramatic statements. The mystery's rather-too-clever solution is still the only saving grace of the plot.

Columbia. D: Lambert Hillyer. SP: Robert Quigley. Ph: John Stumar. Ed: Otto Meyer. Sd: George Cooper. With Ralph Bellamy, June Collyer, Claude Gillingwater, Bradley Page, Betty Blythe, Arthur Pierson, George Cooper, Joseph Crehan, Kit Guard, Bob Kortman, Fred "Snowflake" Toones; 63 minutes

Ref: *AFI catalog*. Tim Murphy.

"Too much of the solution is given over to verbiage"—*Variety* 1/16/34. *New York Times* 1/10/34.

"The horror element is fairly prominent here in the first twenty minutes"— Dave Sindelar (1/12/2004).

The SON OF KONG

The Son of Kong released Dec. 22, 1933: "I wish I'd left him on his island." Don't think of *King Kong* and you won't get too upset. Just think of this as a kiddie movie from 1933, or as the missing Baby Kong and Helen Mack scenes from *King Kong*. *The Son of Kong* begins about a month after the original ends. The "man who gave [Denham] the map of Kong's island"—Helstrom (John Marston)—sets Denham (Robert Armstrong), Englehorn (Frank Reicher), and Charlie (Victor Wong) off on a treasure hunt to Kong's island, where they find a big, but manageable, anthropomorphized ape ("Well, if it isn't a little Kong!"), about 15 feet tall, as well as other beasts, including a styracosaurus, a relatively small bronto/dragon, a sea monster/bronto, and a huge bear. And, again, the beasties all have their distinctive roars.

About all that's to be said of the first 40 pre-beast minutes is that it's good to see Denham, Englehorn, and Charlie again, and it's pleasant to hear Mack's Hilda (or Helene—it's unclear) gamely singing the charmingly corny "Runaway Blues." Armstrong, however, gets reeled into the prevailing cuteness with Baby and Hilda/Helene. It's the crusty Reicher who gives perhaps the best performance this time around.

Willis O'Brien and Max Steiner do the best they can with the material they're handed. O'Brien probably wished he could have handed some of it back, including some low comedy with the son's eyeballs. At least, the Denham/Hilda relationship produces some sweetly idyllic Steiner, and the music for the discovery of the "treasure of the island" is kinda fun. Touching: The last we see of Baby is his bandaged hand. Startling: the sea monster's head and neck rearing up from underwater

RKO. D,P: Ernest B. Schoedsack. SP: Ruth Rose. Ph: Edward Linden, J.O. Taylor, Vernon L. Walker. Mus: Max Steiner. Settings: Al Herman, Van Nest Polglase. SpFX: Willis O'Brien, Harry Redmond, Jr., Harry Redmond, Sr. Ed: Ted Cheesman. Exec P: Merian C. Cooper. With Robert Armstrong, Helen Mack, Frank Reicher, Victor Wong, John Marston, Ed Brady, Steve Clemente, Noble Johnson, Lee Kohlmar, Frank O'Connor, Harry Tenbrook, Clarence Wilson; Fay Wray (voice, archive footage); 70 minutes

Ref: "O'Brien is said to have been unhappy with the "tongue-in-cheek" approach to *The Son of Kong* and was reluctant to discuss it in later years"—*The Making of King Kong*, p204.

"*The Son of Kong* is charming juvenile entertainment, with the most heartbreaking ending of any horror film"—Frank J. Dello Stritto, *Cult Movies* 19:28.

"The guiltiest of guilty pleasures"—Michael Brunas, *Midnight Marquee* 50:5-11.

Highlights of 1934

The ranks kept thinning in 1934—just one major horror film, *The Black Cat*, but one both unique and historically important. (*Black Moon* might be characterized as semi-major.) Unique, thanks to off-kilter performances by Karloff and Lugosi and way-off-kilter art direction by Charles D. Hall and direction by Edgar Ulmer. Historical, because *The Black Cat* marked the first and perhaps finest teaming of Karloff and Lugosi, though cases could be made for *Son of Frankenstein* and *The Body Snatcher*, respectively.

The second-most-interesting horror pic of the year: *The Ninth Guest*, featuring sleek, uncharacteristic (for a horror movie) art direction and a plot that foreshadowed both *The Man They Could Not Hang* (1939) and *And Then There Were None* (1945).

Third-most-interesting 1934 horror movie and second-most-interesting '34 adaptation of *The Black Cat*—the scurvy little alternate take on the Poe story, *Maniac*, an inimitable mating of camp and gore.

1934 was the year for voodoo movies without zombies—*Black Moon*, *Chloe, Louisiana*. And they were sorely missed, as was entertainment.

Notable performances: John Halliday, Sir Guy Standing, Richard Carle, William Frawley (*The Witching Hour*), Karloff, Lugosi, David Manners (*The Black Cat*), Louis Calhern, David Landau (*The Man with Two Faces*), Elspeth Dudgeon (*The Moonstone*), Ted Edwards (*Maniac*), Fay Wray (*Black Moon*)

Notable photography: Mack Stengler (*Chloe*), Benjamin Kline (*The Ninth Guest*), John Mescall (*The Black Cat*), Robert Planck (*The Moonstone*), M.A. Anderson (*The Ghost Walks*), Joseph August (*Black Moon*)

Notable direction: Edgar Ulmer (*The Black Cat*), Roy William Neill (*The Ninth Guest*)

Notable writing: Peter Ruric, Ulmer (*The Black Cat*), Garnett Weston (*The Ninth Guest*)

Notable art direction: Charles D. Hall (*The Black Cat*), uncredited (*The Ninth Guest*)

Notable costumes: Vera West, Ed Ware, Ulmer (*The Black Cat*)

Notable sound: John Stransky, Jr. (*House of Mystery*, *The Moonstone*)

Other films of interest:

Babes in Toyland—aka *March of the Wooden Soldiers*. Ref: *Variety* 12/18/34: "Ape-like nondescripts" of Bogeyland ... "packed with laughs and thrills." *HSF1*: "pretty good fun"

The Beast of Borneo—"You mean vivisection?"/"Not exactly." The orangutang here is a big strong guy, but not really a "monster." Charmless human actors and too much "Why, Boris!" *AFI catalog*: *Panbur*—original title

Big Calibre—the "crazy chemist" villain ("He gives me the creeps"), at one point, resorts to what looks like one of Jerry Lewis' disguises. Lethargic, isn't it?

At another point, an over-eager horse almost tears off without his horseman. Okay stunts by men and horses, and a cool variety of "wipes"

Death Takes a Holiday—Ref: Orpheus 3:45. *Variety* 2/27/34. *HSF2*: Death (Fredric March) makes bad double entendres, but rates ace cloak effects

Double Door—woman locked in soundproof room. "The Female Frankenstein of Fifth Avenue"—ad. *HSF1, 2*: heavy-handed, with okay Grand Guignol riffs. *PV* 29:13

Fog—Tom Weaver, CHFB, "Golden Age Horror" 12/12/12: *HR* review 1/8/34: "cross examination includes ... murdered man's ghost"

Gift of Gab — Karloff ("The Phantom") and Lugosi in unremarkable skit. Ref: Jim Shapiro. *Variety* 10/2/34. IMDb

Jane Eyre—Monogram's Cliff Notes edition of the novel. A thunderstorm and screaming from the "mysterious side of the house" make this Gothic, but not horrific. Virginia Bruce does well as Jane

Love Birds—FD 5/4/34: "ghost scene." *Variety* 5/29/34. *HSF1*

The Love Captive—*Variety* 6/19/34: Universal combines Svengali and the "perfect crime." *HSF1*

The Man Who Reclaimed His Head—IMDb: released 12/29/34. *Variety* 1/15/35: "This isn't a horror picture." Flimsy drama with packaged thematic points, though Claude Rains is good. Lionel Atwill's war "hawk" verges on the comic.

Menace—*Variety* 11/27/34: "phantom murderer." CHFB: Rick: "Not even borderline"; Tom Weaver: compare *13 Women*

Murder in the Museum—One horror moment: the eyes of a mummy in a case seem to be luminously alive. (They actually belong to a cowled, caped skulker.) Mostly local politics and a murder mystery. *Forgotten Horrors*: "diabolical invention." *FD* 6/27/34: "freak museum"

Murder in the Private Car—"strange sounds and voices"; plus a gorilla and tired comedy from Charlie Ruggles

Mystery Liner—radio-tube invention, in routine mystery. *Variety* 4/10/34: demented sea captain

The Mystery of Mr. X—cane-sword killing of British cops. More suspense than horror. Ref: Dave Sindelar

Return of the Terror—rare. *Photoplay* 9/34: "chilling mystery" set in a sanitarium. Super-X-ray machine. *Harrison's* 6/30/34: "eerie" ... Dr. Redmayne "returns to the sanitarium on a stormy night and a series of murders follow [sic]." *AFI catalog*: "print viewed ... [Detective] Bradley then finds Redmayne, perfectly sane, hiding in his x-ray apparatus, where he appears as only a skeleton"

Secret of the Chateau—"I don't know whether I'm the heir, or getting it." Scarecard: one spooky sequence ("Must be a ghost"), an occasional atmospheric shot, and some fair wordplay, in a humdrum mystery

Smoking Guns—*Variety* 8/14/34. CHFB: Mysto: "B-movie Gothic Western"

The Star Packer—"Strange things happen here at night." A face at a window elicits a scream, but there's really no spookiness here. The fistfights are ineptly staged, the music doesn't always fit the action, and the camera doesn't take much advantage of all the galloping, in this John Wayne "B" Western.

Their Big Moment—"Ghosts are bad to monkey with." An "adventure on the astral plane" regarding a doctor of "psychical research" and apparently real spiritualism. ("Someone who was dead spoke to me?") Flat-footed storytelling. Ref: *Photoplay* 10/34. FDY

The Unknown Soldier Speaks—*Variety* 5/29/34: "A voice represented as the spirit [of the U.S.] begins reciting"

A Very Honorable Guy—Brain specialist proves to be escaped lunatic. Incredible story, flat dialogue

1934

The NINTH GUEST

The Ninth Guest released Jan. 31, 1934: "You're about to meet my guest of honor—the ninth guest. His name is Death." Though this is hardly an old-dark-house thriller—it is, rather, a new brightly-lit-penthouse mystery—it has

one thing in common with thunderstorm mysteries: the terror of The Unseen. An unknown person with a "spooky voice" invites eight people to the "most original party ever slated," in a modernistic penthouse. ("Nothing has ever been used.") On "Station WITS"—on an electrified console radio in the living room—the host announces, "Before the clock strikes eleven, one of you will be dead—the one who least deserves to live," and he proceeds to kill the guests, one by one. He's just a voice, but he seems to have both omniscience and prescience. Radio as Mr. Evil.

The most horrific death: a crackling suicide-by-electrocution on an electrified gate. The most unsettling image: the row of coffins below the veranda ("One for each of us.") This film's uncredited remake, *The Man They Could Not Hang*, had one distinct advantage over the original: The avenging host was not one of the guests, and thus no arduous explanations as to how the host was surreptitiously pulling the strings were necessary. Yet this forerunner, also, of the rather milder *And Then There Were None*, is an interesting film in its own right, with superior photography by Benjamin Kline. Note, for instance, how the camera tracks up to and through the gate to catch the looks on the faces of the two survivors, as the madman/host approaches said gate.

Director Roy William Neill and Kline also fashion an oddly elegant "invisible man"-like sequence, in which the unseen opens doors and slips an envelope onto a night stand. The film seems prescient in its introductory Anatomy of a Telegram sequence, in which the invitational telegram is tracked through slots, slats, and tubes, from the Postal Telegraph office to the homes of the prospective guests, which sequence anticipates similar asides/inserts in *You're a Big Boy Now* (1966) and *Stolen Kisses* (1969).

Perhaps not surprisingly, in the mystery novel upon which the film is based—*The Invisible Host* by Gwen Bristow and Bruce Manning—the telegram sequence is just a part of a sentence: "Eight yellow envelopes were briskly on their way toward their eight destinations." Screenwriter Garnett Weston *(White Zombie)* took the cue and ... As a whole, in fact, the movie is an improvement on the book. In the latter, the "ghostly voice" becomes less intimidating the more it speaks, and it speaks a lot. It becomes a vehicle for exposition, finally just a rather tiresome character. The authors do, however, explain the origin of the unidentifiable voice—as the killer instructs, just hold a glass tumbler "so that one side of the rim is pressed to the corner of [your] lips and the other side [is] raised an inch or so ... " The book also relies on an old-fashioned Gothic thunderstorm.

(*The 9th Guest*—ad title) Columbia. D: Roy William Neill. SP: Garnett Weston, from the novel *The Invisible Host* by Bruce Manning and Gwen Bristow and the play of the same name by Owen Davis. Ph: Benjamin Kline. AD: uncredited. Ed: Gene Milford. Sd: George Cooper. With Donald Cook, Genevieve Tobin, Hardie Albright, Edward Ellis, Edwin Maxwell, Vince Barnett, Helen Flint, Samuel S. Hinds, Sidney Bracey; 65 minutes

Ref: IMDb.

"All the necessary elements of the shivery-spine school of fiction"—*Variety* 3/6/34.

HOUSE OF MYSTERY

House of Mystery March 30, 1934: "Hindus! Tom-toms! Apes! Haunted houses!" That exclamatory summing-up tells you pretty much all you need to know about this lackluster thunderstorm mystery, in which the "curse of Kali" seems to follow archaeologist John Prendergast (Clay Clement) for 20 years, from 1913 India to the U.S. In his old house, "great hairy hands" of apparent "ghost apes" break the neck of a Mrs. Carfax (Dale Fuller) ... a medium (Fritzi Ridgeway) invokes the spirit of Pocahontas (one of the first Indian spirit guides on film) ... and a Hindu high priestess ("That woman gives me the creeps!"), Chanda (Laya Joy), is the instrument of Kali's revenge. ("The house is bewitched!")

The emphasis is as much on comedy as horror here. In fact, there are attempts at humor with at least six different characters. The insurance agent hero's (Ed Lowry) spiels are almost immediately annoying, and the bickering husband and wife (Harry C. Bradley and Mary Foy, respectively) just take up running time. The closest-to-risible touch: the joined-at-the-hip movements of the three cops (Irving Bacon, Eddy Chandler, and George Cleveland). Accidental or not, amusement is provided, at one point, by the synched screaming of the three female characters who fall into the arms of three male characters at the sound of tom-toms.

The budget of next-to-nothing yields an occasional little something. The booming tom-toms are a novel element, akin to thunder, but maybe even a little creepier because it's not just noise—there's a human agent behind them. And the supposedly stuffed ape in the living room suddenly coming to life is a pretty good startler.

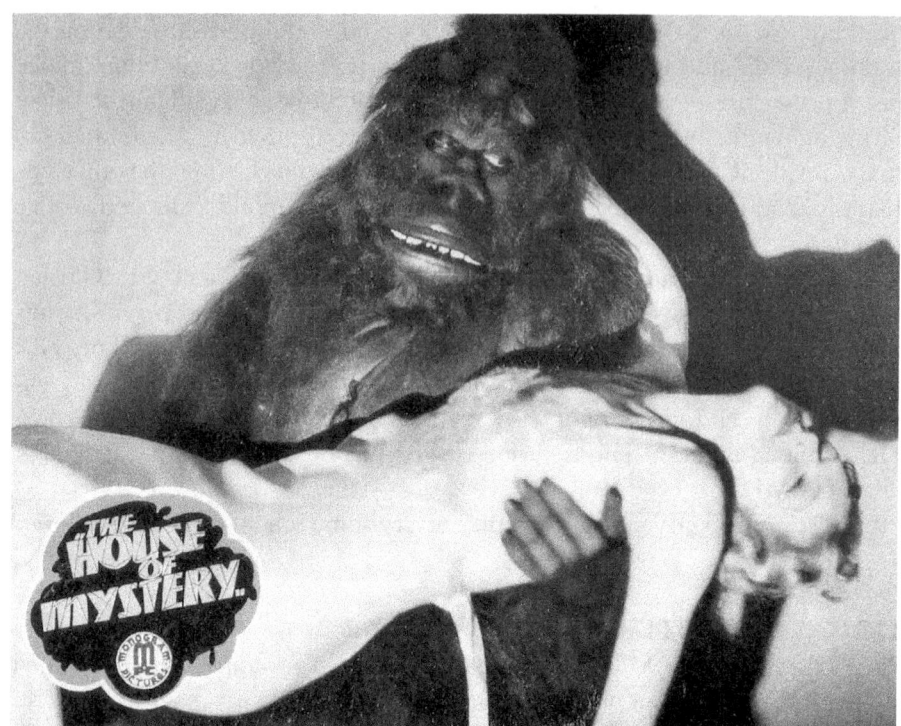

The man in the ape suit once again gets to carry off the girl, in a lobby card from *The House of Mystery*.

Note: Not to confuse matters, but the story seems to include a real live ape, a stuffed, dead ape, and a man in an ape suit ... but no "ape ghosts."

[SPOILER]: Not to give too much away, but there's the expected twist with the crippled Prendergast.

(*The Ape*—working title; *Curse of Kali*—working title). Monogram/Paul Malvern Productions. D: William Nigh. SP: Albert DeMond, from the play *The Ape* by Adam Hull Shirk. Ph: Archie Stout. Tech D: E.R. Hickson. Ed: Carl Pierson. Sd: John Stransky, Jr. Cost: Claire Julianne. With Ed Lowry, Verna Hillie, John Sheehan, Brandon Hurst, Joyzelle Joyner, Fritzi Ridgeway, Clay Clement, George "Gabby" Hayes, Irving Bacon, Mary Foy, Dick Botiller, Eddy Chandler, George Cleveland; 62 minutes

Ref: *TVG*. doctor kiss, CHFB (Golden Age Horrors 9/23/11).

"Nutty comedy mystery"—*PV* 30:10.

L.A. Times 12/27: Marquis Busby review of new Shirk play, *The Ape*, which work seems much closer to *House of Mystery* than to *The Ape* (1940). Ingredients include an "Indian temple in Benares," the curse of a high priest, and an L.A. mansion. "Good entertainment."

"These 'old dark house' mysteries ... can get quite addictive"—Dave Sindelar (11/1/2001).

CHLOE: LOVE IS CALLING YOU

Chloe: Love Is Calling You released April 1, 1934: "Somebody's puttin' the voodoo on you." Mandy, an "old voodoo Negress" (Georgette Harvey), says, "I'm gonna work my voodoo." But does her voodoo doll actually work? A hex on the Colonel (Frank Joyner) seems to amount to nothing. This is voodoo without zombies, or anything supernatural, just an occasional fun line about "boys … voodooin' down in the swamp." Voodoo here is not unfairly summed up as a "mixture of savagery, gin, mumbo jumbo, and drums." For horror fans, then, *Chloe* is a disappointment—the only horrific sequence comes at the end. [SPOILER]: And it's pretty impressive, all fire and smoke, as the swaying revelers dance around a huge bonfire, and the firelight flickers almost hypnotically, in the night. But the ceremony seems indebted as much to Broadway as to Haiti and *Haxan*, and it concludes, predictably, when the bound Chloe (Olive Borden) is saved from sacrifice, in the nick of … ("They've been known to sacrifice enemies and cut out their hearts.")

It may come as no surprise, then, that the film's main cross reference is not *White Zombie*, but *Imitation of Life* (also 1934). What *Variety* said (11/27/34) about the latter could have been said about *Chloe*: "The tragedy of [a] girl born to a white skin and Negro blood. This subject has never been treated upon the

Chloe (Olive Borden) looks ravishing in the title role.

screen before. Girl is miserable being unable to adjust herself to the lot of her race and unable to take her place among the whites." Ultimately, though, *Chloe* cheats, but for most of its length it too is about miscegenation.

Why Chloe is so miserable is not spelled out. Going simply on what we see: Black means a shack; white means a mansion. No wonder Chloe likes to be thought white. Strip away her color-consciousness, and she's just ambitious. What complicates matters, morally, is that the film treats her ambition as admirable. There's no ambiguity—only gain, no sense of loss, in the happy happy, all-white ending.

As drama, *Chloe* is thin, rudimentary. It's rooted, almost comically, in the grand passions. Hate is calling, too. And Fear. Nothing in between. And Olive Borden—co-star of John Ford's 1926 silent *3 Bad Men*—acts by dramatic fits and starts. However—unlike most 1930s "B" and "C" horrors—*Chloe* was shot on location, and that location is occasionally breathtaking. Mack Stengler's long shot (for instance) of Chloe in frilly white, on a wooden bridge, above the water, is genuinely lyrical. Also noteworthy, on a smaller scale: the close shot of Chloe tapping her foot as she embraces her beloved (Reed Howes). The at-first-catchy title music gets to be an unwelcome guest. Charmingly, the "o"s in "Love" and "You," in the subtitle, are hearts.

Pinnacle. D, SP: Marshall Neilan. Ph: Mack Stengler. Mus: George Henninger. AD: Robert Stevens. Ed: Joseph Josephson, Helene Turner. P: J.D. Trop. With Olive Borden, Reed Howes, Mollie O'Day, Philip Ober, Georgette Harvey, Francis Joyner, Augustus Smith, the Shreveport Home Wreckers, Ruth Ford; 62 minutes

Ref: IMDb.

"This whole twisted movie is about fear of black people"—*PV* 27:10.

The WITCHING HOUR

The Witching Hour released April 26. 1934: "So Frank Hardmuth was killed by a thought." Jack Brookfield (John Halliday) has a "pretty weird" talent for "thought transference"—in the course of hypnotizing young Clay Thorne (Tom Brown) out of his fear of looking at a cat's-eye ring, he accidentally plants the idea of shooting "political grafter" Frank Hardmuth (Ralf Harolde) in Clay's mind. Some 12 hours later, Clay again comes under the spell of the ring and proceeds to shoot Hardmuth. ("The cat's eye started it!") The ghost of retired Judge Martin Prentice's (Sir Guy Standing) beloved Margaret (Gertrude Michael) persuades him to take Clay's case.

The third film version of the inexplicably revered Augustus Thomas play ("from the celebrated stage play," it says in the credits) foregrounds the intriguing idea of hypnotic influence, but the story strands of love, young and old, are just frills. "Those Endearing Young Charms" is a lovely tune, but it's used as a crutch—instant nostalgia and romance. And the ring's powers seem incon-

sistent—in between the two demonstrations of its power over Clay, Brookfield has him look at it, no problem. Apparently, the ring is effective only when it lights up.

There's good but rather futile work by Halliday, Standing, and Richard Carle (Lew). And William Frawley has a choice small role as a skeptical juror. The absurdly happy grin of Brookfield's black butler Clarence (John Larkin) summons up a world seemingly built on wishful thinking. ("Lady Luck, I is yo' slave!") File under the cliché of "docile child-men" (in Leonard Pitts' phrase, *Contra Costa Times* 8/22/2011).

Of course, things couldn't have worked out better, politically, if Brookfield had intentionally planted the idea of murdering Hardmuth in Clay's mind …

Note: The "thoughts are dangerous things" idea will become *Fiend Without a Face* 24 years later.

Paramount. D: Henry Hathaway. SP: Salisbury Field, Anthony Veiller, from the play by Augustus E. Thomas. Ph: Ben Reynolds. Mus: John Leipold. Ed: Jack Dennis. Sd: Harold Lewis. P: A. Veiller. With Sir Guy Standing, John Halliday, Judith Allen, Tom Brown, Olive Tell, William Frawley, Richard Carle, Ralf Harolde, Purnell Pratt, Gertrude Michael, Ferdinand Gottschalk, Selmer Jackson, John Larkin, Jack Mower, Oscar Smith, Guy Usher; 69 minutes

Augustus Thomas, "one of our few great native dramatists"—*Variety* 5/1/34.

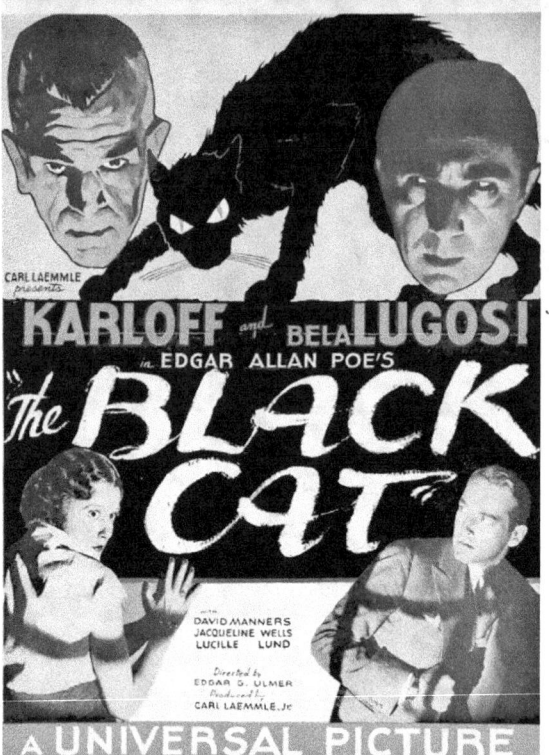

Pressbook cover from *The Black Cat* (1934)

"One of those forgotten gems"—Dave Sindelar (8/30/2001).

The BLACK CAT

Unheimliche Geschichten (1932): "A new addition to the House of Horrors." Stories by Stevenson (*The Suicide Club*) and Poe (*The Black Cat, The System of Dr. Tarr and Professor Fether*) prove a pretext for mild, if weird fun with outré settings—"mad scientist" Morder's (Paul Wegener) chintzy mad lab ... the bricks which house his murdered wife and a howling cat ... a wax museum which springs to (simulated) life one night (one exhibit: Jack the Ripper) ... an insane asylum where the apparent inmates become a chorus of screaming prisoners ... and the local suicide club which Morder runs. And these sites all seem to be on the same city block! Film is just an oddity and a curiosity now. Historical oddity: a Morder and a Murder—Lugosi's Murder Legendre in *White Zombie*—the same year. The huge pendulum at Morder's is perhaps tribute to another Poe story ... and prefigures the art deco "death clock" in the Suicide Club.

The Black Cat released May 7, 1934: "It has been a good game." They're lifelike, but not alive. Fifteen years before the present-day action, master architect Hjalmar Poelzig (Boris Karloff) betrayed Hungarian forces to the Russians and compounded his war crime by spiriting off the wife of fellow officer Vitus Werdegast (Bela Lugosi). He now houses the preserved body of the dead Karen (Lucille Lund)—and the bodies of other, unidentified women—in glass cases, in a corridor of his futuristic mansion, built on the battlefield of Marmaros, the "greatest graveyard in the world." "I wanted to have her beauty always" is his explanation to the avenging Vitus. (Lugosi's Dracula is similarly motivated regarding Mina, and he too must first kill his love before the "always" kicks in.) Like the maiden of Keats' Grecian urn, "she cannot fade."

Boris Karloff as Hjalmar Poelzig

If Poelzig stares at stranded honeymooner Mrs. Alison (Jacqueline Wells), he's impolite; but if he gazes at length at Karen's displayed body, he's simply admiring a work of art, a thing of beauty. In fact, his nocturnal walk through his corridor of beauties is one of the oneiric highlights of *The Black Cat*. Certainly, it's one of the more bizarre putting-out-the-cat sequences on film. Poelzig is most sincere—if not at all comforting—when, a little later, he tells the distraught Vitus, "I have cared for her tenderly and well." For him, the words "tenderly" and "well" have somewhat loose definitions, but he is not, as Vitus accuses him, really a liar here, at least in this regard: He's just morally mis-wired.

Bela Lugosi plays Vitus Werdegast, menacing Jacqueline Wells.

"It's the red switch, isn't it, Hjalmar?" The bad news for Vitus gets worse. He discovers, in quick succession, that Karen's daughter (Lund again), also named Karen, is still alive (Poelzig has told him otherwise), that Poelzig has married her, then that Poelzig has just murdered her. Picture Vitus' mind here: a revolving door of horror. His wild swings from anger to horror lend themselves to camp—and the character was rewritten in the course of filming—but when Lugosi's voice cracks as he asks Poelzig, "Why is she like this?" (embalmed and encased in glass, that is), it's the sound of raw emotion, as opposed to Poelzig's creepily detached "tenderness."

The latter is a surprisingly moving scene—surprising, thanks, in part, to the bizarre setting ... thanks, in part, to the compare-and-contrast effect between the characters of Poelzig and Werdegast. Both profess their love for her, Poelzig quietly, almost sheepishly: "I loved her too, Vitus." But the fact that the scene is played out before a display in the Poelzig Museum of Eternal, Embalmed Beauty rather undercuts Poelzig, indicates the strange nature of his love. Vitus' evident emotion is not qualified ... The unusual hypnotic quality of this sequence derives from the moving camera, the cadence of the background (or foreground) music, and the lulling voice of Karloff.

"What is this place?" Despite the unevenness of the writing of the character of Vitus, this is still perhaps the most satisfying Karloff-Lugosi film, and it's unusual but kind of a treat to see Lugosi as the hero in a 1930s horror movie. (The same year he was also the hero in a serial, *Return of Chandu*.) Part of the unique quality of the experience that is *The Black Cat* is the synthesis of the classical-music score, which draws one in, and the modernistic decor, which works like a distancing device, for the viewer as well as for Mr. Alison (David Manners). And, like the house he designed, Poelzig's severe hair style, stiff movements, and ascetic, formal garb are a little off-putting, while Karloff's calm, measured tones could lull anyone less wary than Vitus into anything. It's a quietly magnificent performance—Imhotep on "wry."

[SPOILERS]: *The Black Cat* is a love story embedded in a horror story. The camera is subjective (approximating the daughter) as Poelzig caresses her face. Anyone's "tender" could be applied here. "You are the very core and meaning of my life," he tells her, and that may be true. But that doesn't mean that he won't kill young Karen and put her in a glass case, all of which he would have done had he survived Vitus' wrath. In the same scene, he abjures her to stay in the bedroom the next day. She doesn't. Thus, he must kill her. Hence, the need for display cases. The dead don't disobey and are easier for control-freak Poelzig to care for. The fate of the daughter suggests that her mother suffered the same fate—Vitus, in fact, seems certain that Poelzig murdered his wife.

At the same time, Vitus is becoming a moral mirror image of Poelzig. To this end, it would seem sufficient for director Edgar Ulmer and Peter Ruric's story to suggest that Vitus is himself transforming into a killer, if on not so grand a scale as Poelzig—he has tried to shoot the latter and, by the end, is flaying him alive. But the story, as originally written, was after even more narrative symmetry: Vitus was to have taken Mrs. Alison for himself, from Poelzig—who had "won" her in a chess game—just as Poelzig took Karen the mother from Vitus. In retrospect, this aborted design begins to become apparent in the first sequence, set on the Orient Express: Vitus gently caresses the hair of the sleeping Mrs. Alison and explains to the watchful Mr. Alison that she reminds him of his long-lost wife. Poelzig's photographically underscored caress of the daughter's face is the formal completion of this particular part of the equation of the two foes. In a sense, Vitus' caress of Mrs. Alison foreshadows *everything*, from the echoing scene with Poelzig and Karen, to Vitus' vengeance, and to the scenes dropped from the film. The gentleness of the gesture is not necessarily misleading—in the picture's context of death and mayhem, it simply seems indicative of the complicatedness of human nature.

Cinematographic puzzle: Poelzig's several grand entrances and appearances are generally dramatic, but his first appearance before his guests is enig-

In the cellar hangs the suspended corpse of Karen (Lucille Lund), before which Werdegast holds a gun on Poelzig.

matic as well: John Mescall uses two consecutive, but fairly unobtrusive, stop-and-start-over tracks—from somewhat different angles—into, first, a close shot of Poelzig, then into a medium shot of him, as he enters the room. It's as if Mescall had been testing which shot his director might like, and Ulmer had said, *both*. Yield: an unobtrusively disorienting camera effect, right at home in this "very tricky house" (as Mr. Alison puts it).

Cinematographic allure: In the most magically mysterious sequence, Poelzig leads the distraught Vitus back up the spiral metal staircase from the fort's chart room (now, in effect, a basement) to the house he built upon it. But we see no one: The camera is not-quite-subjective (that is, not-quite-Poelzig), more like a third, almost sentient presence. The scene is, as noted, all shadow, moving camera, Karloff's voice, Beethoven's Seventh. Two invisible ghosts, in effect—the walking, talking dead.

Hair notes: Poelzig's servant (Egon Brecher), with the fourth-stooge haircut, seems to be having a bad-hair lifetime, while the encased Karen's up-sweeping hair anticipates Elsa Lanchester's Bride's 'do, and Poelzig's widow's-peak hairstyle anticipates Henry Hull's werewolf from *WereWolf of London*.

The other 1934 adaptation of Poe's gruesome but ingenious story of a "Karma" cat (or avenging-angel cat), *Maniac*, actually employs more elements of Poe than does *The Black Cat*.

Quiz: What are the very first words exchanged between Karloff and Lugosi? (Answer: Lugosi's "It has been a long time, Hjalmar! The years have been kind to you.")

Miscellaneous notes: Dramatic crutch, perhaps: The prevalence of the word "death" in the dialogue. Poelzig's finest feature: He likes cats. The felinophobic Werdegast kills them, or seems to.

Universal. D, Story, Set Des, Cost: Edgar G. Ulmer. SP, Story: Peter Ruric. Contributing Writer: Tom Kilpatrick, suggested by Edgar Allan Poe's story. Ph: John J. Mescall. AD: Charles D. Hall. Ed: Ray Curtiss. Mkp: Jack Pierce. Sd: Gilbert Kurland. VisFX: John P. Fulton et al. Cost: also Vera West, Ed Ware. With Boris Karloff, Bela Lugosi, David Manners, Jacqueline Wells, Egon Brecher, Harry Cording, Henry Armetta, Lucille Lund, Luis Alberni, King Baggot, John Carradine, Herman Bing, John George, Michael Mark, Paul Panzer, Paul Weigel; 65 minutes

Ref: *Modern Monsters* 3:18-19: Ulmer regarding Karloff's wardrobe. "You could feel a certain amount of jealousy or tension" between Karloff and Lugosi—Shirley Ulmer, interviewed by Tom Weaver, *Cult Movies* 25:52-61.

"The lines conceived for Karloff and Lugosi ... seem almost to have been story-boarded to take advantage of their accents"—Jim Knusch and Sharon Williams, *Filmfax* 7:32-37.

"A film full of eerie touches, with an all-encompassing aura of perversity"—Mick LaSalle, *San Francisco Chronicle* 3/18/05.

"Lugosi's Werdegast is the heartrending violin and Karloff's Poelzig the sinister bassoon"—Nathalie Yafet, *Midnight Marquee* 52:20.

"Additional scenes and retakes ... [make] Lugosi's Werdegast less aberrated and more tragically heroic"—Gregory Mank, "Universal's Golden Age—Some Facts and Figures," *Midnight Marquee* 35:12.

"The cold, decadent sterility of the film's set perfectly matches Poelzig's psyche and his diabolical intentions"—Steve Kronenberg, "Staged Fright," *Monsters from the Vault*, Spring '97:24." On the counts of story, novelty, thrills and distinction, the picture is sub-normal"—*Variety* 5/22/34.

"The Black Cat," segment of *Tales of Terror* (1962): "The cat—what a charming fellow he is!" Maddened by jealousy, a man (Peter Lorre) walls up his wife (Joyce Jameson) and her lover (Vincent Price). Would-be-droll Richard Matheson adaptation of both *The Black Cat* and *A Cask of Amontillado* features a genuinely bizarre nightmare sequence in which wife and lover play keep away with the husband's head. Director Roger Corman gives Price and Lorre way-too-long leashes, though Lorre has a way with quiet muttering.

DRUMS O' VOODOO

Drums o' Voodoo released May 11, 1934: "I ain't scared of your voodoo!" "Voodoo woman" Hagar (Laura Bowman) invokes the "Voodoo Gods" to strike an evil man (Morris McKenny) blind. Hagar's voodoo chanting ("And the VOO-DOO!") qualifies as camp, but the interminable speechifying here beats almost everything else to death. However, when Elder Amos Berry (Augustus Smith) gets up a full head of steam preachifying, he's pretty impressive. Based on a 49-minute version.

A tip o' the hat to Dave Sindelar.

(aka *Louisiana*; aka *She Devil*): Sack/International Stageplay. D: Arthur Hoerl. SP: Augustus Smith, from his play *Louisiana*. Ph: J. Burgi Contner, Walter Strenge. Ed, P: Louis Weiss. AD: Sam Corso. With Laura Bowman, Augustus Smith, Morris McKenny, Lionel Monagas, Edna Barr, Alberta Perkins; 70 minutes

Ref: "time-killing songfests ... dull exchanges between the [church] parishioners"—Bryan Senn, *Drums of Terror*, pp28-31.

"Cheaply produced and looking it"—*Variety* 5/15/34.

"Lots of high energy preaching and singing"—*PV* 16:13.

"Filmed as unimaginatively as possible"—Dave Sindelar (9/8/2001).

BLACK MOON

Black Moon (novel—Clements Ripley). "The chant was a wailing frenzy—primeval fear, rising to beat against the quiet stars until it seemed that Something must hear. Something ancient and dark and terrible, blackened by the smoke of fires, smeared with the blood of he-goats." Rada (a religion), brujeria (black mass), an ouanga (a dead man's severed fingers), and sacrificial goats, all on the island of San Cristobal. Dr. Almon Perez, a psychologist, brings young Steven Lane to the island to marry his mysterious niece, Amalia.

More wisely than the movie based on the book, the latter maintains the mystery of the "consecrated" Amalia until the middle chapters; the movie re-

In this tense lobby card from *Black Moon*, Dorothy Burgess confronts an unsettled Fay Wray.

veals (the renamed) Juanita's voodoo roots in the very first shot. (Thus no spoiler here.) A pretty fair writer, Clements is occasionally too ambitious, though generally not ambitious enough. Once the mystery of Amalia and the black mass is revealed, the book becomes standard action and adventure. The voodoo here is a matter of intimidation and fear-mongering, not magic and zombies. Movies would continue to go the way of *White Zombie*, not *Black Moon*, book or movie. The book is at its best describing the sensuousness of the tropical atmosphere and the relationship between Amalia and Steven: "Once, while he caught his breath, she flung out her arms and whirled in a slow little dance step, as though something in the night, stronger than her own weariness, was gripping her, compelling her." Clements is good with "something."

More so than the film, the book has an arguably racist undercurrent. Steven feels comfortable in a "sane, ordered world, a white man's world." Head counts like "five whites [and] five hundred blacks"—the population of the island—seem meant to stir up uneasiness regarding a Black Peril. The giveaway: the incidental phrase "the lazy laughter of a gang of darkies."

The child Nancy does not appear in the book.

Black Moon released June 15, 1934: "She tasted blood!" What's a voodoo movie without a zombie? Answer: basically, any voodoo movie made in 1934—

Black Moon, Chloe, Drums o'Voodoo. It was a one-year trend. Credit film and book with doing something different. But this lost backwater of voodoo movies is not remembered for no reason. Both film and book have trouble locating a viable dramatic center. In the middle of the book, Amalia declares her intention of conquering the world with voodoo. Then she pretty much drops out of the action. In the film, Juanita (Dorothy Burgess) is keen on tropical voodoo, and the native chanting is lulling and inveigling, no doubt about it. ("This place is part of me, Steve—every path of the jungle, every shadow.") But it's not clear what the Wells Root screenplay is doing with this "poisoned with voodoo" role, until the concluding sequences [finally, a SPOILER alert]: when Juanita is directed to offer daughter Nancy (Cora Sue Collins) as a sacrifice. There you go. Drama: Love of voodoo; on the other hand, love of daughter. Harry Cohn must have been pleased. It's contrived but at least it's comprehensible.

Most of the movie is just a curious blur, but two things help make it bearable. Fay Wray is quietly radiant in what might have been a thankless role. Her suppressed love for her boss—Juanita's husband (Jack Holt)—is unstressed, affecting, as is her concern for his daughter. The concern is just there, in her face and manner, it seems. The other welcome element: Joseph August's atmospheric photography. Prime shot: Juanita's eyes spotlighted in the dark.

Yes, the movie cites *2,000* blacks on the island, instead of the book's 500. But the screenplay explicitly singles out Dr. Perez (Arnold Korff) as racist, and his manhandling of Ruva (Madame Sul-Te-Wan) is not endorsed. It's a character or two—Perez and Eleanor Wesselhoeft's Anna—not the movie, that are prejudiced. Still, this is the studio that made the occasionally heinous *Night of Terror* (which see) the year before, so lines like "Six times, the blacks have tried to wipe us out" cannot be dismissed outright as perfectly harmless.

Notes: In the movie, the island is called San Christopher.

Good thing Juanita wasn't trying to conquer the world with dance. Her voodoo number is pretty terrible.

It would be some 23 years before Columbia finally made a zombie movie—*Zombies of Mora Tau* (1957).

Columbia. D: Roy William Neill. SP: Wells Root, from Clements Ripley's novel. Ph: Joseph August. Mus: Louis Silvers. Ed: Richard Cahoon. Cost: Robert Kalloch. Sd: Edward Bernds. With Jack Holt, Fay Wray, Dorothy Burgess, Cora Sue Collins, Arnold Korff, Clarence Muse, Madame Sul-Te-Wan, Laurence Criner, Lumsden Hare, Henry Kolker, Ruby Dandridge, Robert Frazier; 68 minutes

Ref: *PV* 37:64.

"Very little happens"—Bryan Senn, *Drums of Terror*, pp32-34.

"Dated and pretty offensive today"—Stephen Jones, *Essential Monster Movie Guide*, p51.

The MAN WITH TWO FACES

The Man with Two Faces released Aug. 4, 1934: "Them scary shows give me the creeps!" The supposedly dead Stanley Vance (Louis Calhern) did well for himself "living on women." He had, in fact, a "strange power" over his wife, Jessica (Mary Astor), and [SPOILER] when he suddenly reappears, returned from the "dead," he virtually freezes his captive audience—including Jessica and her brother Damon Wells (Edward G. Robinson): It's as if he had just stepped out of *Svengali*. Again, Jessica becomes a "colorless automaton."

Cross references include, of course, *Svengali*, "The Pied Piper" (as Vance himself suggests), zombies, robots, and Stepford wives. As Vance, the cad, Calhern does Insufferably Blithe very well. ("I trust I'm not putting a damper on this little party!") But Robinson fails to impress with either of his two faces: He's flavorless as "Chautard," and oddly belligerent as Wells. If Calhern gets the thing off to a good start, David Landau as the empathetic sergeant wraps it up satisfyingly, suggesting to Wells that a strong "performance in the witness box" could save him from [SPOILER] a murder charge. (His victim: Vance of course.)

The problem is the vast middle of the movie—it's just another dead "clever" plot. George S. Kaufman, co-author of the source play *The Dark Tower*, gets an eternal pass: With Morrie Ryskind, he helped launch The Marx Brothers in movies with *The Cocoanuts* [sic] and *Animal Crackers*.

Note: Archie Mayo directed both this film and *Svengali*.

WB-FN. D: Archie Mayo. SP: Tom Reed, Niven Busch, from the play *The Dark Tower* by George S. Kaufman and Alexander Woollcott. Ph: Tony Gaudio. Mus: Bernhard Kaun. AD: John Hughes. Ed: William Holmes. P: Robert Lord. With Edward G. Robinson, Mary Astor, Ricardo Cortez, Mae Clarke, Louis Calhern, Arthur Byron, John Eldredge, David Landau, Emily Fitzroy, Henry O'Neill, Stanley Blystone, Wade Boteler, Joseph Crehan, Milton Kibbee, Dennis O'Keefe, Henry Otho, Guy Usher; 72 minutes.

Ref: IMDb. "If you had the ability to control your husband or wife, boyfriend or girlfriend, would you use it, and how often?"—Mick LaSalle, review of *Ruby Sparks*, *S.F. Chronicle* 7/25/12.

"Sustained in tone and cleverly put together"—Otis Ferguson, *The New Republic*, 8/29/34.

"The Svengali menace, as done by Louis Calhern, is hardly credulous [sic]"—*Variety* 7/17/34.

"Calhern is witty and sinister as the husband"—Dave Sindelar (10/17/2002).

The MOONSTONE

The Moonstone (novel—Wilkie Collins): "What the Sand gets, the Sand keeps for ever." Despite occasional, sudden poetry (regarding, for instance, that Shivering Sand), Collins' book finally seems a bit thin, as mystery or drama. What still shines: the comedy, with, say, Mr. Candy, the doctor, or with Miss Clack and her ubiquitous tracts. The latter is hilariously well-meaning and oblivious, and the tale of the Moonstone takes a back seat, temporarily, to her messianic efforts. The non-comic characters get to be a bit much, too, unintentionally. Now, try to fit a 500-page book into a 50-minute movie ...

The Moonstone released Aug. 20, 1934: "You're all worked up over the silly superstition that misfortune dogs the footsteps of anyone possessing the Moonstone!" The latter is the "famous yellow diamond," the Herncastle Moonstone, stolen from a "sacred idol" in an Indian temple. It "almost hypnotizes" those who gaze upon it, as it changes colors with the gazing angle, and its appearance waxes and wanes with the moon. And now, it disappears from Verinder Manor, "forty miles from nowhere, in the wilds of Yorkshire," England. ("It's murder! It's that cursed Moonstone!")

This very short 1934 film of the book can do little more than capture two incidents from that book—the disappearance of the diamond, and the explanation of that disappearance. Adele Buffington's screenplay reduces the story to an old dark house mystery. In fact, its finest feature is Elspeth Dudgeon's performance—she switched genders in *The Old Dark House* (1932) to play old Roderick Femm. Here, she's Betteredge, the housekeeper, who, oddly enough, in the book, was a man, Gabriel Betteredge, the house steward! Her funniest line (to Inspector Cuff [Charles Irwin]): "Aren't you the little Sherlock!" The above-average cast also features Gustav von Seyffertitz, as the money-lender Lucker, Evelyn Bostock, as the maid (who has a more substantial role in the book), and John Davidson as Yandoo (rhymes with "Chandu")—Davidson majored in usually sinister exotics.

Robert Planck (photography) and J.A. Stransky, Jr. (sound) make the most of the lightning, thunder, and rain. Verinder Manor is all whistling night winds, the first night. (No storm the second night.) Even music from the house radio can't drown out the thunder. At one point, lightning knocks out the lights and yields a scream scene.

Notes: In an anticipation of *Mark of the Vampire*, a new drug makes its user repeat his actions of the night before: Franklin Blake (David Manners) "sleepwalks" down the upstairs hall and finds the Moonstone, or a substitute. In the book, the drug is opium.

In 1934, Manners majored in movies with mysteriously dead phones—this and *The Black Cat*.

The full-length, 62-minute version of the film seems to be lost, according to researcher doctor kiss; this cut-down version runs only 47 minutes.

Monogram. D: Reginald Barker. SP: Adele Buffington, from Wilkie Collins' novel. Ph: Robert H. Planck. AD: E.R. Hickson. Sd: John Stransky, Jr. P: Paul Malvern. With David Manners, Phyllis Barry, Gustav von Seyffertitz, Jameson Thomas, Herbert Bunston, Charles Irwin, Elspeth Dudgeon, John Davidson, Claude King, Olaf Hytten, Fred Walton; 62 minutes

Ref: Sinister Cinema.

Turner/Price, *Forgotten Horrors*.

Okuda/*Monogram*.

Walt Lee.

"This production suggests the early type of vocal mystery story when the talkers were about a year old and the directors were all experimenting with their sound effects"—*Variety* 9/18/34.

The DRAGON MURDER CASE

The Dragon Murder Case (novel—S.S. Van Dine): "The dragon did it!" "Strange and uncanny things" happen at the "old Stamm estate in Inwood" (New York), a "gloomy place." In particular, "many strange and grotesque legends" center on the estate's "old Dragon Pool," the "place of the water-monster." Detective Philo Vance attempts to solve the "voodoo mystery" of two deaths seemingly caused by "some gigantic prehistoric beast": The bodies seem to have been slashed by a huge three-clawed dragon, and claw and hoof prints are found in the silt at the bottom of the pool. Old Mrs. Stamm "haunts this whole house like a ghost." Plus a "gruesome, half-buried tomb" and bottled "sea-monsters," including a "miniature dragon" fish. ("More monsters!")

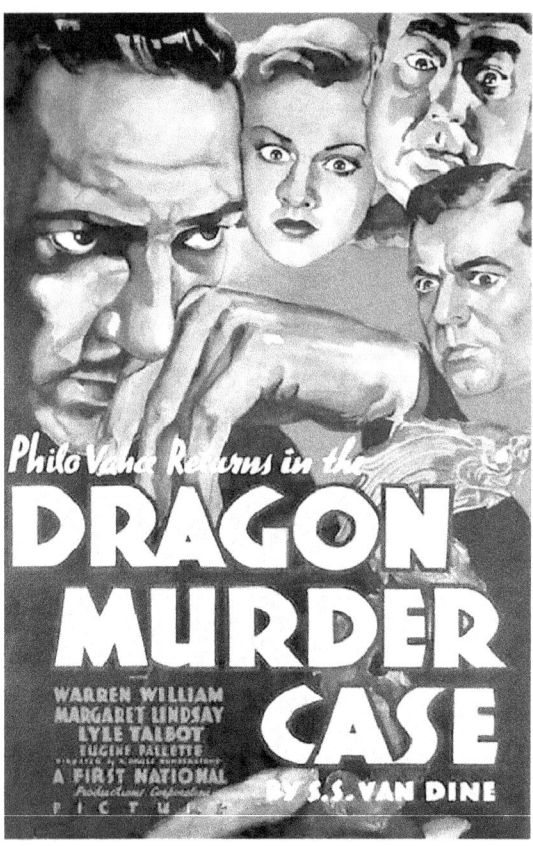

Van Dine gets some creepy mileage out of the dragon pool, including one classic horror passage, in which the pool is slowly drained in order to find the murder victim, and there's "no sign of a body!" And Mrs. Stamm's fanciful tales of a dragon's hiding-places "made for him when the world was young" add flavor. But 300 pages of Vance's nonchalance is a bit much, even if (as narrator Van Dine notes) his jocularity cloaks a certain seriousness.

The Dragon Murder Case released Aug. 25, 1934: "I never saw marks like these, on the throat. They don't look human!" A man (George Meeker) disappears from a swimming pool (actually, a "dammed-up stream"). Later, "three-toed claw marks" are found at the bottom. Behind it all, supposedly: a dragon that hides its victims in a place "older than history, older even than man."

Warren William's Philo Vance is easier to take than Van Dine's. He's smooth, sure, a bit dull, but not annoying or affected. The movie itself, however, is really no better than the book. Just a little musical underscoring would have made key moments—say, the respective discoveries of the bodies and the "dragon" signs—more memorable. As it is, only the credit sequence features any musical excitement. And the movie pretty much throws away the highlight of the book—the draining of the pool: no suspense, no drama, and no revelatory moment.

The F. Hugh Herbert, Robert N. Lee, Rian James screenplay, however, partially atones for these weaknesses by providing a few Monster Movie moments. In the first, a huge "claw" out of *Curse of the Demon* seems to swipe a man swimming underwater in the pool; in a follow-up bit, a "dragon" claw emerges from the pool. The sequence is fairly satisfying, if it seems extraneous to the story. Unfortunately, the line: "Supposing old Stamm, with his pet theories of breeding, had succeeded in producing a new kind of monster, big enough to kill a man" is just a passing red herring.

The maniacally cackling old Mrs. Stamm (Helen Lowell) is actually not as much of a character as the cantankerous medical examiner, Dr. Doremus (Etienne Girardot). Lyle Talbot, as part-Indian Leland, gets the "I can't help it, darling" role. And Eugene Pallette's (Sgt. Heath) comic relief is pretty flat.

Notes: 1934 was a big year for water monsters. There was also the British *Secret of the Loch*. At one point, *The Dragon Murder Case* refers to a "gigantic monster in Loch Ness."

In book and film, drawings are made of the "talons" at the bottom of the drained pool. Why are not photographs taken instead?

At one point, Vance, Sgt. Heath, and Inspector Markham (Robert McWade) flip through Stamm's books on dragons and devils. It's preferable to the equivalent section of the book, in which Vance verbally catalogs every last damn dragon from history and literature.

WB-FN. D: H. Bruce Humberstone. SP: F. Hugh Herbert, Robert N. Lee, Rian James, from S.S. Van Dine's novel. Ph: Tony Gaudio. Mus: Bernhard Kaun. AD: Jack Okey. Ed: Terry Morse. Sd: Leslie G. Hewitt. Cost: Orry-Kelly. With Warren William, Margaret Lindsay, Lyle Talbot, Eugene Pallette, Helen Lowell, Robert McWade, Robert Barrat, Dorothy Tree, George E. Stone, Etienne Girardot, George Meeker, Robert Warwick, William B. Davidson, Arthur Aylesworth, Charles C. Wilson, Milton Kibbee, Wilfred Lucas, Henry Otho, Eric Wilton; 67 minutes

Ref: "poorly paced ... [Williams'] is a colorless performance"—*Variety* 8/28/34.

"A marked horror element ... a mythical 'dragon'"—Dave Sindelar (5/27/2004).

MANIAC

Maniac released Sept. 11, 1934: "It's horrible, I tell you—workin' on the dead! Trying to bring back life—it's not natural!" Dr. Meirschultz (Horace Carpenter) is a "great research scientist," and an inveterate cackler. Meanwhile, the beyond-Renfield subject Buckley (Ted Edwards) scoops up a passing somnambulist, and the cat Satan scoops up a loose living brain. ("You wretch!") Poe-plus, or minus: Don Maxwell (Bill Woods), the itinerant vaudevillian impersonating the doctor, pops one of Satan's eyes out of its socket and into his mouth. He cackles, too. Finally, the walled-up cat cries out from behind a wall, thus alerting police to the doctor's body, which Maxwell has hidden there. A long way from vaudeville ...

The first half is mainly just bad; the second half hits camp heights with its chaotically-lurching plot. Double-exposure clips from *Haxan* and serious inter-titles regarding madness and "fear thought" don't interfere with the festivities. Like *The Raven* (1935), this is a Poe two-fer: It has elements of both *The Black Cat* and *Murders in the Rue Morgue*. It is perhaps not fair to throw Ed-

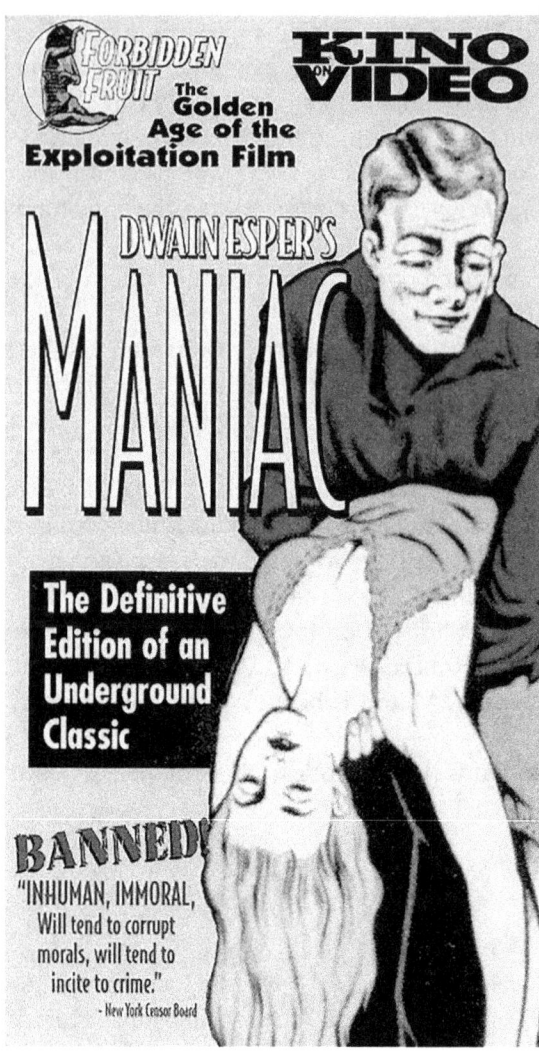

wards' convincingly tortured rant, midway, into the camp catch-all—it could fit, if uneasily, into a serious drama regarding split personality. As he ends his mad spiel, the orangutang in him takes over, and he begins squawking like an ape. A unique film.

(aka *Sex Maniac*) Roadshow. D, P: Dwain Esper. SP, P: Hildegarde Stadie, from Edgar Allan Poe's stories *The Black Cat* and *Murders in the Rue Morgue*. Ph: William C. Thompson. Ed: William Austin. Props: Dan Sonney. With Bill Woods, Horace Carpenter, Ted Edwards, Phyllis Diller, Theo Ramsey; 51 minutes

Ref: IMDb.

FD 1/7/36.

The GHOST WALKS

The Ghost Walks released Dec. 1, 1934: "This old house seems to belong in the rain and thunder." All the men wear bow ties, in the "old, isolated country home" ("supposed to be haunted") outside Cragdale, about 80 miles from New York City. [SPOILERS/STORY TWISTS]: In a story twist, the first 20 minutes of the movie prove to have been simply a rehearsal of an author's (John Miljan) new play, a "bloomin' horror play" titled "The Ghost Walks." But the producer (Richard Carle) and his secretary (Johnny Arthur) think the rehearsal is continuing. In another twist, an asylum guard (Spencer Charters) turns out to be a homicidal maniac, Case 222, the "Professor"—complete with mad-doctor cackle—who specializes in plastic surgery. ("I am the greatest genius you have ever seen.")

Or, *The Old Dark House* Meets *Doctor X*. *The Ghost Walks* is pretty undisciplined—both its weakness and its strength. It's not as staid as most "B" thunderstorm mysteries, but it's also not that amusing. The supposedly psychic

Beatrice (Eve Southern), for instance, is supposed to be kooky-spooky ("That woman gives me goose pimples!"), but the actress is wooden. And the comedy with Carle, Arthur, and Charters is more off than on.

One good scare: the "death-white face" which floats towards the camera when the lights go out. Another plus: the weird chime of the clock, which "strikes any old time" (a "union" clock, as per Arthur). M.A. Anderson contributes an effective tracking shot up to a suddenly empty divan. (Beatrice's body has disappeared.) Thunder considerately waits for gaps in the dialogue. Another oddity: No one dies in the course of the action. The apparent gay subtext to the Carle-Arthur scenes is made pretty explicit when the "guard" tells them, "There's something queer about you both."

Chesterfield/Invincible. D: Frank Strayer. SP: Charles Belden. Ph: M.A. Anderson. AD: Edward C. Jewell. Ed: Roland D. Reed. Sd: L.E. Clark. P: Maury M. Cohen. With John Miljan, June Collyer, Richard Carle, Henry Kolker, Johnny Arthur, Spencer Charters, Donald Kirke, Eve Southern, Harry Strang; 69 minutes

Ref: *Forgotten Horrors*.

"Picture is above the indie norm all around"—*Variety* 4/3/35.

"This one isn't too bad"—Dave Sindelar (5/14/2005).

Highlights of 1935

Universal released its second *Frankenstein*, its first werewolf saga, and its second Karloff-Lugosi co-starrer. April 1935—candidate for greatest month in horror-movie history: *Bride of Frankenstein* and *Mark of the Vampire* opened that month, and made 1935 the last great year of the first part of the Golden Age (which part ended in 1936).

WereWolf of London, though, proved to be pretty much a hack work—and our Dud of the Year—and *The Raven* is beloved mostly as camp, though the two stars have their cherishable moments, in spite of all. Karloff's three best genre performances of the year came in two other movies—*Bride of Frankenstein* and *The Black Room*, where he plays twins.

There were several horror hybrids this year: *Charlie Chan in Egypt* and *The Florentine Dagger* were mysteries with horror scenes. *Vanishing Riders* was a Western with horror scenes. *The Great Impersonation* was a spy flick with horror scenes. *The Black Room* was a costume drama with horror scenes. And *Air Hawks* was an aviation drama with ...

It was the year of Valerie Hobson, lovely in *Bride of Frankenstein*, *WereWolf of London*, and *The Great Impersonation*, not to mention *Mystery of Edwin Drood* and *Life Returns* (see *Other films* of interest, below. for both).

Young Valerie Hobson and Boris Karloff, as the Monster, in *Bride of Frankenstein* (1935)

Notable performances: Robert Barrat (*The Florentine Dagger*), Boris Karloff, Ernest Thesiger, Elsa Lanchester (*Bride of Frankenstein*), Bela Lugosi, Lionel Atwill (*Mark of the Vampire*), Ralph Bellamy, Victor Kilian (*Air Hawks*), Warner Oland (*WereWolf of London, Charlie Chan in Egypt*), Stepin Fetchit (*Charlie Chan in Egypt*), Peter Lorre (*Mad Love*), Lugosi (yes, those two or three scenes, *The Raven*), Karloff (*The Black Room*), Pedro de Cordoba, Mischa Auer (*Condemned To Live*), Valerie Hobson (*The Great Impersonation*)

Notable photography: John J. Mescall (*Bride of Frankenstein*), James Wong Howe (*Mark of the Vampire*), Ernest Miller, William Nobles (*One Frightened Night*), Henry Freulich (*Air Hawks*), Charles Stumar (*WereWolf of London*), Daniel B. Clark (*Charlie Chan in Egypt*), Allen G. Siegler (*The Black Room*), Milton Krasner (*The Great Impersonation*)

Notable direction: James Whale (*Bride of Frankenstein*), Tod Browning (*Mark of the Vampire*), Karl Freund (*Mad Love*)

Notable writing: William Hurlbut, John Balderston (*Bride of Frankenstein*)

Notable music: Franz Waxman (*Bride of Frankenstein*)

Notable photographic effects: John P. Fulton (*Bride of Frankenstein, WereWolf of London*)

Notable art direction: Charles D. Hall (*Bride of Frankenstein*), Cedric Gibbons (*Mark of the Vampire*), Albert S. D'Agostino (*WereWolf of London*)

Notable costumes: Vera West (*Bride of Frankenstein*)

Notable sound: Gilbert Kurland (*Bride of Frankenstein, The Great Impersonation*), Douglas Shearer et al. (*Mark of the Vampire*)

Notable makeup: Jack Pierce (*Bride of Frankenstein, WereWolf of London*)

Notable editing: Ted Kent (*Bride of Frankenstein*), Holbrook N. Todd (*Vanishing Riders*)

Notable mask: Markoff (*One Frightened Night*)

Notable props: Robert Laszlo (*WereWolf of London*)

Other films of interest:

Dante's Inferno—HSF1: hellish footage from 1909 Italian *L'Inferno*

Death from a Distance—"Arcturus is very bright tonight." Bizarre murder in an observatory on a "forsaken hilltop": "The reflected light from the star made the contact and fired the shot." The star in question is Arcturus, aka Job's star, but it seems that any star would have done. Film is just well-enough made to be boring, not campy. Not even quasi-horror

Life Returns—FD 1/2/35—drama regarding attempts to revive the dead

Midnight Phantom—FD 11/21/35; IMDb: just a mystery

Murder by Television—Ref: HSF2: Concerns an "interstellar frequency," or death ray, a conjunction of rays involving a television and a phone. Alternately dull and sweetly clumsy. Lugosi gets to feast on only a few real Lugosi lines.

Mysterious Mr. Wong—Bela Lugosi is probably the only Wong ever to sport a Hungarian accent, though in disguise as "old Li See the herb dealer," Wong affects a stilted Chinese accent. Lugosi gets to do Fu Manchu, sort of. Unhorrific, and breezy in the worst way. Terrible playful dialogue for Lugosi and Wallace Ford. Based on *The Twelve Coins of Confucius* or *The Strange Adventure of the Twelve Coins of Confucius* by Keeler.

Mystery of Edwin Drood—"He haunts my thoughts like a dreadful ghost." Claude Rains' Jasper is the "monster that frightens." The scene with Durdles (Forrester Harvey) and Jasper in the crypt is the closest the film gets to creepy, but this isn't really at all horrific. Rains, though, has some bravura scenes as a man in the grip of opium, tormented by thoughts of strangling people.

Window card from *Mad Love* (1935)

Night Life of the Gods—Ref: *Variety* 2/27/35. Mad doc turns folks into statues. IMDb: Medusa, leprechaun. *FD* 2/23/35

Obeah—Ref: *TV Guide* article. *FD* 2/13/35. *Midnight Marquee* 46:8. *AFI Catalog*: not viewed. Early, lost Jean Brooks horror flick regarding voodoo curse. doctor kiss e-mail: (from *The Daily Gleaner* [Jamaica] 6/1/34 & 6/19/34): *Outside World*—original title. *White Sails*—shooting title. *Jungles of the Night*—intermediate title)

Remember Last Night—"I feel like the bride of Frankenstein!" Hypnosis machine, "spooky" cellar, secret room. It's a fun if a slender James Whale mystery.

Rocky Mountain Mystery—"This place makes me nervous." The deafening noise from the stamp mill (long before *The Fly*) is intimidating, but the black-cloaked skulker in the dark is kind of incidental.

Seven Keys to Baldpate—"I'm a hermit and a ghost, and nothin' else." "Spooks," two black cats, and a secret passage—but the movie isn't even remotely horrific. It's a smooth, dull blend of comedy and crooks.

A Shot in the Dark—"A most uncommon instrument." A cattle-killing, needle-shooting invention is used for gruesome murder. Plus a "rather eerie" auditorium and an "old deserted road house." Mystery features a dollop of suspense and a skulker in cloak and hat.

The Spanish Cape Mystery—Ref: *FD* 10/9/35. Atmospheric mystery in which the horrific content is limited to one line regarding a "bewitched" house, on the California coast, haunted by a "banshee."

While the Patient Slept—"I'm telling you the evil one himself is here!" It's not *Doctor X*, but they pour on the wind and the water. Plus screaming, a clutching hand, a secret passage, a "ghost," and that bane of Warners comedy, Allen Jenkins, surlier than usual. On the verge of spookiness, but it never quite gets there.

1935

SECRETS OF CHINATOWN

Secrets of Chinatown released Feb. 20, 1935: "We've a sinister, evil mind to combat—almost like black magic. Tonight, I saw an image come to life. And then, people vanishing through solid walls!" *Secrets of Chinatown* is a tale of the "hidden world" of Lao-Tsee, the "ancient seer, the father of a strange devil worship." The "evil mind" belongs to the "mysterious head of the Black Robe" (Harry Hewitson), who can cause an idol to transform into a trance-bound woman, Zenobia (Lucile Browne). ("You know I have a way of casting a strange spell over whomever I want.") She has become the "eye of Lao-Tsee": "I am his servant."

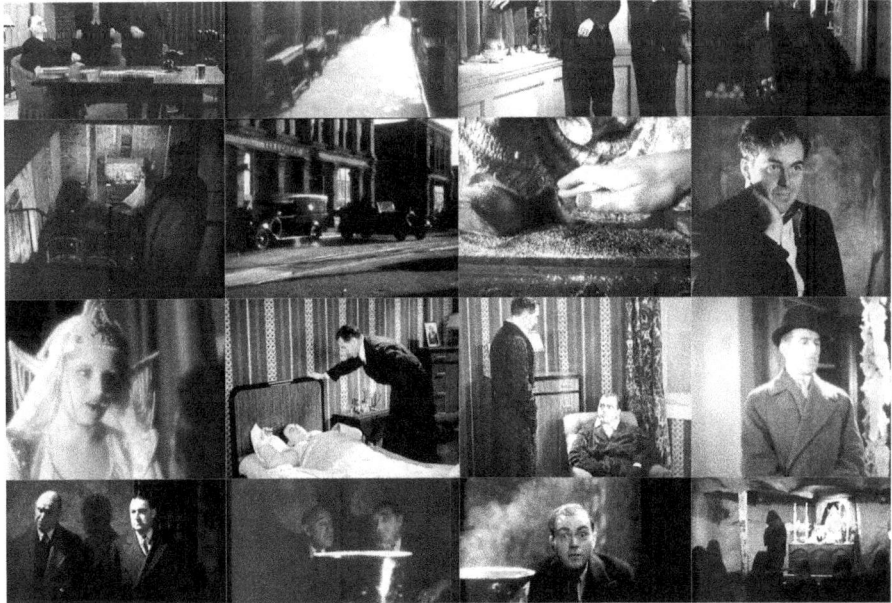

Assorted stills from *Secrets of Chinatown* (1935)

Meanwhile, a "little known," mind-clouding drug (a "strange water") has blotted out a man's (James Flavin) memory. Magically, however, the Yogi of Madrada (Arthur Legge-Willis) un-blots same, and allows a detective (Raymond Lawrence) to "read the hidden section of Brandhma's brain"—until a vision of the Black Robe unhinges the man. ("The human mind is queer—it makes things like this possible.")

Call it what you will—black magic, mind over matter, mind over mind—this movie plays like the boiled-down, feature version of a serial. It's very bad, it moves jaggedly, in fits and starts, but there are few lulls, and Guy Morton's juvenile script (from his novel, *The Black Robe*) doesn't stint on the mystical elements. And the picture is plenty mysterious, at least to look at—half the action is played out in semi-darkness.

Syndicate/Northern Films/Producers Laboratories. D: Fred Newmeyer. SP: Guy Morton, from his novel *The Black Robe*. Ph: William Beckway. Ed: William Austin. Sd: Wallie Hamilton. Tech D: Li-Young. P: Kenneth J. Bishop. With Nick Stuart, Lucile Browne, Raymond Lawrence, James Flavin, Harry Hewitson, James McGrath, Arthur Legge-Willis; 63 minutes

Ref: *Forgotten Horrors*: U.S.-Canadian co-production.

The FLORENTINE DAGGER

The Florentine Dagger (novel—Ben Hecht): "The wraiths of past De Medicis! Inherited phantoms! Bosh!" Signs do point to "inherited homicidal mania" on the part of Julien De Medici. Or is there some "demoniacal stranger" lurking? At any rate, Julien's musings regarding the identity of the murderer of Victor Ballau form the core of the mystery. The key: Florence Ballau's line: "He thought I was the insane one, the double ego and all that." The dual-personality theme here, though, proves not a strong enough peg upon which to hang a book-length story. The denouement is satisfying and surprising, if a little schematic, though that might just be another term for pleasingly designed. There are, in effect, three detectives—an actual detective, Lt. Norton; Julien, and Dr. Lytton. Complete with a *Mark of the Vampire* reenactment-of-murder scene.

The Florentine Dagger released March 30, 1935: A Clue Club Picture. "The ghosts of the Borgias still walk in me!" As the "last of the Borgias," Juan Cesare (Donald Woods) feels himself "cursed with a lethal legacy": "Irresistibly, I feel the urge to kill." But a psychiatrist (C. Aubrey Smith) considers Juan's an "artificial mania." Meanwhile, on stage, Juan's beloved Florence Ballau (Margaret Lindsay) "becomes entirely Lucrezia Borgia." She herself goes so far as to say, "I'm Lucrezia Borgia." Is one of these dueling dual personalities responsible for the murder of Victor Ballau (Henry O'Neill)?

[SPOILERS]: In Hecht's book, the solution to the mystery depends on where the roulette wheel of dual personality stops. Midway, the movie throws out his structural design and substitutes a murderer behind a mask. The mov-

ie's Ballau, it seems, "made a monstrosity out of a beautiful woman" (Florence Fair). We don't get a peek behind the mask, although Floria, at one point, threatens to reveal what's behind it.

If the movie retains the book's killer, it drastically alters her motivations—and the character of Ballau. In the book, there are rumors, but he is shown to be a caring husband and father. In the movie, the rumors regarding his "weird love" for his stepdaughter prove to be true. The changes don't make the movie better or worse—though they do provide for a different, if equally satisfying denouement. The changes simply seem to be aimed at increasing the sensationalism factor.

The main problem with the movie is that all the interesting action seems to occur offstage, or decades (or centuries) ago. And the dialogue we hear, on stage, tends toward: "Oh, if you only knew—it's too awful!" Fortunately, Robert Barrat's full-bodied performance as the vain, flirtatious inspector distracts, and the plot alterations allow him to conclude as a very romantic character.

Note: As in the book, a lady with a dagger strikes in the night, but here she strikes the psychiatrist. In the book, she attacked the hero.

WB. D: Robert Florey. SP: Tom Reed. Addl Dial: Brown Holmes, from Ben Hecht's novel. Ph: Arthur L. Todd. Mus: Bernhard Kaun. AD: Anton Grot, Carl Jules Weyl. Ed: Thomas Pratt. Cost: Orry-Kelly. P: Harry Joe Brown. With Donald Woods, Margaret Lindsay, C. Aubrey Smith, Henry O'Neill, Robert Barrat, Frank Reicher, Charles Judels, Rafaela Ottiano, Paul

Porcasi, Eily Malyon, Egon Brecher, Herman Bing, Henry Kolker, Barlowe Borland, Wheaton Chambers, Olaf Hytten, Charles Lane, William V. Mong, Paul Panzer; 69 minutes

Ref: *Variety* 5/1/35.

BRIDE OF FRANKENSTEIN

Bride of Frankenstein released April 22, 1935: "An audience needs something stronger than a pretty little love story. So why shouldn't I write of monsters?" *Bride of Frankenstein* retains more elements of the Mary Shelley novel than does the 1931 *Frankenstein*. (Which latter Gavin Gordon's Lord Byron recaps in the introductory scenes.) In addition to the "bride," there's the blind old man who plays sweet music, the interlopers who ruin the blind-man/monster idyll (in the book, Felix, Safie, and Agatha; in the movie, the two hunters), and the "young girl" whom the monster rescues from the "rapid stream." And, of course, the creature speaks, as he does in the book, and did not in the earlier movie. Still, apart from these threads of continuity, *Bride of Frankenstein* bears little more resemblance to the book than did its predecessor.

The Monster (Boris Karloff) juxtaposed to the image of Christ suffering on the cross, in *Bride of Frankenstein* (1935)

Why was the Shelley source so drastically rewritten for the screen? In large part, perhaps, because the dialogue and narration of the original would have fallen flat when spoken by actors. Much of the narration of Victor Frankenstein and the monster, in fact, now reads awkwardly. One of the still-eloquent passages: the monster's account of his introduction to the world. ("I was delighted when I first discovered that a pleasant sound, which often saluted my ears, proceeded from the throats of the little winged animals who had often intercepted the light from my eyes.") Another: his farewell to the world. ("Am I to be thought the only criminal, when all humankind sinned against me?") The tale of Frankenstein was ripe for re-imagining.

"I love dead. Hate living." In this direct sequel to the 1931 *Frankenstein*, Henry Frankenstein's (Colin Clive) colleague Dr. Pretorius (Ernest Thesiger)—"a very queer-looking old gentleman," and Henry's old philosophy professor—grows miniature, human-looking beings "from seed." ("You must see my creations!") Dr. Pretorius and the Little People. One of these little perpetual-motion machines looks like the "very devil"—"There's a certain resemblance to me, don't you think?" he asks Henry. Dwight Frye's Fritz, from the original, is dead. (Frye, however, is back, and in fine, sardonic form, as the body-snatcher Karl [commenting regarding a corpse]: "Pretty little thing in her way, wasn't she?") But—like "this strange man you call a Monster" (Boris Karloff)—Fritz lives again, in effect, in the form of Pretorius, the new brain-wrangler: "I have created, by my method, a perfect human brain, already living, but dormant," ready for use in the body of the Bride (Elsa Lanchester). A pessimistic theology: Dr. Frankenstein, aka God, provides the spark of life. ("A mortal man who dared to emulate God.") Pretorius, the devil, brings the brain, and the latter proves to be no more viable than the brain that Fritz brought to the (operating) table.

If, for Pretorius, life—especially, the creation of life—is a lark, for poor manic-depressive Henry it has gotten to be prolonged agony. Haunted by the past—in the form of his monster—and terrified of the future—in the form of Pretorius and his goading—Dr. Frankenstein has, in this film, been recreated in the image of the Victor Frankenstein of the book, who is forever "miserable and overcome by a thousand fears." Here, he simply acts as counterpoint to Pretorius. In retrospect, it seems, in fact, that Henry has been more or less irrelevant since the middle of *Frankenstein*, when he effectively relinquished responsibility for the care and feeding of his creation. Essentially a quitter, he's tormented, and rightfully so, but poor Colin Clive suffers, too, in this fairly thankless, one-or-two-note role. Sour Dr. F's original gusto is really rekindled only near the end here when, on the verge of the Bride's vivification, the camera angles, famously, start going crazy. ("Shall we put the heart in now?")

"I take great relish in savoring each separate horror!" The power now belongs to Pretorius, in effect a mocking mirror reflecting back to Henry his

original enthusiasm, and underlining the strain of callousness in the latter. The role of Pretorius is a brilliant invention, if the role of Henry Frankenstein could have stood some reworking. Instead: another invention, the hermit (O.P. Heggie), who befriends the Monster. Who responds to him, that is, as Henry might have responded, in the first place, in *Frankenstein*. Henry, that is, might have been the one to introduce him, back then, to "food"/"smoke"/"friend"/sweet music. But that's another shorter, sweeter, tamer, less memorable movie … As would be *Frankenstein and the Hermit*, a 43-minute movie ending with the monster smoking a cigar and the hermit playing his violin … The hut is just an oasis of peace.

"Oh, he's quite harmless—except when crossed." The Frankenstein tale is generally considered a tale about a creature with a bad brain. However, as played out, it seems more a tale of a creature with a bad face. Make the Monster handsome … no screaming, many friends. The Bride is a step in this direction—lipstick, drawn eyebrows, etc., applied, one assumes, by Pretorius. Her brain, though, works like a light bulb fritzing out: head one way, then the other … short-circuited screams ... the unladylike hiss. But the Groom's defective brain seems really not so terribly defective. Unsurprisingly, he responds well to kindness, not so well to meanness. And he learns. He approaches the shepherdess (Ann Darling) hopefully. She screams. He approaches the Gypsies hopefully, with open, waving arms. They scream and scatter. The light dawns.

Now, having learned caution, he greets the hermit with a preemptive growl, as he throws open the door to the hut. He quickly readjusts and softens when the hermit warmly welcomes him in. He's not that different from ourselves: tit-for-tat responses. Or, for that matter, that different from Dr. Frankenstein, who automatically snaps out of his funk whenever he picks up the scent of breakthroughs on the AI front of his time—Pretorius' mini-menagerie, the Bride. And that may be the point.

"I cannot see, and you cannot speak." Unwittingly, Pretorius instructs the monster, by example, in deceptive appearances—the monster comes to realize that "friend—good" is just the beginning of that particular lesson. There's no doubting the sincerity of the hermit sequence, a Christian idyll, but the sequence ends with the Monster's new friend taken away from him, the friend's hut in flames, and the Monster himself alone again: "Alone bad, friend good." Karloff—drawing out the words "alone" and "bad"—evokes the whole harrowing history of the Monster in them. The lessons learned during his idyll are quickly unlearned by the Monster. It's Pretorius who unteaches him, who gives him his unsentimental education.

"Woman—friend!" The bad doctor assures him he's his friend, but the assurance is only a means to an end, the enlisting of Henry in the plan to create a mate for the Monster. Pretorius is not his friend; the bride proves not to be his friend, though Pretorius has promised she'll be a "friend for you." Acute pathos and portent of the film's conclusion: the monster gesticulating helplessly and crying "Friend!" after the hunters whisk the hermit away from the burning hut. So much for the hermit's claim, "Fire—good!" So much to unlearn ...

"The kites! The kites! Get 'em ready!" Pretorius is not necessarily a butterfingers as a scientist. The problem with the bride's brain isn't technical, the William Hurlbut screenplay suggests—it's elemental. Pretorius' science is a dead end, creation for creation's sake, certainly not for the Monster's sake. Pretorius and Frankenstein (in spite of himself) agree—the creation of life is "enthralling"—and the climactic sequence, the fashioning of the bride, seems at first to endorse their view: The crash of machinery, the thunder, the careening storm kites, the disorienting camera angles (John J. Mescall, photography), the wildly celebratory music (Franz Waxman), and the operating table's ascent to the sky ("It's coming up!") enthrall, make us complicit in the creators' excitement. Just when you think it can't get any more electrifying (in any sense you like), the lightning itself seems to plummet down the coils to the body on the operating table. Just when you think that the combination phallic-coil-gizmo and operating table can't go any higher—after reaching the roof—two cables are hastily attached to same and the electric vessel soars further into the sky, and would have soared indefinitely, apparently, if not for the anchoring cables.

"We belong dead." In fact, this sequence endorses the scientists' view, but the shorter, follow-up coda: the end-of-the-affair hiss of the bride, the tears

The Monster juxtaposed to the image of Death/The Grim Reaper

of the groom, as he pulls the doomsday switch, endorses the Monster's view: There's more to it than enthrallment, gentlemen. Creation is just the beginning. The Whale/Hurlbut/John Balderston film encompasses both views. It's at once exultant and despairing. The Monster's achingly hopeful, simple gesture—patting his "mate's" hand—makes her rejection of him all the more crushing. In immediate retrospect, it's nastily poignant. The earlier scene where Waxman's stirring music mirrors the righteous fervor of the angry townsfolk, as the bound Monster flails helplessly in the bottom of the cart and is carried away, foreshadows the magnificent climatic sequence and its sobering coda.

Notes: The perpetually cloudy or foggy backdrops in *Frankenstein* and its sequel evoke (cheaply, it's true) a most inhospitable environment.

Organized religion takes it on the chin here, in the form of Pretorius' disapproving little "archbishop" and the like statue in the cemetery, which the monster angrily topples. Disorganized religion, however—the hermit's simple faith—shines through, if its power proves very circumscribed.

Bride of Frankenstein re-situates the story to around 1900—the young woman whose bones are ticketed for the Bride "died 1899." Thus can the plot introduce a telephone.

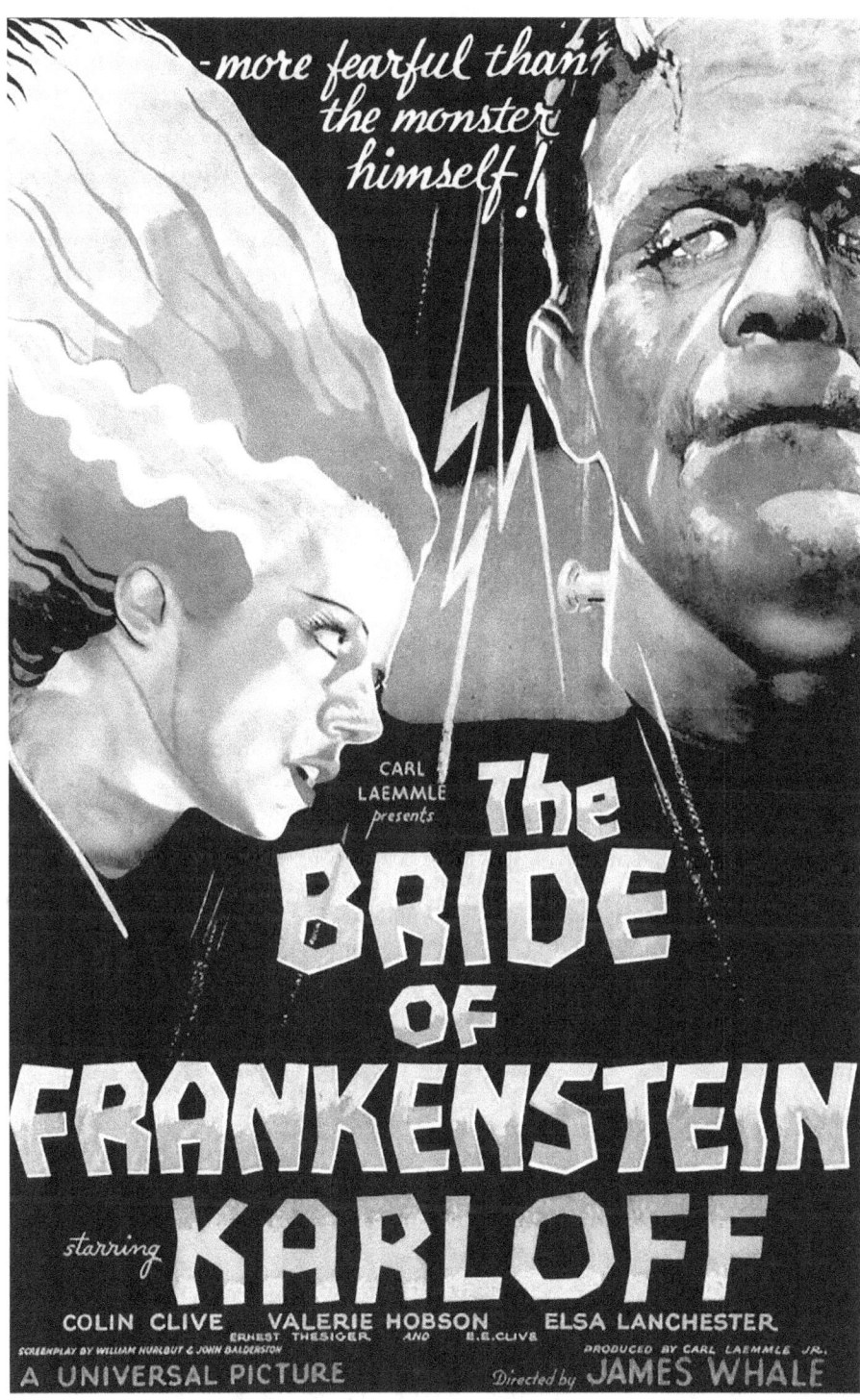

1-sheet poster from *Bride of Frankenstein*

Whale and company seem to be having fun with their signature line from *Frankenstein*. Minnie (Una O'Connor) shrieks "It's alive!" when she finds the Monster still alive; she shrieks "He's alive!" when she sees the doctor reviving. Later, another variation: Dr. Frankenstein cries "She's alive!" when he hears his kidnapped baroness (Valerie Hobson) on the phone. Finally, the doctor cries "She's alive!" regarding the other bride.

"Yes, there have been developments since he came to me." Note how Pretorius, here, takes credit for teaching the Monster how to speak ("Frankenstein!")—but it was the hermit who began the vocabulary lessons.

Look for the old Gypsy woman. ('We've got no pepper and salt!') It's Elspeth Dudgeon, from *The Old Dark House* and *The Woman Who Came Back*.

Karl and torch get the same treatment, which the Monster gave Fritz and torch in *Frankenstein*.

The too-sweet organ music threatens to send the hermit sequence into sentimentality, but, in context, the latter is decidedly unsentimental.

Valerie Hobson has the flavorless role of the other bride, Henry's. ("We are not meant to know those things!")

There was another memorable use of off-angle photography the same year, in the "Lullaby of Broadway" number in *Gold Diggers of 1935*. *Bride of Frankenstein* might be Grave Diggers of 1935.

(*The Return of Frankenstein*—original title; *Frankenstein Lives Again!*—another alternate title). Universal. D: James Whale. SP: William Hurlbut. Adap: Hurlbut, John L. Balderston, from Mary Shelley's novel *Frankenstein*. Ph: John J. Mescall. Mus: Franz Waxman. AD: Charles D. Hall. Mkp: Jack Pierce. PhFX: John P. Fulton. SpFX: Kenneth Strickfaden, David S. Horsley. Ed: Ted Kent. Sd: William Hedgcock. Cost: Vera West. P: Carl Laemmle, Jr. With Boris Karloff, Colin Clive, Ernest Thesiger, Elsa Lanchester, Valerie Hobson, Gavin Gordon, Douglas Walton, Una O'Connor, E.E. Clive, Lucien Prival, O.P. Heggie, Dwight Frye, Reginald Barlow, Mary Gordon, Anne or Ann Darling, Ted Billings, Billy Barty, Walter Brennan, John Carradine, D'Arcy Corrigan, Grace Cunard, Jack Curtis, Elspeth Dudgeon, Helen Jerome Eddy, John George, Marilyn Harris, Rollo Lloyd, Torben Meyer, Edward Peil, Sr., Tempe Pigott, Joan Woodbury; 75 minutes

Ref: "A lot of jollification, nice fancy, elegant mounting—there is, in short, beauty as well as the beast"—Otis Ferguson, *The New Republic*, 6/29/35.

Scarlet Street 26:28-33: Bob Madison interview with Christopher Bram, author of *Father of Frankenstein*, filmed as *Gods and Monsters*.

Film Quarterly, v36 #4:42: author's review of James Curtis' book *James Whale*.

"It is this excellent camera work coupled with an eerie but lingering musical score by Franz Waxman (one of Hitler's gifts to Hollywood) that gives a great deal of the film its real horror"—*Variety* 5/15/35.

"Satirical, exciting, funny, and an influential masterpiece of art direction"—rogerebert.com

"There has never been another movie that looks quite like this one ... It showcases probably the finest performance of Boris Karloff's movie career"—Bill Warren, avrev.com 10/19/99.

MARK OF THE VAMPIRE

Mark of the Vampire released April 26, 1935: "It is the darkness." Key personnel from the two 1931 versions of *Dracula* returned in one or the other of two follow-ups in 1935 and 1936, respectively. And one person—John Balderston—figured in all four films. He of course co-wrote the source play for the two *Dracula*s, and (uncredited) was a contributing writer for *Mark of the Vampire* and (again uncredited) a treatment author for *Dracula's Daughter*. And the latter film reunited scriptwriter Garrett Fort and actor Edward Van Sloan from the Lugosi *Dracula*, and George Robinson (cinematography) and Heinz Roemheld (music) from the Spanish version of *Dracula*. Charles D. Hall's sets were used for all three *Dracula* films. Finally, *Dracula* director, Tod Browning, and star, Bela Lugosi, returned for *Mark of the Vampire*.

A lobby card showing Luna (Carroll Borland) and Count Mora (Bela Lugosi) from *Mark of the Vampire* (1935)

Back cover of the pressbook for *Mark of the Vampire,* showing various style posters

Czechoslovakia after midnight ... In some ways, the 1935 Browning film is the laziest of the four; in some ways, it's the most impressive. Lionel Barrymore's Professor Zelen performs the same walking-guidebook function as Edward Van Sloan's Professor, in *Dracula* and *Dracula's Daughter,* and is more mechanical in the role than is Van Sloan. Mina (Helen Chandler) here becomes Irena (Elizabeth Allen), Jonathan (David Manners) becomes Fedor (Henry Wadsworth), and the two new actors repeat most of the same old scenes. And with stunning blatancy, verging on plagiarism, the stone staircase of Castle Dracula becomes the stone staircase of Castle Mora, complete with Son of Giant Spider Web. The bugs, bats, and possums are back, too, right down to that plucky spider clambering up the stone wall.

Yet, the walking-undead sequences seem, at the same time, wholly original. The scenes with Count Mora (Lugosi) and his daughter, Luna (Carroll Borland), "in her grave clothes," may begin on the carbon-copy staircase, but they're more in the spirit of *Dracula*'s cellar scenes, the ones in Castle Dracula and Carfax Abbey. That is, they're dialogue-free and eerier for it. They're like an inspired extension of the comparable scenes in *Dracula.* The silence of the vampires seems almost ... supernatural. Yes, the Lugosi voice is missed. Here, he just gazes at the children of the night—the beetles and the bat—rather than speaking admiringly of them.

The "voice" of the undead: the unusual sound effects. At various points in the film, the wind effects blend with singing and the music of a pipe organ. In this film, the wind is orchestrated—at least, it seems partly wind, but also partly some kind of subdued howling, or whirring, the sound of some supernatural "motor," as it were—an aural undeath or unlife force. The wind and fog *follow* Mora and Luna, even into the rooms of the house—a script dated

January 5, 1935 (when the production was still called *The Vampires of Prague*) notes that the "mist seems to cling to [Luna] and follow with her." You'd think that the other characters would catch on and be tipped off to her presence by the mist and wind. It seems only right to mention everyone connected with sound effects and editing here, from Douglas Shearer (director) to G.A. Burns (uncredited, sound mixer), to James Graham, T.B. Hoffman, and Michael Steinore (uncredited, sound effects editors).

The January version of the screenplay (by Guy Endore and Bernard Schubert, with additional dialogue by Ornitz, Kraft, and Balderston) contains virtually no hint of these sound effects, though most of the finished film's visual wonders (James Wong Howe, photography) are already in place, including the transformation of Luna from bat to human form: "Her wings closely fold before her, becoming part of her shroud-like garment." (The long-lost silent version of *Mark of the Vampire*, *London after Midnight* [1927], also apparently included this effect. See page 144 of Philip J. Riley's book of the film.) And that inimitably creepy background touch (as seen from the cemetery vault), the wandering dog, is described here as a "shaggy wolf-like beast"; but the shot of the spec-

tral onlookers, Mora and Sir Karell (Holmes Herbert), in the same scene, would be added later. Fortunately, two or three limp comic scenes were dropped.

Unfortunately, some horror scenes were also lost: The movie's short sequence with the "old crone" (Jessie Ralph), in the graveyard, continues—in the script—in her "tumbledown, weather beaten shack," where a bat ("a vampire!") flutters outside her window, only to "retreat angrily" when confronted

Pressbook herald for *Mark of the Vampire*

by an anti-vampire charm, wolf's-claw (a "thorny herb"), which weapon becomes, in the film, bat-thorn. In a scene only reported verbally in the film, a "shadow [which] detaches itself from the surrounding shadows swoops down upon Fedor." In the screenplay, the vampires' introductory scene also includes the "third vampire" (James Bradbury, Jr.), who seems to be "on a quest of his own" and who "exits out of scene."

Also dropped: a continuation of the castle day scene in which Zelen directs everyone's attention to a bat hanging from a tapestry rod, a scene dropped perhaps because it came off a bit silly: Zelen stands up on a chair and "brings his head on a level with the bat—stands there, studying it. Slowly the little beady eyes of the bat open—and stare at the Professor ... Into the scene comes the Professor's hand, holding a magnifying glass ... INSERT MAGNIFYING GLASS, behind which, magnified, are seen the terrifying eyes and face of the bat. Professor: 'I wish there were some way to tell ... if this bat is one of them!'"

Dramatically, *Mark of the Vampire* has few, if any, wonders. Mind-numbing scenes with Barrymore, Allan, Jean Hersholt, and Wadsworth alternate—with maddening regularity—with the above "demons of the castle" aural/visual treats. It's like peas and carrots/dessert/peas and carrots/dessert. If only one could mix a Renfield in with the peas and carrots. The vacuous all-a-hoax ending consumes the last 10 minutes or so, though a brief coda with the vampire actors at least allows Lugosi to speak: "I was greater than any *real* vampire!" Luna the Bat Woman: "Sure, sure, but get off your makeup!" There is, however, a bizarre integrity to the way the film switches gears. It's Irena who breaks the spell. She can't work with the actor who plays and strongly resembles her dead father. And just as she cries, "I can't do it!," the wind effects cease. And the cobwebs are gone! Something completely different—an odd reverse-magic ...

File the fabulously forbidding presences of Lugosi and Borland under Visual rather than Dramatic. Of the other, non-vampire actors, Lionel Atwill, as Inspector Neumann, is virtually the only one who escapes the general malaise. In a warm-up for his Inspector Krogh, in *Son of Frankenstein*, he provides perfectly clipped briskness for lines like (to Donald Meek's doctor): "You're no moon-flower—you're a morning glory."

A tip of the hat to Eric Hoffman.

Note: Barrymore's is the only name above the title, natch.

Question: Left unresolved: Is our Professor in fact a vampirologist or just a private detective?

(*The Vampires of Prague*—working title): MGM. D, P: Tod Browning. SP: Guy Endore, Bernard Schubert. Story, *The Hypnotist*, by Browning. Contributing Writers: John L. Balderston, H.S. Kraft, Samuel Ornitz. Ph: James Wong Howe. AD: Cedric Gibbons. Ed: Ben Lewis. Mkp: Jack Dawn, William Tuttle. PhFX: Warren Newcombe. Sd: Douglas Shearer, G.A. Burns, James Graham, T.B. Hoffman, Michael Steinore. Gowns: Adrian. P: also E.J. Mannix. With Lionel Barrymore, Bela Lugosi, Lionel Atwill, Jean Hersholt, Elizabeth Allan, Henry Wadsworth, Carroll Borland, Donald Meek, Jessie Ralph, Ivan Simpson, Leila Bennett, June Gittelson, Holmes Herbert, Michael Visaroff, Eily Malyon, James Bradbury, Jr., Egon Brecher, John George, Robert Greig, Torben Meyer, Christian Rub; 60 minutes

Ref: *Ecran Fantastique* 49:10,11.

Weldon.

Hardy/*HM*.

"The two vampires, Count Mora and Luna, are father and daughter. Their incestuous relationship in life, followed by Mora's killing Luna and then himself, damned them to rise from their graves as the Undead. Nothing survives of this in the final cut."—Frank J. Dello Stritto, "The British Horror *Ban* of 1937" (*Cult Movies* 14:25).

"Wonderfully atmospheric"—John Stell, *Monsters from the Vault*, Spring '97:67.

"Atmospherically photographed by the great James Wong Howe"—Stephen Jones, *Essential Monster Movie Guide*, pp241-243.

"In many ways, a dazzler of a horror movie"—Gregory Mank, *Midnight Marquee* 44:4-15.

"[Borland] almost takes the picture away from Lugosi on the chiller end"—*Variety* 5/8/35.

"Some very moody and effective moments"—Dave Sindelar (11/4/2001).

ONE FRIGHTENED NIGHT

One Frightened Night released May 1, 1935: "It wasn't human!" After the Tracking Delight opening shots, it's all pretty much downhill. Even the slick camerawork of Ernest Miller and William Nobles can't save a standard thunderstorm mystery. Even a "monster" ("There it was—that face!") can't save it. Not even Rafaela Ottiano (Malita in the 1936 *The Devil-Doll*) ...

The idea of the big-eyebrowed-monster-masked murderer is quite okay, but the mask is discarded almost as soon as it's introduced. An exhaustive search for highlights produced only the thunder and lightning, which attend two new arrivals at the front door of the old house. That said, this is at least livelier than most low-budget old-dark-house movies.

Note: The cantankerous old millionaire's (Charley Grapewin) trophy room features a sarcophagus complete with Egyptian mummy. Jasper's take on the relatives flitting about him as a "lot of mummies walking around" isn't far off.

Mascot. D: Christy Cabanne. SP: Wellyn Totman. Story: Stuart Palmer. Ph: Ernest Miller, William Nobles. Set Des: Edward G. Boyle. Ed: (sup) Joseph H. Lewis; Ray Curtiss. Sd: Terry Kellum. SpFX: John T. Coyle, Howard Lydecker. Mask Des: Markoff. P: Nat Levine. With Charley Grapewin, Mary Carlisle, Arthur Hohl, Wallace ("Wally" in credits) Ford, Lucien Littlefield, Regis Toomey, Hedda Hopper, Clarence Wilson, Evalyn Knapp, Rafaela Ottiano, Fred Kelsey, Roger Pryor; 66 minutes

Ref: *TVG*.

"The atmospheric opening credits are great"—*PV* 31:10.

"They've dragged in all the spook, storm, hidden door and shrieking heroine stuff, but well joined together"—*Variety* 10/9/35.

"Has more than its share of fun performances"—Dave Sindelar (5/12/2004).

AIR HAWKS

Air Hawks released May 7, 1935: "The person who buys my invention will control the skies!" Action, drama, sentiment (with a small dog and a doll), science fiction, and seven minutes of an old-dark-inn movie. Setting: Mountain View Inn. Atmosphere: night, a thunderstorm. Maniacal scientist Shulter's (Edward Van Sloan) greeting: "How do you like my workshop?" The main gizmo in the lab: a ray machine that destroys a model plane. How you know that Shulter is mad: the look on his face as he walks into a weird, spotlighted close-up. ("Give me enough money to build this in full scale, and I will destroy barracks, battleships, airplanes, anything!") That's actually only about six minutes, but a later, one-minute night scene at the inn features more cobwebs, scare music, and out-sized shadows.

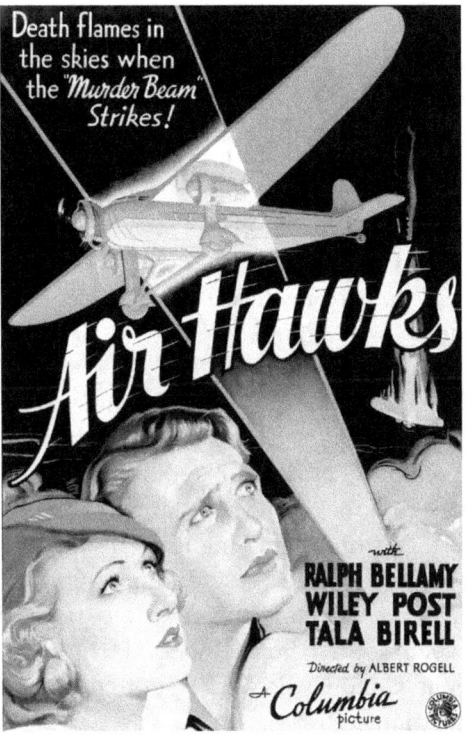

Those seven minutes are engagingly Gothic, but the prevailing drama is pretty routine flyboy stuff, if the acting is generally above average. Ralph Bellamy (as Barry Eldon) navigates his way through his longer speeches reasonably well and does some pioneering method acting with hands and fingers. (Sample speech: "Otto's been spending large sums of money for electrical equipment that could never be used in a night club!") Victor Kilian ingratiates, too, as Eldon's newspaperman buddy. Tala Birell is capable as chanteuse Renee. Douglass Dumbrille is his usual effortlessly hissable self. And aviator Wiley Post has a few minutes, as himself; he died in a plane crash with Will Rogers three months after *Air Hawks* was released. The little actress who plays Dorothy wins the Donnie Dunagan Prize for 1935.

A tip of the hat to Tom Weaver (yes, "barracks" not "Daleks") …

A second tip of the hat to Jim Shapiro.

Notes: And a kickier version of that intro line here would have been: "The person who buys my invention buys the skies!"

Score one point for the shot of Shulter's eye as seen through the machine's scope (photography: Henry Freulich).

Columbia. D: Albert Rogell. SP: Griffin Jay, Grace Neville, from Ben Pivar's story *Air Fury*. Ph: Henry Freulich. Mus: Howard Jackson. Ed: Richard Cahoon. Sd: Edward Bernds. P: Harry Cohn. With Ralph Bellamy, Tala Birell, Edward van Sloan, Wiley Post, Douglass Dumbrille, Robert Allen, Billie

Seward, Victor Kilian, Robert Middlemass, Wyrley Birch, Geneva Mitchell, Egon Brecher, Gino Corrado, Inez Courtney, William Irving, John Irwin, Charles King, Frank O'Connor, Joe Sawyer, Harry Strang, Guy Usher, Charles C. Wilson; 68 minutes

Ref: Jim Shapiro.
Hardy/*SF*.
Walt Lee.
"Exciting entertainment"—*Variety* 6/12/35.
"One of my favorite ray-guns-taking-down-airplanes movies"—Dave Sindelar (1/11/2004).

WEREWOLF OF LONDON

WereWolf of London released May 13, 1935: "There is a werewolf abroad in London." A bright full moon high in the background. An illuminated Tibetan ridge of rocks jutting up at 45 degree angles in the middle ground. A botanical expedition busying itself in the foreground. Charles Stumar's panoramic first shot promises a grand and glorious horror-adventure, along the lines of *The Mummy*. Unfortunately, *WereWolf of London* is not that picture. Main blame would seem to go to Robert Harris, who associate-produced his own story, and John Colton, who saddled both this film and *The Invisible Ray* with tired romantic triangles.

Henry Hull is neither sympathetic (as Dr. Glendon), nor scary (as the werewolf). And director Stuart Walker's staging of his full-moon attacks is pedestrian. The flora here is actually more intriguing than the fauna. Glendon's horticultural "zoo" features tentacled and sucker plants, which recall a similar scene in Murnau's *Nosferatu*, and they succeed in furthering the fantastic aura here. And his invisible-ray-ish moonlight machine makes, first, a moon vine, then the crucial mariphasa lumina lupina—or "phosphorescent wolf flower"—do quick, eerie time-lapse blooms. WereFlower of London. Warner Oland's understated, insinuating manner, as the other werewolf, Dr. Yogami, of the University of Carpathia, gives quiet portent to lines like: "In workaday modern London, today, at this

very moment, there are two cases of werewolfery known to me." Oddly, he calls his affliction "lycanthrophobia" (fearwolfery?), rather than the more-commonly-accepted "lycanthropy." Spring Byington provides a little more *December Bride* than one would want here, as a tipsy, dipsy socialite.

Credit Harris or Colton with a near-Bunuelian scene in which men in tuxes and women in gowns, at a dinner party, are unnerved by the off-screen howling of some "lost soul." And credit art director Albert S. D'Agostino with some cobwebs-and-shadows atmosphere for the Monk's Rest scene, in which Glendon has himself locked up for the night to protect his wife, Lisa (Valerie Hobson): "The werewolf instinctively seeks to kill the thing it loves best." Credit someone's artistic desperation with the culminating shots of an unexplained plane soaring into the clouds and segueing into the good old Universal, round-the-world airplane.

Universal. D: Stuart Walker. SP: John Colton. Story, Assoc P: Robert Harris. Ph: Charles Stumar. Mus: Karl Hajos. AD: Albert S. D'Agostino. Mkp: Jack Pierce. SpFX: John P. Fulton. VisFX: David S. Horsley. Ed: Russell Schoengarth. Sd: Gilbert Kurland. With Henry Hull, Warner Oland, Valerie Hobson, Lester Matthews, Lawrence Grant, Spring Byington, J.M. Kerrigan, Ethel Griffies, Zeffie Tilbury, Reginald Barlow, Egon Brecher, Tempe Pigott, Harry Stubbs; 75 minutes

Ref: *Midnight Marquee* 57:29-30.

"[*WereWolf of London* and *The Invisible Ray*] contain the same moving scene: standing on opposite sides of a doorway the wife begs the husband to join her. He can only refuse, for only he knows passing through means her death"—Frank J. Dello Stritto, "The British *Ban* on Horror Films of 1937," *Cult Movies* 14:25.

"Scenes of the hairy creature putting on his hat and coat before going out are simply laughable"—Stephen Jones, *Essential Monster Movie Guide*, p410.

"Hollywood can certainly use another Lon Chaney, and here is one [Hull] right in its lap"—*Variety* 5/15/35.

CHARLIE CHAN IN EGYPT

Charlie Chan in Egypt released June 21, 1935: "Ghost of Sekhmet disappears in room of mystic symbols." The supposed ghost of the Egyptian goddess of vengeance, Sekhmet, is employed to scare intruders away from the recovered treasure of Ahmeti, a priest of the 21st Dynasty, 3,000 years ago. ("The ancients endowed her with many supernatural powers, Mr. Chan.") For a good half its length, *Charlie Chan in Egypt* does seem to be a horror-fantasy, until ghosts and apparitions are explained away, and the rather desultory mystery story takes over. In fact, the three-minute introductory sequence apes the introductory scenes of Universal's *The Mummy*—another 3,000-years-ago movie—as an Egyptian worker (John George) pokes his head into the just-opened tomb

Pressbook herald from *Charlie Chan in Egypt* (1935)

of Ahmeti, clutches his throat, and falls dead. Thus begins a King Tut-like "superstition of the tomb," as Daniel B. Clark's camera pans up, down, and around the tomb, and ends with a flashlight-illuminated shot of the bottom of a stone sarcophagus.

In the first of two big scare sequences, the lab lights go out, the eyes of the statue of Sekhmet begin glowing, a gong sounds, and music shrieks. The all-at-once of the sight and sound effects is effectively disorienting. Yes—a pre-Lewton "bus." A later scene in the tomb, in the dead of night, more or less repeats these shock tactics. As noted, the supernatural is explained away, though it's not explained how the murderer managed to synchronize the lab effects with the simultaneous, drug-induced hallucinations of the heroine, Carol (Pat Paterson): Just as the eyes of the "piece of carved stone" light up, she "sees"—in the hall above—a "horrible head coming towards [her] out of the darkness— the head of Sekhmet!" Yow!

Charlie Chan in Egypt is a riot of inventive, politically-incorrect casting. Swedish Warner Oland, of course, plays the great Chinese detective. Briton Nigel de Brulier is Edfu Ahmad, Egyptian servant, craftsman, and apparent descendant of Ahmeti. Sicilian Paul Porcasi plays an Egyptian police inspector. Spanish Rita Cansino, whose name would be changed to Rita Hayworth, plays Nayda, Egyptian servant. And Stepin Fetchit plays the terrified Negro handyman Snowshoes. Something for everyone …

Oland brings a light gravity to his role, which sees Chan at first seemingly disgraced, then redeemed. Everything seems to be right at Oland's fingertips, dramatically speaking—he gives key words easy emphases, and underlines his bigger pronouncements by understating them. ("Every detail most important where murder concerned.")

Snowshoes is a terrible stereotype, but Stepin Fetchit's stylized approach yields intermittent delights, like his funny, prolonged muttering regarding "all them hants." His chronic whine is an extreme aesthetic tactic, like Virginia O'Brien's deadpan in Red Skelton movies. Two other characters treat Snowshoes rather rudely, perhaps to set them up as meanie murder suspects. At any rate—apart from Warner Oland and Stepin Fetchit—the movie is stiffly acted.

The key "very thin glass vibrate to certain sound" idea (in Chan's words) was "always technically feasible," according to film historian Bill Warren, "since a loud sound at the right pitch really can shatter some glass, if the glass is quite thin." While the shattering idea, that is, sounds novel, it's not science fiction, and was used again in *Mr. Wong, Detective* (1938) and its Chan remake, *Docks of New Orleans* (1948).

The composer of the "simple" Egyptian melody, which Barry (James Eagles) plays on the violin, has apparently never been identified.

Fox. D: Louis King. SP: Robert Ellis, Helen Logan. Ph: Daniel B. Clark. AD: Duncan Cramer, Walter Koessler. Ed: Alfred DeGaetano. Sd: Albert Protzman. Cost: Helen A. Myron. P: Edward T. Lowe. With Warner Oland, Pat Paterson, Thomas Beck, Rita Hayworth, Stepin Fetchit, Jameson Thomas, Frank Conroy, Nigel De Brulier, Paul Porcasi, James Eagles, Frank Reicher, George Irving, John Davidson, John George; 73 minutes

Ref: *Variety* 6/26/35.

"The drugged cigarettes [plot device] was most likely inspired by a cleverer use of the same device in Ben Stoloff's 1933 horror film, *Night of Terror*"—Ken Hanke, *Charlie Chan at the Movies*.

"Lively and entertaining ... Stepin Fetchit ... the master of slow motion"—Andre Sennwald, *NYT* 6/24/35.

The VANISHING RIDERS

The Vanishing Riders released July 3, 1935: "There ain't no such thing as ghosts." In a plot to scare baddie Wolf Lawson (Wally Wales) and his gang, Bill Jones (Bill Cody) and young Tim Lang (Bill Cody, Jr.) don white-painted shrouds and bring the vaunted "ghosts of Silver City" to life. ("This town is supposed to be full of hants, ghosts of the former citizens.") Indeed, two ghosts on ghost-horses laugh and seem to vanish, and then momentarily reappear a few yards away, getting the jump on Godardian jump cutting. And Junior's ghost, at one point, disappears, inexplicably—magic and the supernatural were not supposed to be part of the plot. ("This is a spooky spot.")

Ghostly humans as well as ghostly horses appear in *The Vanishing Riders* (1935).

The behind-the-credits drawing of a scythe-wielding skeleton on a skeletal horse promises horror; the two men and their two horses in ghost costumes deliver Camp, as "the spooks" scare the bad guys—grown men!—although both men and horses are accidentally adorable, in a Happy Halloween sort of way. Complete with a very unconvincing fist fight, rope-expert Junior, and singing bad guys.

Spectrum. D: Robert F. Hill. SP: Oliver Drake. Ph: Bill Hyer. Ed: Holbrook N. Todd. P: Ray Kirkwood. With Bill Cody, Bill Cody, Jr., Ethel Jackson, Hal Taliaferro, Donald Reed, Budd Buster, Milburn Morante; 58 minutes

Ref: *FD* 7/2/35.

"One of the weaker weird Westerns"—Dave Sindelar (7/3/2012).

The RAVEN

The Raven (poem—Edgar Allan Poe): This lament for a lost love, Lenore, is rather a trifle, but oh! that rhythm. And, no, it's not "Night's Plutonium shore."

The Pit and the Pendulum (short story—Poe): "But what mainly disturbed me was the idea that [the pendulum] had perceptibly *descended*." Or, the Pit, the Pendulum, the Rats, and the "Closing Walls." The solid core: Poe's description

Window card from *The Raven* (1935)

of the insinuating movement of the pendulum, and of the Inquisition prisoner's various reactions to same. Most dire: the thing *hisses* ... The rest of the story is mostly typical Poe fear and loathing. The ending is absurdly happy, but it's also a sort of reward for the protagonist's admirable ingenuity.

The Raven (1915): Edgar Allan Poe (Henry B. Walthall) suffers wine-engendered visions regarding Lenore, a floating skull, and a raven (as the poem unfolds, in inter-titles), ending in her leading his spirit away. This sequence is oddly evocative, partly thanks to the ominousness of the verse. There's not much more to be had in this 45-minute version of the 57-minute movie

The Raven released July 8, 1935: In *The Raven*, Bela Lugosi has one of the great mad, bad roles, as surgeon Richard Vollin, and one of the great mad, bad lines: "Poe, you are avenged!" The doctor's madness takes the form of the torture of others, physical and psychological: "A man of genius ... begins to think of torture, torture for those who have tortured him." And it helps that the actor—who clearly loves the sound of certain words—finds new oratorical juice in words like "torture" and "horror." He makes them his own, although the super-campy dialogue ultimately fails Lugosi—his best moments here are actually wordless.

Vollin is his own worst psychotherapist: "I tear torture out of myself by torturing you!" he informs his nemesis, Judge Thatcher (Samuel S. Hinds), who finds him a singularly unsuitable match for his daughter, Jean (Irene Ware). Of necessity, Vollin's method fails. The screams from Jean (in the diminishing room) and the groans from her father (under the pendulum) offer, at best, temporary relief. Vollin just gets madder, more self-tortured.

In fact, his helpless, climactic mad cackling is the closest he comes to a sympathetic moment—the closest the movie comes to illuminating the apparent fact that, ultimately, he's at the mercy of the merciless ... himself. This fact perhaps explains the oddity of Vollin's abbreviated death scene, in the diminishing room, which would seem to have been a fine occasion for Lugosi to emote. The end, for Vollin, actually—in retrospect—came a little earlier, in complete, untreatable, flailing-arms madness. In this light, his death, then, is, properly, anticlimactic. The Lugosi flailing-arms business comes just after the "avenged" line, and it's curiously uncomfortable for the viewer. It seems uncontrolled, almost as if Lugosi were no longer just feigning madness, almost as if, yes, he were actually going ... Oh, right, yes—that's acting, of a rather naked sort.

Generally, one does not look to Lugosi for subtlety, but there is another amazing moment in *The Raven*, which apparently got past the censors because it is only a moment, a fleeting look on the actor's face, as he tells his prospective henchman, Bateman (Boris Karloff), "So you put the burning torch into [the bank clerk's] face ... into his eyes." Note the momentary empathy—it's in Vollin's eyes, the sick there-and-gone smile—just before "into his eyes," as if Vollin sensed a kindred twisted spirit. This perverse moment is perhaps not often noted because it comes in the middle of the famous, accidentally hilarious "acetylene torch" scene. (Bateman: "Sometimes you can't help things like that.")

In this lobby card from *The Raven* (1935), Lester Matthews and Boris Karloff confront one another.

Jean shows Bateman some kindness, and the latter finds he can't take part in having her diminished. He frees her and thus redeems himself (and angers Vollin), at the end—and, so, twice, in 1935, Karloff throws a switch and dooms himself. (See, too, *Bride of Frankenstein*, in which he also dooms others.) In part, the movie is a slapdash homage to Poe, but the Vollin-Bateman relationship has a crazy, zany integrity to it. The crux (Vollin to Bateman): "I can use your hate." Karloff's talents, however, are not put to their best use with this paranoid, simple-minded thug—the searing, Frankenstein-monster pathos (again it's the eyes) seems out of place. His is a miscalculated performance, buried by its camp aspects.

Meanwhile, Hinds' Thatcher is unalloyed camp. See him try, most haplessly, to cool the Vollin-Jean relationship: "You don't want a young girl like Jean falling in love with you." If there is a level of obviousness beyond David Boehm's dialogue, Hinds finds it.

Notes: In one respect, *The Raven* is perhaps unique. It introduces its stars, in large letters, as KARLOFF and LUGOSI. Boris was given this royal treatment more than once, but this seems to have been the only time for Bela.

Unfortunately, Universal's repeated good cast—both before and after the film proper—is in error, as the cast/character credits switch the roles of Ian

Wolfe (Geoffrey) and Spencer Charters (Col. Grant).

The movie uses more of *The Pit and the Pendulum* than it does of *The Raven*—there's much play with the pendulum and some play with a diminishing room (from the story), and there's a bit with a door that opens into a pit.

Acting-wise, Karloff is at a triple disadvantage, limited as he is by bad writing, heavy makeup, and the use of only one eye. Early on, Vollin turns one of Bateman's eyes into a sort of dysfunctional omelet.

Universal. D: Lew Landers. SP: David Boehm (uncredited), Guy Endore, et al., from Edgar Allan Poe's poem *The Raven* and short story *The Pit and the Pendulum*. Ph: Charles Stumar. Mus: Clifford Vaughan. AD: Albert S. D'Agostino. Mkp: Jack Pierce. VisFX: John P. Fulton. Ed: Albert Akst. Sup Ed: Maurice Pivar. Chor: Theodore Kosloff. Assoc P: David Diamond. With Boris Karloff, Bela Lugosi, Irene Ware, Samuel S. Hinds, Lester Matthews, Spencer Charters, Inez Courtney, Ian Wolfe, Maidel Turner, Anne Darling, June Gittelson, Jonathan Hale, Walter Miller, Bud Osborne; 61 minutes

Ref: "A good horror flicker"—*Variety* 7/10/35.

Midgit window card from *The Raven*

The Raven (1963): Magician Scarabus (Boris Karloff) vs. magician Erasmus Craven (Vincent Price), with help from Peter Lorre's "dismal little fat man," Dr. Bedlo, whom Scarabus has transformed into a raven. It's all pretty much downhill after Lorre's ice-breaking first line: "How the hell should I know?" although Lorre has a delightful throwaway bit distractedly dusting a coffin with his out-sized wing. (Craven: "Thank you.") The belatedly-introduced Karloff's reassuringly commanding voice reminds one who's in charge—he's just about the only actor who doesn't succumb to the prevailing vacuousness. The climactic duel is alternately playful and insipid. This lackadaisical horror-comedy is a low point for, at least, Roger Corman, Richard Matheson, and Jack Nicholson. Note to this note: The 1987 Hong Kong horror-comedy *Ghostbusting* is partly an homage to the 1963 film; in 1987, the raven's line is: "Why are you so stupid?," and there's a duel of wizards.

MAD LOVE

Mad Love released July 12, 1935: "I, a poor peasant, have conquered science! Why can't I conquer love?" It's not surprising that it took some seven credited and uncredited writers (including Guy Endore, John L. Balderston, and Edgar Allan Woolf) to fashion a workable screenplay out of Maurice Renard's novel *The Hands of Orlac* (*Les Mains d'Orlac*). If the movie is still very uneven, it's a giant step up from the maddeningly convoluted book, which presents spiritualistic phenomena in unnecessarily great detail, then explains away same in unnecessarily great detail. One of the more intriguing phenomena—an "exteriorized" nightmare—proves to be, simply, a projected image; another, however—the strangling of a painter by a puppet supposedly inhabited by the soul of a criminal ("a criminal puppet!")—seems to have escaped explanation. [SPOILER]: In the novel's last, curious twist, pianist Stephen Orlac is revealed not to have had a murderer's hands grafted onto his wrists, after all—they were, it transpires, the hands of a man *framed* for murder. In the movie, the grafted hands of Orlac (Colin Clive) are indeed those of a murderer (Ed Brophy), a knife thrower, and they come in handy, at the end, in dispatching mad Dr. Gogol (Peter Lorre).

Dr. Gogol (Peter Lorre) from *Mad Love* (1935)

Peter Lorre's performance itself is uneven. His ultimately full-blown madman is no match, histrionically, for Lugosi, Laughton, and Clive, in comparable roles. But his earlier, muted-mad love scenes with Frances Drake's Yvonne Orlac are quietly unique. Already, the madman is there, but in the disarming form of a polite little love struck boy. The latter, of course, proves to be simply the other, repressed side of his later "Pygmalion"—to Yvonne's "Galatea." In the backstage-party scene, his abrupt, unwanted passionate embrace of Yvonne is sandwiched, beforehand, by a shy lips-slightly-parted-in-adoration look at her and, afterwards, by an embarrassed, oh, why did I do that? downward glance.

The sweet, sincere Gogol is there in the script, in, for instance,

Dr. Gogol and Yvonne Orlac (Frances Drake) embrace front and center, in this lobby card from *Mad Love*.

his explanation to Yvonne of his decision to go ahead with the long-shot graft: "I had to find a way—because you trusted me." And Lorre clearly and wonderfully comprehends and embodies the intertwining, in the character, of the perverse and the sweet. The sequence in which Yvonne admits to the doctor that he frightens her results in a double reaction: "You are cruel," he begins, angrily, but an insight changes his thought in midstream, and he concludes, "But only to be kind." The kindness may or may not be only in the mind of the beholder. Yes, she is honest here, but to save *him* grief, or her? Or both? Either way, Gogol is generous. For the second reaction, Lorre reins in his voice almost to an admiring, astonished whisper.

At the end, the hallucinating Gogol mistakes Yvonne for his wax statue of her: "My love has made you live!" But another idea: "Each man kills the thing he loves" creeps into his head, and he of course must be stopped, as described above. A less formulaic, perhaps even crueler, ending would have had the doctor incarcerated (for murdering Orlac's father [Ian Wolfe]), separated from his "Galatea."

Drake and Clive are not bad at all, in their respective roles, but theirs is a relatively cut-and-dry, sane love here. The worst that can be said of their relationship, in the movie, is that it takes up running time. In the book, the viv-

id but monotonous internal lives of Stephen and his wife (there called Rosine) are reduced to "her poor persecuted husband." Finally, note that, from one angle, *Mad Love* is a variation on *Frankenstein*, in which Clive now plays the "monster"—with bad hands rather than a bad brain, or bad face—rather than the creator, whom he succeeds in killing.

(*The Mad Doctor of Paris*—working title. *The Hands of Orlac*—British title): MGM. D: Karl Freund. SP: P.J. Wolfson, John L. Balderston. Adap: Guy Endore, from Maurice Renard's novel *Les Mains d'Orlac*. Ph: Chester Lyons, Gregg Toland. Mus: Dimitri Tiomkin. AD: Cedric Gibbons. Mkp: Norbert A. Myles. Ed: Hugh Wynn. Sd: Douglas Shearer. Cost: Dolly Tree. P: John W. Considine, Jr. With Peter Lorre, Frances Drake, Colin Clive, Ted Healy, Sara Haden, Edward Brophy, Henry Kolker, Keye Luke, Harold Huber, Isabel Jewell, Sam Ash, Hooper Atchley, Cora Sue Collins, Frank Darien, Billy Gilbert, Otto Hoffman, Robert Emmett Keane, Murray Kinnell, Rollo Lloyd, Michael Mark, Edward Norris, Sarah Padden, Carl Stockdale, Charles Trowbridge, Clarence Wilson, Ian Wolfe; 68 minutes

Ref: *Midnight Marquee* 45:25-29.

Fangoria 123:35: *Dr. Cyclops* review.

"Every ounce of horror has been wrung from the *Hands of Orlac* property"—*Variety* 8/7/35.

"A classic of Grand Guignol cinema"—Stephen Jones, *Essential Monster Movie Guide*, p235.

"I like this movie more each time I see it"—Dave Sindelar (3/25/2002).

The BLACK ROOM

The Black Room released July 15, 1935: "The house began with murder. It will end the same way." Baron Gregor (Boris Karloff) rules the House of de Berghman with an iron hand. ("Gregor is a monster!") A "fiend" in a "gloomy" Hungarian castle, circa 1800, he lives in fear of a prophecy, which holds that his younger (twin) brother Anton (Karloff) will kill him. ("I end as I began.") He dares to thwart the prophecy by killing Anton and taking his place.

The next best thing to a movie with Boris Karloff and Bela Lugosi is a movie with Boris Karloff and Boris Karloff. Unfortunately, it's two Karloffs

Pressbook herald from *The Black Room*

and about 50 stick figures here. This is a handsome but rather hollow costume drama with a dash of Poe—The Pit and the Prophecy. (The de Berghmans have a history of tossing enemies into a pit in their infamous Black Room.) If Karloff's early Universal classics did not take full advantage of his commanding, deep voice, Columbia's *The Black Room* makes up for that. As Gregor, his voice is full, rich, and menacing; as Anton, it's full, rich, and reassuring. And though they are not triplets, there is a third Karloff presence here—Gregor impersonating Anton, which impersonation entails quick, amusing switches between personae. However, Karloff's finest scene is all Gregor, when he is doing his best to ignore Mashka's (Katherine DeMille) passionate entreaties, by addressing the pear that he is eating. He proceeds to kill her, but his callous focus on the pear seems equally despicable. ("Adam should have chosen a pear.") The movie's second-most-notable element—after Karloff's performances—is the lyric sung, first, by Thea (Marian Marsh), then, by Mashka. It's simple, and speaks of "sweet music from nowhere." But it is both sweet and somehow eerie, cold, distant—distant in time as well as emotion. It's like an ancient echo, or at least a 200-year-old echo. One or more of the movie's three uncredited composers—Louis Silvers, Milan Roder, and R.H. Bassett—apparently composed it.

"One of the most beautiful melodies ever to grace a horror film"—Don G. Smith, in *Boris Karloff*, p137.

Notes: One curiosity—the opening credits list Karloff only as "Anton." The rocky exteriors seem more Southern California than Hungary.

The Raven of the same year made much use of a pendulum; *The Black Room* foregrounds a pit.

Allen G. Siegler's nimble camerawork contributes to the film's handsomeness.

(*The Black Room Mystery*—British title): Columbia. D: Roy William Neill. Story, SP: Arthur Strawn. SP: also Henry Myers. Ph: Allen G. Siegler. AD: Stephen Goosson. Ed: Richard Cahoon. Sd: Edward Bernds. VisFX: Jack Cosgrove, Roy Davidson. Cost: Murray Mayer. With Boris Karloff, Marian Marsh, Robert Allen, Thurston Hall, Katherine DeMille, John Buckler, Henry Kolker, Colin Tapley, Torben Meyer, John Beck, Sidney Bracey, Egon Brecher, John George, George Burr Macannan, Michael Mark, Robert Middlemass, Edward van Sloan, Frederick Vogeding, Paul Weigel; 70 minutes

Ref: "Roy William Neill has directed as well as possible a tawdry and obvious story"—*Variety* 8/21/35.

"A magnificent double (actually triple!) performance from Boris"—Joe Karlosi, dvddrive-in.com

CONDEMNED TO LIVE

Condemned To Live released Sept. 15, 1935: "The bat's abroad tonight!" A man whose mother was bitten by a vampire bat, in Africa, the night he was born, fears that he turns into a bat—"some huge, loathsome thing"—in the dark. ("It never happens in the light!") Bodies of villagers are found "drained of blood," with "great gaping holes" in their throats.

Condemned To Live might be a course in Bad Filmmaking 1A. It's a very odd "B" movie, a combination period piece and supernatural horror movie. The writer, Karen DeWolf, tended more towards *Blondie* and *Jones Family* movies, but she does come up with a novel monster, a sort of lycanthropic/Mr. Hyde vampire. ("The monster is a man!")

Most of the Good people here—Prof. Kristan (Ralph Morgan), Marguerite (Maxine Doyle), her father (Carl Stockdale), David (Russell Gleason)—are insufferably so. Only Pedro de Cordoba's Dr. Anders Bizet and Mischa Auer's hunchback Zan bring off the Good thing. De Cordoba's playing is quietly idiosyncratic. His manner and voice are effortlessly Wise, reassuring. ("The old superstition—a vampire bat.") Auer's performances always seem slightly off-kilter. His Good here is unexpected, out of left field. ("What good can there be in a hunchback?") And there's something balmily iconic about Auer as the hunchback carrying a woman's dead body into Bronson Caverns—it almost seems planned as a loopy image for the ages. The over-enthusiastic old villager (apparently Jean Handel) is loud fun. She's Invincible's answer to Una O'Connor.

If there's a creepy-in-spite-of-itself aspect to the movie, it's because so much of it takes place at night, in the dark—add to that the crazy, wild wind sounds as the professor carries the lamp through the woods. But the big "scary" out-go-the-lights sequence between the vampire man and Marguerite is so transparent it's just plain camp. Don't blow out that candle. And for heaven's sake, don't turn off the lamp! Oh, has the fireplace fire gone out? No, not the other candle! And oh my here come the clouds to cover the moon.

Notes: One oddity: The villagers run about with torches all through the movie, for the light, not just at the end, for a march on the castle.

The 1915 *The Inner Brute* has a similar premise. In same, the son of a woman scared by a tiger "inherits the instincts" of a tiger (*Motion Picture News* 7/3/15).

(*Life Sentence*—working title. *Demon of Doom*—reissue title). Chesterfield/Invincible. D: Frank Strayer. SP: Karen De-Wolf. Ph: M.A. Anderson. Title music: David Broekman. AD: Edward C. Jewell. Ed: Roland D. Reed. Sd: Richard Tyler. P: Maury M. Cohen. With Ralph Morgan, Pedro de Cordoba, Maxine Doyle, Russell Gleason, Mischa Auer, Lucy Beaumont, Carl Stockdale, Barbara Bedford, Robert Frazer, Ted Billings, Horace B. Carpenter, Dick Curtis, Jean Handel, Paul Seigel, Slim Whitaker; 67 minutes

Ref: *Variety* 10/9/35.

3-sheet poster from *Condemned to Live*

The CRIME OF DOCTOR CRESPI

The Premature Burial (short story—Edgar Allan Poe): A recounting of the horrors endured by cataleptics, including the narrator. In the most imaginative passage, *Shadow* has "thrown open the graves of all mankind" for the protagonist to see, and the buried alive outnumber the truly dead "by many millions": "From out the depths of the countless pits there came a melancholy rustling from the garments of the buried." A little heavy, at times, on the wretchedness of the afflicted. But, surprisingly, a happy ending!

The Crime of Doctor Crespi released Sept. 24, 1935: "He's been dead ... for a day and a half, and rigor mortis hasn't set in yet." Macabre on the cheap. An impossibly hokey love-triangle plot yields some bizarre premature-burial and back-from-the-virtually-dead scenes. Erich von Stroheim's Crespi is the one who commits the crime of burying romantic rival Stephen Ross (John Bohn) alive. His monologue ("Feel the cold of your own grave") over Ross's barely-alive body is sufficiently fiendish, and, yes, it's kind of Poe. It winds up, natch, with a "Pleasant dreams!" [SPOILERS]: Ross' later coming back to life and sitting up is fun, if not quite Imhotep. Finally, there's Crespi's droll, unstartled reaction to the walking dead man, as the latter limps into his office: "So you've come back to haunt me?"

There are also a few *Vampyr*-ish traveling shots of treetop boughs, and dirt gets thrown on the camera, suggesting that Ross's coffin sports a window. At one point, the film intercuts action on three fronts—doctor's office, doctor's

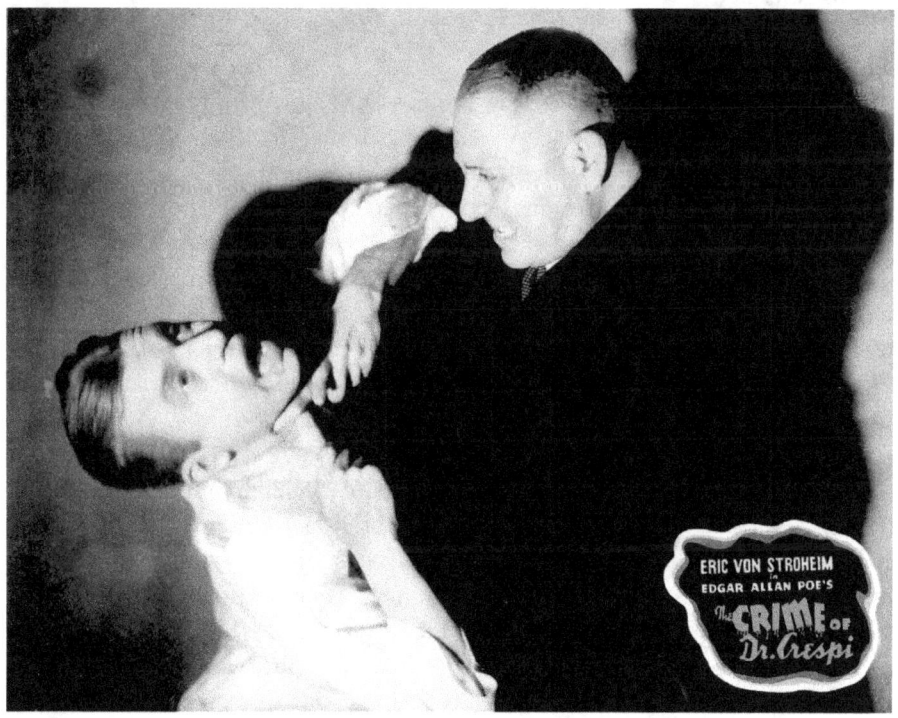

Erich von Stroheim as Crespi has his hands on the throat of Dwight Frye, in this lobby card for *The Crime of Doctor Crespi*.

house, and cemetery. It's not *Intolerance*, but it's ambitious, in an unambitious way. Von Stroheim and Dwight Frye are a potentially memorable team. But much von Stroheim time is given to flicking a little skeleton's head and sitting down and writing a report. It's a modernist performance, of sorts—he's very casual with the more functional dialogue, and barks his dramatic lines. Frye gives his "Will there be anything else tonight?" more undertone than it deserves, but he has little else to do.

Notes: The credits misspell the original author's name as "Edgar Allen Poe."

This rudimentary picture makes a sort of companion piece to the Poe cheapie of the year before, *Maniac*.

Republic/Liberty. D, SP, P: John H. Auer. SP: also Edward Olmstead, Lewis Graham, from Edgar Allan Poe's story, *The Premature Burial*. Ph: Larry Williams. AD: William Saulter. Ed: Leonard Wheeler. Sd: Clarence R. Wall. Mkp: Fred C. Ryle. With Erich von Stroheim, Harriet Russell, Dwight Frye, Paul Guilfoyle, John Bohn, Jean Brooks [as Jeanne Kelly]; 63 minutes

Ref: *Famous Monsters of Filmland* 10:20.

"As a baby scarer this is a weak entry"—*Variety* 1/15/36.

"Stroheim as Dr. Crespi is a wonder to behold"—Dave Sindelar (9/28/2001).

The GREAT IMPERSONATION

The Great Impersonation (novel—E. Phillips Oppenheim): "The ghost of Roger Unthank still haunts the Black Wood ... " Norfolk, England. A "most appalling and unearthly cry"—at once human and non-human—haunts Dominey Hall, where Sir Everard Dominey is believed to have killed Roger Unthank years ago. ("Any ghost alarms last night?") Has the latter's "spirit ... been taken possession of by some sort of great animal"? No—spirits "do not leave tracks ... " At any rate, the "ghoulish noises" of this "demon"—"half beast, half man"—provide the welcome Gothic counterpoint to the prevailing, tepid international intrigue. Is the German Baron von Ragastein impersonating the British Everard Dominey, or vice versa? The plot twists are pretty unbelievable, though the writing isn't bad.

The Great Impersonation released Dec. 9, 1935: "He'll haunt you out of this house!" Norfolk, England, 1914. The ghost of Roger Unthank (Dwight Frye) seems to haunt Dominey Hall ("The devil walks that part of this house by night, sir"), and his agonized shrieking unnerves Sir Everard Dominey's (Edmund Lowe) unstable wife, Eleanor (Valerie Hobson). [SPOILER]: At the end, Roger is seen mainly as a menacing shadow on the walls of the Hall.

This quasi-spy movie begins in East Africa, but turns left, into a horror movie ("ghosts and murders and whatnot"), intermittently, at Dominey Hall. The international intrigue is of no interest now, but the Gothic elements are

Edmund Lowe and Wera Engels strike a cute pose from *The Great Impersonation*.

fun, and they were not just added to capitalize on the horror boom of the mid-1930s. They were there in the book (see above).

Dwight Frye seems to be doing those half-human screams outside the mansion, but other unidentifiable sounds seem to be intermixed with his voice (sound: Gilbert Kurland). In long and medium shot, in heavy hairy makeup, he's visually unrecognizable. His mother Mrs. Unthank (Esther Dale) looks like a cross between Dracula's daughter and her advisor Sandor. Lowe, as usual, is The Great Blank, but Valerie Hobson, as his wife Eleanor, is sweet and touching, trying to regain her sanity. Milton Krasner's photography makes her nightgown, in one scene, a marvel of light and shadow. Look for bits and pieces of the sets of *The Old Dark House*, *Dracula*, *Frankenstein*, and *Bride of Frankenstein*.

Notes: In a sense there's another spoiler, above, but you wouldn't know it, thanks to the cockeyed game of impersonation, in both book and film.

In the book, the semi-villain von Ragastein was German; in the movie he's Austrian (and his name is spelled "Ragostein"). Was someone afraid of offending Germany (though not Austria)?

Universal. D: Alan Crosland. SP: Eve Greene, Frank Wead, from E. Phillips Oppenheim's novel. Ph: Milton Krasner. Mus: Heinz Roemheld, Clifford Vaughan. AD: Charles D. Hall. Ed: Philip Cahn. Sd: Gilbert Kurland. VisFX: John P. Fulton. Mkp: Jack Pierce. Cost: Brymer; (uncredited) Vera West. P: Edmund Grainger. With Edmund Lowe, Valerie Hobson, Wera Engels, Murray Kinnell, Dwight Frye, Esther Dale, Brandon Hurst, Henry Mollison, Ivan F. Simpson, Spring Byington, Lumsden Hare, Charles Waldron, Leonard Mudie, Claude King, Frank Reicher, Nan Grey, Henry Kolker; 68 minutes

Ref: "Will seem okay ... in the sectors where sophistication isn't too rife"—*Variety* 12/18/35.

"Dwight Frye makes it official by playing the bogy-man of the Black Bog"—Andre Sennwald, *NY Times* 12/14/35.

Highlights of 1936

In March, Warners released the last good American-made horror movie before the bleak years of 1937 and 1938—*The Walking Dead*, with Boris Karloff in an unusual role, even for him. In July, MGM released Tod Browning's *The Devil-Doll*, which was uneven, but it was a horror movie, and that was that, until 1939 ...

For the Philo Vance mystery *The Garden Murder Case*, writer Bertram Millhauser came up with an unsettling idea regarding induced "suicide," which he later re-used in the Sherlock Holmes mystery *The Spider Woman*. Universal paired Karloff and Lugosi one last time before the drought, but *The Invisible Ray* was otherwise a major disappointment, as was the studio's follow-up to *Dracula*, *Dracula's Daughter*, which featured only scattered salvageable scenes. The Halperins' follow-up to *White Zombie*, *Revolt of the Zombies*, might have done in horror movies if censorship hadn't.

The year in fear began (*Charlie Chan's Secret*) and ended (*Charlie Chan at the Opera*) with, yes, Charlie Chan.

Notable performances: Frieda Inescort (*The Garden Murder Case*), Boris Karloff, Ricardo Cortez, Marguerite Churchill (*The Walking Dead*), Nan Grey (*Dracula's Daughter*), Lionel Barrymore and Maureen O'Sullivan (*The Devil-Doll*), Sidney Blackmer (*The House of Secrets*), Warner Oland and Karloff (*Charlie Chan at the Opera*)

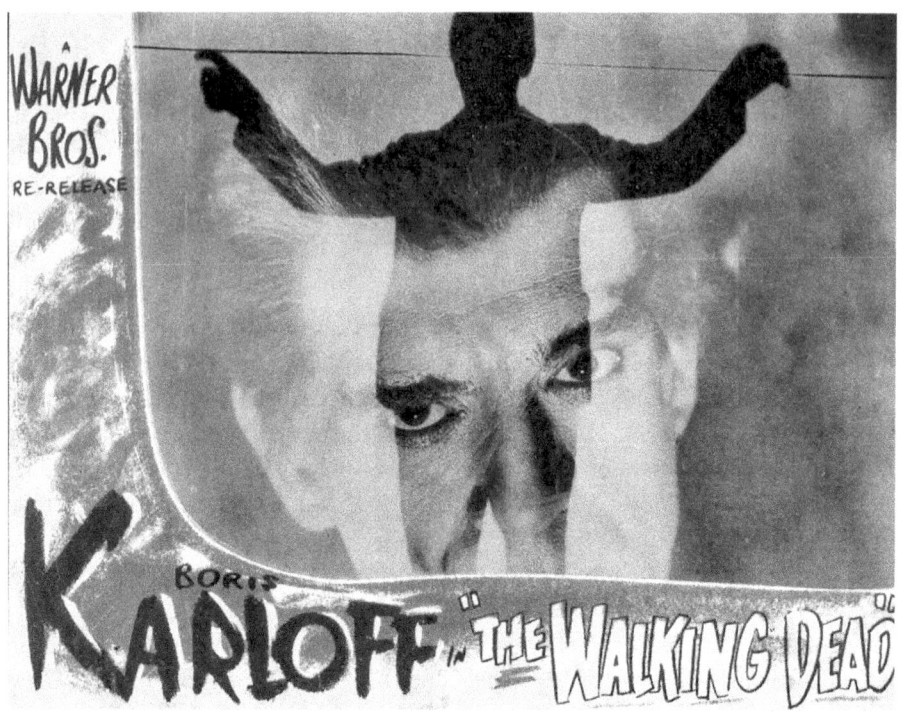

Notable direction: Michael Curtiz (*The Walking Dead*)

Notable writing: Bertram Millhauser (*The Garden Murder Case*), Robert Andrews et al. (*The Walking Dead*), Garrett Fort et al. (*The Devil-Doll*)

Notable photography: George Robinson (*The Invisible Ray* and *Dracula's Daughter*), Bill Hyer (*A Face in the Fog, Kelly of the Secret Service* and *The Rogues Tavern*), Hal Mohr (*The Walking Dead*)

Notable special photography: John P. Fulton, David S. Horsley (*The Invisible Ray*), uncredited; perhaps cinematographer Leonard Smith (*The Devil-Doll*)

Notable music: Heinz Roemheld (*Dracula's Daughter*)

Notable art direction: Van Nest Polglase (*Mummy's Boys*)

Notable sound effects: J.S. Westmoreland (*The Rogues Tavern*), Harry Jones (*Ghost-Town Gold*)

Notable mask: Herschel (*Charlie Chan at the Opera*)

Other films of interest:

Desert Phantom—a locked-house murder mystery regarding the "phantom of the old El Monte Mine." But there's no scene with the phantom! "Always been interested in ghosts"

Ellis Island—Ref: DVD: semi-spooky scene in cemetery

Ghost Patrol—invention "controls all electricity"

Helivision or *Hellevision*—TV invention, footage from 1909 Italian film *L'Inferno*. Ref: FJA. *FM* 67:11. *Cult Movies* 12:32. *Filmfax* 23:40-41

Jaws of the Jungle—"Winged demons of disaster—vampire bats! [These] horrible creatures ... blacken the skies." A shot or two at the beginning try to make this horror, but ... spliced-together thrills.

Killer at Large—*Variety* 10/28/36: "spook material," cemetery scene, Chaney, Jr. as the second coffin man ...

Last of the Warrens—scene in which a supposed dead man confronts the villain: "I've come to take you with me." And the speaker does seem to be impervious to bullets.

The Leavenworth Case—"fiendish doctor ... monkey he employs to turn loose gas"—*Variety* 1/22/36

The Man Who Lived Twice—*HSF1:* operation eliminates man's criminal tendencies

Moonlight Murder—*HSF4*: Generally mundane mystery features a voodoo-doll "curse" and a swami's (Pedro de Cordoba) death threat.

The Murder of Dr. Harrigan—*Variety* 1/22/36: "Patient, scared to death, goes to the morgue."

Pennies from Heaven—"I'm afraid the house is full of ghosts." An "old house in New Jersey" is turned into the Haunted House Cafe. Cool shadow effects for the Louis Armstrong number, which is actually more atmospheric than the haunted-house sequence.

Pilot X—the "Sky Murderer" here has a "split personality" and seems like a "winged demon." But there's no spookiness, despite a thunderstorm. Rudimentary

The Preview Murder Mystery—*Motion Picture Reviews*: "eerie atmosphere"

Trouble for Two—"I never saw anything like it—monstrous, weird, distorted minds!" Some seven creepy minutes here, at the Suicide Club, where the film's lighting and music darken. Mainly action, adventure, and romance. *Bride of Frankenstein* music for the credits

1936

CHARLIE CHAN'S SECRET

Charlie Chan's Secret released Jan. 10, 1936: "Will call on spirit world for message from great beyond." Is it an "old boogeyman" or "Bowan's spooks" that are responsible for the "spook business" in San Francisco's Colby House, a "strange house" with "funny rooms" and a "tinge of the graveyard"? At any rate, the chief suspects are Professor Bowan (Arthur Edmund Carewe), psychic researcher, and Carlotta (Gloria Roy), medium, when the body of a murdered man (Jerry Miley) turns up at a séance. A second séance prompts the hapless killer to throw a knife at a "spirit reflection in [a] mirror." ("I know now the one who fears discovery, the one who murdered.")

Thin Chan mystery regarding supposed "malevolent spirits in [an] ancient house." The séance provides the one bit of excitement when what appears to be your usual "phony ghost" turns out to be the above dead body, somehow fixed in a standing position before it topples to the floor. It's a well-engineered two-part shock: the ghastly, ghostly face, then the crumpled body. Ultraviolet-ray-goosed quinine sulfate on the corpse's face produces the main spectral effect, while the background music also seems to be a "manifestation from the world beyond."

In a later scene, Chan (Warner Oland) seems to be comforting Alice (Rosina Lawrence) with spiritual wisdom when he says [SPOILER]: "Though loved one seem to be taken away, remain always near"; in retrospect, he proves to have been speaking more literally. Herbert Mundin's butler Baxter takes over the scared-shitless role from Stepin Fetchit, in *Charlie Chan in Egypt*. The first time Baxter's jitters are amusing, but there are many more times. Perhaps the best Chan aphorism here: "Necessity mother of invention, but sometimes stepmother of deception."

Fox. D: Gordon Wiles. SP: Robert Ellis, Helen Logan, Joseph Hoffman. Ph: Rudolph Mate. AD: Duncan Cramer, Albert Hogsett. Ed: Nick DeMaggio. Sd: Albert Protzman. Cost: Helen Myron. With Warner Oland, Rosina Lawrence, Charles Quigley, Henrietta Crosman, Edward Trevor, Astrid Allwyn, Herbert Mundin, Jonathan Hale, Egon Brecher, Gloria Roy, Ivan Miller, Arthur Edmund Carewe, Francis Ford, Bud Geary, Jerry Miley; 72 minutes

Ref: *Variety* 1/22/36.

"What remains in the mind ... is the great stylized atmosphere [director Gordon] Wiles brings to the film—long, lingering tracking shots through Colby House, the gigantic Whalean close-ups, the delight taken in the actual mechanics of the film's séances"—Ken Hanke, *Charlie Chan at the Movies*, p64.

"This one isn't one of the best, but it's still quite good"—Dave Sindelar (5/28/2005).

The INVISIBLE RAY

The Invisible Ray released Jan. 20, 1936: Before the first, fine cycle of Universal horror ended in 1936, there would be official follow-ups to both *Dracula* and *Frankenstein*, and an unofficial follow-up—*The Invisible Ray*—to both *The Invisible Man* (the man with the power who goes mad) and *The Mummy* ("curse" on a scientific expedition). *The Invisible Ray* is also Universal's third and least interesting major pairing of Boris Karloff (as Janos Rukh) and Bela Lugosi (as Dr. Benet), and the opening credits tell it all about the course their respective careers were taking: The word "Karloff" is all you need, and all you get, and it's in larger lettering than "Bela Lugosi."

Janos Rukh (Boris Karloff) says goodbye to his mother (Violet Kemble Cooper) in this lobby card from *The Invisible Ray* (1936).

Boris Karloff, Bela Lugosi and Frances Drake in a lobby card from *The Invisible Ray*

The latter's performance is more even than Karloff's, and there is at least one notable Lugosi moment—his calculatedly casual delivery of the line: "They die," when asked what happens when the ray-infected Rukh touches his victims. Karloff is overbearing and obvious with bad dialogue like: "They'll never laugh at me again!"—his vocal heavy artillery just emphasizes the badness. But his breathless narration excitingly propels the movie's one outstanding sequence, the film-as-planetarium trip to "the nebula in Andromeda," which enables Rukh and assembled onlookers (including Benet) to see Earth "as it existed long ago." (They also *hear* this young Earth: A sound effect marks the crashing to earth of a meteorite, in Africa.) Their experience of the spectacle "recorded on that beam of light" is a phenomenon somewhere between a motion picture and a time machine.

Interestingly, the script—in effect, at least, if not intent—situates Rukh's discovery in a world where—in Sir Francis Stevens' (Walter Kingsford) words—the "theory of reproducing vibrations from the past is not new." Yes, the idea of "vibrations from the past" may not have been new in 1936; as scientist George Carlisle writes (5/2005 e-mail), we view such vibrations "when we see light coming from distant stars and galaxies." But the idea of *reproducing* same,

The masters of Universal horror—Bela Lugosi and Boris Karloff, from *The Invisible Ray*

and casting them on a ceiling, with the aid of a projector, would have been new to the real world of 1936, or 2006.

Unfortunately, after this sterling introductory sequence—set in Rukh's lab in the Carpathian Mountains—the film crashes to earth in Africa, and becomes a mixture of safari horror and treacle. If *The Raven* was a glorious miscalculation, *The Invisible Ray*, for the most part, is simply the work of dull minds. Frances Drake, as Rukh's wife, has the tortured look down cold, but she and fellow romantic interest Frank Lawton contribute little else. Violet Kemble Cooper, as Rukh's mother, anticipates Maria Ouspenskaya's Gypsy woman, in *The Wolf Man*—old, wise, forever forecasting tragedy. As uneven as Karloff's performance, Franz Waxman's score is alternately trite and tantalizing.

Instead of a ray-generated trip to early Earth, the 100%-utilized brain of a woman (Scarlett Johansson) takes us back to Tyrannosaurus time, in *Lucy* (2014).

(*The Death Ray*—original title) Universal. D: Lambert Hillyer. SP: John Colton. Story: Howard Higgin, Douglas Hodges. Ph: George Robinson. Mus: Franz Waxman. AD: Albert S. D'Agostino. SpPh: John P. Fulton; (asst) David S. Horsley. Mkp: Jack Pierce, Otto Lederer. Ed: Bernard W. Burton. P: Edmund Grainger. With Boris Karloff, Bela Lugosi, Frances Drake, Frank Lawton, Violet Kemble Cooper, Walter Kingsford, Beulah Bondi, Frank Reicher, Paul Weigel, Georges Renavent, Ernie Adams, Ted Billings, Etta McDaniel, Walter Miller, Fred "Snowflake" Toones, Nydia Westman, Lloyd Whitlock; 80 minutes

Ref: *Scary Monsters* 26:14-19. Bill Warren.

"Arguably the most overrated Universal horror from the 1930s"—Bryan Senn, *Filmfax* 61:44-45.

"Different and fairly entertaining"—*Variety* 1/15/36.

A FACE IN THE FOG

A Face in the Fog released Feb. 1, 1936: "It's the Fiend! He's here!" The cloaked skulker who likes to creep in through open windows is the Fiend, a madman who has targeted members of a theater group for murder. The Fiend's use of bullets of frozen "concentrated poison" seems driven less by any sort of logic than by sheer vengefulness: The victims die a more hideous death.

Everything's off here, from Al Martin's dialogue ("Gosh, it's spooky in here") to Bob Hill's staging of the fistfights. And the Sam Katzman budget did not provide for fog. Bill Hyer's lighting, however, insures that the scenes with the "mysterious fiend" are pretty mysterious, all right.

In the lobby card, Lloyd Hughes and June Collyer appear deep in their thoughts, from *A Face in the Fog*.

Victory. D: Bob Hill. SP: Al Martin, from Peter B. Kyne's story *The Great Mono Miracle*. Ph: Bill Hyer. Sets: Fred Preble. Ed: Earl Turner. Sd: J.S. Westmoreland. With June Collyer, Lloyd Hughes, Lawrence Gray, Jack Mulhall, Al St. John, John Elliott, Sam Flint, Forrest Taylor, Lane Chandler; 66 minutes

Ref: *Castle of Frankenstein* 9:32.

"On the debit side is the expected cheapness of production (Sam Katzman's specialty)"—*Forgotten Horrors*, p179.

"Quite silly, but fun in its hokey way"—Dave Sindelar (10/8/2001).

LOVE WANGA

Love Wanga released 1936: "You've got to help me—I need zombies." "An actual case history." Paradise Island, in the West Indies—"devil country," where "nature becomes ghostly and unearthly" at night. Clelie (Fredi Washington), a high priestess, employs a "voodoo death charm" to take Adam Maynard (Philip Brandon) away from her rival, Eve Langley (Marie Paxton). "I'll show you what a black girl can do!" Then: "I'm not afraid of your voodoo!" Finally: "So, the voodoo priestess has been out-voodooed!"

Some visual interest, thanks to the scenery and the camerawork. But, as Bryan Senn notes, "Authentic locales are not enough" (*Drums of Terror*, p38). No dramatic interest, thanks to dialogue that is mainly exclamations. See above, as well as: "If I can't have him, no one else will!" and "It's a voodoo death charm!" Award: Most Casual Zombie-Making Scene on film. Clelie just waves her arms and draws two rather well preserved bodies out of their coffins. ("They looked like dead men?") But dig those strange looking tree trunks and cool "windshield" wipes. The print looks like someone put in way too much bleach. Birth of a Nation of Zombies: The black zombies are tasked to abduct the white woman. Semi-remake: *The Devil's Daughter* (1939).

(aka *Ouanga*-British title. *Drums of the Night*-original title. *Drums in the Night*-shooting title.

aka *Crime of Voodoo*. *Drums of the Jungle*-alternate title): British Paramount. D, SP, P: George Terwilliger. Ph: Carl Berger. With Fredi Washington, Sheldon Leonard, Philip Brandon, Marie Paxton, Winifred Harris, Babe Joyce, George Spink, Sidney Easton; 70 minutes

Ref: *Something Weird Video* ('93 Special Edition); 56 minutes.

IMDb. 61-minute 1942 Hoffberg re-release. *HSF2*. *PV* 20: 7,13.

"This may help an indie in building a double bill but his patrons won't thank him"—*Variety* 1/7/42.

"Some nice atmosphere here and there"—Dave Sindelar (11/21/2002).

The GARDEN MURDER CASE

The Garden Murder Case (novel—S.S. Van Dine): "Devilish things have been happening in the garden this afternoon." This generally pallid mystery novel occasionally turns smooth and engaging, when it gets down to business—in the middle, for instance, when detective Philo Vance interviews all the suspects, or, at the very end, when he retrospectively documents the killer's actions and intentions. Regulation whodunit business, but well done. At its most exasperating, the book is padded out with extensive notes on the history and practice of horse racing—interruptions, really, like Harpo's solos. The *Garden* in the title refers both to a family name and a rooftop site. And "S.S. Van Dine" is both a pen name and a character in the story, the "patient and retiring chronicler" of Vance's exploits. Retiring is right—"Van" is as quiet as a mouse here. It's Willard Huntington Wright's curious little joke. At one point, he acknowledges Ogden Nash's renown comment on Vance ("needs a kick in the pance"), and good-naturedly praises it. Meanwhile, Bertram Millhauser introduces a new and fascinating element into the film version of the book ...

The Garden Murder Case released Feb. 21, 1936: "I have the weirdest story." [SPOILERS]: Scattered about the movie *The Garden Murder Case* are conventional Gothic elements—a violent thunderstorm, a black-cat scare at midnight, a screaming woman. And this Philo Vance (Edmund Lowe) mystery generally plays like your typical movie whodunit. Intermittently, however, the story anticipates the melancholy and fatalism of the Val Lewton films of the 1940s like *The Seventh Victim*. A disconsolate jockey (Douglas Walton) mutters, "I've got to ride—and I've got to break my neck!" He does and he does. A driven woman (Frieda Inescort) announces, "I've got to go. I'm going to get killed." She does and she does. Is it murder? Or suicide? Or hypnotically-suggested murder? Is Millhauser channeling the character Jacqueline (Jean Brooks) from *The Seventh Victim*?

Walton's Floyd Garden "seems so miserable." He walks around in a disconsolate daze. "You've been so strange," Inescort's Madge tells him. His father (Henry B. Walthall) blames the "vicious and immoral influence" of the unlovely Lowe Hammle (Gene Lockhart) for corrupting his son with "fast women

and filthy money." Later, the observant Madge ("I think I'm going out of my mind!") goes into a glazed daze herself, as she walks, zombie-like, out onto the boulevard, then falls from the top of a double-decker bus. These tantalizing passages are ultimately undermined by a cockeyed all-an-hypnotic-trance ending, but Millhauser has, at least momentarily, conjured up a dysfunctional society haunted by moral lemmings, where the determinedly disillusioned all but "run to death."

The movie also anticipates a few other 1940s films—*The Spider Woman* and *Black Magic* (both 1944). Not surprisingly, in the case of the former film: Millhauser wrote the screenplay for it.

MGM. D: Edwin L. Marin. SP: Bertram Millhauser, from S.S. Van Dine's novel. Ph: Charles G. Clarke. Mus: Dr. William Axt. AD: Cedric Gibbons. Ed: Ben Lewis. Sd: Douglas Shearer. Cost: Dolly Tree. P: Lucien Hubbard, Ned Marin. With Edmund Lowe, Virginia Bruce, Benita Hume, Douglas Walton, Nat Pendleton, Gene Lockhart, H.B. Warner, Kent Smith, Grant Mitchell, Frieda Inescort, Henry B. Walthall, Jessie Ralph, Charles Trowbridge, Etienne Girardot, William Austin, Olaf Hytten, Rosalind Ivan, Fred Kelsey, Wilbur Mack, Duke York; 61 minutes

Ref: *Photoplay* 4/36.

"Millhauser's screenplay, which changed about everything of the book except its title, is the slower-upper"—*Variety* 3/4/36.

1-sheet poster for Warner Bros.' *The Walking Dead* (1936)

The WALKING DEAD

The Walking Dead released March 14, 1936: "You can't escape what you've done." "World famous scientist" Dr. Evan Beaumont (Edmund Gwenn) restores "miracle man" pianist John Ellman (Boris Karloff) to life, after he is executed for a murder he did not commit. Ellman becomes the "instrument of some supernatural power," which tells him *who* the gangsters are that were responsible for framing him and exactly *where* to find them, and his intimidating presence somehow scares them into killing themselves. Meanwhile, the doctor is trying to pry "secrets from the beyond" out of John …

Satisfying fantasy of celestial justice. Ellman's "favorite piece," Rubinstein's moving "Kamenoi Ostrow," becomes the unexpected force behind John's strange crusade, in a bravura sequence in which he plays the piece as, first, his fixed, terrible eyes are highlighted, then the faces of his "enemies" are highlighted. Ordinarily, such a sequence would have invited ominous, even horrific music, to match the sweaty, terrified looks on the lit-up faces of the victims-to-be. But this is not a revenge saga. It's a story oddly situated on the edges of the province of the divine—in great music, in an unblinking gaze, in ultimate justice.

Retribution works through Ellman, just as the music does. He has the power, or rather two powers—or they have him. He's not playing God. He's not even aware of what's happening. His eyes remain fixed, penetrating, as—one after the other—his foes die. As soon as each new deed is done, he "awakens," not at all sure what has happened. "You can't escape … "

It's hard to say who should get the credit for the occasional brilliance of *The Walking Dead*—the director Michael Curtiz and/or one or more of the several writers. Just say that one of the latter, Robert Andrews, worked on some interesting projects, particularly in the 1940s—*The Man from Colorado*, *The Cross of Lorraine*, *The Mayor of 44th Street*, and another, sporadically imaginative Karloff vehicle, *The Devil Commands*.

[SPOILER]: The deaths of the last of Ellman's "enemies"—Nolan (Ricardo Cortez) and Loder (Barton MacLane)—electrocuted in a car accident, and not in Ellman's presence—may seem simply fortuitous, but there's a suggestion of supernatural intervention here too: Their driver, the flunky Betcha (Eddie Acuff), was not among Ellman's divinely-designated enemies, and he is not in the car with them when they die. He was booted out when his driving was deemed unsatisfactory. Just before the "accident."

In a sense, the movie is Nancy's (Marguerite Churchill) story, too. At first, she seems just a sweet young thing, but she weasels out of becoming a witness for Ellman. However, she breaks down when he's executed, and obsessively cares for him afterwards. She atones for her desertion, and Ellman's cosmic directive never includes her.

Reissue 1-sheet for *The Walking Dead*

Who's the last actor you'd want to see as a mad doctor? Based on *The Walking Dead*—Edmund Gwenn. Or perhaps it's just that the role as written is wholly uninspired. Cortez, however, is exactly right as suave slime Nolan.

Warners apparently did not want to step on any Universal toes, though this film includes Karloff as the "man who returned from the dead." Plus a "He's alive" line, off-angle shots, and a lively operating table which, however, does not ascend through the roof. It just kind of seesaws.

Notes: In 1936, bow ties were apparently in; the more discerning Ellman, however, favors ties.

A tip of the hat to Jim Shapiro, who notes that the Rubinstein music also appeared in the 1934 film *The Scarlet Empress*.

Compare *The Walking Dead* to the 1984 *Brother from Another Planet*, featuring another guy (Joe Morton) with a direct, extra-natural line to do-badders.

In the credit sequence, a walking-dead shadow rises from a lying to a standing position. Cool, eh?

Reedited footage entitled "Young Dr. Jekyll Meets Frankenstein" featured in *Ensign Pulver* (1964)—Don Glut, *The Frankenstein Legend*, p133.

WB. D: Michael Curtiz. SP: Robert Andrews, Peter Milne, Lillie Hayward, Ewart Adamson. Story: Adamson, Joseph Fields. Ph: Hal Mohr. Mus: Bernhard Kaun. AD: Hugh Reticker. Ed: Thomas Pratt. Mkp: Perc Westmore. Cost: Orry-Kelly. P: Louis F. Edelman.   With Boris Karloff, Ricardo Cortez, Marguerite Churchill, Edmund Gwenn, Warren Hull, Barton MacLane, Henry O'Neill, Joe King, Addison Richards, Paul Harvey, Robert Strange, Joe Sawyer, Eddie Acuff, Kenneth Harlan, Miki Morita, Wade Boteler, Sarah Edwards, Edward Gargan, Crauford Kent, Milton Kibbee, Paul Panzer, Syd Saylor; 66 minutes

Ref: "The film's message is one of reassurance and as such is rather appealing and, ultimately, satisfying"—Bryan Senn, "The Horror Films of Michael Curtiz," *Midnight Marquee* 58:34.

"[Art director Hugh] Retiker ... secured some laboratory equipment ... that was of a more authentic nature than the usual 'Mad Medico' apparatus seen in films of the time"—Bryan Senn, in *Boris Karloff*, p173.

"*The Living Dead* [sic] lets [Karloff] down badly on opportunities"—*Variety* 3/4/36.

"I love the lost and confused look that goes over [Karloff's] face after each confrontation, as if he himself doesn't even know what's going on"—Dave Sindelar (12/19/2001).

DRACULA'S DAUGHTER

Dracula's Daughter released May 11, 1936: "The spell is broken." Is it genetic or hypnotic? The vampiric Count Dracula has been staked, and his daughter, Marya Zaleska (Gloria Holden), has burned the body. She longs to be free of the "curse of the Draculas," and to join the "bright world of the living." But she still sleeps in a coffin, and goes out at night for a bite. The spell is not broken. Like Renfield (whose dead body is briefly seen here), she's ever-tormented by the curse of blood. She even expresses her torment in a line that is a variation on a Renfield line from the Spanish-language version of the 1931 *Dracula*: "I need you to save my soul," she tells the psychiatrist, Garth (Otto Kruger). She feels the "superhuman mentality" of her dead father still shaping her life,

Title lobby card from *Dracula's Daughter* (1936)

Montage lobby card featuring Gloria Holden front and center as *Dracula's Daughter* (1936)

and ultimately gives in to his power, as Renfield never wholly could. In effect, she takes over the roles of both Renfield *and* Dracula.

Unfortunately, Holden plays Gloom in a pretentious monotone, and Irving Pichel, as her companion Sandor, is likewise a monotonous Doom. Meanwhile, Kruger and Marguerite Churchill (as Janet) represent the bright world of the living with insufferably cutesy byplay, and Edward ("the strength of the vampire") van Sloan is back, as Von Helsing (it's really the same character), now with the added burden of recapping the story of *Dracula* for those who were not a part of it. The sole memorable performance is Nan Grey's as the vulnerable Lili. Even when terrified by a thirsty Dracula's daughter, she's polite: "I think I'll go, if you don't mind." The quiet melancholy of her two or three scenes anticipates the Lewtons—they're like a Val Lewton film in miniature.

Heinz Roemheld's (uncredited) score is generally serviceable, occasionally creditable. His music for the funeral scene evokes sadness, solitude, finality, false hope. George Robinson photographs his second *Dracula*—he did the 1931 Spanish-language version—and he's dependable with fog and shadows. But the film's tremendous treat is an encore for the Castle Dracula stone-stairway set. A less-long long shot of the latter shears off a little of the shadowy majesty of set and glass shot, but the lower angle makes the stone steps perhaps even more imposing. The gigantic spider web looks like huge rope-spewing spiders made it.

Albert S. D'Agostino's art direction incorporates signs of the ravages of time: The branches growing through the castle's windows are now bigger and more plentiful. Apparently, Dracula's brides did not keep up the place. And, apparently, one of those brides was Marya's mom.

Universal. D: Lambert Hillyer. SP: Garrett Fort. Story: John L. Balderston. Ph: George Robinson. Mus: Heinz Roemheld. AD: Albert S. D'Agostino. Mkp (uncredited): Jack Pierce. VisFX: John P. Fulton. Ed: Milton Carruth. Sd: Gilbert Kurland. Cost: Brymer. With Gloria Holden, Irving Pichel, Otto Kruger, Marguerite Churchill, Edward van Sloan, Nan Grey or Gray, Gilbert Emery, Halliwell Hobbes, Billy Bevan, Claude Allister, Edgar Norton, E.E. Clive, Hedda Hopper, Eily Malyon, Christian Rub, Fred Walton, Paul Weigel; 71 minutes

Ref: "Could it be that the Countess is possessed by Dracula's spirit at times ... ? Many a critic detects a lesbian subtext to this picture[however] ... I personally don't see it"—Dwight Kemper, *Videoscope* 42:57.

"Marya's seduction of Lili ... [contains] strong unmistakable overtones of lesbianism"—Frank J. Dello Stritto, "The British *Ban* on Horror Films of 1937," *Cult Movies* 14:25.

"Lugosi made more money from *not* being in *Dracula's Daughter* than he had for starring in the original." Bram Stoker's story "Dracula's Guest" dropped as source.—CHFB (Universal Horrors 5/5/15), Gary J. Satterlee, from TCM.

"Only an interesting curio"—Stephen Jones, *Essential Monster Movie Guide*, p118.

"Rates tops among recent horror pictures ... Robinson apparently grasped every opportunity to highlight the story with his camera"—*Variety* 5/20/36.

The ROGUES TAVERN

The Rogues Tavern released June 4, 1936: "Everyone here is in the shadow of death!" The Red Rock Tavern, where the wind "sounds like the wailing of ghosts." ("This place is spooky!") At first, it seems as if a "part-wolf" police dog is slaughtering the guests.   [SPOILER]: But it's really a human who expertly wields "false dog teeth": "Look at those marks on his throat!" The throat action apparently accounts for the strange, strangled gasps/screams/moans of the victims. (Sound: J.S. Westmoreland.) Instead of a clutching hand, it's a clutching dog's-head thing.

Director Robert F. Hill is helpless at staging both dialogue and action scenes, and Dan Milner's lax editing leaves the actors to meander like cows in a pasture. The only time it looks as if someone knows what he's doing is when Bill Hyer moves the camera. His big, showpiece tracking shot introduces both

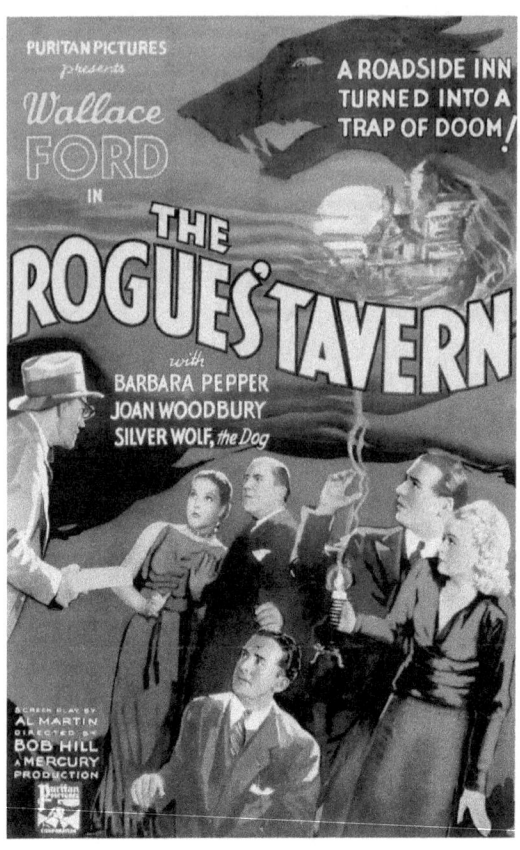

setting and characters. And he achieves "spooky" in the shot of the dog's head looming out of the darkness of a doorway. Earl Dwire's Morgan's face is typically weirdly lit, but he spends most of his time skulking [SPOILER #2] and proves to be a red herring.

Fortunately, the film goes camp in the character of Joan Woodbury's "boogie boogie!" Gloria—a card reader by way of Gloria Holden's daughter of Dracula—and in the climactic, off-screen cackling of the killer. ("You're all going to die! Heh heh heh heh heh heh …!") Listen for the line about the killer's being there in the room *now*, and appreciate the irony, later, when the identity of said killer is revealed. At Mercury Pictures, Wallace Ford gets his name above the title.

(aka *The Rogues' Tavern*) Puritan/Mercury. D: Bob Hill. SP: Al Martin. Ph: Bill Hyer. Sets: Fred Preble. Ed: Dan Milner. Sd: J.S. Westmoreland. P: Sam Katzman. With Wallace Ford, Barbara Pepper, Joan Woodbury, Clara Kimball Young, Jack Mulhall, John Elliott, Earl Dwire, Ed Cassidy; 67 minutes

Ref: "Fluid dolly and lateral tracking shots enhance many scenes"—*Forgotten Horrors*, p184.

"First half is a little stiff, but as story unreels it improves … series of freak murders"—*Variety* 7/15/36.

"Way too many shots of people looking suspiciously at each other"—Dave Sindelar (9/19/2002).

REVOLT OF THE ZOMBIES

Revolt of the Zombies released June 4, 1936: "Find the secret of the zombies—destroy it!" In what would come to be called World War I, a "regiment of French Cambodians from the lost city in Angkor [arrives] on the Franco-Austrian front. It is in fact composed of "zombie-soldiers" who—although repeatedly shot—still advance, bayonets ready. The International Expedition for Archaeological Research in Angkor is formed for the express purpose of destroying the secret of the zombies/robots.

The distance between the Halperins' *White Zombie* and their follow-up film, *Revolt of the Zombies*: Here the heroine Claire (Dorothy Stone) simply says of her beloved, Cliff Grayson (Robert Noland), "Loving each other, we are no farther apart than our thoughts can reach." In *White Zombie*, a series of elaborate dissolves imaginatively says the same thing regarding Madeline (Madge Bellamy) and Neil (John Harron). The gist: Love is stronger than voodoo. But, in *White Zombie*, you see it, you don't just hear it.

Dean Jagger's zombie master, Armand Louque, in *Revolt of the Zombies*, combines Legendre  (Bela Lugosi) with Beaumont (Robert Frazer) and Neil—he even rates inserts of Lugosi's hypnotic eyes to represent his power over his subjects. At the end, the Beaumont in Louque allows the latter to renounce his power. It's a grand idea—but the context is far from grand. Instead of a memorable sendoff for Louque ... a prosaic execution: The ex-zombie soldiers just shoot him. Earlier, Louque had recalled, for Claire, the legend of a priest-king who "promised to give up his power, release his subjects for this woman he loved." This is supposed to add some mythic dimension to the proceedings, but, again, it's just words.

A sense of disproportion ... The mainspring of the plot is pure balminess. The resolute Cliff advises the initially tentative Armand, "If you want anything, ride roughshod over everything." And Armand takes his advice to heart ... In his suddenly-found drive to "become the greatest force in the world," Louque creates "hordes of supermen" and hypnotizes everyone who comes near him (except, mainly, Claire, this film's White Non-Zombie) to do his bidding. His campiest riding-roughshod line (to his servant [Teru Shimada]): "Buna! We're learning to be ruthless!" Near the end, the chastened Cliff tells Claire, "Both of us taught him the lesson of being ruthless."

A line in *White Zombie* inspires Louque's line here (to his zombie regiment): "No doubt you would all tear me limb from limb should I ever relinquish control." In neither movie, however, is there any such tearing of a limb from a limb, nor even from a torso—*Island of Lost Souls* actually comes a lot closer to visualizing fears such as Legendre's and Louque's. The actual Revolt of the Ex-Zombies, at the end, pales in comparison to the revolt of Moreau's subjects. It's pretty pale even without the comparison ...

The script can't even get its premises straight. At various times, the zombie-control key seems to be (a) a vapor, (b) the master's right hand held to the forehead (imitating the third eye of Siva), and/or (c) Bela Lugosi's eyes.

Notes: In an odd sequence, a Cambodian acolyte wades through a swamp, to a temple, carrying an apparently-stone carving. Arthur Martinelli's nice camerawork here would be more atmospheric if the back projection were not so obvious.

Roy D'Arcy's General Mazovia at first seems to be ticketed to become the Legendre of the movie, but gives way to Louque's sudden ambitions. D'Arcy hardly rates third billing—as *Variety*'s Chic (6/10/36) noted, "Just where Roy D'Arcy comes in never becomes apparent."

(aka *Revolt of the Demons*) Academy/Halperin. D, SP: Victor Halperin. SP: also Howard Higgin, Rollo Lloyd. Ph: Arthur Martinelli AD: Leigh Smith. Ed: Douglass Biggs. SpFX: Ray Mercer. Sd: G.P. Costello. P: Edward Halperin. With Dorothy Stone, Dean Jagger, Roy D'Arcy, Robert Noland, George Cleveland, E. Alyn Warren, Carl Stockdale, Teru Shimada, Selmer Jackson; 65 minutes

Ref: *FM* 8:29.
Photon 21:11.
TVG.
Ecran F 31:17,51.
FD 6/5/36.
"Pretty bad, but very entertaining"—*PV* 11:12.
"Almost a total disappointment"—*Forgotten Horrors*.

The DEVIL-DOLL

Burn Witch, Burn! (book—A. Merritt): Piecing together the early publishing history of Merritt's work is no easy matter. But two sources—the 1951 Avon edition of the book and the unattributed August 9, 1932 edition of the "West Coast Story Department Bulletin" suggest that it was first published as a serial in 1932 under the title, *The Dolls of Madame Mandilip*, then published and copyrighted the next year as a book, *Burn Witch, Burn!* The serial title stems from the book's Foreword, in which the narrator, Dr. Lowell, refers to a heading in one of his case-books as "The Dolls of Mme. Mandilip." The book itself is not quite as interesting as its genesis, though it begins tantalizingly with "terror and horror" in the eyes of several victims of ... what, exactly, is not at first known. What the problem boils down to is that the eyes have it, the dolls don't. Neither the latter nor Madame Mandilip can quite live up to the promise of those eyes of horror. Consider "little Anita," with "terror in her fixed gaze": "The aspect of the child after death was peculiarly disturbing ... She was conscious *after physical death!*" Yow-plus!

The Devil-Doll released July 10, 1936: "It is lifelike, isn't it?" A scientist (Henry B. Walthall) has found a way to shrink people and other animals to one-sixth their size. His aim: an easier-to-feed world population. (Smaller portions.) But his friend Paul Lavond (Lionel Barrymore) hijacks the process to wreak revenge on the businessmen who framed him and sent him to prison. A list of contributors to the entertaining but patchwork screenplay—which has little to do with the book—reads like a Who's Who in 1930s horror—Tod Browning, Garrett Fort, Guy Endore, Erich von Stroheim, and Richard Schayer. Merritt, however, makes the main contribution—the living dolls. Strange but true: Only a single character from the book makes it to the screen—Madame Mandilip's niece, Laschna. (Her name in the movie is spelled "Lachna" [Grace Ford].) That's right: In the film, there is no Madame Mandilip—it's just Lavond in disguise. In the book, she seems to be off on some kind of evil, if rather nebulous, cosmic power trip; in the movie, Lavond's motivation is simple revenge. Either way, the yield is living, threatening dolls.

Fortunately, Barrymore's amusing turn as "Madame Mandilip"—complete with a shades-of-Julia-Child voice—makes up for the lack of a real Madame M. The actor was a drag, as the inspector, in Browning's previous thriller, *Mark of the Vampire*; here, in drag, he's pretty nearly the film's highlight. His mock-French accent lends itself very well to covert insolence, in the presence of his intended victims and the police. Maureen O'Sullivan, as Lavond's daughter, gives the movie's other fetching performance. Her quiet Humiliated, in the

Pressbook ad from *The Devil-Doll* (1936)

wake of her father's disgrace, is touching, where her role could have been just another gear in the plot.

The closest that the movie gets to the best of the book: Lavond's reading from a newspaper story: "Police are baffled by what they consider a look of constant terror in Monsieur Coulvet's expression." Then, later, Matin's (Pedro de Cordoba) question regarding the paralyzed Coulvet: "What could have frightened him so? What could he have seen?" But we know what the police and Matin don't—we already know what Coulvet saw—and thus the book's most horrific sequences are dissipated. Cart before horse. And the dolls, although riveting as bizarre spectacle, are not very scary. They're more on the charming side, like the tiny dogs and horse.

Notes: Rafaela Ottiano's bug eyes are almost parodistic. She might be a Killer from Space.

The Devil-Doll has echoes of *Bride of Frankenstein*—in Franz Waxman's score, in the idea of miniature people, and in the white streak in Ottiano's hair. Most of this seems inadvertent, except perhaps for that white streak.

The Devil-Doll was the last full-fledged American-made horror movie released before The Great Horror Drought of 1937-1938.

(aka *Devil Doll*; aka *The Witch of Timbuktu* or *The Witch of Timbuctoo*). MGM. D, P, Story: Tod Browning. SP: Garrett Fort, Guy Endore, Erich von Stroheim. Dial: Richard Schayer, from A. Merritt's novel *Burn Witch, Burn!* Ph: Leonard Smith. Mus: Franz Waxman. AD: Cedric Gibbons. Ed: Fredrick Y. Smith. Sd: Douglas Shearer. Mkp: Robert J. Schiffer. Cost: Dolly Tree. P: also E.J. Mannix. With Lionel Barrymore, Maureen O'Sullivan, Frank Lawton, Raffaela Ottiano, Henry B. Walthall, Robert Greig, Lucy Beaumont, Grace Ford, Pedro de Cordoba, Arthur Hohl, Rollo Lloyd, E. Alyn Warren, King Baggot, Egon Brecher, Billy Gilbert, Edward Keane, Wilfred Lucas, Eily Malyon, Frank Reicher; 78 minutes

Ref: "The picture ... has about everything an adult-scarer needs except story ... Process shots ... indicate considerable advancement has been made lately in the blending line"—*Variety* 8/12/36.

"Despite the fact that I have several problems with this movie, I really like it"—Dave Sindelar (8/30/2001).

"Grotesque, slightly horrible and consistently interesting"—Frank S. Nugent, *New York Times* 8/8/36.

KELLY OF THE SECRET SERVICE

Kelly of the Secret Service released July 22, 1936: "I'll make a killer out of anyone I choose!" Ingredients include hypnotizing hands from nowhere, which direct a man to kill ("The man's hypnotized!") and cloud another victim's mind ... a secret panel used "for scarin' people," a woman who seems to "evaporate into thin air," "pictures jumpin' off of the wall," and an "aerial bomb" (or

"radio controlled death bomb") which destroys a "robot controlled battleship" at sea. ("I've completed the secret room—the apparatus will always be safe there. And I dare anyone to find the secret panel.")

Occasionally likeably hokey programmer. Lloyd Hughes takes the Stiff Acting prize; meanwhile, Forrest Taylor does to dialogue what Hughes does to facial expressions. Fuzzy Knight and Syd Saylor provide the weak comedy, while the farfetched hypnotism sequences tie those in *Revolt of the Zombies* for the *White Zombie* memorial award of 1936. The best madlab gizmo: the circular thing which pinwheels out apparently animated zaps from its hub.

More murder and hypnotism, the same year as *The Garden Murder Case*. Bill Hyer uses some fancy lighting for the face of the villain, in the climactic sequence. "You can't pull that trigger, Kelly! You can't! You can't!"

Note: Another line we like: "Something spooky about this place."

Victory. D: Bob Hill. SP: Al Martin, from Peter B. Kyne's story *On Irish Hill*. Ph: Bill Hyer. Sets: Fred Preble. Ed: Dan Milner. Sd: Hans Weeren (or Weerin—credits). P: Sam Katzman. With Lloyd Hughes, Sheila Manors, Forrest Taylor, Jack Mulhall, John Elliott, Fuzzy Knight, Syd Saylor, Miki Morita, Tom London; 69 minutes

Ref: *Forgotten Horrors*, pp196-198.

MUMMY'S BOYS

Mummy's Boys released Oct. 2, 1936: "One of them mummies just moved!" Egypt. The story, told in a King Tut-inspired headline: "Curse of King Pharatime's Tomb Claims Ninth Victim." Lackluster ingredients include a man (Moroni Olsen) impersonating a mummy ("I've seen Dr. Sterling's ghost!") ... poison which eventually causes seemingly-natural death ... a bat attack ... a rough-looking hyena ... a secret tomb room ... and an early shooting-through-fireplace-flames shot.

Bert Wheeler, Robert Woolsey and Barbara Pepper in a lobby card from *Mummy's Boys*

It takes this comedy half its running time just to get to the desert and the tomb, and even then it's still not at all spooky or funny. Bert Wheeler's bad memory is a tired running gag, and the Wheeler-Robert Woolsey wordplay is pretty pallid. (Wheeler is the one with the tie; Woolsey, the one with bow tie and glasses.) Sample: "Mum's the word"/"What word?"/"Mum." The "crow flies" routine is okay, but not up to Groucho's "Lodge with my fleas" business. It's Egypt, Part II, for Willie Best, who wide-eyed it through *Charlie Chan in Egypt* the year before, and again gets the willies re "ghosts." Van Nest Polglase's statuary, caskets, and corridors for the mummy's tomb pass muster, but Jack Mackenzie's photography is atmosphereless.

Apparently, the only American feature of the 1930s and 1940s, outside of Universal, to feature living mummies was Eddie Cantor's *Kid Millions* (1934). In it, the mummies in a "mummy room" do a "Let My People Go" number. In *Mummy's Boys*, there are three fake mummies, if you count the drawings of Wheeler and Woolsey in the credits. Cartoon shorts like *Gypped in Egypt* (1930), *Egyptian Melodies* (1931), and *Betty Boop's Museum* (1932) featured living mummies and skeletons. *Kalkoot* (1935) was an East Indian version of *The Mummy* (1932).

RKO. D: Fred Guiol. SP: Jack Townley, Philip G. Epstein, Charles Roberts. Story: Townley, Lew Lipton. Ph: Jack Mackenzie. Mus: Roy Webb. AD: Van Nest Polglase. Ed: John Lockert. Sd: James G. Stewart. Cost: Edward Stevenson. P: Lee Marcus. With Bert Wheeler, Robert Woolsey, Barbara Pepper, Moroni Olsen, Frank M. Thomas, Willie Best, Frank Lackteen, Mitchell Lewis, Frederick Burton, John Davidson, Noble Johnson, Edward Keane, Ethan Laidlaw, Frank Moran; 68 minutes

Ref: *Filmfax* 30:63,64. *PV* 16:15.

"Net result of the dialog is about four snickers"—*Variety* 12/16/36.

"So thoroughly and uneventfully commonplace that I find it hard to say anything about it"—Dave Sindelar (1/21/2003).

GHOST-TOWN GOLD

Ghost-Town Gold released Oct. 26, 1936: "Town's givin' me the willies!" This is one-third Western, one-third boxing pic, and one-third spook show. Actually, the latter third is more like three minutes, but it's a jim-dandy three minutes. [SPOILER]: In a cobwebbed "old mine tunnel," Uncle Jake (Milburn Morante) is using some kind of weird bullhorn to produce screeches to scare the local thugs. ("Probably a few ghosts.") Yes, it seems there be banshees here. The sound does seem to be produced by some sort of ungodly ghost/beast. ("It's no wonder Jake's a little bit goofy.")

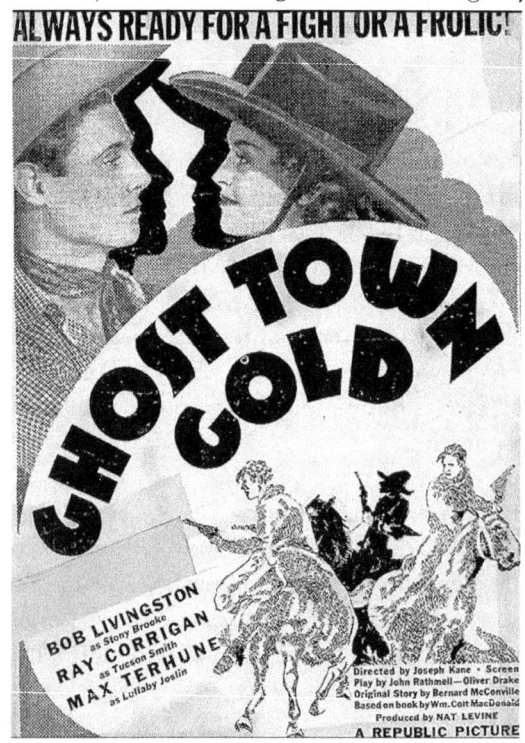

The Three Mesquiteers Westerns were coming up with some ace sound effects (courtesy of Harry Jones) in the mid-1930s, in this movie and in *Riders of the Whistling Skull* (1937). For the record, Lullaby (Max Terhune) acquires "big doll" Elmer as a prize here. With *Obeah*'s F. Herrick Herrick and *The Searchers*' Hank Worden. Fun stunt: two on a lasso. Unconvincing fisticuffs, in or out of the ring.

Republic. D: Joseph Kane. SP: John Rathmell, Oliver Drake. Story: Bernard McConville. Based on characters created by William Colt MacDonald. Ph: Jack Marta. Ed: Lester Orlebeck; (sup) Murray Seldeen. Sd: Harry Jones. P: Nat Levine.

With Robert Livingston, Ray Corrigan, Max Terhune, Kay Hughes, LeRoy Mason, Burr Caruth, Bob Kortman, Milburn Morante, Frank Hagney, F. Herrick Herrick, Yakima Canutt, Bob Burns, Horace B. Carpenter, I. Stanford Jolley, Bud Osborne, Edward Peil, Sr., Harry Tenbrook, Hank Worden; 55 minutes

Ref: *Variety* 2/10/37. YouTube.

The HOUSE OF SECRETS

The House of Secrets (novel—Sydney Horler): "It is said to be haunted—and certainly some strange things are supposed to have happened there." The Durdles—a "haunted house in the Thames Valley," England—was originally called Eagle's Nest (or Neste). Vying for the strangest character in this "house of strange happenings" are an "unnaturally strong ... hairy creature," or "mad baboon"—a "creature whose face was covered with such a dense growth of hair that he looked like a baboon"—and Dr. Daniel Kenwit, who intends to "cure [a] man of his criminal instincts" by operating on his brain—an idea resurrected in the 1939 film *Torture Ship*. The prevailing "uncanny atmosphere" is furthered by the presence of the psychic hero, Barry Wilding ... "nerve-shattering maniacal laughter," a secret passage ... and a clutching hand.

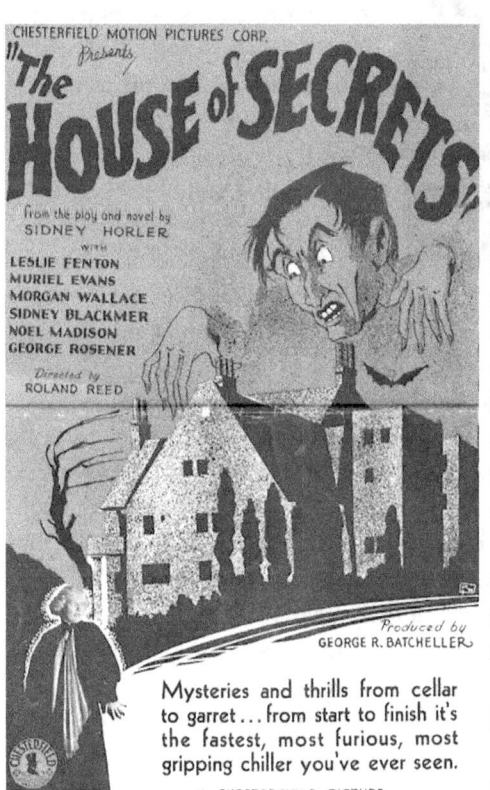

Yes, this otherwise unremarkable book features science fiction, fantasy, and a hint of horror. (The baboon thing is explained away.) Horler seems infected with a mild case of camp—lots of "he would go mad." The book is so thin that it's more to be skimmed than read, and it's infected with a strain of racism: The "nigger servant" Starkey's eyes regularly roll. True, though, it's a certified thug who boasts, "As an American, I confess to having a rooted aversion to negroes," but it's our hero who uses the former slur.

Genre books and movies of the era seemed bound by some passing sense of duty to poetry, or doggerel, and this book's rhyme is:

By this hearthstone I swear to lie, All my days until I die.

The House of Secrets (1929 film): "Mysterious and spooky house ... "

As the synopsis in *Forgotten Horrors* suggests, this long-lost first movie version was apparently dismayingly faithful to Horler's book, although the doctor and "baboon" of the book seem to have become one here. And the doc is just working on a new poison gas. *Variety* (10/23/29) called it a "junkwagon full of mongrelized hoke": "The dialog is indie awful," the "lighting is terrible," and the "performers ... wouldn't rate very high in a backwoods revival of Unk Tom's hut."

The House of Secrets released Oct. 28, 1936: Again, this second adaptation follows the book's plot pretty closely, for better or worse, mostly worse. This for-the-most-part-interminable mystery, set in and around a country estate outside London, concludes on a surprising science-fictional note: [SPOILER]: An inventor's (George Rosener) "formula which would instantly destroy all poison gas" indeed does just that, as the hero (Leslie Fenton) shoots a hole in a tank of the anti-gas, and the rest of the cast is saved from a cellar-full of deadly fumes.

The estate itself is reputed to be "haunted" by "good old, chain-clanking ghosts," but the spooky elements are few and far between—a secret panel, a clutching hand, a *Dracula*-ish stone stairway, midnight skulking, and off-screen screaming. The most effective ingredient is the periodic (off-screen) mad cackling, revealed to have come from the inventor. ("And leave you here with that *thing*, whatever it is?") As in the book, a doctor works to bring back the mind of said inventor, but apparently through standard psychiatric methods.

The name of the estate is variously spelled "Hawk's Nest," "Hawks Nest," and (in old English) "Hawkes Neste." There's hardly even any fog, oddly enough, considering the setting. Smooth-as-silk Sidney Blackmer is the most watchable actor here. Director Roland D. Reed later produced the *Rocky Jones, Space Ranger* TV series. Here, the book's rhyme becomes:

"By ye blood that cometh from my heart,
I swear to keep ye Hawk's Nest till death do us part."

Chesterfield. D: Roland D. Reed. SP: John Krafft, from Sydney Horler's novel and play. Ph: M.A. Anderson. AD: Edward C. Jewell. Ed: Dan Milner. Sd: Richard Tyler. P: George R. Batcheller. With Leslie Fenton, Muriel Evans, Noel Madison, Sidney Blackmer, Morgan Wallace, Holmes Herbert, Jameson Thomas, Syd Saylor, George Rosener, Olaf Hytten, Edgar Norton; 70 minutes

Ref: *Variety* 2/24/37.

"A more unnerving atmosphere than was achieved in 1929"—*Forgotten Horrors*, pp202-203.

PHANTOM OF THE RANGE

Phantom of the Range released Nov. 28, 1936: "People say the ranch is haunted ... Some people say that the old man couldn't sleep easy in his grave." Ghost Western's ghost is just a man in a raincoat on a horse. ("I do all the dirty work—fighting, ghost riding.") He's supposed to "scare the daylights out of any galoot that comes near" Tower Rock, where there's some buried treasure.

The British valet (Sammy Cohen) out west is supposed to remind you of *Ruggles of Red Gap* (1935). Four years later, hero Tom Tyler was Kharis in *The Mummy's Hand*. Heroine Beth Marion's forte was not acting, but she gets the best spook lines: "Maybe grandfather's ghost really does ride the range. He was a strange man, from what my mother told me. Never gave up anything that once belonged to him. Maybe he won't give it up even when he's dead."

At one point, a coyote's yowl is made to sound like a scream. ("Blimey! A banshee.") Cameraman Bill Hyer's forte: panning shots. He seemed to photograph every third thriller in 1936. Sam Katzman made this and a million others.

Victory. D: Bob Hill. SP: Basil Dickey. Ph: Bill Hyer Sets: Fred Preble. Ed: Charles Henkel. Sd: Herb Eicke. P: Sam Katzman. With Tom Tyler, Beth Marion,

Sammy Cohen, Soledad Jimenez, Forrest Taylor, Charles King, John Elliott, Richard Cramer; 59 minutes

Ref: Alpha Video.

"Juve trade will relish this hillside scamper"—*Variety* 6/15/38.

CHARLIE CHAN AT THE OPERA

The Black Camel (book by Earl Derr Biggers): None of the spookier Chan mystery movies—spooky enough, that is, to land in this book—is based directly on a Chan mystery novel. So we detour now through *The Black Camel* (book and film) to get an idea of the written Chan. Why *The Black Camel*? No compelling reason, but the film does pair Warner Oland with Bela "Dracula" Lugosi—as *Charlie Chan at the Opera* later, famously, paired Oland with Boris "Frankenstein's Monster" Karloff. (Karloff had a small role in an earlier, non-spooky, non-Oland Chan movie, 1929's *Behind That Curtain*.) Biggers describes "phony fortune-teller" Tarneverro the Great—Lugosi's role in the film—as one of the "voodoo men" of Hollywood, as Lugosi would later become the "voodoo man" of Monogram. There's "something uncanny, inexplicable and oddly disturbing" about Tarneverro and his "rather disquieting" eyes. "What was the secret of this dark man's power ... ?" He is both the "king of mystery" and, possibly, a hypnotist.

The Inspector Chan of Biggers' book is resolute and firm with suspects. ("Attempt by any one of you to go aboard ship will be instantly known to us, and regarded with dark suspicious eye.") But he's empathetic with young lovers and affectionate with his many children, though dismayed by their Americanization. (They're "all American citizens.") Featured are college-age Henry, the eldest son; Rose, the eldest daughter; 15-year-old Evelyn; and the "small Barry." "Jolly-looking" Mrs. Chan also makes a brief appearance. "Maybe I should put my 11 children on this case," Chan muses, at one point, but it's the Japanese Kashimo who takes

Pressbook herald from *Charlie Chan at the Opera* (1936)

on the role of the bumbling, amateurish detective generally reserved, in the films, for the Chan offspring.

In the early passages, the details regarding the suspects' various alibis seem rather dry, but about midpoint, the tale begins to get, page by page, more and more intriguing, as Biggers interweaves mystery, drama, and human interest, and one apparent solution kaleidoscopically replaces another—the *Rashomon* effect. It's a feature of any decent mystery, but Biggers employs it more skillfully than most writers.

The Black Camel (1931 movie): "Wages of stupidity is hunt for new job." Yes, it's grand seeing Warner Oland's Chan and Bela Lugosi's Tarneverro ("world famous mystic") together, investigating a murder. They're a dream team. As in *Charlie Chan at the Opera*, Oland is quietly forceful, even-keeled, and he lets his more mercurial co-star here soar, then plummet, like a comet, or kite. Lugosi has the one really successful dramatic sequence, early on, the sequence in which he verbally terrorizes Dorothy Revier's Shelah Fane, as they're lit from below, weirdly, and only by a crystal ball (Joseph August and Daniel Clark, camera). The way he intones: "But you fear something!" indeed guarantees

Boris Karloff as he appeared in *Charlie Chan at the Opera*

that she fears something—him. In the book, the corresponding passage is a more conventional interview. Director Hamilton MacFadden and writers Barry Conners et al. perhaps revamped it the better to accommodate the stage and screen Dracula. Good move.

Unfortunately, the story—though it sticks fairly closely to Biggers—proceeds haphazardly, revelation by revelation. The movie is now largely just a museum piece, with Oland, Lugosi, and Dwight Frye the main exhibits. At the end, MacFadden and company crank up the drama for Frye, too—there's a hint of Renfield in Jessop's ranting at Chan ("You know too much!"), in a scene not in the book. Everyone cranks up the comedy for Otto Yamaoka's Japanese detective Kashimo, too—he's absurdly energetic, and the absurdity is occasionally amusing.

Charlie Chan at the Opera released Dec. 4, 1936: [SPOILERS]: "This opera is going on tonight even if Frankenstein walks in!" Or, Frankenstein Meets the Wolf Man of Tibet. Or, Fu Manchu vs. Fu Manchu. It's a twofer—Karloff horror and Chan (Warner Oland) mystery. There's a "madman loose in the house"—by name, Gravelle (Boris Karloff), an amnesiac opera star, thought dead for the seven years he has been in the Rockland State Sanitarium. ("Everybody thinks I'm mad!") The presence of Karloff as the "homicidal maniac" or "ghostly visitor" ("All I could see were his eyes—they were horrible!"), a thunderstorm, a bloodcurdling scream, and some skulking in cobwebby rooms are the scattered horror elements here.

There's also, of course, mystery, as well as suspense, drama, romance, and sentiment. It's really a sixfer. Not surprising, then, that this mélange is alternately workmanlike and uninspired. What's surprising is that it's on occasion inspired. The height of inspiration: Karloff as Gravelle as Mephisto—in Oscar Levant's production-within-a-production of "Carnival." It's not just his horrible eyes and frozen grin—it's the bright but oddly sinister mask (costumes by Herschel) which sets off eyes and grin.

Karloff as Gravelle also has his moments—observe his threatening smile when he visits Mme. Barelli's (Nedda Harrigan) dressing room, or his mad glee when he visits Barelli's (Gregory Gaye) room: "Yes, Barelli, I have come back to take your place tonight!" But what everyone wants to see is what's above the title: Warner Oland vs. Boris Karloff. (Simply "Oland vs. Karloff" up there might have been even more thrilling.) It's only one scene, and Karloff seems to be giving Oland lessons in acting, and overacting: There's an uncomfortable echo or two of *The Raven*. Meanwhile, Oland does an impeccable Unflappable. It's a bit of a letdown, but it is an historic scene: Karloff vs. Oland, camp and grandeur vs. cool.

Someone else (Tudor Williams) too obviously does Karloff's singing. And, as Ken Hanke notes, in *Charlie Chan at the Movies* (page 83), the boldness with which Gravelle is fashioned as a red herring is sometimes stunning. William Demarest, as Sgt. Kelly, is already plying his patented Exasperation.

Gravelle went missing from a Chicago opera house in 1923, which would seem to put the film's action back in 1930.

There's some ambiguity as to whether Gravelle actually kills anyone. The orderly (John Bleifer) whom he overpowers—in the opening sequence—seems to be still moving about as Gravelle leaves the sanitarium, and it makes no mystery-movie sense if Gravelle is both a red herring and a killer.

Fox. D: H. Bruce Humberstone. SP: Scott Darling, Charles S. Belden. Story: Bess Meredyth. Ph: Lucien Andriot. AD: Duncan Cramer, Lewis H. Creber. Ed: Alex Troffey. With Warner Oland, Boris Karloff, Keye Luke, Charlotte Henry, Thomas Beck, Margaret Irving, Gregory Gaye, Nedda Harrigan, Frank Conroy, Guy Usher, William Demarest, Maurice Cass, Stanley Blystone, Benson Fong, Bud Geary, Selmer Jackson, Fred Kelsey, Marc Lawrence, Eddie Parker, Lee Shumway, Harry Strang, Emmett Vogan, Mary Wickes, Joan Woodbury; 68 minutes

Ref: Walt Lee.

Variety 12/16/36.

"Karloff holds the unique position of being the only actor to ever receive the above-the-title billing with Oland in the series"—Ken Hanke, *Charlie Chan at the Movies*, p83.

Highlights of 1937-1938

"In 1936 horror films went out of style, and *Bluebeard* (along with *Phantom of the Opera*, *The Electric Man* and other thrillers Universal was planning) went down the tubes"—Tom Weaver, *Poverty Row Horrors*, p188.

"Horror Films Taken off Universal Sked"
"Universal ... [has] no chiller pictures contemplated for 1936-1937 release. Reason ...: European countries, especially England, are prejudiced against this type product."—*Variety*, May 6, 1936.

"By mid-year, horror film production had entirely ceased ... The London County Council ... announced that as of January 1, 1937 children under 16 could not attend "H" rated films. Other county councils soon did the same, and across Britain "horrific" films were virtually banned ... No horror films would be produced in America for almost three years ... In 1938 Universal ... re-released *Dracula* and *Frankenstein* on a double bill. The gimmick exceeded all expectations, and convinced the studio that the domestic market could support a resurgence of horror."—Frank J. Dello Stritto, "The British "Ban" on Horror Films of 1937," in *Cult Movies* 14 (1995), pp.20-27.

Reading between the lines here, then, it seems that the U.S. did not really have to suspend production of horror movies, in the first place, in 1936. The "domestic market" could have sustained itself. The immediate real test of this new-found conviction: the release, in January 1939, of *Son of Frankenstein*. (No new Universal *Dracula*, however, would be undertaken for some four years, although Bela Lugosi would seem to have been available, dammit.)

See also the book *Censored Screams: The British Ban on Hollywood Horror in the 1930s*, by Tom Johnson (reviewed in *Midnight Marquee* 58:56). And also *Scarlet Street* 26:69-74, 80-81: "A Hunger for Horror!" by Garydon Rhodes, regarding the *Dracula/Frankenstein* revival of 1938. And *Cult Movies* 20:26-33: "Boris Karloff and the Horror Ban," by Tom Weaver.

Small consolation: In 1937 and 1938, there were scattered quasi-horror movies, disguised as mysteries: *The Thirteenth Chair*, *The Black Doll*, *The Missing Guest*. The latter two were Universal's token semi-shockers during the lull. There was also a comedy-fantasy with a sort of monster, *Sh! the Octopus*, and a Western which seemed to fancy itself as a sort of reworking of the 1932 *The Mummy*—*The Riders of the Whistling Skull*. But the closest thing to an actual, live (as opposed to animated; see below) horror movie was *London by Night*—the Umbrella Man would have to do as a monster until Dr. Frankenstein's eventual return.

Notable performances: Donald Woods and Nan Grey (*The Black Doll*), George Zucco (*London by Night*), Hugh Herbert (*Sh! the Octopus*), William Lundigan (*The Missing Guest*)

Title lobby card from *Night Must Fall* (1937)

Notable photography: Jack Marta (*The Riders of the Whistling Skull*), Leonard Smith (*London by Night*), Arthur L. Todd (*Sh! the Octopus*)

Notable writing: George Bricker (*Sh! the Octopus*)

Notable editing: George Boemler (*London by Night*)

Notable sound effects: Charles Carroll (*The Black Doll*), Harry Jones (*The Riders of the Whistling Skull*), Bernard B. Brown (*The Missing Guest*)

Other films of interest:

Border Phantom (1937)—"man who disappeared like a ghost"

Bulldog Drummond Comes Back (1937)—"haunted"-house bit

Bulldog Drummond Escapes (1937)—eerie manor house

Devil Diamond (1937)—cursed gem

The Girl from Scotland Yard (1937)—*HSF1*: madman. *Variety* 6/2/37. Press sheet: death ray that shoots down two military planes ... "waxwork museum"

Making the Headlines (1938)— Ref: Tom Weaver (AFI): abandoned house with a secret panel—reading of the will at midnight ...

Mystery House (1938)—quasi-premonition, wailing wolf, Elspeth Dudgeon "driving everybody crazy." Routine mystery

Mystic Circle Murder (1938)—phony mystic

Night Key (1937)—stick which emits web-like ray. Tepid Karloff vehicle

Night Must Fall (1937)—psychopath. Mild thriller that might have been made more horrifically a few years earlier

Sky Racket (1937)—death ray. Hilariously inept early Sam Katzman actioner. *PV* 36:13. *HSF4*

Snow White and the Seven Dwarfs (1937)—the forest, the witch, the apple. Horror goes animated

Super-Sleuth (1937)—spooky house

They Drive by Night (U.S.-British, 1938)—"But spooks ain't cops." Just when the film seems to be turning into a horror picture, it ends. Long live Ernest Thesiger!

Wake up and Live (1937)— Jim Shapiro e-mail: "Mike fright" makes Jack Haley see the radio microphone "as a "monster" face a la Moloch"

1937-1938

RIDERS OF THE WHISTLING SKULL

Riders of the Whistling Skull (book—William Colt MacDonald): "It shore whistles skeery." The only things that the book and the film adaptation have in common: the Three Mesquiteers and the Whistling Skull. No other characters from the book are in the movie. Latter with a completely revamped story. In MacDonald's book, a secret society/counterfeiting ring wants to take over the United States. No hint of such a scheme in the movie. But both book and movie prominently feature a "huge boulder shaped like a human skull ... now ghastly in the moonlight." And both feature that "uncanny whistling [which rose] to piercing heights hurling waves of tortured sound across the desert floor. Gradually the tones dissolved to faint sepulchral whisperings ... " But only in the book is it suggested (then dismissed) that the whistling is a manmade phenomenon. All the hard ridin' here is hard readin' now. The height of the tough-hombre act: "It was said that the Guadalupe Kid was one-quarter Spanish and three-quarters hell." And has any living person ever said "Gosh all hemlock!"? The plot, though, is serviceable and features some surprises. (See above for examples.)

The Riders of the Whistling Skull released Jan. 4, 1937: "The legends of the Whistling Skull were true!" A "remarkable mummy," a rocky "skull" atop a mountain, and wind effects to rival *Doctor X*—this is Republic's 1937 horror movie masquerading as a "B" Western, in a year which saw very few even semi-horror movies, thanks to the British horror-film "ban."

The Riders of the Whistling Skull recalls a prominent feature of *King Kong*'s Skull Island, and the movie is rife with echoes of the 1932 *The Mummy*. And not just the "mummy" which gets up and sneaks off. ("That mummy was moving away!") Nor just the mummy that "talks," thanks to ventriloquist Lullaby

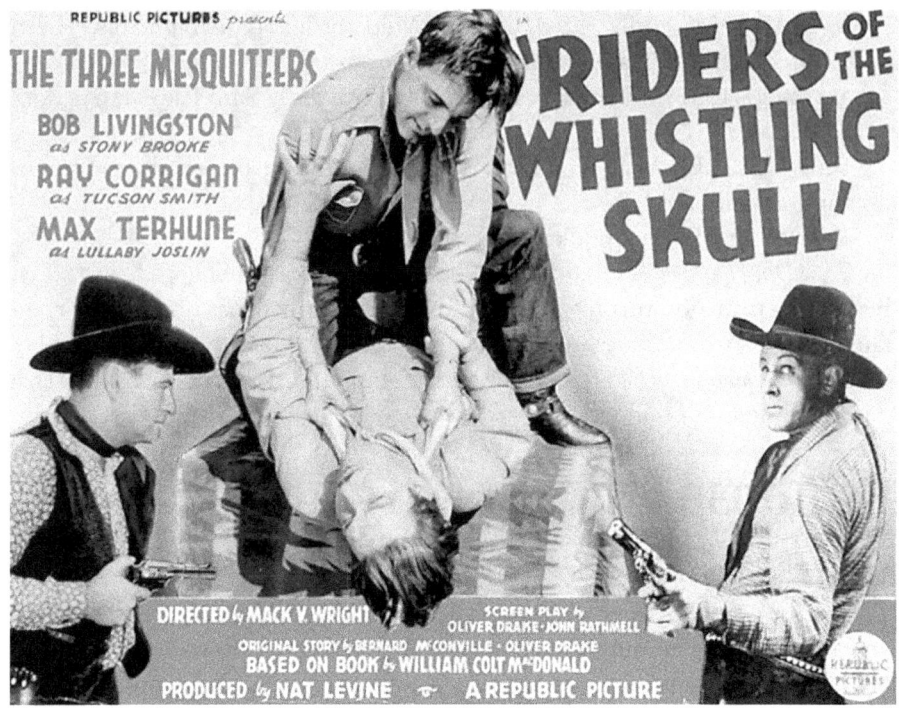

Joslin (Max Terhune). I submit that the most interesting link to the 1932 film is actually Professor Flaxon's (C. Montague Shaw) display of abject fear when confronted with a human skull: "The Whistling Skull! I can't stand it! It howls in my ears, day and night." Compare Norton's (Bramwell Fletcher) crazed cackling at the sight of the living mummy ("You should have seen his face!") at the beginning of *The Mummy*. Other Gothic elements include a lights-out murder and the match cut from the close shot of the Indian dancer's skull-masked face to that human skull. All this and the Lost City of Lukachuke, too.

Cameraman Jack Marta seems to have been inspired by the rugged settings. About 20 minutes in, the movie goes outdoors and pretty much stays outdoors, and he photographs the action against picturesque hills, trees, bushes, clouds. It must have been pretty breathtaking on the big screen. Of course, the uniformly stilted acting may have been magnified there, too.

Notes: The 1948 remake, *The Feathered Serpent*, retains only one semi-spooky element, occasional whistling winds, and adds three Chans, Charlie and two sons. As Charlie Chan, Roland Winters seems to be doing a stilted impression of earlier movie Chans. It's a really dreadful movie.

(*The Golden Trail*—British title) Republic. D: Mack V. Wright. SP: Oliver Drake, John Rathmell. Story: Drake, Bernard McConville, based on the William Colt MacDonald books *Riders of the Whistling Skull* and *The Singing Scorpion*. Ph: Jack Marta. Mus: William Lava, David Tamkin, Cy Feuer. Ed: Tony Martinelli. Sd: Harry Jones. P: Nat Levine. With Robert Livingston, Ray Corrigan, Max Terhune, Mary Russell, Roger Williams, Fern Emmett, C. Montague Shaw, Yakima Canutt, John Ward, George Godfrey, Chief Thundercloud, Iron Eyes Cody, Jack Kirk, Edward Peil, Sr., Wally West; 58 minutes

Ref: *Forgotten Horrors*, pp205-206. IMDb.

"A cool looking giant skull ... impressive stunts"—*PV* 25:11.

"Some eerie effects provided by the sound department ... This film will keep the kids on the front two inches of the seat"—*Variety* 4/21/37.

The THIRTEENTH CHAIR

The Thirteenth Chair released May 7, 1937: "I believe that woman has a power of some sort." Ingredients: medium Mme. La Grange (Dame May Whitty), who at one point seems to be speaking in the voice of a dead man ... her spirit control, Laughing Eyes ... a "living" dead man (Henry Daniell) at a séance ... murder in the dark at an earlier séance ... unexplained table levitation ... a scream which turns out to be an "idiot bird" cry ... dialogue references to ghosts ... and regulation eerie music for eerie scenes.

Fearfully faithful to the play, this is a basically inert mystery, except for the hokey but fun [SPOILER] scene in which Wales (Daniell) seems to return to life and point to the murder weapon. It's a nice macabre idea only suggested by the play. And it's introduced with a sort of pre-*Cat People* "bus," as screams and the jarring sound of falling window blinds accompany the pointing corpse. There's a little *Stella Dallas* sentiment in the relationship between the medium ("I didn't want to shame her") and her daughter (Madge Evans). Lewis Stone, as the inspector, is not exactly Mr. Electricity. Okay comic relief from Elsa Buchanan's featherbrained Grace Stanby, who is prone to attacks of nerves, and her only-slightly-less-featherbrained brother (Robert Coote, remembered as one of the stars of TV's *The Rogues* [1964]).

Note: *The Thirteenth Chair* (1917 play—Bayard Veiller): "I can't fight the dead." A man is killed during a séance. Later, the dead man's voice is heard, and that voice, the man's "spirit," and the sudden appearance of the murder weapon, a knife—together—scare the killer into confessing. Slight mystery play, with hints of the supernatural and dollops of sentiment. The presence of the knife is apparent to the audience early on here; it's 56 minutes into the 1937 movie version before its (odd) location is disclosed.

MGM. D: George B. Seitz. SP: Marion Parsonnet, from Bayard Veiller's play. Ph: Charles G. Clarke. Mus: David Snell. AD: Cedric Gibbons. Ed: W. Donn Hayes. Sd: Douglas Shearer. With Dame May Whitty, Madge Evans, Lewis Stone, Elissa Landi, Thomas Beck, Henry Daniell, Janet Beecher, Ralph Forbes, Holmes Herbert, Charles Trowbridge, Robert Coote, Elsa Buchanan, Lal Chand Mehra, Neil Fitzgerald, Matthew Boulton, Heather Thatcher; 66 minutes

Ref: "Whitty ... cuts through the film's dull moments with some fine character study"—*Variety* 6/9/37.

LONDON BY NIGHT

London by Night released July 30, 1937: "It's almost as though Casey never existed." It's 1937, and there are no horror movies on the horizon. *Dracula's Daughter* and *The Devil-Doll* are distant memories, or at least seem distant. The British horror-movie "ban" has wreaked its havoc. The situation is bleak. But then along comes *London by Night*, a happy near-exception to the rule of un-horror, a semi-oasis in the desert of 1937 and 1938.

I say "near" and "semi" because The Umbrella Man is not Jack the Ripper. He uses an impersonal gun, not a knife. But the man under the umbrella scurrying about the London night fog is really pretty eerie. ("He gives me the creeps, he does!") To onlookers, he seems seven-feet tall, with "arms like a gorilla" and a "face like a demon." The intent, at least, is Monster. Umbrellas themselves begin to seem sinister. The "mysterious Umbrella Man" is a "homicidal maniac," a "strange malefactor," and, in one scene, a disappearing whistler. And there's some question as to whether several characters here—including the above Casey, Von Kranz, and the Rabbit Man—ever existed. Yes, the Rabbit Man. The Men Who Never Were ... Semi-sweetly, the key to the identity of the killer proves to be the dog Jones (as played by the estimable Corky).

London by Night has two claims to a sort of fame, two scenes of good old-fashioned horror. In one—an inventive evocation of a city in panic—the ghostly-white, double-exposed figure of The Umbrella Man looms larger and larger, screen center, as it approaches the camera and dominates a montage of the panic-stricken (Leonard Smith, photography; George Boemler, editing). In the other—a rough sketch for a scene from *Psycho*—the barmaid Bessie

(Virginia Field) walks up the back stairs, toward the camera, when—near the top—she recognizes the man with the gun before her, just as he shoots her, and she tumbles back down. In a third, quietly chilling moment, Bessie tends to her drunken Bill (Eddie Quillan), in the bar, as she happens to notice The Weaver's Arms' front doors swinging slightly, dead of night, no one visible.

The Umbrella Man plot itself is a fairly intriguing puzzle, and the George Murphy/Rita Johnson scenes are smooth but mild romantic-comedy filler. George Zucco is capable as the inspector, but this pre-dates his mad-doctor period, so he is not, in fact, the one who cries, "You think I'm mad, don't you? But I'm not!"

(*The Umbrella Man*—working title): MGM. D: William Thiele. SP: George Oppenheimer, from Will Scott's play *The Umbrella Man*. Ph: Leonard Smith. Mus: William Axt. AD: Cedric Gibbons. Ed: George Boemler. Sd: Douglas Shearer. P: Sam Zimbalist. With George Murphy, Rita Johnson, Virginia Field, Leo G. Carroll, George Zucco, Montagu Love, Eddie Quillan, Leonard Mudie, J.M. Kerrigan, Neil Fitzgerald, Harry Stubbs, Ivan F. Simpson, Leyland Hodgson; 69 minutes

Ref: IMDb.

"[Eddie Quillan's] drunk bit is excellent and his English accent worthy. Another whose work is more than ordinarily competent is George Zucco"— *Variety* 8/4/37.

SH! THE OCTOPUS

Sh! the Octopus released Dec. 11, 1937: Heckzapoppin' [SPOILERS]: An old dark lighthouse is the setting for this surreally cheesy horror-comedy-fantasy, with an all-a-dream ending. Tame comic beginnings don't prepare one for some wild plot developments. An apparently dead body drips blood, but turns out to be merely a dummy. No sooner does one character declare that there are no stairs in the lighthouse than a panel lifts to reveal a flight of stairs. An octopus that can apparently stand on its hind tentacles while waving other tentacles drags victims through doorways and trap-doorways. A few lighting and makeup effects, and a "helpless old woman" (Elspeth Dudgeon) becomes, in an instant, the wicked witch of Octopus Island, the super-criminal The Octopus, with a gnarled, blasted countenance. But the resident (supposedly real) octopus lassos The Octopus. An ignominious end for someone who wanted to "rule the world" with a death ray. And that other octopus is still at large ...

Almost all of the characters have at least two identities. In the haunting dream, The Octopus is also Nanny. At the end, however, she's just Kelly's (Hugh Herbert) mother-in-law. "Clancy," the supposed police commissioner (Eric Stanley), is really Vesta Vernoff's (Marcia Ralston) father, although his name is really Harriman, not Vernoff. Captain Hook (George Rosener) proves to be an intelligence agent. Polly Crane (Margaret Irving) works for the Peace League. Paul Morgan (John Eldredge), a marine painter, turns out to be a sort of FBI agent. About the only characters who are who they say are the detectives, Kelly and Dempsey (Allen Jenkins). Herbert is his usually personable screen self; Jenkins is his usual one-note self—comically gruff.

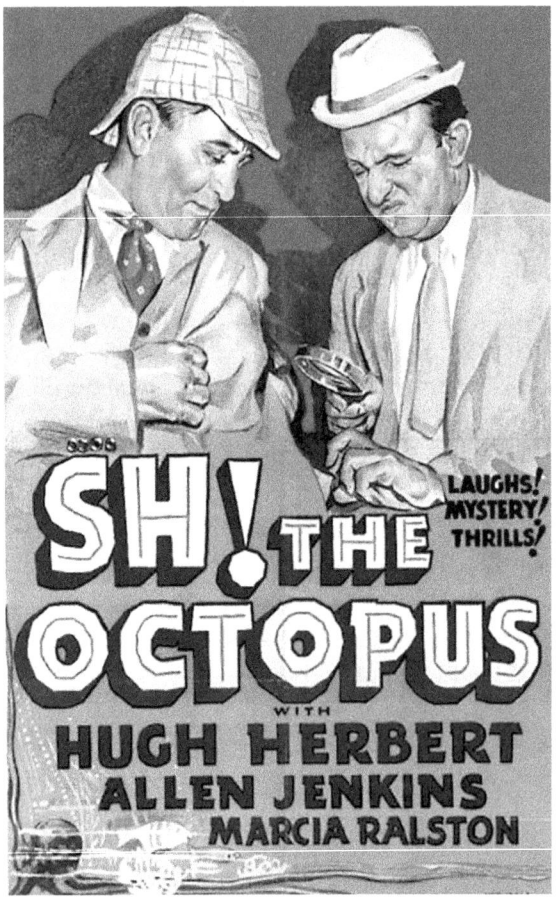

Notes: The mysteriously moving candle gag did not originate with Abbott and Costello. It makes an appearance here and goes back, at least, to Harold Lloyd's *Welcome Danger* (1929). Here, it's on the back of a turtle, or tortoise.

There's actually a third octopus, if only figuratively. The phrase the "giant octopus of crime which grips the city" turns up in a newspaper story.

Actors named Clifford Dempsey and Harry Kelly played Dempsey and Kelly, respectively, in the original stage production of *Sh, the Octopus*, in 1928.

The only connection to the movie's second source, the play *The Gorilla*—at least as represented by the 1939 film adaptation—is the presence of a couple of detectives.

Elspeth Dudgeon worked for many notable directors, including King Vidor, Rouben Mamoulian, Mervyn LeRoy, George Cukor, Hitchcock, Robert Siodmak, Chaplin, Lang, and, of course, James Whale.

WB-FN. D: William McGann. SP: George Bricker, from the play *The Gorilla* by Ralph Spence and a play by Ralph Murphy and Donald Gallaher. Ph: Arthur Todd. Mus: Heinz Roemheld; (title music) David Raksin. AD: Max Parker. Ed: Clarence Kolster. Sd: Francis J. Scheid. Assoc P: Bryan Foy. With Hugh Herbert, Allen Jenkins, Marcia Ralston, John Eldredge, George Rosener, Brandon Tynan, Eric Stanley, Margaret Irving, Elspeth Dudgeon, Frank Hagney; 54 minutes

Ref: *TVG*.
IMDb.

"So feeble even the actors seem embarrassed"—*Variety* 12/8/37.

"One of the most strikingly effective villain unmaskings I've ever seen in a movie of this ilk"—Dave Sindelar (1/5/2006).

The BLACK DOLL

The Black Doll released Jan. 30, 1938: "It's Barrows, all right—he's come back to life!" A Crime Club picture. An unseen "ghost" tosses a knife into Nelson Rood's (C. Henry Gordon) back, then tosses a rag, or straw doll, at the body. ("She means death.") Yes, the periodic little jolts here involve a thrown doll rather than a clutching hand. There's also thunder throughout, as a storm rages. The best use of the thunder: Peals of same twice drown out the sheriff's (Edgar Kennedy) impression of a "bloodcurdling scream."

In the most harrowing sequence, the screaming heroine, Marian Rood (Nan Grey), runs into a masked killer, thunder and lightning raging, and rooms suddenly go dark. In another fun, semi-shock scene, with a semi-"bus," father Rood throws the doll down in front of semi-enemies Mallison (Addison Richards) and Walling (John Wray), and music blares. [SPOILER]: In an incidental (but possibly prophetic narrative stroke) scream scene, the Doc's (Holmes Herbert) unexpected presence hovering over Marian startles her.

In the amusing windup, semi-pro sleuth Nick Halstead (Donald Woods) rounds up the suspects, feeds them breakfast, and goes at them one by one.

Universal Picture's "Crime Club" entry, *The Black Doll*.

Woods seems to be doing a good imitation of William Powell as Nick Charles, in similar Thin Man climactic roundups—it's the vocal timing and emphases. He's his characteristically forthright self. Nan Grey's understandable fear, as Marian, echoes her lost soul in *Dracula's Daughter*. Edgar Kennedy does his familiar "slow burn" thing, and his pipe caddy (Syd Saylor) is a wry running gag.

Notes: Music from *Bride of Frankenstein* accompanies the opening credits.

There's a passing hint of the supernatural in the line: "If that doll could get out of that ravine, anything could happen!"

Universal. D: Otis Garrett. SP: Harold Buckley, from William Edward Hayes' novel *The Black Doll*. Ph: Stanley Cortez, Ira Morgan. AD: Ralph Berger. Ed: Maurice Wright. Sd: Charles Carroll. Cost: Vera West. P: Irving Starr. With Donald Woods, Nan Grey, Edgar Kennedy, C. Henry Gordon, Doris Lloyd, John Wray, Addison Richards, Holmes Herbert, William Lundigan, Syd Saylor; 66 minutes

Ref: *Variety* 2/9/38.
Mystery File (9/14/2010), online.
Rare Nightmare DVD.

The MISSING GUEST

The Missing Guest released Aug. 12, 1938: "The house is haunted." In this fourth film version of the *Secret of the Blue Room* story, Old Man Kirkland was found dead 20 years ago, in a "terrible house," Baldrich Manor, on Long Island. The "original owner" of the "ghost mansion" went missing from the Blue Room "and was never heard from again ... Other owners were also done away with in that same room, at three in the morning, the identical hour Mr. Kirkland was murdered in that self-same Blue Room." In the present, young Larry Dearden (William Lundigan) disappears from the room, and Dr. Carroll (Edwin Stanley) is shot dead in it ...

Creditably, *The Missing Guest* substantially reworks the script of the first American version, *Secret of the Blue Room*, but with much less interesting actors, although Lundigan is an improvement over his counterpart, William Janney. Hero Paul Kelly is the familiar wise-cracking reporter, and three other actors (Billy Wayne, George Cooper, and Pat C. Flick) inflict much comic damage.

The movie, however, is fraught with inventive sound and music effects, courtesy of Bernard B. Brown, Karl Hajos & company: the non-player-piano acting like a player piano, during a lights-out interlude at a costume party ... the cobwebbed pipe organ mysteriously playing ("Why, there's nobody here!") ... the Blue Room door suddenly creaking open (the room has been "closed and locked for 20 years") ... the mood-setting howling wind ... the (initially) unexplained voices ... and a loud whirring/howling noise. Milton Krasner's subjective shot of a "ghost" entering the manor is a good introduction to the place, and later there's an odd "apparition" scene in which Kelly's "Scoop"

simply yanks out his camera when an intimidating "ghost" appears at a window.

Universal. D: John Rawlins. SP: Charles Martin, Paul Perez. Ph: Milton Krasner. AD: Jack Otterson. Ed: Frank Gross. Sd: Bernard B. Brown. Assoc P: Barney Sarecky. With Paul Kelly, Constance Moore, William Lundigan, Edwin Stanley, Selmer Jackson, Billy Wayne, George Cooper, Harlan Briggs, Pat C. Flick, Guy Usher; 68 minutes

Ref: *MFB* 38:261.

"This one is so bad it can't even be viewed as a gag"—*Variety* 9/14/38.

"As a time killer, it's pleasant enough, but it's pretty routine"—Dave Sindelar (8/23/2005).

Highlights of 1939

Horror returned in 1939, just in time to make its contribution to Hollywood's greatest year. And if it wasn't horror's greatest year, it wasn't a bad one, although many of the films in question were really mysteries in disguise: *Hound of the Baskervilles, The Adventures of Sherlock Holmes, Miracles for Sale* (Tod Browning's last film), *The Witness Vanishes, The House of Fear, Charlie Chan at Treasure Island, The Cat and the Canary,* and *The Gorilla.*

In fact, two of the best horror sequences of the 1930s turned up in *Charlie Chan at Treasure Island* (see entry below). But what made all the difference, between the sad lean years of 1937 and 1938 and the comeback of 1939: *Son of Frankenstein* was released on January 13th, and it made gaudy promises which, as it transpired, Universal couldn't keep in the coming years, though *The Wolf Man* (1941) seemed briefly to rekindle those promises ...

Lionel Atwill was arguably the horror star of the year. He notched *Son of Frankenstein, Hound of the Baskervilles,* and *The Gorilla.* The two finest single performances, however, were perhaps Charles Laughton's in *The Hunchback of Notre Dame* and Bela Lugosi's in *Son of Frankenstein*—the two hunches ...

Other notable performances: Basil Rathbone, Nigel Bruce, Wendy Barrie (*Hound of the Baskervilles*), Rathbone again in *The Adventures of Sherlock Holmes,* William Gargan (*House of Fear*), Gloria Holden (*Miracles for Sale*), Boris Karloff

(*The Man They Could Not Hang*), Bob Hope, George Zucco, Gale Sondergaard (*The Cat and the Canary*), Hamtree Harrington (*The Devil's Daughter*), Edmond O'Brien and Harry Davenport (*The Hunchback of Notre Dame*)

Notable photography: George Robinson (*Son of Frankenstein*), J. Peverell Marley (*Hound of the Baskervilles*), Edward Cronjager (*The Gorilla*), Benjamin Kline (*The Man They Could Not Hang*), Leon Shamroy (*The Adventures of Sherlock Holmes*), Virgil Miller (*Charlie Chan at Treasure Island*), Jack Greenhalgh (*Torture Ship*)

Notable direction: Joe May (*House of Fear*), Rowland V. Lee (*Son of Frankenstein*)

Notable writing: Willis Cooper (*Son of Frankenstein*), Peter Milne (*House of Fear*), Robertson White (*The Witness Vanishes*), John Larkin (*Charlie Chan at Treasure Island*)

Notable musical scores: Frank Skinner (*Son of Frankenstein*), David Raksin et al. (*The Adventures of Sherlock Holmes*), Dr. Ernst Toch (*The Cat and the Canary*), Bernard Kaun, Max Steiner (*The Return of Dr. X*)

Notable art direction: Jack Otterson (*Son of Frankenstein*), Richard Day, Hans Peters (*Hound of the Baskervilles*)

Notable makeup: Perc Westmore (*The Return of Dr. X, The Hunchback of Notre Dame*), Jack Pierce (*Son of Frankenstein*)

Notable special effects: perhaps cinematographer Milton Krasner (*House of Fear*), John P. Fulton (*Son of Frankenstein*)

Notable costume: Herschel (for Dr. Zodiac, *Charlie Chan at Treasure Island*)

Other films of interest:

Another Thin Man—If Phil Church (Sheldon Leonard), the "dream butcher," dreams something three times, it comes true—C. Aubrey Smith's Col. MacFay does in fact die a bloody death. Church's glee describing his dreams is engaging, in a macabre way

Beware Spooks!—Coney Island spook house

Bulldog Drummond's Secret Police—Very lightweight comedy-adventure features a cobwebbed chamber of descending spikes and the line, "You vine-climbing Dracula!"

Charlie Chan in Reno—"sleeping ghosts" supposedly haunt Dead Man's Canyon. Transparent mystery wastes Ricardo Cortez.

Death Rides the Range—"Noises comin' up through the fireplace" prove to originate in a cave under a cabin. "This place give me the creeps!" Just this one scene with "spooks."   Ref: Mysto (CHFB, "Poverty Row")

The Invisible Killer—Lee: death-by-phone. IMDb: "fiendish killer." *Showmen's* 2/10/40. *HSF1*

On Borrowed Time—Death (Sir Cedric Hardwicke) up a tree. Ref: *Variety* 7/5/39

Tarzan Finds a Son!—And the son (Johnny Sheffield) finds a horde of nasty spiders, who surround him in one scene. Well, really, they find him.

Tower of London—"Don't try to escape from old Mord." Boris Karloff's Mord loves to torture, and his scenes are great fun-horrific punctuation. Otherwise, the horror is soft-pedaled. Watch for Donnie Dunagan as a baby prince.

The Wizard of Oz—the witch and her monkeys, oh yeah, as horror goes fantasy

Wuthering Heights—Ref: Lee: ghost sequence. IMDb

1939

SON OF FRANKENSTEIN

Son of Frankenstein released Jan. 13, 1939: "He does things for me." In a "little mountain village" called Frankenstein ... *Son of Frankenstein* is at once tremendously exciting and somewhat of a letdown, half rousing entertainment and half gorgeous Gothic bore. The dialogue suggests that both the Monster

Midget window card for *Son of Frankenstein*

(Boris Karloff) and the doctor (Basil Rathbone) are "sons" of Henry Frankenstein: Asks the doctor, Wolf, of resident hunchback, or hunchshoulder, "that crazy Ygor" (Bela Lugosi), "Are you suggesting that *he* is my *brother?*" And yet the doctor-monster story in this third entry in the Universal series seems played out. The doctor's role had diminished somewhat, already, two thirds into *Frankenstein*. And Henry was a virtual stick figure, a Dismal Desmond, through most of *Bride of Frankenstein*.

"What strange looking country!" Here, Wolf is a mechanical reprise of both early and late Henry—the initial exhilaration, the subsequent testiness ("a bundle of uncontrollable nerves")—though another actor might have made more of the drama of a man torn between science and family. Rathbone is as helpless in the role as Colin Clive was, as Henry, in *Bride of Frankenstein*. And Baron Wolf's role is neither happily nor succinctly dialogued.

"Considerable osteodermia in the frontal region." The Monster, too, is reduced nearly to decoration. Only briefly, once or twice, does the film become the Monster's story again ... first, when he compares himself to his "brother," Wolf, in the mirror, and laments his lot, waving his arms as if to wave away the image ... and, later, when he learns that he has lost another friend, Ygor—as he lost the hermit in *Bride of Frankenstein*—and howls in agony. The two scenes seem to belong to another, finer *Son of Frankenstein*. They were not enough to keep Karloff from swearing off the role. His angry/tortured grunting in the mirror sequence is supremely expressive. Only Karloff ...

"Nobody can mend Ygor's neck." In effect at least, this movie proves a vehicle for two characters new to the series. Ygor is to this film what Pretorius was to *Bride of Frankenstein*, a revitalizing addition. Body snatcher, ex-blacksmith, and caretaker of both the Frankenstein estate and its monster, Ygor uses the latter to wreak revenge on those who sentenced him to hang, but couldn't quite finish the job. Legally, then, (as he says) "Ygor is dead." Willis Cooper provides Lugosi with some of his best dialogue since *Murders in the Rue Morgue*. And while Ygor's head, neck, and shoulders may be nearly immobile, the actor's voice is in fine rasp. For the line, "I stole bodies—they said," Lugosi emphasizes, but does not over-emphasize, "they said." One quibble: a little too much Ygor cackling.

"We Frankensteinians are as nervous as cats!" Lionel Atwill's Inspector Krogh is the other fresh note. He, too, plays off his character's physical infirmities. The monster has torn off Krogh's right arm, and Atwill's relationship to his wooden arm seems to inform his whole performance, physically as well as emotionally, seems to explain both his over-perfect posture and enunciation (hear him enunciate "parboiled to the bone" and make the "b"s therein seem to rhyme), and his double-edged concern for the Frankenstein family: He wants to protect Wolf and his wife and son almost as much as he wants to eradicate the Monster. ("There's a monster afoot, and you know it!")

"What awful lightning!" George Robinson's photography and Frank Skinner's score make the Monster intimidating before the latter even opens his eyes.

Basil Rathbone as Wolf von Frankenstein confronts a very sympathetic Monster (Boris Karloff), in this lobby card from *Son of Frankenstein*.

At one point, the music—building anticipation as it does—makes the opening of a heavy-duty stone-slab door a little whirlwind adventure, as Ygor struggles to pull back the door to the inner lab chambers—the "Monster's home," as the villagers put it. Skinner seems to have been enjoying himself, relishing his role in the affair, as much as does Lugosi. If, by this time, the philosophical dimensions of the Universal Frankenstein films are pretty much history, there are the sumptuous, monster-scale sets (Jack Otterson) and the impressive shadow play to drink in ...

Notes: The ultimate cool: "Basil Rathbone/Boris Karloff/Bela Lugosi," before the title.

Wolf's "I'll not be halted by anything!" might apply equally to dead-alive Ygor and the dead-alive Monster.

Even the castle's front-door knocker is huge. ("That awful knocker!")

"Cosmic rays" are now said (by Wolf) to have given life to the Monster, originally.

Once heard, Donnie Dunagan's "Well, hello!" cannot be unheard.

Both Elsa (Josephine Hutchinson's Mrs. Frankenstein) and Peter (Dunagan as the son of the son of Frankenstein), respectively, create awkward moments attempting to shake Krogh's right hand.

Peter's one saving-grace line: "I like lightning." He's definitely a Frankenstein.

Not quite buyable turnabout: In the coda, the perpetually angry villagers cheer the Frankensteins and see them off.

Universal. D, P: Rowland V. Lee. SP: Willis (or Willys) Cooper. Ph: George Robinson. Mus: Frank Skinner. AD: Jack Otterson. Mkp: Jack Pierce. SpFX: John P. Fulton. Ed: Ted Kent. Sd: Bernard B. Brown. Cost: Vera West. With Bela Lugosi, Lionel Atwill, Boris Karloff, Basil Rathbone, Josephine Hutchinson, Donnie Dunagan, Emma Dunn, Edgar Norton, Perry Ivins, Lawrence Grant, Lionel Belmore, Michael Mark, Gustav von Seyffertitz, Ed Cassidy, Ward Bond, Harry Cording, Jack Curtis, Clarence Wilson; 99 minutes

Ref: IMDB.

"Lugosi finally got to play Rasputin, a role MGM denied him a few years earlier"—Frank J. Dello Stritto, *Cult Movies* 21:35.

"[Lugosi's Ygor] is considered by many to be his *tour de force*"—Susan Svehla, in *Bela Lugosi*, p122.

"Value of latest Frankenstein feature has recently been enhanced through reissues of former pictures in the series ... Story is slow and draggy in getting under way prior to first appearance of Karloff, but from that point on, sustains interest at high pitch"—*Variety* 1/18/39.

"It's not the equal of the first two movies, but it's still pretty good"—Dave Sindelar (4/26/2002).

The HOUND OF THE BASKERVILLES

The Hound of the Baskervilles (short novel—Sir Arthur Conan Doyle): "I don't think I'll get that cry out of my head." The "bogie hound" or "demon dog," which haunts the Baskerville estate in Devonshire, England, is a "huge creature, luminous, ghastly, and spectral"—a "foul thing, a great, black-beast, shaped like a hound, yet larger than any hound that ever mortal eye has rested upon." Fire seems to "burst from its open mouth." (Dr. Watson: "Phosphorous.") And its cry is the "weirdest, strangest thing … " The estate itself is somber "enough to scare any man." Renowned Sherlock Holmes tale is a trifle uneven, but well written, with little chaff. Suspense highlight: Conan Doyle's description of the climactic onslaught of the fog, which is the "one thing upon earth which could have disarranged" Holmes' plans to trap the murderer. Yes, the fog is as scary as the dog. The high point of wit: Holmes' "a more lively evening" comment regarding Sir Henry Baskerville's disappointment at having stayed at home and had a (blessedly) dull evening.

Der Hund von Baskerville (German film) 1936 Sinister Cinema: The hound here rates snarling and growling as well as the usual howling sound effects. But if he sounds decently fearsome, glimpsed, he looks like Fozzie Bear after an ill-advised shearing. Willy Winterstein contributes some slick moving-camera work, but his money shot is the one in which a woman runs past the stationary camera, and her translucent, light-woolen cape (a tip of the hat to Mo) falls

In this lobby card from *The Hound of the Baskervilles*, Sherlock Holmes (Basil Rathbone) and Dr. Watson (Nigel Bruce) discover a corpse.

over the camera, like an evanescent, elegant filter. Atmospheric wind, sight, and sound effects also help. No English.

The Hound of the Baskervilles released March 31, 1939: "In all England there is no district more dismal than that vast expanse of primitive wasteland, the moors of Dartmoor in Devonshire." The story peg, as in the novel: "For centuries past, every Baskerville who's inherited the estates [in Devonshire] has met with a violent and sudden death." In other words, a "bogie story" regarding a "wild, supernatural monster," in a setting of "dreadful eeriness." The film's snarling hound—first seen in the flashback to Sir Hugo (Ralph Forbes)—doesn't live up to the image of the "beast of the Baskervilles," which the original tale planted in the reader's mind. Here, he's just the fairly menacing, relatively big dog of the Baskervilles—an "ordinary dog," as Holmes (Basil Rathbone) notes. And the dog doesn't glow. The closest the movie gets to scary: the cry of the hound alarming, simultaneously, near the end, (a) Holmes and Dr. Watson (Nigel Bruce), on the moor; (b) Sir Henry Baskerville (Richard Greene), elsewhere on the moor; and c) Beryl Stapleton (Wendy Barrie), left behind in her bedroom.

Arguably, however, the film's main drawback is its lack of a musical score. Apart from the beginning, the end, and the flashback sequence: no music. Of course, some people resent being hit over the head by Max Steiner (I'm usually not one of them, but there is *Gone with the Wind*) or Dmitri Tiomkin (I'm sometimes one of them), but *The Hound of the Baskervilles* seems adrift, airless, and uninvolving, without background music. Sins of omission. Art directors Richard Day and Hans Peters take up some of the slack with an unending series of moor rocks and ruins and tombstones and underbrush and clouds—a touch of Stonehenge here, a touch of a Universal *Frankenstein* graveyard there.

Another, perhaps less serious, drawback is the dumbing down of the relationship between the Stapletons, Beryl and John (Morton Lowry), and the related omission of Mrs. Laura Lyons. These changes bland out some of Conan Doyle's story and issue in a formula happy ending. At the same time, story-wise, Ernest Pascal's addition of a séance goes nowhere, but J. Peverell Marley lights, or darkens, the séance room ominously. Rathbone, Bruce, Lionel Atwill (Dr. Mortimer), and Barrie contribute solid performances. Atwill delivers the famous line, "Mr. Holmes, they were the footprints of a gigantic hound!" As the butler Barryman (Barrymore in the book), John Carradine looks like he just stepped out of the Addams family.

(*Sherlock Holmes in The Hound of the Baskervilles*—TV ad title) Fox. D: Sidney Lanfield. SP: Ernest Pascal, from Doyle's book. Ph: J. Peverell Marley. Mus: David Buttolph et al. AD: Richard Day, Hans Peters. Ed: Robert Simpson. Sd: W.D. Flick, Roger Herman. Cost: Gwen Wakeling. Assoc P: Gene Markey. With Basil Rathbone, Nigel Bruce, Richard Greene, Wendy Barrie, Lionel Atwill, John Carradine, Barlowe Borland, Beryl Mercer, Morton Lowry, Ralph Forbes, E.E. Clive, Eily Malyon, Nigel De Brulier, Mary Gordon;   80 minutes

Ref: *TVG. Variety* 3/29/39.

Dave Sindelar (11/7/2004).

"Succeeding marvelously in making real characters of both Holmes and Watson"—Otis Ferguson, *The New Republic* 7/5/39.

The GORILLA

The Gorilla released May 26, 1939: "There's no tellin' what that ape will do." "Three morons" (Al, Harry, and Jimmy Ritz) from the Acme Detective Agency confront the "maniac murderer" The Gorilla, who is terrorizing Westchester. Lame horror-comedy features better-than-average production values for an old-house mystery, including deft camerawork by Edward Cronjager. It has thunder and lightning, rain, shadows, faces and figures at windows, screams, a clutching paw, Lionel Atwill, and Bela Lugosi—it has the basics. But the comedy is represented mainly by the Ritz Brothers. Three problems: It's hard to tell them apart. There's nothing at all special about their delivery, of dialogue in general or punch lines in particular. And there are three of them. Conversely, Patsy Kelly's advantage is that there's only one of her, though she attacks comedy like a fourth Ritz Brother.

6-sheet poster from *The Gorilla*

The horror half of this horror-comedy fares better. Atwill's edgy bluster carries the opening sequences. In terms of dialogue, Peters is not one of Lugosi's better roles. His quietly threatening "May-be" is one of the scattered highlights. But his unflappability proves welcome counterpoint to the efforts of the more frenetic cast members.

An unusual bit of fantasy: The Ritz Brothers, at one point, hear what sound like footsteps going past them, up to a closed door, which then opens, as if by the hand of an incidental invisible man. Confronted a little later, Peters says, "Yes, I did just walk through the room." And that's that.

Notes: The Gorilla sends messages via a large Zenith radio. Product placement 1939?

Score one for the menacingly shiny eyes and vicious look of the hired gorilla (Art Miles).

On the screen, the Ritzes did much better in musical comedy.

Fox. D: Allan Dwan. SP: Rian James, Sid Silvers, from Ralph Spence's play. Ph: Edward Cronjager. Mus: David Buttolph. AD: Lewis Creber, Richard Day. Ed: Allan McNeil. Sd: Roger Heman, George Leverett. Mkp: Perc Westmore. Assoc P: Harry Joe Brown. With Jimmy, Harry and Al Ritz, Anita Louise, Patsy Kelly, Lionel Atwill, Bela Lugosi, Joseph Calleia, Edward Norris, Wally Vernon, Paul Harvey, Art Miles; 66 minutes

Ref: *Variety* 5/24/39.

"As a horror comedy, I consider it an atrocity ... The Ritz Brothers are IMHO the worst of the movie comedians ... "—Dave Sindelar (9/20/2001).

The HOUSE OF FEAR

The House of Fear released June 30, 1939: "Some person [or persons] is playing ghost, and doing an uncanny job of it." The plot of this remake of *The Last Warning*, in newspaper-headline inserts:

"Woodford Case Baffles Police; And No Corpse—No Clues!!"
"Woodford's Ghost Said To Haunt Theater"
"Watchman Quits, Claiming Spook Sat in His Lap"
"Hoodoo House Dark Whole Year"

The excellent news here is that Peter Milne, the man who wrote the movie, actually read the book of the same title, and incorporated a couple of its best ideas. In one of the resulting sequences, producer/detective Arthur McHugh

(William Gargan) and stage director Dick Pierce (Harvey Stephens) "spend the night in the theater, just to see if that ghost walks." The fast advancing, expanding, and garishly-illuminated face of Woodford is a visual humdinger, so much so that it might seem to be original with the movie, but it's adapted from the "ghastly light" of the book. It actually starts as three mysterious balls of light and smoke, but two of them quickly fade out. Though much of the mystery plot is explained at the end, this ghost light is not, though it's partly accounted for by a life mask of Woodford (Donald Douglas). It anticipates, in its modest but effective way, the fiery force that chases Holden in the woods, outside Karswell's house, in *Curse of the Demon*. When McHugh finally shoots the ghost light, it seems to explode.

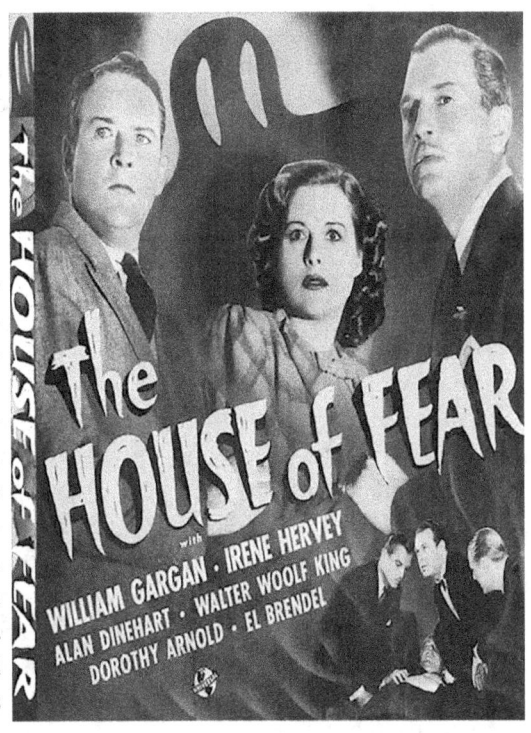

The other idea from the book: the mysterious voice on the telephone. In the book, the "queer sound," or "unearthly ringing" of the phone was achieved [BOOK SPOILER] (according to McHugh's last-chapter explanations) by "barely making the connection in the exchange and breaking it continually ..." Then—after the cosmic ringing—the "name *Woodford* had sighed across the wire"... an untraceable sigh, of course. In the movie, McHugh hears someone say, "This is John Woodford speaking," on a dead telephone. ("Dead as a graveyard.")

Milne himself comes up with one unearthly device, worthy of Wadsworth Camp—the voice coming from nowhere, as it seems, at first. ("That's Woodford's voice!") As the actor Carleton (Walter Woolf King) is about to speak, on stage in rehearsal, the echoing voice of the dead Woodford takes over, preempting—and startling—Carleton, and everyone else. Almost immediately Milne explains away this disembodied voice, but it has had its effect. In all, there are some half dozen good chills, three or four of them originating in the film itself.

Director Joe May makes full use of the theater set, from top to bottom. Every prop, curtain, rope, chair, elevator, ladder, and rafter comes into play, at one time or another. But, apart from the above-noted ghostly highlights, this is still a pretty routine mystery, with (as with the 1929 adaptation, *The Last Warning*) little story or character interest. The "ghost notes" (ostensibly from the dead Woodford)—e.g., "You will never play my part"—left for the principals, can sustain interest only so long. An energetic Gargan almost succeeds in holding it all together.

Notes: The Barbara Morgan of the book *The House of Fear*—who became Doris Terry in *The Last Warning*—is now Alice Tabor.

The well-done first scare: the apparently optically-enhanced, ultra-bright eyes in the dark of a black cat.

The "Minneapolis mockingbird" Jeff is played by El Brendel, he of the "Yumpin' yiminy!" accent.

Universal. D: Joe May. SP: Peter Milne, from the book (aka *Backstage Phantom*) by Wadsworth Camp and the play *The Last Warning* by Thomas F. Fallon. Ph: Milton Krasner. AD: Jack Otterson. Ed: Frank Gross. Sd: Bernard B. Brown. Cost: Vera West. Assoc P: Edmund Grainger. With William Gargan, Irene Hervey, Dorothy Arnold, Alan Dinehart, Harvey Stephens, Walter Woolf King, Robert Coote, El Brendel, Tom Dugan, Jan Duggan, Donald Douglas, Hobart Cavanaugh, William Gould, Harry Hayden, Holmes Herbert, Milton Kibbee, Emory Parnell, Charles C. Wilson; 67 minutes

Ref: *Motion Picture Herald* 6/10/39.
Film Daily 6/5/39.
IMDb.

"Both script and director brought in several weird situations and spooky effects to make the theater as haunted as possible"—*Variety* 6/14/39.

"Slightly better than average for this kind of thing, with some interesting and surprising plot twists"—Dave Sindelar (7/26/2003).

MIRACLES FOR SALE

Miracles for Sale released August 14, 1939: Cesare Sabbat and his Manhattan apartment provide most of the "spook atmosphere" in Clayton Rawson's mystery novel, *Death from a Top Hat*. ("There was a Lon Chaney-Boris Karloff feel to him.") He's into "such things as vampires, werewolves"—and he's the first murder victim, found strangled in the center of a "Voodoo trick" star on the floor, ringed by chalk-scribbled demonic incantations. ("Come Surgat!") Suspects include the "large, huskily-built" Madame Rappourt, who claims to be a real "20th-century witch," and David Duvallo, escape artist. Surprises include a mysteriously-typed note from "the Invisible Man." And the inscription on the door of magician-sleuth Merlini's Magic Shop provides the film version its title: *Miracles for Sale*.

Rawson's book is single-mindedly clever, a kaleidoscope of clues, alibis, and puzzles. And, give it its due—it is darned ingenious, certainly, at least, "good of kind," in *Parents Magazine*'s phrase. In a paean-to-puzzles book such

as this, the coda—chock-full as it is of explanations—is actually the main thing. The mystery, however, has little but lesser mysteries to keep itself going: The protagonist trio—Merlini, ever-exasperated Inspector Gavigan, and the narrator Harte—don't do much except juggle those alibis and clues.

"Sabbat invoked some demon out of hell, who got sore and wrung his neck." Hollywood filmed two of Rawson's Merlini novels, but there really isn't a Merlini movie as such. Both times the name was changed, both times to Michael ... here, Michael Morgan (Robert Young) and, in *The Man Who Wouldn't Die*, Michael Shayne. Here, at least, The Great Morgan is a magician, though the script retains little of the flavor of the book, whose whodunit intricacies arguably wouldn't have translated well to the screen anyway—they're developed in talk and written, and furiously re-written, lists.

As in the original, victim Dr. Sabbat (Frederick Worlock) wrote "books on demonology—vampires and devils and things." The dead "Dr. Demonology" seems to appear, first, as a "horrible face" at a window, then as a misty figure at a séance ("It's Dr. Sabbat!") Despite the tantalizing references to demons and other "weird things"—like souls leaving and returning to bodies—this is a predictable MGM mixture of comedy, action, and human, or family, interest. The same year that Tarzan and Nick Charles, also at MGM, found sons, Morgan welcomes a father (Frank Craven) to New York City. Judge Hardy, anyone?

The only improvement on the book: Gloria Holden's Madame Rapport, who seems to be in a hypnotic trance even when she is not. Her cosmic stare matches her cosmic lines: "There is death in this place—death from the other world." In essence, yes, Tod Browning—for his last film—returns to direct "Dracula's daughter," though the movie as a whole might have been helmed by anyone in the studio stable ...

MGM. D: Tod Browning. SP: Harry Ruskin, Marion Parsonnet, James Edward Grant, from Clayton Rawson's novel *Death from a Top Hat*. Ph: Charles Lawton. Mus: William Axt. AD: Cedric Gibbons. Ed: Frederick Y. Smith. Sd: Douglas Shearer. Mkp: Jack Dawn. Cost: Dolly Tree. Magic Tutor: Paul Le Paul. P: J. J. Cohn. With Robert Young, Florence Rice, Frank Craven, Henry Hull, Lee Bowman, Cliff Clark, Astrid Allwyn, Walter Kingsford, Frederick Worlock, Gloria Holden, William Demarest, Harold Minjir, Eddie Acuff, Truman Bradley, Chester Clute, John Davidson, Edward Earle, Suzanne Kaaren, Charles Lane, Richard Loo, Claire McDowell, Matt McHugh, John Picorri, William Tannen, Phillip Terry, E. Alyn Warren; 71 minutes

Ref: *PV* 14:44.
FM 22:40.
Motion Picture Herald 8/5/39.
Variety 8/16/39.

"Lacks the moodiness you expect from a Browning film"—Dave Sindelar (9/23/2006).

The MAN THEY COULD NOT HANG

The Man They Could Not Hang Aug. 17, 1939: "I have the perfect alibi—I am legally dead." 1939 was quite a movie year for the living hanged—Ygor (Bela Lugosi), in *Son of Frankenstein*, and Dr. Henryk Savaard (Boris Karloff), in this film. Yes, literally speaking, the title has it reversed. They hanged him. But there's really an implied title, too, something like The Man They Couldn't Keep Dead. And they couldn't.

Reissue (Favorite Films) title lobby card from *The Man They Could Not Hang*

This well-made "B" picture was a fairly auspicious beginning for Karloff's Columbia series. [SPOILER]: Dr. Savaard's "mechanical heart" invention brings, first, himself, then, at the end, his daughter (Lorna Gray), back to life. Its success vindicates him, as a scientist, but mainly it allows him—as a man tried and executed—to wreak revenge on those who helped convict him of the murder of his assistant, Roberts (Stanley Brown), who might also have been scientifically revived if not for the interference of a nurse (Ann Doran) and the police.

Plot-wise, the script (Karl Brown, screenplay; G.W. Sayre and Leslie White, story) is functional, but it's a most effective vehicle for Karloff. In the courtroom sequences, he plays, first, the visionary who aims to "make death our servant," then (after the wrong verdict is returned) the prophet of doom, the accused who accuses the judge, jury, etc. of humanistic myopia. Later, after Savaard's associate (Byron Foulger) revives him, he holds captive his accusers, in a macabre variation on the Gracious Host.

Karloff seems to relish the role of a man "beyond the reach of any law," or graciousness. With sepulchral irony, Savaard lets his victims know the "exact hour and moment of the end" for each of them. He wants them to feel what he felt. And Benjamin Kline's high-angle shots of their living-room

"prison" echo Savaard's god-like, second-floor point of view. One quiet, standout shot catches the terrified look on the faces of three captives as the clock strikes seven, the time which had been scheduled for the judge's (Charles Trowbridge) death. It's a look of dire realization. In addition to Savaard's voice, the elements of terror here are everyday items such as a telephone receiver, an iron-grill gate, a microphone, and chimes. The immediate inspiration for this film seems to have been the publication of Agatha Christie's mystery novel, *Ten Little Indians*, also 1939.

Note: After *Son of Frankenstein*, this was the second full-fledged American sf/horror movie of the Return of the Golden Age.

Columbia. D: Nick Grinde. SP: Karl Brown. Story: George W. Sayre, Leslie T. White. Ph: Benjamin Kline. Ed: William Lyon. Sd: George Cooper. Mkp: Clay Campbell. P: Wallace MacDonald. With Boris Karloff, Lorna Gray, Robert Wilcox. Roger Pryor, Don Beddoe, Ann Doran, Charles Trowbridge, Byron Foulger, Dick Curtis, James Craig, Sam Ash, Stanley Blystone, Harlan Briggs, Stanley Brown, John Dilson, Walter Sande, Robert Sterling; 64 minutes

Ref: *FM* 2:32.

"Feels like a filmed play with two sets"—John Stell, "Hail Columbia?"— *Monsters from the Vault* Spring 1997:44.

"Plot is inconsistent with the deep interest of Karloff in promoting life by his discovery to deliberately turn murderer in the end"—*Variety* 9/27/39.

The WITNESS VANISHES

The Witness Vanishes released Aug. 22, 1939: "He's threatened to kill us—all of us!" Lucius Marplay (Barlowe Borland) escapes from Hillsdale Sanitarium and threatens to kill the "four scoundrels who stole [his] newspaper"—Mark Peters (Edmund Lowe), Ambrose Craven (Walter Kingsford), Sinclair Ellis (Boyd Irwin), and Nigel Partridge (Vernon Steele). To that end, he sets himself up at the abandoned site of the old London *Evening Sun*. ("They do say the old building's haunted.")

Uncannily, Marplay's notebooks regarding his enemies' respective demises seem prophetic—the victims die exactly as indicated therein, including one, Craven, who (according to "The Fortunate Finish of Ambrose Craven"), it was suggested, could be "scared to death"—hence, the further suggestion that a ghost or an avenging angel lurks. When Peters scoffs that "no living man" can walk through concrete, Partridge queasily counters, "*If* he is a living man, which I'm beginning to doubt." Partridge, again, later: "But if Marplay's alive, why is it everyone can see the things he does and no one can see the man himself?"

More a "ghost" story than a whodunit, *The Witness Vanishes* falters only at the end, when it awkwardly resolves itself as a who-

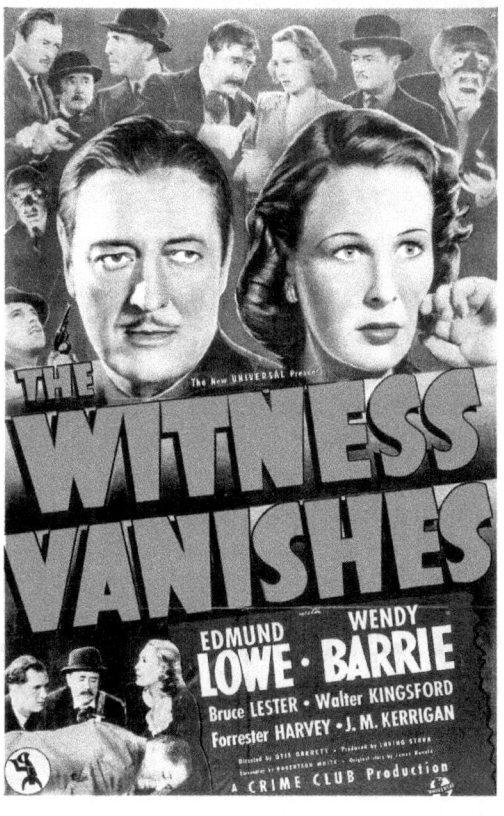

dunit. Up to that point, it's an intriguing little offbeat anecdote, featuring that *Son of Frankenstein* mounting-horror musical theme and a thunderstorm-accompanied, lantern-lit walk through the old newspaper building.

The book, which is the basis of *The Witness Vanishes*—James Ronald's Crime Club mystery *They Can't Hang Me*—is also told, in part, as a "tale of horror," in which Marplay seems to be a "ghost," a "supernatural force," a "ubiquitous but disembodied spirit" or an invisible man, in an overt nod to the H.G. Wells novel. But, though Craven (as in the movie) is "out of his mind with fear," he does not die of fright. And the old *Evening Echo* building is not said to be haunted. The MacNab character (Forrester Harvey in the movie) is more complicated here than in the Robertson White-scripted film, but Ronald's characters are generally dimensionless. The book is not badly written—in particular, Ronald has a knack for striking similes—but it's drawn out, and the finale in which the cornered killer explains how-he-did-it is a tad too ingenious.

Universal. D: Otis Garrett. SP: Robertson White, from James Ronald's novel *They Can't Hang Me*. Ph: Arthur Martinelli. AD: Jack Otterson. Ed: Harry Keller. Sd: Bernard B. Brown. Cost: Vera West. P: Irving Starr. With Edmund Lowe, Wendy Barrie, Bruce Lester, Forrester Harvey, Walter Kingsford, J.M.

Kerrigan, Barlowe Borland, Boyd Irwin, Vernon Steele, Reginald Barlow, Leyland Hodgson, Robert Noble, Phyllis Barry, Hal E. Chester, Anne Nagel; 66 minutes

Ref: "Fifth and final production in the first Crime Club series ... a first-rate whodunit ... Forrester Harvey ... provides a sparkling character study which stands out all the more because of dismal surrounding performances"—*Variety* 10/25/39.

The ADVENTURES OF SHERLOCK HOLMES

The Adventures of Sherlock Holmes released Sept. 1, 1939: "There's something grotesque about this business." Professor Moriarty (George Zucco) is out to swipe the crown jewels, but first he must distract super-sleuth Sherlock Holmes (Basil Rathbone) with a murder or two ... The movie's weakness is that the "distraction" has more drama and suspense than the main item on the dramatic menu. Zucco would go on to become a specialist in this sort of urbane villainy, but Moriarty here basically just sets the co-plots in motion.

What survives in *The Adventures of Sherlock Holmes*: the swirl of fog, music, and photography (Leon Shamroy) of the scattered "grotesque" sequences. In one, a man is swallowed up in the fog of a London park, and the last we hear of him is a strangled cry. In another, a club-footed killer stalks the heroine (Ida Lupino) through the grounds of a semi-remote estate. And the most unsettling element of grotesquerie: the "ancient Inca funeral dirge," which seems to herald death. ("There's death in every note of it.") In the context of the film's special circumstances—fog, darkness, quiet—the little tune seems fraught with menace: The Tune at Midnight.

Its composer is not credited, though at least five people—R.R. Bennett, David Buttolph, Cyril Mockridge, David Raksin, and Walter Scharf—worked on the score. Film music researcher Jim Shapiro's best educated guess is that Raksin wrote it. Perhaps one of them got the idea of giving the audience the wind-instrument willies after seeing *Son of Frankenstein*, earlier in the year, in which film Bela Lugosi's Ygor essays provocative flute solos.

Artistically, Universal did not seem to agree with Basil Rathbone. In *Son of Frankenstein* and Universal's later continuation of the Holmes films, he's often stolid. In *The Adventures of Sherlock Holmes* and *Hound of the Baskervilles*, at Fox, he thrives. He actually breathes. He's Sherlock Holmes. Nigel Bruce plays Dr. Watson as Holmes' pet here—psychologically speaking, Watson's sense of self-worth seems completely dependent on emotional crumbs from Holmes.

(*Sherlock Holmes*—British title) Fox. D: Alfred Werker. SP: Edwin Blum, William Drake, from the play *Sherlock Holmes* by William Gillette. Ph: Leon Shamroy. Mus: David Raksin, David Buttolph et al. AD: Richard Day, Hans Peters. Ed: Robert Bischoff. Sd: W.D. Flick, Roger Heman. Cost: Gwen Wakeling. P: Darryl F. Zanuck. With Basil Rathbone, Nigel Bruce, Ida Lupino, Alan Mar-

6-sheet poster for *The Adventures of Sherlock Holmes*

shal, Terry Kilburn, George Zucco, Henry Stephenson, E.E. Clive, Arthur Hohl, Mary Gordon, Holmes Herbert, George Regas, Mary Forbes, William Austin, Ted Billings, Harry Cording, Neil Fitzgerald, Leyland Hodgson, Boyd Irwin, Leonard Mudie, Ivan F. Simpson, Eric Wilton; 85 minutes

Ref: IMDb.

"An exciting story told with more real movie art per foot than seven reels of anything the intellectual men have been finding good this whole year or more"—Otis Ferguson, *The New Republic*, 9/20/39.

"About the neatest package in several attempts to make Sherlock Holmes exciting on the screen ... George Zucco offers a splendid characterization as the arch-criminal"—*Variety* 9/6/39.

"Some people say it's the best of the series, and quite frankly I agree ... Zucco's performance as Moriarty is one of the high points of his career ... The horror elements are fairly slight, but an exciting chase that ends in a graveyard adds an ample amount of horror atmosphere"—Dave Sindelar (3/8/2005).

CHARLIE CHAN AT TREASURE ISLAND

Charlie Chan at Treasure Island released Sept. 8, 1939: "It is Dr. Zodiac—he is not dead!" Charlie Chan (Sidney Toler)—the "world's foremost whodunit celebrity"—investigates the case of the "great Dr. Zodiac," "doctor of the occult" and the "Eye of Allamata." His "spook room" séances may be fraudulent, but Eve Cairo (Pauline Moore)—the "world's greatest living mind reader"—seems to be the real thing. ("Under hypnosis, Miss Cairo becomes a delicate radio receiving apparatus, tuned to every forceful mind.") Her control: Rhadini (Cesar Romero), who claims that he is out to expose Zodiac.

Or, oddly: Up with mind readers, down with mediums. The film's endorsement of ESP pays off, dramatically, at least. *Charlie Chan at Treasure Island* has two of the more cherishable horror scenes of the 1930s. In the first, a mental intruder interrupts the hypnotized Eve's act: "There's someone else! I can't go on!" ... she cries, at first. She jumps up and: "I hear death among us! I'm frightened! There's evil here! Someone here is thinking murder!" Instant Scary, not just for her, but for everyone in attendance. Anyone could be the killer, anyone could be the victim. A unique telepathic "Boo!" Thousands of possibilities ... (The dagger flying past Chan and into the trunk of a palm tree proves a little anticlimactic.) It's a moment that anticipates similar scenes in *The Crawling Eye* and *Scanners*.

In the second sequence, at the end, Chan instructs Eve, onstage with him, to read his thoughts "until dominant thought of killer" comes to her. Yes, from one angle, it's as if he is rather ungallantly taping a "Kill me" sign on her back. But it's good theater, or ESP. "Mr. Chan, there is a mind here that is fighting me," she says—"trying to keep your thoughts from me." All we see is a pair of eyes in a blacked-out face. Mystery-movie conventions may have dictated this Eyes without a Face tactic—the better of course to preserve the mystery until the last minute—but the Psychic Monster side effect is pretty creepy. And the Good Mind vs. Bad Mind battle is unusual for its time. A tip of the hat to the screenplay writer, John Larkin.

Unfortunately, the rest of the movie is largely a glossy bore. Sidney Toler is not necessarily a lesser actor than Warner Oland, but he has little in the way of presence. And Sen Yung as Jimmy Chan is a lightweight, too. For the most interesting casting notes, you have to go behind the scenes. June Gale (Mrs. Rhadini) would go on to marry Oscar Levant, composer of the opera scenes for the previous Chan spooker, *Charlie Chan at the Opera*. She was one of a quartet of actress sisters, also including Jane Gale, Jean Gale, and Joan Gale. (Adorable, isn't it?) Curiously enough, Sally Blane (Stella Essex here) also had three sisters who were actresses, most prominently Loretta Young, as well as Georgiana Young and Polly Ann Young. Sally was featured in an early Bela Lugosi talkie, *Night of Terror*; Polly Ann, in a later Lugosi, *The Invisible Ghost*. Small world, by gum ...

Half-sheet poster from *Charlie Chan at Treasure Island*

Virgil Miller contributes some slick lighting effects for the séances. Costume designer Herschel contributes a parade-float get-up for Dr. Zodiac. And J. Edgar Hoover might have gotten some ideas from Zodiac's file cabinets full of damaging secrets regarding various individuals—"All kinds of dope about all kinds of people." ("Organized blackmail!")

Fox. D: Norman Foster. SP: John Larkin. Ph: Virgil Miller. Mus: Samuel Kaylin. AD: Lewis Creber, Richard Day. Ed: Norman Colbert. Sd: William H. Anderson, E. Clayton Ward. Cost: Herschel. Assoc P: Edward Kaufman. With Sidney Toler, Cesar Romero, Pauline Moore, Victor Sen Yung, Douglas Fowley, June Gale, Douglass Dumbrille, Sally Blane, Billie Seward, Wally Vernon, Donald MacBride, Charles Halton, Trevor Bardette, Louis Jean Heydt, Heinie Conklin, John Elliott, Bud Geary, Fred Kelsey, Al Kikume, Kay Linaker, Hank Mann, Gerald Mohr, Harry Strang, Charles Tannen; 74 minutes

Ref: *Film Daily Yearbook.* Fox Cinema Classics.

Treasure Island was the setting here for the World's Fair of the West ... tie-in with Chan comic strip—pressbook.

"*Charlie Chan at Treasure Island* is considered the finest of all Toler Chans"—Ken Hanke, *Charlie Chan at the Movies*, p123.

"Maze of weird and spooky episodes"—*Variety* 8/23/39.

TORTURE SHIP

"I became quite accustomed to dying." In Jack London's short story *A Thousand Deaths*—the source for the movie *Torture Ship*—the hero all but drowns in San Francisco Bay but is revived "by means of his [father's] aerotherapeutical apparatus." His father then forces him to undergo a series of experimental deaths and resurrections. ("The easiest deaths were by asphyxiation ... ") [SPOILER]: At the end, our hero—a scientist himself—counters by inventing "two powerful batteries, connected with magnets," which vaporize his father. ("Puff! It was like the wind sighing among the pines.") Balmy, wry s.f. anecdote is outrageous, yet modest in its dramatic scope. If you buy the father's inventions, you pretty much buy the son's.

In *Torture Ship*—released Oct. 28, 1939—the scientist, Dr. Herbert Stander (Irving Pichel), operates on his nephew, Bob Bennett (Lyle Talbot) ... and that's the only point at which short story and movie come close to intersecting. Dr. Stander wants to "make better men and women" of a batch of "vicious criminals [with] mental disorders," including Harry, The Carver (Russell Hopton), a "machine gun slayer" (Skelton Knaggs), a "Blue Beard" (Leander De Cordova), an "alien strangler" (Adia Kuznetzoff), and "Poison Mary" (Sheila Bromley). On a yacht "cruise to nowhere," he injects his subjects with ingredients isolated from the endocrine glands, but fails abjectly with Krantz, the strangler, who promptly proceeds to strangle a sailor. ("Not the reaction I'd hoped for.")

He takes the opposite tack with his normal "free from criminal taint" nephew, who—post-op—gets a wicked glint in his eye and promptly attacks poor Joan (Jacqueline Wells). [SPOILER]: This is apparently chalked up as a success, but Stander goes too far, and Bob seems to turn into a virtual zombie, though he's really only fooling and pretending. The fulfilled but dying doc lives just long enough to hear the no-longer-murderous Mary declare, "Something has come over me. I feel as if I had been born again." Compare this to the post-lycanthrope Larry Talbot of *House of Dracula*.

Jack Greenhalgh photographs the rampaging Krantz as a monster, and the post-endocrined Bob as a "brute." And he even dares, at one point, to bring Knaggs' camp horror face (he looks like a Dick Tracy villain) into alarming close-up. But director Victor Halperin is a long way from his glory day of *White Zombie*. Mary's marvelous transformation shouldn't be the dramatic highlight, but it's about the only plot development that makes some kind of sense. It's scientifically-achieved Sweetness and Light. The cool, calm Pichel was of course Dracula's daughter's evil adviser Sandor, and Wells was another Joan in *The Black Cat* (1934).

Notes: Sinister Cinema's full-length, 57-minute version is nice and glossy, but the extra seven minutes of running time (over the more-familiar version) doesn't make much difference dramatically.

The idea of "curing" criminals goes back, in film, at least to 1913 and *Doctor Maxwell's Experiment*. Ref: Bioscope 4/10/13.

Producers Pictures (Sigmund Neufeld). D: Victor Halperin SP: (uncredited) Harvey Huntley, George W. Sayre, from Jack London's short story *A Thousand Deaths*. Ph: Jack Greenhalgh. AD: Fred Preble. Ed: Holbrook N. Todd. Sd: Hans Weeren. With Lyle Talbot, Irving Pichel, Jacqueline Wells, Sheila Bromley, Anthony Averill, Russell Hopton, Wheeler Oakman, Stanley Blystone, Leander De Cordova, Skelton Knaggs, Carleton Young, Adia Kuznetzoff, Fred Walton; 57 minutes

Ref: *Showmen*'s 9/9/39.

Film Daily 11/22/39. Solano Public Library.

"A fun little film"—Dave Sindelar (4/23/2002).

"Should be seen"—*PV* 11:12.

"Yarn has so many unreasonable and unexplainable points that it will annoy even the most juve-minded"—*Variety* 11/29/39.

The CAT AND THE CANARY

The Cat and the Canary (play—John Willard): "It came from the dark ..." Glencliff Manor, a "spooky old place" on the Hudson. ("This house is haunted.") Ingredients in this rather dated 1922 stage thriller include a "monster" with a "claw-like hand," a "homicidal maniac" supposedly escaped from an asylum, the "rather weird ... voodoo woman" Mammy Pleasant, from the West Indies—and her "friends from the shadow world"—a madman who suffers "spells," and a "weird gong." A play that spawned numerous "cats" and "canaries" now seems very thin, though it has occasional ingenuity. Florence Eldredge was the first Annabelle West, and author Willard was the first Harry Blythe. Henry Hull, the "werewolf of London," was the original Paul Jones.

The Cat and the Canary (1927 silent): "Ghosts are murdering people in the Cyrus West house!" The latter is a "grotesque mansion" on the Hudson. ("Gosh what a spooky house!") And Mr. West's ghost has supposedly been haunting the place for 20 years, until the reading of his will ... The beginning is imaginative, and the climactic scenes are lively. The in between, though, is only a little better than the play, better thanks mainly to evocative tinting.

In this lobby card from *The Cat and the Canary* (1939), Paulette Goddard cowers at the approach of "The Cat" (William Abbey, uncredited).

Highlights include the emblematic image of a miniature Cyrus surrounded by cats somewhat larger than he is ... a gloved hand wiping away cobwebs and dust to reveal the title ... strangely-shaped shadows on a wall, which resolve into more ordinary shadows of humans ... and the Hall of Billowing Curtains. Cinematographer Gilbert Warrenton may have been responsible for the shots of the strangely-illuminated model mansion—he similarly lights a model New York City in *Lonesome* (1928). Disappointingly, at the end, the Cat simply indulges in fisticuffs. More happily, he sports a bulging eye, two fangs, and a "hand, like a claw or a spider."

The Cat and the Canary released Nov. 10, 1939: "The demon in this house has got him." The "old Norman place"—situated in the "strange solitude" of the Louisiana bayous—proves to be a "house full of maniacs," including (supposedly) an escaped madman with claw-like fingernails called The Cat by his fellow inmates. At the end, the house proves also to be full of secret panels, passages, stairs, trapdoors, and cellars. ("It's awful spooky down here.")

If, occasionally, this generally unremarkable comedy thriller begins to seem downright eerie, it may be because Dr. Ernst Toch's musical score is doing some of its better work almost subliminally. There's the more familiar suspense and shock music here, too, all the better it seems to set off the subtler, more elusive choirs of angels, or devils, which quietly get on the nerves, in three or four scenes. In the main such sequence, it's at first just Joyce Norman (Paulette Goddard) going to the window and putting out the lamp, while, in the background, a secret panel opens, and the Cat lurks. But those barely heard, edgy voices have started in, and they return, shortly, when housekeeper Miss Lu (Gale Sondergaard) fiddles with a pistol, as Joyce unravels a bit. (Randall D. Larson calls this aural effect an "eerie high vocal ambiance.") The sotto voce music is so damn spooky because at first you don't even notice it. By the time you do, it has done its subterranean damage. Like the Cat, early in this sequence, it's there hovering in the background. True, there are comparable diabolical choruses in films like *Supernatural* and *Invaders from Mars*, but those are hardly subtle.

In fact, the movie is rife with offbeat sight-and-sound effects, including also the lights with "jitters," which inspire musical "jitters," and the gong sounds. Yes, the 1939 *The Cat and the Canary* restores the gong, which was featured in the play, but understandably not in the silent *The Cat and the Canary*.

Bob Hope, as Wally—the one-note Paul character in the play and silent-film versions—is a breath of brash air, and he gets a still-funny line now and then. Paulette Goddard's Joyce seems genuinely amused by him. And there are some pleasing American Gothic shots of George Zucco's Crosby and Miss Lu together—they're sort of a Ma and Pa Horror. Miss Lu seems to be behind every door and peering out every window.

Note: This movie brings back one of the best lines from the play: "The hand—it came from the dark!" And it throws in a variation on it: "A hand—it came out of the wall!"

Paramount. D: Elliott Nugent. SP: Walter DeLeon, Lynn Starling, from John Willard's play. Ph: Charles Lang. Mus: Dr. Ernst Toch. AD: Hans Dreier, Robert Usher. Ed: Archie Marshek. Sd: Richard Olson, Philip Wisdom. Cost: Edith Head. P: Arthur Hornblow, Jr. With Bob Hope, Paulette Goddard, John Beal, Douglass Montgomery, Gale Sondergaard, George Zucco, Elizabeth Patterson, Nydia Westman, John Wray, George Regas, Milton Kibbee, Charles Lane, Chief Thundercloud; 72 minutes

Ref: Jim Shapiro. Clarens.
Orpheus 4:57.
FM 31:59. *COF* 9:23.
Modern Monsters 3:32.

"Both this and *The Ghost Breakers* have real scares and tension in them"—Dave Sindelar (2/22/2002).

"There's the low-key lighting, drifting shadows, eerie music, sliding panels and secret passages"—*Variety* 11/1/39.

The RETURN OF DOCTOR X

The Return of Doctor X released Dec. 2, 1939: "Merrova's got that same cold, graveyard look." Why are people who look "like something dead" walking about New York City? Retired stage star Angela Merrova (Lya Lys) miraculously rebounds from an apparently deadly knife wound, but she's still the walking "dead white," with a striking drained-of-blood look. And Marshall Quesne's (Humphrey Bogart) face looks "like a piece of white marble," which complements the streak of white in his hair, an affectation borrowed from the bride of Frankenstein.

The two are not just making a fashion statement. In fact, in a cannier movie—say, a variation on the Val Lewton *The Seventh Victim*—they would prove to be figurative as well as literal walking-dead souls, and Merrova's line, "I feel cold," would have more resonance. It does have some emotional resonance as it is. And there could be white marble-like visual hints of creeping spiritual-moral decay.

Unfortunately, the answers to the provocative questions that the Lee Katz script raises, or seems about to raise, are pretty pat science fiction regarding a series of "blood murders." [SPOILER]: Seems that Dr. Flegg's (John Litel) "synthetic blood" sustains reanimated corpses only "for a short period." Hence, his main subject, undead citizen Quesne, requires infusions of human

Half-sheet poster from *The Return of Doctor X* (1939)

blood. The "pasty-faced" Quesne proves to have been "medical genius" and "child slayer" Dr. Maurice Xavier, executed in 1937.

The occasionally rousing Max Steiner-Bernhard Kaun score makes it sound as if something's going on, though it rarely is. The quieter musical highlight: the eerie-plaintive background music for Dr. Rhodes (Dennis Morgan) and Wichita Garrett's (Wayne Morris) questioning of Merrova. As shot by Sid Hickox, Dr. Flegg's lab is sleek and rather spare, unlike the three-ring affairs at Universal. The climactic sequence takes place at an "abandoned duck club," in a New Jersey swamp, a club, one assumes, frequented, in its heyday, by Donald, Daisy, and Daffy.

WB. D: Vincent Sherman. SP: Lee Katz. Story: William J. Makin. Ph: Sid Hickox. Mus: Bernhard Kaun, Max Steiner. AD: Esdras Hartley. Ed: Thomas Pratt. Sd: Charles Lang. Mkp: Perc Westmore. Gowns: Milo Anderson. Assoc P: Bryan Foy. With Humphrey Bogart, Wayne Morris, Rosemary Lane, Dennis Morgan, John Litel, Lya Lys, Huntz Hall, Charles C. Wilson, Vera Lewis, Howard Hickman, Olin Howland, Creighton Hale, John Ridgely, Joseph Crehan, Glenn Langan, William Hopper, John Harron, Jack Mower, Paul Panzer, Ian Wolfe; 60 minutes

Ref: *HSF1*. IMDb.

"Addicts of the gory and the macabre should get a kick out of this chip off the Frankenstein block … Humphrey Bogart exudes plenty of menace and pitches a makeup that should give Boris Karloff a hot run for honors"—*Variety* 11/2/39.

The DEVIL'S DAUGHTER

The Devil's Daughter released Dec. 7, 1939: "And remember, we were only having a little pocomania." Is it Haitian voodoo, in Jamaica, or is Sylvia "only drugged—she'll be all right in a few moments"? Apparently, it's only "obeah trickery," designed by one sister, Isabelle (Nina Mae McKinney), to spur the other, Sylvia (Ida James), into returning to New York City. The above is not a spoiler—Isabelle makes it plain that she'll only be fooling and pretending, that Sylvia will undergo only an herb-induced trance. But Isabelle's fooling sounds pretty serious, at the time: Okay, now, a [SPOILER]: During the climactic ritual, she vows to send her sister's soul to the "black pit." "Let her breath become shorter and shorter. Dissolve the living flesh from her bones." Only here does she bear any resemblance to the "devil's daughter."

The casual, loopy comedy scenes with "house man" Percy (Hamtree Harrington) are easier to take than the stilted dialogue sequences, and Harrington is the only engaging member of the cast. ("They ain't gonna put my soul in no pig!") The scrappy but breezy singing-and-dancing sequence, at the beginning, is actually the best of it, before story and dialogue set in.

Note: The movie features one of the least convincing fist fights on film.

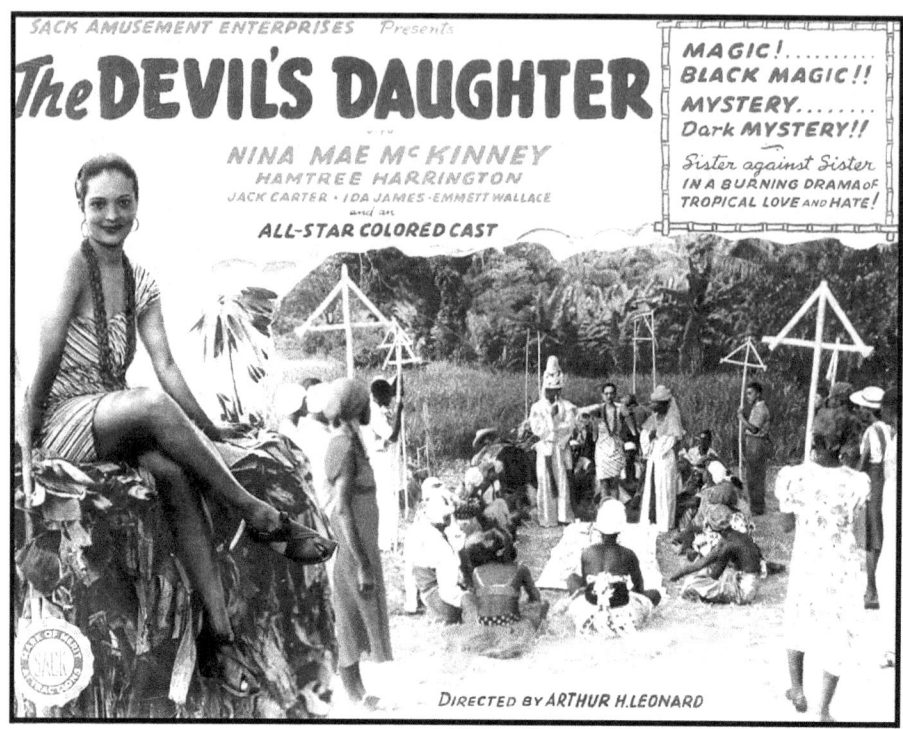

(aka *Ouanga.* aka *Drums of the Jungle.* aka *Pocomania. Daughter of the Isle of Jamaica*—original title): Sack/Lenwal. D, Assoc P: Arthur Leonard. SP: George Terwilliger. Ph: Jay Rescher. Mus: John Killam. Ed: Samuel Datlowe. Sd: Dean Cole. Mkp: Richard Willis. Cost: Renee. P: Harry M. Popkin. With Nina Mae McKinney, Jack Carter, Ida James, Hamtree Harrington, Willa Mae Lang; 52 minutes

Ref: *HSF1.*
Showmen's 12/9/39.
Film Daily 12/14/39. IMDb.

"Even less successful than its indifferent model, *Ouanga*"—Bryan Senn, *Drums of Terror*, p42.

"Touches of what feels like authenticity scattered throughout"—Dave Sindelar (4/19/2002).

The HUNCHBACK OF NOTRE DAME

The Hunchback of Notre-Dame (novel—Victor Hugo): "He looks like a devil riding a ghoul ... " Hugo's renown tale of the "sublimely monstrous" hunchback Quasimodo—a "real monster of abomination" even as a little boy ... his guardian the Archdeacon Claude Frollo—a study in abnormal psychology bordering on camp ... the lovely gypsy Esmerelda ... and her "guardian," the goat Djali. Meanwhile, a "goblin-monk" haunts the streets of Paris ... Grand

pathos, with time-outs for histories of Paris, Notre-Dame, and world architecture. These detours are occasionally quite artful, but in the end yield a somewhat diluted masterpiece. At any rate, the first 100 pages are a helluva read, and what follows is intermittently killingly poignant. A for-instance: the deaf Quasimodo "listening to [Esmerelda's] song with his eyes." The insufferable Frollo reduces to "Woe is I," but even he has his moments. But did Djali live? The philosopher Gringoire (Esmerelda's husband, in name only), at least, "tried to save the goat," from hanging.

The Hunchback of Notre Dame (1923 silent): "Swift run the sands of life except in the hour of pain." Lon Chaney plays Quasimodo—"a monstrous joke of Nature"—as a manic, acrobatic child. Somewhat amazingly, his elaborate makeup does not seem to make him any less expressive. Patsy Ruth Miller is a little plain to be playing the dazzling Esmerelda. The script wildly scrambles bits and pieces of Hugo's story and characters. The distance between this movie and Hugo can best be indicated by the happy ending, which unites Esmerelda and Phoebus. It was apparently an era and city of terrible hats for women.

The Hunchback of Notre Dame released Dec. 29, 1939: Rife with [SPOILERS] for film and book: "Why was I not made of stone like these?" This curtain-call line for Quasimodo (Charles Laughton) is not Hugo's, but it's just as good as—and certainly more terse than—the latter's more mysterious send-off for the hunchback. Fortunately, yes—if the scriptwriters savage most of Hugo—

they retain the hunchback, not surprisingly considering the title. And, again fortunately, it's Laughton as Quasimodo. If most of the novel is lost, the heart of it is retained. And if the makeup for Laughton's face is innocuously smooth and rubbery, it was someone's (perhaps makeup artist Perc Westmore's) inspired touch to have Quasimodo's unruly hair always at the mercy of any breeze. It's a visual equivalent of his: "But I am deaf, too." Hunchbacked, ugly, one-eyed, deaf, and unkempt. But Laughton's one working eye and quivering voice are enough, and movements and gestures such as his pathetically flailing arms seem unique to his character.

The other notable performance is Edmond O'Brien's. He's all youthful exuberance and idealism as the poet-philosopher Gringoire. He always seems to be looking up at clouds. His helpless, joyous laughter at Quasimodo's Tarzan-style rescuing of Esmerelda (Maureen O'Hara) is a minor marvel. Gringoire's union, at the end, with her, however, is the payoff of an ongoing fraud. The latter begins with the introductory title, "The people under Louis XI felt free to hope again." Hugo's assessment of Louis XI was somewhat less positive. ("Kings such as Louis XI take care to have the pavement speedily washed after a massacre.") Compounding the crime, Harry Davenport makes a most affable Louis, elevated here from a minor character almost to a main character. And, ah! yes, this nice king would pardon Esmerelda. (She seems to have been accused of being a Gypsy.) Voila!—a happy ending. In the book, Esmerelda dies.

In the movie, Esmerelda proves more realistic regarding Phoebus. In other words, she gets over him. In still other words, she's really the anti-Esmerelda. The book's main characters—Quasimodo, Esmerelda, Frollo—are absolutes. They don't evolve. They don't resolve their differences. It's rather terrifying. And the writers must have worked overtime coming up with bad dialogue for Esmerelda and Frollo (Sir Cedric Hardwicke). (She: "My own silly heart betrayed me!") The presence of both Frollo and George Zucco's procurator ensures that there's a surfeit of unctuousness.

Notes: If this movie is any indication, it was a bad hair era for men, though Quasimodo did not choose his hair style.

This was the first of Rondo Hatton's six horror movies. He's the first applicant for the King of Fools. This is just one of many roles in horror movies for Zucco.

RKO. D: William Dieterle. SP: Sonya Levien. Adap: Bruno Frank, loosely based on Victor Hugo's novel *The Hunchback of Notre-Dame*, or *Notre-Dame de Paris*. Ph: Joseph H. August. Mus: Alfred Newman. AD: Van Nest Polglase. SpMkp: (uncredited) Perc Westmore. Ed: William Hamilton, Robert Wise. Sd: John E. Tribby. Cost: Walter Plunkett. SpFX: Vernon L. Walker. P: Pandro S. Berman. With Charles Laughton, Sir Cedric Hardwicke, Thomas Mitchell, Maureen O'Hara, Edmond O'Brien, Alan Marshal, Walter Hampden, Harry Davenport, Katharine Alexander, George Zucco, Fritz Leiber, Etienne Girardot, Minna Gombell, Arthur Hohl, Curt Bois, George Tobias, Rod La Rocque, Spencer Charters, Siegfried Arno, Lionel Belmore, Barlowe Borland, Edmund Cobb, Harry Cording, Laura Hope Crews, Jack Curtis, Charles Drake, Ralph Dunn, Peter Godfrey, Alexander Granach, Charles Halton, Rondo Hatton, Al Herman, Louis Jean Heydt, Otto Hoffman, Cy Kendall, Victor Kilian, Nestor Paiva, Gail Patrick, Tempe Pigott, Dewey Robinson, Norbert Schiller, Louis Zamperini; 117 minutes

Ref: "My candidate for the worst-made class-A film of the year"—Otis Ferguson, *The New Republic*, 1/22/40.

"*Hunchback* is one of the greatest horror tales of literature ... Laughton's over-emphasis of his characterization in the early sequences is too vividly ugly and bestial"—*Variety* 12/20/39.

"The film is almost unrelievedly brutal and without the saving grace of unreality which makes Frankenstein's horrors a little comic"—Frank S. Nugent, *NY Times* 1/1/40.

"This is one of my favorites, and it always leaves me somewhat speechless"—Dave Sindelar (2/27/2003).

Afterword

Universal. The years 1931 to 1935 were almost too good to be true for what would come to be called horror movie fans. Even what would come to be called the British horror film "ban" couldn't spoil the decade. And *Son of Frankenstein*, in January of 1939, marked the beginning of a resurgence of the genre, which would last until 1946.

The most important name in horror between 1931 and 1935 was Carl Laemmle, Jr., who produced all of Universal's horror pictures from *Dracula* to *Bride of Frankenstein*. (He got a head start, in 1930, with *The Cat Creeps*.) Take Laemmle out of the picture, and the 1930s might have been very different for us. After 1935, Universal would continue to dominate the genre, but the magic would become intermittent. Even so, no studio could rival Universal, until RKO arrived with Val Lewton and *Cat People* (1942).

The beauty of horror, 1930s style. Many of those moments and images cited in the Introduction here—the tower light reflected in the monster's eyes,

A smiling Carl Laemmle, Jr.

in *Frankenstein* ... the highlighted eyes of Juanita, in the dark, in *Black Moon* ... the supernatural hum of the wind, in *Mark of the Vampire* ... the oddly intimidating sweet music, in *The Walking Dead* ... the glowing death mask floating down the darkened hall, in *Before Dawn*—have as much to do with beauty as with horror. The finer writers and directors of the time were not just trying to scare people, though they did that pretty well. They had a somewhat more complicated artistic agenda.

Mad Love, for instance, features ineffably sweet scenes with little boy-shy Dr. Gogol (Peter Lorre). Ah!—one might conclude—the beauty of human simplicity. But that adorable shyness is the flip side of Gogol's more sinister face. It's just part of the whole psychological package. And the complicated Dr. Gogol, in turn, is representative of one of the main subjects of the horror films of the 1930s and 1940s—the split personality, whether the split is psychological, supernatural, or science-fictional.

This theme infuses films from the *Dr. Jekyll and Mr. Hyde* adaptations to *The Wolf Man* and *Cat People*, to *Bewitched* and *The Brighton Strangler*, and *Hangover Square*. Unfortunately, these movies usually, unintentionally, slight the "good" half of the split personality. Has there ever been a great Dr. Jekyll performance? (In Jerry Lewis's comedy *The Nutty Professor*, Lewis gives a very funny Dr. Kelp performance.) On the "good" side of the split, Lorre's Gogol, Lorre again in *Stranger on the Third Floor*, Stanley Ridges' Professor Kingsley (*Black Friday*), Simon Simone's Irena Dubrovna (*Cat People*), and Phyllis Thaxter's Joan, in *Bewitched*, successfully embody the sweeter side of human nature, in these Tales of Two Personae.

The seed. I found the impetus for this book in volume four of my *Horror and Science Fiction Films* (1997). When I first looked through the finished product I found that I was mainly interested in revisiting what I had written (I have a short memory) about the films of the 1930s and 1940s—and, to a lesser extent, silents and the films of the 1950s. Yes, I had to work through four volumes to discover myself. And there I was, back in 1932 ... The sheer number of new horror and science-fiction films in the 1980s and 1990s was beginning to put the idea of a fifth volume in the H&SFF series out of my reach. And I had taken so many notes in darkened theaters that my right thumb had begun to lose all feeling (The computer—the greatest invention since the pencil.) The Classic Horror Film Board and IMDb would have to take over ... And boy do I thank them.

Stay tuned for our second volume, covering the 1940s, coming within the next year.

Acknowledgments

Many thanks to Dave Sindelar, the late Tim Murphy, the late Bill Warren, Jim Shapiro, J.C. Michel, Rick and Wich2 & the gang at CHFB, Sean, Susan & Mo, Andy Gregg et al., and Greg Luce of Sinister Cinema.

About the Author

My interest in horror began about 1955, when I was 7, when our YMCA Day Camp counselor told us the tale of Dracula, which, as I recall, went pretty much according to Stoker. By 1959, my fate was sealed: I was mesmerized by *Horror of Dracula*, *Curse of the Demon*, and *The Fly* on the big screen. In the next few years, I discovered both a magazine (at our local pharmacy) called *Famous Monsters* and—happily and complementarily—a series of old horror films on the small screen. This film package was called, unprepossessingly enough, *The Late Show*, in Sacramento, but elsewhere, I found out it was known as *Shock Theatre*! I began writing for fanzines such as *Photon* and *Gore Creatures*, and, with Les Otis, assembled a film series at UCLA, which we called Great Films of Fear and Fantasy, and featured several of the movies found in this book. Just about every day, after classes, I would journey to the UCLA Film Library or the Academy of Motion Picture Arts and Sciences Library to research the sometimes-arcane movies that would become, in 1972, the subject of the first installment of my four-volume *Horror and Science Fiction Films*. I also began to contribute book and film reviews to *Sight and Sound*, *Film Quarterly* and *Take One*. In 2002, now in Vallejo, California (home some 100 years ago to Boris Karloff), I began work on the current project. And here it is …

www.ingramcontent.com/pod-product-compliance
Lightning Source LLC
Chambersburg PA
CBHW052011070526
44584CB00016B/1703